Canadian Corrections

FOURTH EDITION

Canadian Corrections

FOURTH EDITION

CURT T. GRIFFITHS
SIMON FRASER UNIVERSITY

DANIELLE J. MURDOCH
SIMON FRASER UNIVERSITY

NELSON / EDUCATION

NELSON / E D U C A T I O N

Canadian Corrections, Fourth Edition
by Curt T. Griffiths and Danielle J. Murdoch

Vice President, Editorial Higher Education:
Anne Williams

Executive Editor:
Lenore Taylor-Atkins

Marketing Manager:
Terry Fedorkiw

Developmental Editors:
Caroline Winter and Katherine Goodes

Photo Researcher:
Melody Tolson

Permissions Coordinator:
Melody Tolson

Production Service:
Sykam Sreemannarayana Reddy, diacriTech

Copy Editor:
Matthew Kudelka

Proofreader:
diacriTech

Indexer:
diacriTech

Manufacturing Manager:
Joanne McNeil

Design Director:
Ken Phipps

Managing Designer:
Franca Amore

Interior Design:
Brenda Barratt

Interior Design Image Credit:
Redshinestudio/Shutterstock

Cover Design:
Brenda Barratt

Cover Image:
Chris Hill

Compositor:
diacriTech

Library and Archives Canada Cataloguing in Publication Data

Griffiths, Curt T. (Curt Taylor), 1948–

  Canadian corrections / Curt T. Griffiths & Danielle J. Murdoch. — 4th ed.

Includes bibliographical references and index.

ISBN 978-0-17-652921-5

  1. Corrections—Canada—Textbooks. I. Murdoch, Danielle J., - II. Title.

HV9507.G75 2013
364.60971C2013-900471-8

ISBN-13: 978-0-17-652921-5
ISBN-10: 0-17-652921-7

To my mentor: Dr. Robert W. Balch
and
To Dr. William J. Griffiths (Will), M.D., Ph.D.
my brother, my hero
—C.T. Griffiths

To Michael J. Redhead
—D. Murdoch

To the memory of Dr. Elizabeth "Liz" Elliott
A true champion of social justice
—C.T. Griffiths and D. Murdoch

BRIEF CONTENTS

CONTENTS

PART I CANADIAN CORRECTIONS: SETTING THE FRAMEWORK 1

Chapter 1 Perspectives on Crime and Punishment 2

Chapter 2 The Origins and Evolution of Canadian Corrections 24

Chapter 3   Contemporary Canadian Corrections 45

Chapter 4   Sentencing: Beginning the Corrections Process ...64

PART II   CORRECTIONS IN THE COMMUNITY: ALTERNATIVES TO CONFINEMENT 87

Chapter 5   Alternatives to Confinement 88

Chapter 10 Classification, Case Management, and Treatment 199

PART IV   RETURNING TO THE COMMUNITY: RELEASE AND REENTRY 227

Chapter 11 Release from Incarceration 228

PART V   SPECIAL POPULATIONS IN CORRECTIONS . . . 281

Chapter 13   Women Offenders 282

Chapter 14   Aboriginal Offenders 302

Chapter 15 Young Offenders 330

PART VI   GOING FORWARD: REFORMING CORRECTIONS 359

Chapter 16 Creating Effective Systems of Corrections ... 360

List of Boxes

List of Figures

List of Tables

List of "AT ISSUE" Features

List of "Research File" Features

PREFACE TO THE FOURTH EDITION

This text is designed to provide a comprehensive overview of corrections in Canada. It attempts to capture the dynamics of corrections in this country and to explore the unique attributes of the Canadian correctional enterprise. The materials presented in this text are descriptive and analytical. We have endeavoured to present them in a way that will stimulate your thinking about corrections and capture the intensity of the issues surrounding the response to criminal offenders by systems of corrections.

The public, criminal justice and corrections personnel, and offenders have expressed a considerable amount of frustration, anger, and disappointment with the response to criminal offenders and the operations of correctional systems in Canada over the past 200 years. It often appears that, despite the expenditure of considerable time, effort, and money, we are no further ahead in our quest to find successful strategies for preventing and correcting criminal behaviour. Given the pessimism that often surrounds corrections, it would have been quite easy to write a text that focused only on the failures, of which there have been enough to fill volumes. However, to have done so would have been to tell only part of the story. In recent years, there have been some exciting initiatives in corrections, many of which hold great promise.

This text avoids the pessimism that so often characterizes discussions of corrections. It describes community-based and institutional programs and, as well, includes the latest research findings. No doubt, the text may raise more questions for you than it answers. This is the nature of scholarly inquiry and of any study of corrections.

It is also important to keep in mind that corrections systems have been assigned a very difficult role: to sanction offenders while providing programs and services designed to reduce the likelihood that the offender will return to a life of crime. The response of correctional systems to offenders in carrying out this mandate has ranged from the brutal to the humane. Nearly always, it has been controversial.

Correctional institutions continue to be beset by violence. HIV/AIDS, hepatitis, and an aging inmate population are among the more significant health-related challenges confronting systems of corrections. For correctional officers and inmates, correctional institutions continue to be unsafe places in which to work and live. The breakdown of the traditional inmate code of conduct has created more unpredictability, and a considerable amount of violence—much of it related to the illicit drug trade—continues as a feature of daily life in correctional institutions.

On the treatment side, Canada continues to be a world leader in the development of effective correctional programs, and there has been some success in implementing programs for Aboriginal offenders and female offenders. The research evidence is substantial that correctional treatment programs, if properly implemented, can reduce rates of reoffending. The reentry of offenders into the community remains an area of concern, and there is increasing scrutiny of parole board decision making alongside efforts to meet the needs of and to manage the risk posed by special categories of offenders, including sex offenders.

For this edition, many of the chapters from the third edition have been heavily updated and revised. In addition, there are five new chapters: probation practice, women offenders, Aboriginal offenders, young offenders, and a concluding chapter that sets out the challenges and opportunities for Canadian corrections.

Every attempt has been made to make this text student-friendly and to ensure that it complements well-taught corrections courses. At the beginning of each chapter, a number of objectives are identified. Boxes highlight research findings and present important issues. Key words are highlighted and defined in the margins and are included in the Glossary. Questions for review are located at the end of each chapter. Links to online resources are provided throughout the text. Liberal use is made of figures and charts to illustrate important information.

Also the instructor supplements have been revised for this new edition. These supplements are downloadable on the book's Companion Website at www.nelson.com/cancorrections4e.

We hope we have succeeded in our efforts. Should you wish to comment on any aspect of this book or have suggestions on how it can be improved, you can contact us at griffith@sfu.ca and dmurdoch@sfu.ca.

Thanks
Curt T. Griffiths
Danielle J. Murdoch
Vancouver, British Columbia
May, 2013

INSTRUCTOR SUPPLEMENTS

The **Nelson Education Teaching Advantage (NETA)** program delivers research-based instructor resources that promote student engagement and higher order thinking to enable the success of Canadian students and educators.

Instructors today face many challenges. Resources are limited, time is scarce, and a new kind of student has emerged: one who is juggling school with work, has gaps in his or her basic knowledge, and is immersed in technology in a way that has led to a completely new style of learning. In response, Nelson Education has gathered a group of dedicated instructors to advise us on the creation of richer and more flexible ancillaries and online learning platforms that respond to the needs of today's teaching environments. Whether your course is offered in-class or online or both, Nelson is pleased to provide pedagogically driven, research-based resources to support you.

In consultation with the editorial advisory board, Nelson Education has completely rethought the structure, approaches, and formats of our key textbook ancillaries and online learning platforms. We've also increased our investment in editorial support for our ancillary authors. The result is the Nelson Education Teaching Advantage and its key components: *NETA Assessment* and *NETA Presentation*. Each component includes one or more ancillaries prepared according to our best practices and may also be accompanied by documentation explaining the theory behind the practices.

NETA Assessment relates to testing materials. Under *NETA Assessment*, Nelson's authors create multiple-choice questions that reflect research-based best practices for constructing effective questions and testing not just recall but also higher order thinking. Our guidelines were developed by David DiBattista, a 3M National Teaching Fellow whose recent research as a professor of psychology at Brock University has focused on multiple-choice testing. All Test Bank authors receive training at workshops conducted by Professor DiBattista, as do the copy editors assigned to each Test Bank. A copy of *Multiple Choice Tests: Getting Beyond Remembering*, Professor DiBattista's guide to writing effective tests, is included with every Nelson Test Bank/Computerized Test Bank package. (Information about the NETA Test Bank prepared for *Canadian Corrections*, Fourth Edition, is included in the description of the Companion Website.)

NETA Presentation has been developed to help instructors make the best use of PowerPoint® in their classrooms. With a clean and uncluttered design developed by Maureen Stone of StoneSoup Consulting, NETA Presentation features slides with improved readability, more multimedia and graphic materials, activities to use in class, and tips for instructors on the Notes page. A copy of *NETA Guidelines for Classroom Presentations* by Maureen Stone is included with each set of PowerPoint slides. (Information about the NETA PowerPoint® prepared for *Canadian Corrections*, Fourth Edition, is included in the description of the Companion Website.)

COMPANION WEBSITE

Key instructor ancillaries have been revised and updated by Danielle Murdoch, Simon Fraser University, one of the text's co-authors, and are downloadable from the Companion Website (www.nelson.com/cancorrections4e). They provide instructors with the ultimate tool for customizing lectures and presentations. Downloadable supplements for *Canadian Corrections*, Fourth Edition, include the following:

- **NETA Assessment:** The NETA Assessment Test Bank includes approximately 320 multiple-choice questions written according to NETA guidelines for effective construction and development of higher order questions. These Test Bank files are provided in Word format for easy editing and in PDF format for easy printing.
- **NETA Presentation:** Microsoft® PowerPoint lecture slides average approximately 20 to 25 slides per chapter, many featuring key figures,

tables, and photographs from *Canadian Corrections*, Fourth Edition. NETA principles of clear design and engaging content have been incorporated throughout.

- **Instructor's Manual:** The Instructor's Manual to accompany *Canadian Corrections*, Fourth Edition, contains chapter-specific outlines, summaries, learning objectives, key terms, essay questions, discussion questions, and additional ideas to give you the support you need to engage your students in the classroom.
- **Day One:** Day One—Prof InClass is a PowerPoint presentation that you can customize to orient your students to the class and their text at the beginning of the course.

ACKNOWLEDGMENTS

We would like to acknowledge the many people in the field of corrections who have contributed information and ideas that have been incorporated into this edition. We would also like to thank the reviewers, whose comments and suggestions on the third edition of the text provided guidance in preparing the current edition:

- Josh Barath, University of Western Ontario
- Beth de Beer, Douglas College
- Carla Cesaroni, University of Ontario Institute of Technology
- Henry Chow, University of Regina
- Doug King, Mount Royal University
- Elana Sokolov, University of Winnipeg

We would also like to acknowledge the students in our corrections courses in the School of Criminology. Their curiosity and criticisms have been a continual source of inspiration. A further debt of gratitude is owed to those offenders and correctional officers and administrators who have shared their experiences and observations of corrections over the years.

As always, it has been a pleasure to work with the outstanding publishing team at Nelson: Lenore Taylor-Atkins, Executive Editor; Katherine Goodes, Developmental Editor; Caroline Winter, Developmental Editor; Melody Tolson, Permissions Editor; Terry Fedorkiw, Marketing Manager; and Susan Calvert, Director of Content & Media Production. All brought a high level of enthusiasm, energy, and professionalism to the project and helped make it happen. And special thanks to the world's best manuscript editor, Matthew Kudelka, for his outstanding work.

ABOUT THE AUTHORS

Curt T. Griffiths is a Professor and Coordinator of the Police Studies Program in the School of Criminology at Simon Fraser University.

Danielle J. Murdoch is completing her doctorate in the School of Criminology at Simon Fraser University.

PART I

CANADIAN CORRECTIONS: SETTING THE FRAMEWORK

The chapters in this opening section of the text provide the foundations for examining the various facets of Canadian corrections. Chapter 1 explores how punishment has evolved since early times and discusses the factors that have influenced responses to criminal offenders. Also presented are the competing perspectives on crime, criminal offenders, and the criminal justice system, as well as the features of crime and punishment in the early 21st century. One of these features is restorative justice, which offers an alternative to the traditional criminal justice process.

Chapter 2 describes the origins and evolution of Canadian corrections, identifying a number of eras and using prison architecture as an approach to reflect on how the philosophy of corrections has evolved over the decades. Chapter 3 sets out the "who" and the "what" of contemporary Canadian corrections and describes a number of challenges confronting corrections systems. The corrections process begins at the sentencing stage of the criminal justice system, and in Chapter 4 the purposes and principles of sentencing as well as sentencing options, including restorative justice approaches, are discussed.

CHAPTER 1

PERSPECTIVES ON CRIME AND PUNISHMENT

CHAPTER OBJECTIVES

After reading this chapter, you should be able to:
- *Discuss the indicators of correctional change.*
- *Discuss the objectives of punishment.*
- *Discuss how punishment has evolved since early times and the influences of punishment on criminal offenders.*
- *Compare and contrast the conservative, liberal, and radical perspectives on crime, criminal offenders, and the criminal justice system.*
- *Discuss the features of crime and punishment in the early 21st century.*
- *Discuss the rise of (1) punitive penology and (2) penal populism.*
- *Discuss the principles and practices of restorative justice.*

How societies and groups have chosen to respond to those who violate norms, mores, and laws has varied over the centuries. A review of the history of punishment and corrections reveals several distinct trends. There has been increasing centralization and professionalization of punishment and corrections, with formal agents of control assuming responsibility for identifying, responding to, and sanctioning offenders. Concurrent with this has been an expansion of surveillance and control over offenders, both in the community and in the correctional institutions. Also, the role of the community has diminished.

CORRECTIONAL CHANGE

We can say that correctional change has taken place when one or more of the following occurs: (1) the severity of punishment of convicted offenders is modified; (2) explanations of criminal behaviour change; (3) new structural arrangements, such as the penitentiary, are established in order to sanction offenders; and (4) the number or proportion of offenders involved in the correctional process changes.[1] Why do these changes occur? And why were prisons invented in the 18th century? Scholars of penal history study correctional change from a number of perspectives. Some have focused on early reformers' humanitarian ideals; others have argued that prisons were designed primarily to control people who were perceived as threatening the emerging capitalist system of an industrializing Europe. Prisons were not intended to be a humane alternative to the death penalty and corporal punishment; rather, they were designed for isolation and punishment.

In this chapter, we examine the perspectives on crime, offending, and punishment. Then in Chapter 2, we look at the origins and evolution of Canadian corrections.

Historically, responses to criminal offenders have been reactive, with little attention paid to the circumstances or factors that precipitated criminal behaviour. It can be argued that even the contemporary corrections system often fails to address the needs of offenders.

THE EARLY DAYS

Before there were states and written laws, personal retaliation was the primary response to criminal behaviour. This practice was later augmented by the "blood feud," in which the victim's family or tribe avenged themselves on the family or tribe of the offender. Before the Middle Ages (i.e., before 500 CE), the responses to criminal offenders were predicated mainly on punishment. The death penalty was carried out by hanging, live burial, stoning, boiling alive, crucifying, or drowning. Corporal punishment was also used, as were exile and fines.

Punishment by imprisonment was rare, confinement being employed mainly to hold those awaiting trial, execution, or corporal punishment or to compel the payment of fines. Ecclesiastical prisons run by the Catholic Church existed as early as the 6th century and were common by the 9th century. At a time when torture and execution were commonly resorted to in many countries, the Catholic Church used imprisonment as a form of punishment. Centuries later, prison design would be influenced by these church prisons, which isolated prisoners, fed them a strict diet, and provided time for self-reflection.[2] In the 1200s, during the Inquisition, accused persons were often held for months or years. Punishment by imprisonment was rarely resorted to until the 1500s in England and the early 1600s in Continental Europe.

The first house of correction in England opened in a former royal palace at Bridewell, in London, in 1557. This facility operated on the principle that subjecting offenders to hard labour was the best solution to the rising population of criminals.

The 1700s saw the start of the Industrial Revolution, which led to the breakdown of England's feudal, rural-centred society. Courts increasingly resorted to the death penalty in an attempt to stem the rise of what the emerging middle class saw as the "dangerous classes." By 1780, under what had become known as the Bloody Code, more than 350 offences were punishable by death.

England disposed of a large number of offenders through transportation, a form of banishment (often resulting in death) that for centuries had been used as a sanction. Between 1579 and 1776, England sent as many as 2,000 offenders every year to her American colonies. Convicts were also confined in hulks—that is, in decommissioned sailing vessels that had been converted into

© The Print Collector/Alamy

The *Warrior*, a hulk anchored off Woolwich in 1848, was a floating prison.

floating prisons, anchored in rivers and harbours. At its peak, the hulk prison system comprised 11 ships holding more than 3000 prisoners.

There is no simple explanation for why imprisonment became such a core part of the sanctioning process. That it did can be attributed at least in part to a desire to maintain the social order, often at the expense of society's lower classes. That would explain why the use of imprisonment continued to expand even though there was evidence, very early on, that it did little to reduce criminal behaviour.

During the late 1700s, John Howard pioneered efforts to reform conditions in English prisons. In his classic work, *The State of Prisons in England and Wales* (1777), he proposed a number of prison reforms, including providing single sleeping rooms for convicts, segregating women and young offenders from men, building facilities for bathing, and employing honest and well-trained prison administrators. Positive changes that resulted from Howard's work and that of other reformers included the prohibiting of alcohol sales within prisons and improvements to sanitary conditions.[3]

Although well intentioned, some of Howard's proposals—for example, that offenders be placed in solitary confinement to protect them from the corrupting influences of other convicts and to provide the proper solitude for moral reflection—contributed to the deprivations that convicts experienced. Even so, his humanitarian ideals live on in Canada through the work of the John Howard Society.

PERSPECTIVES ON CRIME, OFFENDERS, AND PUNISHMENT

Criminologists have pointed out that underlying all of the justifications for punishment are certain assumptions about human nature. Explanations of crime and responses to criminal offenders have always been strongly influenced by social, political, religious, economic, and demographic factors. The types of actions defined as criminal, the explanations for criminal behaviour, the types of sanctions imposed on offenders, and the objectives of those sanctions are always changing. The particular perspective that is taken as to why individuals engage in criminal behaviour influences the sanctions imposed and the objectives of those sanctions.

There are many competing perspectives on crime and criminal offenders and on what the objectives of corrections should be. Generally, these approaches can be categorized as conservative, liberal, or radical (see Box 1.1). The conservative and liberal perspectives are grounded respectively in the classical and positivist schools of criminological thought; the radical perspective is reflected in the writings of Karl Marx and today's critical criminologists.

The Classical (Conservative) School

During the 18th century, later known as the Age of Enlightenment, a number of ideas emerged that would strongly influence Western society's perception of and response to criminal offenders. During this time, a transition occurred from corporal punishment to imprisonment as a frequent form of punishment. This change was due in large measure to the writings of Enlightenment philosophers such as Montesquieu, Voltaire, Cesare Beccaria, and Jeremy Bentham, who embodied the **classical school** of punishment and correction.

The classical school held that offenders were exercising free will and that they engaged in criminal behaviour as a result of rational choices. Offenders engaged in a "hedonistic calculus" that maximized pleasure and minimized pain; therefore, if they were to change their behaviour, the costs of crime needed to outweigh any benefits (i.e., crime must not pay). In this view, criminal behaviour was not influenced by external societal factors or by deterministic forces internal to the offender; rather, the offender was responsible for his or her crimes.

In his major work, *Essay on Crime and Punishments* (1764), Beccaria argued that the gravity of the offence should be measured by the injury done to society and that certainty of punishment was the most effective deterrent against criminal behaviour. Furthermore, punishments that were too severe served only to embitter offenders and perpetuate criminal conduct.

It was Jeremy Bentham, the leading reformer of English criminal law during the 18th century, who coined the term *hedonistic calculus*. He held that

Classical (conservative) school
A perspective on criminal offenders and punishment based on the view that offenders exercise free will and engage in criminal behaviour as a result of rational choice and that punishment must be swift, certain, and severe.

BOX 1.1

Perspectives on Crime, Criminal Offenders, and the Criminal Justice System

	Conservative	Liberal	Radical
View of capitalism and the Canadian political system	Principles fundamentally sound	Principles need improvement; need greater economic and social equality	Principles fundamentally unsound and exploitive; need to change to socialism
Reason for crime	Social disorder—lack of discipline in society Traditional institutions and values have broken down Lenient criminal justice system—"crime pays"	Poverty, racism, and other social injustices Society is not meeting the human needs, and crime is a manifestation of this inadequacy in our system	Capitalist exploitation: the rich exploit the poor and the poor prey on one another
Ways to stop crime	Re-establish social order and discipline Reassert traditional values that made Canada great Increase the costs of crime through stiffer punishments	Make a better social order through reform Establish social programs to meet the needs of the disadvantaged Establish a more humane and just criminal justice system Focus on rehabilitation of the offender	Eliminate the capitalist system and establish a new social order

Focus of corrections	On the victim of crime and on innocent citizens Offender commits crime through free will	On the criminal—help the disadvantaged criminal and prevent future victimization of society Crime is a result of adverse social conditions, though increasingly, the attention is on the individual offender, who is easier to change than underlying social conditions	On the inherent inhumanity of the system Crime is a result of the way society is structured; any attempt to reduce crime must focus on the system rather than on individual offenders Criminal justice system is used to repress the lower classes
Source of crime problem	Street crime	Street and white-collar crime	The crime of capitalism and the rich
Primary values	Social order—"law and order"	Protection of individual rights and humane treatment of the less advantaged—"doing justice" and "doing good"	Total economic and social equality—"no classes and no exploitation"
Historical influences	The classical and neoclassical schools of criminology The notion of deterrence	The positivist school of criminology	The writings of Karl Marx and contemporary critical criminologists, including Welch and Lynch, Michalowski, and Groves

(continued)

	Conservative	Liberal	Radical
Strengths of the perspective	Focuses on efforts to maintain social order as a determinant of correctional strategies Emphasizes the role of free will in criminal behaviour	Considers the role of environmental factors in crime Attempts to treat and rehabilitate offenders by giving them skills to manage their lives	Highlights the roles of economics and politics in the development and operation of justice systems Considers the role of race and class in crime and administration of justice and highlights the over-representation of Aboriginals and visible minorities in corrections Examines systems of corrections as an industry
Weaknesses of the perspective	Fails to consider any external causes of crime Ignores the role of societal conditions such as poverty, race, and discrimination as contributors to criminal behaviour Relies on reason alone to explain and respond to crime	Fails to consider the role of free will in crime Ignores the potential role of psychological and biological factors in crime May result in net-widening and more persons under supervision in an attempt to meet their needs Exclusive focus on individual offender may distract from an examination of broader social injustices	Few empirical studies Socialist agenda ignores broad public support for most laws Gives little attention to victims

Source: Adapted from M. Welch, *Corrections: A Critical Approach.* 3rd ed. (New York: Routledge, 2011).
For a critical-historical perspective, see also M. Lynch, R. Michalowski, and W.B. Groves, *The New Primer in Radical Criminology: Critical Perspectives on Crime, Power, and Identity* (New York: Criminal Justice Press, 2000).

the main objective of intelligent human beings was to achieve the most pleasure while receiving the least amount of pain. Sanctions, it followed, should be applied to ensure that the pain resulting from the punishment outweighed any pleasure derived from committing the offence; also, the punishment should be no greater than necessary to deter the potential offender. For Bentham, imprisonment was a more precise measure of punishment than corporal punishments: the more heinous the crime, the longer the period of confinement.

According to the classical school, the primary goal of the criminal justice system should be deterrence, not revenge, and to be effective, punishment must be certain and must fit the crime. A person can be dissuaded from committing a crime by the spectre of certain, swift, and measured consequences. This has been the perspective of recent "tough on crime" approaches of the sort that involve mandatory minimum sentences (see Chapter 4) and mass incarceration to reduce crime rates.

A number of criticisms have been levelled at the classical school with its emphasis on free will. Foremost among them that it ignores the role of external factors such as poverty and racism.[4] Also, there is no evidence that tougher sanctions and zero-tolerance policies in themselves contribute to specific or general deterrence, in the absence of attempts to address other, more individualized factors that may have contributed to criminality (e.g., addiction). Also, incarceration policies are expensive, especially when you consider that many offenders who thereby land in prison would otherwise have been diverted to other, less costly forms of supervision in the community. The recent fiscal crisis in the United States has prompted legislators and policy makers to reconsider laws and policies that rely heavily on incarceration and in some cases to roll them back (see below).

In retrospect, Beccaria and Bentham and their contemporaries were somewhat successful in mitigating the severity of punishments imposed on offenders.

The Positivist (Liberal) School

The **positivist school**, as set out in the writings of Cesare Lombroso, Enrico Ferri, and Raffaelo Garafalo in the 1800s, held that criminal behaviour was determined by biological, psychological, physiological, and/or sociological factors. It followed that the scientific method should be used to study criminal behaviour and identify criminal types.

From the positivist perspective, criminal offenders are fundamentally different from others in society, so explanations for crime should centre on the individual rather than on society. Sanctions should focus on treatment and be individualized so that they reflect the unique qualities of the offender. The positivist perspective calls for "selective incapacitation," whereby only serious offenders likely to commit heinous crimes are sent to prison. This is contrary to the mass incarceration that often results from laws and policies informed by the classical perspective.

One weakness of the positivist perspective is that it fails to consider the role of free will in criminal offending.

Positivist (liberal) school
A perspective on criminal offenders and punishment based on the view that criminal behaviour is determined and that offenders require individualized treatment.

The Critical (Radical) School

Critical (radical) school
A perspective on crime, offenders, and punishment that highlights the role of economics, politics, power, and oppression in the formulation of laws and the administration of justice.

In contrast to the preceding, the **critical school** focuses on power and control. Its explanations of crime centre on the exploitative nature of the capitalist system, which uses the justice system to oppress the lower classes. This perspective was first set out by Karl Marx and is reflected to this day in the work of critical social theorists, including convict criminologists (i.e., those with a criminal background).

Proponents of this perspective point out that for centuries, the justice system has drawn into its clutches a disproportionate number of persons who are impoverished and who live on society's margins. These people also suffer high rates of mental illness, addiction, and homelessness and often have few skills. A prominent theme among critical social theorists has been the emergence of a prison-industrial complex that profits from laws and policies (e.g., the war on drugs) that render marginal people more susceptible to punishment. This in turn leads to mass incarceration, which does nothing to contribute to a safer society.[5]

A weakness of this perspective is that it can fail to consider individual factors that may be related to criminal behaviour. Another is that it pays little attention to the victims of crime and the impact of criminal offending on communities. See At Issue 1.1.

"I was just thinking, where would the criminal justice system be without guys like us."

Bernard Schoenbaum/The New Yorker Collection/www.cartoonbank.com

Issue 1.1: Perspectives on Crime

Which perspective on crime, criminal offenders, and the criminal justice system is most valid?

The conservative, liberal, and critical approaches are quite different in their focus. Which perspective comes the closest to your view of crime and justice?

The Objectives of Punishment

Closely related to the perspectives on crime and criminal offenders are the objectives of punishment. There are four principal justifications for punishing criminal offenders: retribution, deterrence, incapacitation, and rehabilitation/reintegration (see Table 1.1). These, in turn, are associated with how criminal behaviour is viewed.

Table 1.1   Key Elements of the Different Perspectives on Punishment

	Retribution	Deterrence	Incapacitation	Rehabilitation/ Reintegration
Justification	Moral	Prevention of further crime	Risk control	Offenders have deficiencies
Strategy	None: Offenders simply deserve to be punished	Make punishment more certain, swift, and severe	Offenders cannot offend while in prison Reduce opportunity	Treatment to reduce offenders' inclination to reoffend and assist in reentry into the community
Focus of Perspective	The offence and just desserts	Actual and potential offenders	Actual offenders	Needs of offenders
Image of Offenders	Free agents whose humanity we affirm by holding them accountable	Rational beings who engage in cost/benefit calculations	Not to be trusted but to be constrained	Good people who have gone astray Will respond to treatment

Source: M. Stohr, A. Walsh, and C. Hemmens, "Summary of Key Elements of Different Punishment Perspectives," *Corrections: A Text/Reader.* (Thousand Oaks, CA: Sage Publishing, 2009). Pg. 13.

As we will see throughout the text, Canada's laws and systems of corrections have long been influenced by the various punishment perspectives. There is a "swinging pendulum" wherein at certain points in history, there has been an emphasis on one punishment perspective, while at other times, other perspectives have predominated. In Chapter 2, to illustrate these changing perspectives on crime, offenders, and punishment, we will trace the emergence of the prison in Canada and show how prison architecture reflects philosophies of corrections.

PUNISHMENT AND CORRECTIONS IN THE EARLY 21ST CENTURY

Several key features of punishment and corrections in the early 21st century provide the backdrop for our discussions of Canadian corrections throughout the text.

The Risk-Focused Society and Corrections

Risk assessment and risk management are the mantras of contemporary corrections. Personnel at all stages of the correctional process, from institutional staff to parole board members to parole officers, have access to theoretically or empirically based assessment tools. Those instruments provide correctional workers with information with which they can develop effective management and treatment plans; they also reduce the liability and culpability of personnel should the offender commit serious crimes in the community.

The extensive use of risk assessment instruments can have a significant impact on offenders, by defining them in ways that hinder efforts at self-determination. Many of these instruments have validity as predictors of risk and the likelihood of reoffending; too often, though, they are not accompanied by an equal amount of attention to the development of personal relationships with offenders.[6] "Assessment is simply 'done to them' in the interests of public protection, and they have very limited opportunities to present alternative versions of life events and self-identity."[7] Offenders with specific challenges such as addiction, mental illness, and/or fetal alcohol spectrum disorder may have little ability to counter the identity created by correctional professionals. Risk assessment is discussed in more detail in Chapter 10.

Systems of corrections have also been heightening the surveillance of offenders. Psychoactive drugs control behaviour in institutional and community settings; electronic tracking and location systems supervise offenders in the community; genetic and neurobiological risk assessments focus on genetic predispositions to violent or criminal behaviour. In 2012 the Corrections and Conditional Release Act, which is the federal law for Canadian corrections, was amended to provide for the electronic monitoring (EM) of federal offenders on conditional release, a strategy that had previously been rejected by the government. Techno-corrections, which includes surveillance within institutions and the global positioning system monitoring of offenders under supervision in the community, focuses on security and order at the possible expense of rehabilitation and treatment.[8] In correctional institutions, inmates are being more heavily restricted in their movements and are being watched over by closed-circuit televisions (CCTVs). The increasing use of surveillance may be having a negative impact on offenders.[9]

Concurrent with the stronger focus on risk has been the persistence of the mantra that "nothing works" in corrections. Politicians and legislatures have often resorted to that view to justify more punitive crime and corrections policies. In fact, as this text will reveal, some interventions do work with offenders, but success requires effort not only on the offender's part but also on the part of correctional personnel: probation officers, correctional officers, treatment staff, correctional managers, and others. When a program fails to have a significant impact on the behaviour of an offender, it may be for a variety of reasons other than the motivation of the offender.

Punitive Penology and the Rise of Penal Populism

Correctional scholars have documented the rise of a "punitive penology" that includes **penal populism** and a shift toward laws that increase the severity of criminal sanctions and that expand the control exercised over offenders by systems of corrections. Penal populism arises when politicians advance "tough on crime" policies that appeal to the public in order to improve their chances of re-election but that do little to reduce crime rates or to ensure that justice is done. These policies often do not reflect public opinion, or they are formulated in the absence of an informed public.[10]

Penal populism is visible in calls for more severe sanctions, such as mandatory minimum sentences and American-style three-strikes-you're-out laws. It has resulted in significant increases in prison populations to the point that *one in nine* black American men between 20 and 34 is a prisoner at any given time and *one in four* either has been or presently is in prison.[11]

Citizens' frustrations with the criminal justice system and their increasing feelings of insecurity are channelled by politicians into criminal laws and social policies that place an increasing emphasis on risk assessment and the management of offenders, both inside institutions and in the community.

> **Penal populism**
> Corrections policies formulated in pursuit of political objectives, often in the absence of an informed public or in spite of public opinion and that are centred on being "tough on crime."

Punitive Corrections in the United States

A brief examination of law and corrections policy in the United States will provide insights into the factors that influence the specific model of punishment and corrections that operates at a given point in time. It also provides the backdrop for recent developments in Canada (see Chapter 2).

In the 1970s, criminal justice policies in the United States began to shift their focus away from rehabilitation toward retribution. This was driven by legislators, who assumed a more prominent role than criminal justice policy makers in determining the response to criminal offenders.[12] Punishment had emerged as a political issue. As a result, indeterminate sentences were replaced with determinate (fixed) ones, including mandatory minimum sentences; also, habitual offender laws were passed, such as (in many states) "three-strikes-you're-out" laws—that is, three felony convictions meant life with no possibility of parole. A "war on drugs" was declared, and zero-tolerance charging policies were introduced. Correctional officer unions played a significant role throughout this period in pushing for more severe penalties and in resisting any efforts to downsize institutions and to explore alternatives to confinement.[13]

The purpose of these initiatives was to reassure the public that something was being done about the crime problem.[14] Incapacitation, rather than rehabilitation, became the strategy whereby communities would be made safe. The Province of Ontario was the first Canadian jurisdiction to express interest in this approach.[15] Ontario also experimented, albeit briefly, with private prisons (see Chapter 7), which raised concerns about "punishment for profit" and the growth of a corrections industry.

By the early 21st century, however, many American states were confronting the fiscal realities associated with their "get tough" policies. The escalating costs of growing prison populations and the nation-wide economic downturn, coupled with the deficits confronting many state governments, led to a major shift in laws and policies. In 2009, California's state auditor estimated that three-strikes offenders would cost the taxpayers an extra $19.1 billion for the time they spent incarcerated.[16] Around this time, a review of 49,000 of the 134,000 inmates incarcerated in California correctional institutions found that drug addiction was the major problem these offenders were facing. Yet statistics indicated that only 15 to 20 percent of all offenders were receiving any treatment, which placed them at risk of committing further offences when they were released.

In response to these challenges, many state legislatures shortened their lists of mandatory minimum sentences, increased opportunities for the early release of nonviolent offenders, and shifted their focus to reintegration and community-based treatment programs.[17] Also, in several states, three-strikes laws were amended to give prosecutors and judges more discretion at sentencing, and legislators reduced the penalties for many drug offences. Many state legislatures had found the price of incarceration too high and the deterrent value of it too low. As of 2013, it is difficult to determine whether the decarceration movement in the United States will continue. Powerful forces, including correctional officer unions, may resist efforts to reform sentencing laws and to move away from punitive penal policies.[18]

Concurrent with these developments, a number of courts—including the U.S. Supreme Court—have ruled that when prison overcrowding reaches a certain threshold, it violates the constitutional rights of inmates, and have directed states to reduce prison populations. As a result, thousands of inmates have been released early, thereby overwhelming community corrections programs and their staffs. In 2009, California's prison population fell to its lowest level in 38 years, largely due to the early release of offenders from custody.[19]

The move toward decarceration has also been prompted by statistics pointing to high rates of reoffending among inmates released from confinement when their treatment needs have been largely unaddressed. There is also evidence that three-strikes laws have not been a deterrent to serious crime.[20] Highly publicized cases of wrongful conviction have led to the reduced use of the death penalty and even to its abolition in several states. Many observers see these developments as marking the advent of "penal moderation"—that is, a shift toward less punitive and retributive sanctions.

All of these developments provide an opportunity for American correctional authorities to begin implementing evidence-based programs that hold the potential to reduce reoffending and that provide a continuum of supervision and assistance between the prison and the community. These strategies are discussed in Chapters 10 and 12.

Crime, Punishment, and the Canadian Public

The impact that public perceptions have on laws and on corrections policies and practices is difficult to determine. What is known is that the Canadian public has little confidence in corrections systems to protect communities, to supervise released offenders with any effectiveness, or to help offenders become law-abiding citizens. To some degree, these perceptions arise from the fact that the general public knows very little about corrections.

For most Canadians, the media are the primary sources of information about crime and criminal justice. However, the media tend to be biased toward sensational crimes and to simplify crime and justice issues, and the public for its part tends to generalize from specific events. All of these have contributed to an uninformed and misinformed public.[21] For example, there is a general lack of public knowledge about the parole system. Surveys have found that the public overestimates the number of offenders who have been released on parole, their revocation rates, and the recidivism rate generally.[22] Despite the ongoing decline in official crime rates, the Canadian public views the state as being too lenient with offenders.[23]

A major obstacle to correctional programming in the community is the **NIMBY (Not In My Back Yard)** syndrome. That term refers to the resistance communities generate to correctional systems' efforts to establish community programs and residences for offenders. Far too often, corrections personnel find themselves in crisis management mode—reacting to the accusations of citizens' interest groups; struggling to reassure a nervous public following an escape or the commission of a serious crime by an offender on parole; or attempting to justify the release of a high-risk offender into the community. These tense relationships are due in part to the failure of corrections systems to educate the public and to develop effective proactive strategies that might counter the myths that surround offending and offenders.

It is interesting, though, that during the recent economic downturn, many North American communities worked hard to attract correctional institutions, in anticipation of the jobs and other economic benefits they would bring.

Chapter 2, about Canada's corrections history, will reveal that in the early days, most offenders were punished in public view. Back then, community residents could actually witness sanctions, including hangings; indeed, they

NIMBY (Not In My Back Yard) The resistance of community residents to efforts of corrections systems to locate programming and residences for offenders in the community.

could often participate in sanctions by showering offenders with insults (as well as the occasional rotten vegetable). Today, with a few notable exceptions—such as the involvement of community residents as volunteers in correctional institutions and in community programs—the public's role in corrections is mainly reactive. Community sentiment is often expressed through interest groups that lobby for harsher sanctions for criminal offenders, longer periods of incarceration, and more stringent requirements for release. See At Issue 1.2.

Penal populism may make it difficult to secure funding and support for treatment and rehabilitation programs within correctional institutions and in the community. In community corrections, programs may be "in" the community but not "of" it, the way community-focused policing programs often are.[24]

As political entities, corrections systems have generally failed to work proactively to counter their media image and to correct statements made about them by politicians. This has allowed politicians and legislatures free reign to direct correctional policy based on ideological rather than empirical grounds. One could ask why corrections systems have not developed better relationships with communities and why corrections officials seem constantly to be playing defence. A cynical view would be that an uninformed public is more pliable and directs fewer questions at politicians and corrections policy makers.

Recent years have witnessed the increasing involvement of the private sector in corrections services. This has been driven primarily by the ongoing fiscal crisis facing governments rather than by evidence-based practices. Private, for-profit companies are involved today in a variety of corrections activities, including monitoring offenders on electronic surveillance, operating institutions (in the U.K. and the United States), and supervising offenders completing community service as a condition of probation (in the U.K.). The U.K. intends to farm out 60 percent of the entire budget for probation to private contractors.[25]

These firms are different from not-for-profit organizations such as the St. Leonard's Society, the John Howard Society, and the Elizabeth Fry Society, which provide services for provincial/territorial and federal offenders across the

Video Link
Punishment:
A Failed Social
Experiment
**www.youtube
.com/watch?
v=zDsSiMpslVQ**

AT ISSUE

Issue 1.2: The General Public and Corrections

Should the general public be involved in corrections?

Generally speaking, corrections systems have not attempted to develop community partnerships. It is often argued that responding to criminal offenders should be left to professionals. For their part, those who favour increased community involvement contend that the community is an underutilized resource. What is your view on this debate? If you support the increased participation of community residents, what initiatives would you take to accomplish this? If you were asked to volunteer for a program for offenders one evening a month at a halfway house or in a correctional institution, would you accept? Why or why not?

country. So far, there has been no examination of the potential benefits and possible pitfalls of outsourcing corrections to private companies. This resort to private companies raises a number of issues, including whether they are effective. It also calls up a moral question: Should profit be related in any way to society's response to offenders? This issue is explored in greater depth in Chapter 7.

RESTORATIVE JUSTICE: AN ALTERNATIVE PERSPECTIVE ON CRIME AND PUNISHMENT

Concerns about the effectiveness of the traditional adversarial system of criminal justice and a variety of other influences have led to the search for alternative ways to respond to people in conflict with the law. **Restorative justice** is based on the principle that criminal behaviour injures not only victims but also communities and offenders and that efforts to address and resolve the problems created by criminal behaviour should involve all of these parties. Key notions in restorative justice are healing, reparation and reintegration, and the prevention of future harm.[26] See Figure 1.1.

Restorative justice
An approach to responding to offenders based on the principle that criminal behaviour injures victims, communities, and offenders and that all of these parties should be involved in efforts to address the causes of the behaviour and its consequences.

Figure 1.1

The Relationships of Restorative Justice

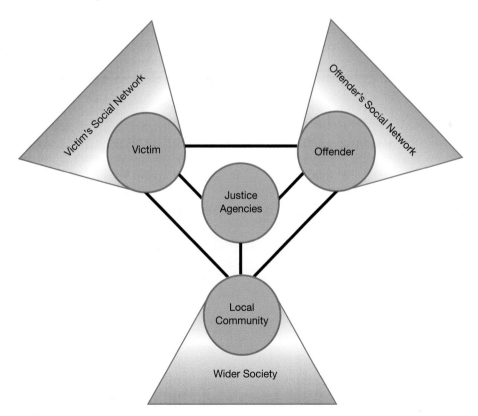

Source: T. F. Marshall (1999). *Restorative Justice: An Overview.* Home Office Occasional Paper 48. (London: Home Office).

Video Link
Four Goals of
Punishment and
Restorative Justice
**www.youtube
.com/watch?
v=MPIQ9aFg5xw**

Restorative justice differs in significant ways from traditional adversarial justice. The key differences are listed in Table 1.2.

The primary objectives of restorative justice are to fully address the needs of victims of crime and to prevent reoffending by reintegrating offenders back into the community. Offenders are required to acknowledge and take responsibility for their behaviour, and efforts are made to create a "community" of support and assistance for the victim and the offender and to address the long-term interests of the community. Table 1.3 compares the traditional criminal court process with restorative justice.

Table 1.2   Comparison of Retributive and Restorative Justice Principles

Retributive Justice	**Restorative/Community Justice**
Crime violates the state and its laws.	Crime violates people and relationships.
Justice focuses on establishing guilt so that doses of pain can be meted out.	Justice aims to identify needs/obligations so that things can be made right.
Justice is sought through conflict between adversaries in which the offender is pitted against state rules, and intentions outweigh outcomes— one side wins and the other loses.	Justice encourages dialogue and mutual agreement, gives victims and offenders central roles, and is judged by the extent to which responsibilities are assumed, needs are met, and healing (of individuals and relationships) is encouraged.

Source: H. Zehr, *Changing Lenses: A New Focus for Crime and Justice.* (Scottsdale: Herald, 1990).

Table 1.3   Comparison of the Criminal Court Process and Restorative Justice

	Traditional Justice	**Restorative Justice**
People	Experts, nonresidents	Local people
Process	Adversarial State v. offender	Consensus Community v. problem
Issues	Laws broken	Relationship broken
Focus	Guilt	Identify needs of victim, offender, and community
Tools	Punishment/control	Healing/support
Procedure	Fixed rules	Flexible

A key feature of restorative justice is the community's involvement in addressing the issues surrounding criminal offending. This moves residents into a proactive, participatory role, one that is not available in traditional justice processes. This involvement reflects survey findings that when provided with information, the public supports treatment and prevention programs.[27] Examples of community involvement will be presented throughout the text.

There are a number of "entry" points in the criminal justice system where restorative justice approaches can be used: police (pre-charge); Crown (post-charge); courts (post-convictions/pre-sentence); corrections (post-sentence); and following sentence expiry. See Figure 1.2.

Figure 1.2

Restorative Justice: Entry Points in the Criminal Justice System

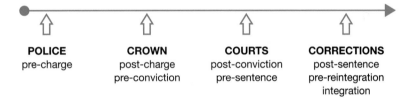

POLICE	CROWN	COURTS	CORRECTIONS
pre-charge	post-charge	post-conviction	post-sentence
	pre-conviction	pre-sentence	pre-reintegration
			integration

Source: J. Latimer and S. Kleinknecht, *The Effects of Restorative Justice Programming: A Review of the Empirical Research Literature*, Pg. 7. Found at: http://www.justice.gc.ca/eng/pi/rs/rep-rap/2000/rr00_16/rr00_16.pdf. (Department of Justice Canada, 2000). Reproduced with the permission of the Minister of Public Works and Government Services Canada, 2012.

The Dimensions and Effectiveness of Restorative Justice

Throughout the text, we will be examining the role of restorative justice programs at various stages of the corrections process. Among the more common restorative justice initiatives that operate at the provincial/territorial level are victim–offender mediation, circle sentencing (see Chapter 4), circles of support and accountability (COSAs, see Chapter 12); community holistic healing programs (often found in Aboriginal communities; see Chapter 14), and family group conferences (often used for youth in conflict with the law; see Chapter 15). Research File 1.1 summarizes what is known about the effectiveness of restorative justice.

Note, in particular, the finding from evaluation studies that restorative justice seems to work best with more serious offenders and in cases involving serious, violent crime. This suggests that there is considerable potential for using it at all stages of the justice process and in those cases that have long been deemed unsuitable for alternative approaches.

Challenges in Restorative Justice

The challenges facing restorative justice include resistance by criminal justice and corrections personnel, the perception that it is "soft" on

Video Links
A Police Officer Speaks about Restorative Justice
www.youtube.com/watch?v=R914YmYYnI

Restorative Justice Is the Law
www.heartspeakproductions.ca

RESEARCH FILE 1.1

The Effectiveness of Restorative Justice

Does RJ have an impact on crime victims? RJ approaches that provide an opportunity for the victim to meet face-to-face with the offender receive high marks from crime victims; there is a positive impact on the psychological and physical health of crime victims.[a]

Does RJ have an impact on offenders? There is higher satisfaction with justice; offenders are more likely to assume responsibility for offending and for the harm they have caused. Also, they are more likely to comply with RJ agreements than with court orders.[b]

Does RJ reduce reoffending? RJ can result in significant reductions in repeat offending for property and violent crime; it is more effective with serious and violent crimes than with property offences; it is more effective than incarceration in reducing reoffending.[c]

Does community involvement have an impact on RJ? RJ provides an opportunity for community residents to involve themselves in responding to criminal offenders in a proactive, problem-solving context; it can contribute to healthier communities and improved quality of life.[d]

Does RJ have an impact on the justice system generally? RJ strategies have the potential to reduce the costs of justice and the amount of time it takes to conclude a case; it is most effective at reducing costs when used as a strategy for diversion.[e]

Sources:

[a] L.W. Sherman and H. Strang, *Restorative Justice: The Evidence* (London: Smith Institute, 2007), http://www.smith-institute.org.uk/file/RestorativeJusticeTheEvidenceFullreport.pdf.

[b] Ibid.

[c] Ibid.

[d] T. Rugge and T.-L. Scott, *Restorative Justice's Impact on Participants' Psychological and Physical Health* (Ottawa: Public Safety Canada, 2009), http://www.publicsafety.gc.ca/res/cor/rep/_fl/2009-03-rjp-eng.pdf.

[e] Y. Dandurand and C.T. Griffiths, *Handbook on Restorative Justice Programmes* (Vienna: UN Office on Drugs and Crime, 2006), http://www.unodc.org/pdf/criminal_justice/06-56290_Ebook.pdf; Sherman and Strang, *Restorative Justice: The Evidence.*

offenders, and a lack of public awareness. For example, an Alberta survey found that only 11 percent of those polled were aware of any places or people in the community that used restorative justice.[28] As well, there have been few evaluations of the effectiveness of restorative justice programs, especially in Canada.

One obstacle has been that many of the key principles of restorative justice are unfamiliar to politicians, policy makers, and criminal justice personnel, including judges. Terms such as *forgiveness, community, empowerment, healing,* and *spirituality* are not found in Canada's Criminal Code and are foreign to many criminal justice practitioners. This has slowed the development of restorative justice programs.

Another challenge is ensuring that the victims of crime are not revictimized through their involvement in restorative justice programs. Aboriginal women, for example, have voiced concerns about the high rates of sexual and physical abuse in their communities and have questioned whether restorative justice provides adequate protection for victims of violence and abuse and whether the sanctions imposed are appropriate.[29] Another concern is that community dynamics, especially in rural and remote communities, may make it difficult to implement restorative justice approaches. In correctional institutions, restorative justice faces a challenge from the dynamics of institutional life (see Chapter 10).

SUMMARY

This chapter has examined the perspectives on crime, criminal offenders, and punishment that have been utilized in response to criminal offending. Explanations of crime and responses to criminal offenders have always been strongly influenced by social, political, religious, economic, and demographic factors and are constantly changing.

The late 20th and early 21st centuries were marked by a move toward punitive penology in the United States, a rise in penal populism, mass incarceration, and the increasing involvement of the private sector in punishment. Ill-informed communities have generally responded negatively to offenders, and this has hindered efforts at reintegration. These trends appear to be developing in Canada and are discussed in Chapter 2.

Restorative justice provides an alternative framework for responding to criminal offenders. It focuses on problem-solving, addressing the needs of victims and offenders, involving the community on a proactive basis, and fashioning sanctions that reduce the likelihood of reoffending.

KEY POINTS REVIEW

1. There are a number of explanations for correctional change.
2. How societies and groups have chosen to respond to those who violate norms, mores, and laws has varied over the centuries.
3. Imprisonment as a form of punishment was not used to any great extent until the 1500s in England and the early 1600s in Continental Europe.
4. There are competing perspectives on crime and criminal offenders and on what the objectives of corrections should be.
5. Generally speaking, the Canadian public is uninformed or misinformed about corrections, and this has often resulted in resistance to offenders and corrections initiatives.

6. Restorative justice provides an alternative framework for responding to criminal offenders.

7. Key principles in restorative justice include healing, reparation, reintegration, and the prevention of future harm.

KEY TERM QUESTIONS

1. What are the basic tenets of the *classical* (conservative). *positivist* (liberal), and *critical* (radical) perspectives on crime, offenders, and the criminal justice system?

2. What is *penal populism* and what role does it play in punitive penology?

3. What is meant by the term *NIMBY*, and what is the importance of that term for any study of corrections?

4. Describe the key principles of *restorative justice* and compare it with the traditional adversarial system of criminal justice.

NOTES

1. N. Shover, *A Sociology of American Corrections* (Homewood: Dorsey, 1979).

2. N. Johnston, "Evolving Function: Early Use of Imprisonment as Punishment," *Prison Journal* 89, no. 1 (2009): 10S–34S.

3. Ibid.

4. M. Welch, *Corrections: A Critical Approach*, 3rd ed. (New York: Routledge, 2011).

5. S. J. Hartnett, *Challenging the Prison-Industrial Complex* (Urbana: University of Illinois Press, 2011).

6. B. Crewe, "Depth, Weight, Tightness: Revisiting the Pains of Imprisonment," *Punishment and Society* 13, no. 5 (2011): 509–29.

7. Ibid., 517.

8. Welch, *Corrections*.

9. Crewe, "Depth, Weight, Tightness."

10. J. V. Roberts, L. J. Stalans, D. Indermaur, and M. Hough, *Penal Populism and Public Opinion: Lessons from Five Countries* (New York: Oxford University Press, 2003).

11. J. Forman, "The Black Poor, Black Elites, and America's Prisons," *Cardozo Law Review* 32, no. 3 (2011): 791–806 at 793.

12. S. Steen and R. Bandy, "When the Policy Becomes the Problem: Criminal Justice in the New Millennium," *Punishment and Society* 9, no. 1 (2007): 5–26.

13. J. Page, "Prison Officer Unions and the Perpetuation of the Penal Status Quo," *Criminology and Public Policy* 10, no. 3 (2011): 735–70.

14. Ibid.

15. W.S. DeKeseredy, "Canadian Crime Control in the New Millennium: The Influence of Neo-Conservative US Policies and Practices," *Police Practice and Research* 10, no. 4 (2009): 305–16.

16. M. Lagos and R. Gabrielson, "Drug Rehab Called Key to Avoid 3rd Strike," *San Francisco Chronicle*, September 29, 2012, http://www.sfgate.com/crime/atricle/Drug-rehab-called-key-to-avoid-3rd-strike-3906024.php.

17. A. F. Rengifo, D. Stemen, B. D. Dooley, E. Amidon, and A. Gendon, "Cents and Sensibility: A Case Study of Corrections Reform in Kansas and Michigan," *Journal of Criminal Justice* 38, no. 4 (2012): 419–29; Steen and Bandy, "When the Policy Becomes the Problem."

18. Page, "Prison Officer Unions."

19. J. Petersilia, "Beyond the Prison Bubble," *Federal Probation* 75, no. 1 (2011): 2–4.

20. J. L. Worrall, "The Effect of Three-Strikes Legislation on Serious Crime in California," *Journal of Criminal Justice* 32 (2004): 283–96.

21. J. V. Roberts, *Fear of Crime and Attitudes to Criminal Justice in Canada: A Review of Recent Trends* (Ottawa: Solicitor General, 2001), http://www.publicsafety.gc.ca/res/cor/rep/_fl/2001-02-fer-crime-eng.pdf.

22. Parole Board of Canada, *Performance Monitoring Report, 2010–2011* (Ottawa: 2011), http://www.pbc-clcc.gc.ca/rprts/pmr/pmr_2010_2011/pmr_2010_2011-eng.pdf.

23. M. Kennedy, "Despite Falling Crime Rates, Many Canadians Believe Justice System Is Too Lax: Pollster," *Postmedia News*, July 24, 2012, http://www.ottawacitizen.com/Canadians+feel+justice+system/6984558/story.html.

24. C. T. Griffiths, *Canadian Criminal Justice: A Primer*, 4th ed. (Toronto: Nelson, 2011).

25. *The Guardian*, "Serco Wins First Private Probation Contract," July 13, 2012, http://www.guardian.co.uk/society/2012/jul/13/serco-first-private-probation-contract/print.

26. R. B. Cormier, *What Is Restorative Justice?* (n.d.), http://www.collaborativejustice.ca/about_e.php.

27. J. Latimer and N. Desjardins, *The 2007 National Justice Survey: Tackling Crime and Public Confidence* (Ottawa: Department of Justice, 2007), http://www.justice.gc.ca/eng/pi/rs/rep-rap/2007/rr07_4/rr07_4.pdf.

28. Alberta Solicitor General and Public Security, *2011 Survey of Albertans* (Edmonton: 2011), http://www.solgps.alberta.ca/Publications1/Survey%20of%20Albertans/2011%20Survey%20of%20Albertans.pdf.

29. L. Presser and P. Van Voorhis, "Values and Evaluation: Assessing Process and Outcomes of Restorative Justice Programs," *Crime and Delinquency* 48, no. 1 (2002): 162–88.

CHAPTER 2
THE ORIGINS AND EVOLUTION OF CANADIAN CORRECTIONS

CHAPTER OBJECTIVES

After reading this chapter, you should be able to:
- *Describe the influences and events that resulted in the building of the first penitentiary in Canada in 1835.*
- *Discuss the conditions of early provincial prisons and local jails across the country.*
- *Highlight the key developments in efforts to reform penitentiaries and the move toward a treatment model of corrections following World War II.*
- *Describe the models of corrections that have been developing for the past two decades.*
- *Discuss the various commissions of inquiry on corrections and their impact on correctional policy and practice.*

This chapter discusses the origins and evolution of Canadian corrections. It examines the creation of penitentiaries in the early 1800s, traces the shifts in Canadian correctional practice from the 1600s to the present day, and discusses how the architecture of correctional institutions reflects changes in corrections philosophies.

THE CREATION OF THE CANADIAN PENITENTIARY

Pennsylvania model (for prisons)
A separate and silent system in which prisoners were completely isolated from one another, eating, working, and sleeping in separate cells.

Recall from Chapter 1 that a key indicator of correctional change is the creation of new structural arrangements for sanctioning offenders. The events surrounding the building of Canada's first penitentiary—in Kingston, Ontario, in the early 1800s—illustrate how changes in responses to crime and criminal offenders can be influenced by social, economic, and political forces. There were influences from the United States, where, between 1790 and 1830, crime came to be viewed as a consequence of community disorder and family instability rather than a manifestation of individual afflictions. The Americans built penitentiaries in an attempt to create settings in which criminals could be transformed into useful citizens through religious contemplation and hard work. Some of these institutions operated on a "separate and silent" system, in which prisoners were completely isolated from one another in their cells. This came to be known as the **Pennsylvania model**.

In other penitentiaries, in what became known as the **Auburn model** (originating in New York State), prisoners worked and ate together during the day and slept in individual cells at night. A system of strict silence, which forbade prisoners from communicating or even gesturing to one another, was enforced at all times. Most prisons in the United States and Canada were patterned on the Auburn model.

In Canada, the building of the first penitentiary in Kingston, Ontario, was the result of a number of influences, including developments in the United States, overcrowding in the local jails (where there was also a lack of classification of inmates), and the view that corporal punishment was improper and degrading.[1] When completed in 1835, the Kingston Penitentiary was the largest public building in Upper Canada. It symbolized a **moral architecture**, one that reflected the themes of order and morality.

Kingston was to be a model for those confined in it as well as for society. Among its goals were the eradication of the underlying causes of crime: intemperance, laziness, and a lack of moral values. Within the penitentiary, hard labour and a strong emphasis on religion were core elements of the reformation process.

The prisoners in Kingston were separated by gender and type of offence. They were allowed to have their own bedding, clothing, and food. Generally, however, their lives centred on hard labour and discipline. Strict silence was maintained at all times; the inmates walked in lockstep; their days were controlled by the constant ringing of bells. Breaches of prison regulations brought swift and harsh punishment, including flogging, leg irons, solitary confinement, and rations of bread and water (see Box 2.1). Male inmates who violated

Auburn model (for prisons)
A system that allowed prisoners to work and eat together during the day and housed them in individual cells at night.

Moral architecture
The term used to describe the design of the first penitentiary in Canada, the intent of which was to reflect themes of order and morality.

BOX 2.1

Entries from The Punishment Book of the Prison (1843)

Offence	Punishment
Laughing and talking	6 lashes; cat-o'-nine-tails
Talking in wash-house	6 lashes; rawhide
Threatening to knock convicts' brains out	24 lashes; cat-o'-nine-tails
Talking to Keepers on matters not relating to their work	6 lashes; cat-o'-nine-tails
Finding fault with rations when desired by guard to sit down	6 lashes; rawhide, and bread and water
Staring about and inattentive at breakfast table	bread and water
Leaving work and going to privy when other convict there	36 hours in dark cell, and bread and water

Source: First Report of the Commissioners of the Royal Commission on the Provincial Penitentiary, 1849, Pg. 185.

prison regulations were generally whipped; female convicts who did so were placed in solitary confinement. The same punishments were applied to children, some as young as eight.

The conditions in Kingston led to the creation of a Royal Commission in 1848, thirteen years after it opened. The **Brown Commission** investigated charges of mismanagement, theft, and mistreatment of convicts. It found that the warden, Henry Smith, had indeed mismanaged the institution and that there was excessive use of corporal punishment, including the flogging of men, women, and children, some as young as eleven. The warden was fired and attempts were made to reform the prison. Though changes were made, corporal punishment, the silent system, and hard labour remained prominent features of life in Kingston. In retrospect, the Brown Commission is perhaps best viewed as a missed opportunity for Canadians to reconsider the use of imprisonment and to explore potentially more effective ways to prevent crime and reform offenders.

In penitentiaries, the bell was the symbol of discipline and controlled the convict's day. Box 2.2 presents the daily schedule of the Manitoba Penitentiary in 1879. Box 2.3 presents the typical coarse diet for convicts confined during the 1880s.

Brown Commission
An investigation into the operations of Kingston Penitentiary that condemned the use of corporal punishment and emphasized the need for rehabilitation.

BOX 2.2

Symbol of Discipline: The Bell

5:50 a.m.	Bell. Prisoners rise, wash, dress, make beds.
6:00 a.m.	Officers parade. Keys issued, slops collected. Cells, walls, halls, and passages swept. Lamps collected and cleaned. Prisoners unlocked and escorted to work. Names of the sick taken. Night tubs [chamber pots] cleaned and placed outside the prison. Fuel distributed and ashes emptied. Random search of cells. Water pumped into tank.
7:30 a.m.	Bell. Prisoners marched to dining halls in groups of three.
7:40 a.m.	Bell. Breakfast over. Prisoners marched back to their cells and locked in. Guards had breakfast.
8:30 a.m.	Bell. Officers parade. Outside gangs unlocked and escorted outside. Inside workers escorted to their jobs. Surgeon attends the sick.
10:00 a.m.	Office hours. Convicts on report were taken to the warden.
12:15 p.m.	Bell. Prisoners marched back to their cells and locked up.
12:20 p.m.	Bell. Prisoners unlocked and marched to the dining room for lunch.
12:45 p.m.	Bell. Prisoners marched back to cells and locked up. Officers had lunch.
12:50 p.m.	Eligible prisoners unlocked for school.
1:30 p.m.	Bell. Officers parade. Prisoners unlocked and marched off to work. Random search of cells.
5:40 p.m.	Night tubs brought back into the prison.

5:50 p.m.	Bell. Prisoners marched to cells and locked up. Supper delivered to each cell. Convicts with special requests may use "signal sticks" to summon guards.
6:00 p.m.	Bell. Prisoners' clothing collected and placed outside cell door. All cells searched. Prisoners begin their meals. Guards on night shift take over. Keys collected. Chief keeper read out daily orders.
7:00 p.m.	Patrol guards supply water to convicts who signal for it. Kitchen and dining hall locked up.
9:00 p.m.	Lights in cells turned down.
10:00 p.m.	Lights in passages turned down. Dampers of heating stoves closed. Lights out in officers' room.

(The bell, which was centrally located in the prison, was so hated by the inmates that it was destroyed during the 1971 riot at Kingston.)

Source: Reproduced from *"Crime and Punishment: A Pictorial History Part III,"* Correctional Service of Canada. Reproduced with the permission of the Minister of Public Works and Government Services Canada, 2012.

BOX 2.3

A Typical Daily Menu for Inmates in the Manitoba Penitentiary in the Late 1880s

Breakfast	1 pint	pease coffee (sweetened with 1/2 oz. brown sugar)
	1/2 lb.	brown bread
	1/2 lb.	white bread or 1/2 lb. potatoes
	1/4 lb.	beef or pork (with beets and vinegar twice a week)
Dinner	1-1/2 pint	soup
	1/2 lb.	white bread or 3/4 lb. potatoes
	1/2 lb.	brown bread
	1/2 lb.	beef, mutton, or pork
Supper	10 oz.	white or brown bread
	1 pint	coffee (with 1/2 oz. brown sugar)

The food allowance for women inmates was generally smaller due to their lighter workload.

Source: Reproduced from *"Crime and Punishment: A Pictorial History Part III,"* Correctional Service of Canada. Reproduced with the permission of the Minister of Public Works and Government Services Canada, 2012.

Local Jails and Provincial Prisons

Conditions in local jails and provincial institutions at this time were generally deplorable. Prisoners were required to pay for their meals, liquor, and rent— and, upon release, for the jailer's fee for his services. Those inmates unable to pay the fee were often confined for additional periods of time or allowed to panhandle on the streets to raise the necessary funds.[2]

LATE 1800s AND EARLY 1900s

In the 1880s, efforts were made to improve the operations of prisons. Various federal laws provided for the appointment of prison inspectors and outlined their powers and duties; addressed the need for the separate confinement of female offenders, mentally disordered inmates, and young offenders; and permitted the use of solitary confinement in federal penitentiaries. However, inmates continued to be subjected to a variety of physical disciplinary sanctions, many of which continued in use until the 1930s.[3]

In 1906, a Penitentiary Act was passed that included, among other provisions, the removal of youthful inmates and the mentally disordered from general penitentiary populations and the powers and duties of the federal penitentiary inspectors. Despite this legislation, there was little change in the philosophy of corrections or in how prisons were operated. Punitive practices documented by the Brown Commission nearly half a century earlier continued. Inmates were subjected to a variety of harsh disciplinary sanctions, many of which continued in use until the 1930s.

THE BEGINNINGS OF MODERN REFORM: 1930–1970

During the 1930s, there were some initial signs, particularly at the federal level, that the harsh regimen of the penitentiary was changing, albeit slowly. Prisoners displaying good conduct were given lighting in their cells in order to read, were permitted to write one letter every three months to their families, and were allowed half-hour visits by relatives once a month. The strict rule of silence was modified and inmates began to be paid for work performed in the institution at a rate of five cents per day.

Contributing to the shift in penal philosophy was the report of the Royal Commission on the Penal System of Canada, which concluded that the goal of prisons should be not only to protect society by incarcerating offenders, but also to reform and rehabilitate offenders. This increasing focus on the treatment of offenders was to provide the basis for the post-World War II era in Canadian corrections.

Following World War II, there was a shift toward a treatment model of corrections. The federal prison system introduced vocational training, education, and therapeutic intervention techniques, such as group counselling and individual therapy. Concurrent with these developments was an increase in the numbers of psychologists and psychiatrists on prison staffs. The emerging rehabilitation model of corrections received additional support from the findings of a committee of inquiry, which argued that the basic principles of Canadian corrections should include: a well-developed and extensive system of adult probation, specialization of institutions and methods of treatment, and the recruitment of professional staff.

This and other reports highlighted the shift toward rehabilitation under what became known as the **medical model of corrections**. In brief, the medical model held that the offender was ill—physically, mentally, and/or socially. Criminal behaviour was a symptom of illness. As in medicine, diagnosis and treatment would ensure the effective rehabilitation of the offender.

The decade of the 1960s was the height of the treatment model in Canadian corrections. A number of new medium- and minimum-security facilities were constructed across the country, all of which were designed to hold small populations of offenders. Prisons expanded visiting privileges, as well as education and training opportunities, and included prison physicians as part of the treatment team in an attempt to address the offender's criminal behaviour. A number of other commissions of inquiry, profiled in Box 2.5, contributed to this shift in correctional philosophy.

Medical model of corrections
The view that criminal offenders were ill—physically, mentally, and/or socially and that treatment and diagnosis would ensure rehabilitation.

LATE 20th AND EARLY 21st CENTURY: THE AMERICANIZATION OF CANADIAN CORRECTIONS

By the late 20th century, Canadian corrections had become a multibillion-dollar conglomerate, requiring massive fiscal and human resources. Systems of corrections have grown even more rapidly than police services and court systems.

This has been accompanied by significant increases in the costs of housing inmates in federal prisons and in the numbers of correctional personnel. The cost of the federal prison system rose 86 percent between 2007 and 2012. More than 80 percent of corrections budgets are for custodial expenses, even though less than 5 percent of sentenced offenders are sent to prison. The cost of housing a male inmate in a maximum security institution is more than $100,000 per year; for female inmates it is even higher. The average annual cost per offender for community supervision is about one-quarter that of an inmate in a minimum security institution ($113,974 for an offender in an institution; $29,537 for an offender in the community).[4] An analysis of data for one federal woman offender serving a 21.5 year sentence estimated the total cost at $7.4 million.[5]

A major development in Canadian corrections has been the emergence of a conservative, American-style approach to correctional policy and practice. This new approach is a radical departure from the more liberal model of corrections practice that has prevailed in Canada in recent decades. Ironically, this shift in Canadian practice has been happening at the same time that the United States is beginning to abandon punitive penology and mass incarceration (see Chapter 1), mainly because of the costs associated with these practices and the realization that community-based treatment programs are more effective and less costly than incarceration.

The cornerstone of the new penology in Canada has been a series of legislative bills, which include the following provisions:

- Elimination from the Criminal Code of the "faint hope" clause, which allowed offenders convicted of first degree murder a hearing before a jury to determine whether a reduced date for parole eligibility was possible (Bill C-48: The Protecting Canadians by Ending Sentence Discounts for Multiple Murders Act, 2011).
- Restrictions on judges as to what types of offences can be considered for a conditional sentence, which is generally served at home (see Chapter 5).
- Elimination of "two-for-one" (two days credit for one day served) for time served by offenders in pretrial custody (Bill C-25: The Truth in Sentencing Act, 2010).
- The introduction of mandatory minimum sentences for some drug crimes as well as for sexual offences (Bill C-10: The Safe Streets and Communities Act, 2012).
- Provisions that encourage Crown counsel to consider adult sentences for young offenders who have committed certain offences, and changes in the rules of pretrial detention for this offender population (Bill C-10: The Safe Streets and Communities Act, 2012).
- An increase in the waiting period to apply for a record suspension (previously referred to as a "pardon") to five years for persons convicted of summary offences and ten years for indictable offences. Persons convicted of sexual offences against minors and persons convicted of three or more indictable offences are now ineligible for a record suspension (Bill C-23: Eliminating Pardons for Serious Crimes Act, 2010).
- Abolition of accelerated parole review, which had allowed parole boards to fast-track the release of nonviolent offenders from federal institutions (Bill C-59: The Abolition of Early Parole Act, 2011).

Also, Bill C-10 altered the wording in the Corrections and Conditional Release Act, replacing the principle that the CSC must "use the *least restrictive measures* consistent with the protection of the public, staff members, and offenders," with the principle that the measures "are limited to what is *necessary and appropriate* to attain the purposes of this Act" (laws-lois.justice.gc.ca/eng/acts/C-44.6).

Bill C-10 generated a heated debate, with provincial and territorial governments arguing that the legislation would result in overcrowding, significant increases in corrections costs, and increased expenditures for criminal justice systems that the federal government would not cover. Also, concerns were expressed by Crown counsels that increases in the number of cases would further overload the justice system, extend case backlogs, and result in offenders walking away from court due to lengthy delays in getting to trial.

These concerns were not unjustified. The Parliamentary Budget Office researched what the fiscal impact of the changes to eligibility for conditional sentence orders would have been if Bill C-10 had been in effect in the 2008–9 fiscal year. It found that those changes would have cost the provinces and territories an additional $137 million for prosecutions, court cases, incarcerations, and parole reviews. Furthermore, the average cost per offender would have increased from $26,000 to $41,000. And these projected costs did not include all of the provisions in Bill C-10, or the capital costs, including constructing new prisons.[6] Additional projected costs of the new legislation included the following:

- A 27 percent increase in the CSC budget.
- Construction of nearly 500 new cells in federal institutions.
- Hiring of 4,000 new corrections staff and parole officers across the country.
- An increase in the average *daily* costs of confining an inmate, which in 2008–9 reached $578 for a federal female offender and $312 for a federal male offender.[7] See At Issue 2.1.

Corrections experts have noted that Bill C-10 and the other recent pieces of federal legislation are only some of the components of the federal government's get-tough approach to crime—an approach that has proven to be ineffective in the United States. A concern is that the shift away from rehabilitation and reintegration toward incarceration will be, as in the United States, a costly failure. According to many observers, decision making on criminal justice policy in Canada has moved from professionals to politicians, as occurred in the United States during it's tough-on-crime era. And all of this at a time when crime rates are declining.[8]

In response to these concerns, the federal Minister of Justice expressed a populist penology: "Canadians have been telling us that this is what they want to see."[9] Surveys have found, however, that more than 90 percent of Canadians are satisfied with their personal safety and that Canadians are generally misinformed about the nature and extent of crime.[10] See At Issue 2.2.

Video Link
Former Prisoner on Prison Changes
**www.youtube
.com/watch?
v=xaEa_ioDsKc**

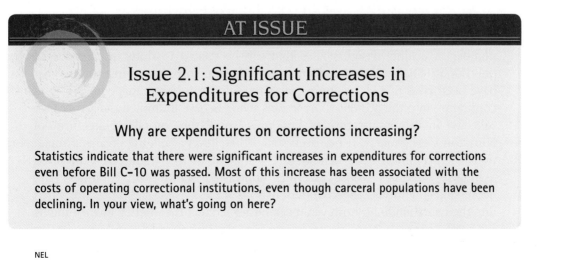

AT ISSUE

Issue 2.1: Significant Increases in Expenditures for Corrections

Why are expenditures on corrections increasing?

Statistics indicate that there were significant increases in expenditures for corrections even before Bill C-10 was passed. Most of this increase has been associated with the costs of operating correctional institutions, even though carceral populations have been declining. In your view, what's going on here?

Issue 2.2: Bill C-10

Does the public really want tougher laws?

Arguing in support of Bill C-10, the federal Justice Minister stated that the bill's provisions reflected public sentiment in favour of getting tougher on criminal offenders. Yet findings from the General Social Survey found that over 90 percent of respondents over the age of fifteen were not concerned about their personal safety. What does this discrepancy indicate about how penal policy is formulated and the factors that may influence laws that affect systems of corrections?

Observers have suggested that these new developments may be merely a recycling or reinvention of previous punishment-oriented policies, rather than representing substantive correctional change.[11] As of mid-2013, it was impossible to determine Bill C-10's impact on prison populations and corrections expenditures. However, Criminal Court judges have ruled in a number of cases that mandatory minimum sentences violate Charter of Rights provisions against cruel and unusual punishment (see Chapter 4). And in 2012, an Ontario Superior Court judge ruled that a provision in the Criminal Code was unconstitutional. Section 753(1.1), the provision in question, provides that a person who is convicted of a third serious personal injury offence and who has received a sentence of at least two years is deemed to have met the criteria to be designated a dangerous offender. Dangerous offenders can be held for an indeterminate period of time in custody.[12] These developments suggest that the judiciary may play a major role in mitigating the impact of Bill C-10 and in undermining the federal government's tough-on-crime strategy.

THE FUNCTIONS AND SYMBOLISM OF PRISON ARCHITECTURE

One way to track changes in corrections philosophy is by examining prison architecture. A review of the history of prison architecture in Canada reveals a number of distinct design phases that can be related to shifts in correctional philosophy. These eras are reflected in the federal correctional institutions that have been constructed, beginning with the Kingston Penitentiary in 1835 and continuing into the present. Corrections scholars have examined the symbolism reflected in the architecture of buildings (recall the "moral architecture" of Kingston Penitentiary). It has been stated that: "every building creates associations in the mind of the beholder."[13] For prisons, this traditionally involved grandiose buildings whose exteriors contrasted starkly with drabness and depressing conditions inside. Modern prisons are less visible and more integrated into their surroundings; however, it can be argued that the internal environments are much more sterile and desensitizing than their historical counterparts.[14]

Note that the timelines presented in Box 2.4 are general rather than definite. Also, only some of the more distinctive attributes of each era have been identified.

One issue is how the changing composition of federal inmate populations, along with laws such as Bill C-10, which may result in more offenders being incarcerated for longer periods of time, may affect prison architecture. The passage of Bill C-10 and other legislation may result in significant increases in federal and provincial prison populations; this in turn may accelerate the shift toward "big box" facilities.

BOX 2.4

The Eras of Prison Architecture and the Philosophies of Corrections

Design	Philosophy
Pre-1835	
Imprisonment not used as a sanction; little consideration given to the structure in which offenders were housed while awaiting trial or punishment; congregate housing with little or no separation of offenders by age gender, or offence	Holding facility
1830s–Early 1900s	
Auburn plan—inmates worked and ate together during the day and housed separately in cells at night; rigid silent system; tiers of small, barred, windowless cells like stacked cages overlooking a tall common space	Reformation through hard labour and discipline
Early 1900s	
No change in design; punitive practices continued	Reformation through hard work and discipline

Kingston Penitentiary, 1919.

Canada. Patent and Copyright Office/Library and Archives Canada/PA-030472

(continued)

Design	Philosophy
### 1930s–1940s	
No change in design; harsh regimen of prison modified	Initial shift toward including rehabilitation as a goal of incarceration
### 1950s	
Emphasis on privacy, with smaller tiers and larger cells with a solid door and a view window; static security with little staff–inmate interaction	Emerging focus on rehabilitation and treatment
### 1960s	
Efforts to "dilute" the prison as a distinct building form; attempts to normalize the institutional environment and reduce inmates' isolation and loss of personal dignity; some facilities incorporate a campus-style layout with residential-scale buildings for living units; increase in the use of dynamic security to encourage positive staff–inmate interaction	Treatment and rehabilitation

Springhill Penitentiary.

Correctional Service Canada

1970s

Physical spaces are designed to increase interaction with staff; treatment, rehabilitation, and living units are overseen by a unit management team; space is provided for rehabilitation programs   Treatment and rehabilitation

Mission Institute.

Correctional Service Canada

Design	Philosophy
1980s	
Mixed design; some institutions are designed to increase security and control over inmates; others, to increase inmate responsibility and staff–inmate interaction	Treatment and rehabilitation
1990s	
Several federal institutions are renovated to create "neighbourhood housing"—small, autonomous housing units for five to eight inmates with reduced direct surveillance; small regional facilities are constructed for female offenders; several healing lodges are built for Aboriginal offenders, incorporating elements of Aboriginal culture and spirituality	Treatment and rehabilitation

© Pê Sâkâstêw Institution (Alberta), Correctional Service of Canada. Reproduced with permission of the Minister of Public Works and Government Services Canada, 2013.

Pê Sâkâstêw Institution.

Design	Philosophy
Early 2000s	
Mixed designs; some federal institutions have housing clusters in which inmates live in individual bedrooms and share a common living area; a "moral architecture" designed to facilitate positive interactions and to prepare inmates for life outside the institution; other institutions are "big boxes": high-tech, with electronic security and video-surveillance technology; reduction of staff–inmate interaction contributes to warehousing (see Chapter 8)	Transition period between (1) a liberal European model emphasizing proactive intervention with inmates and treatment in the community and (2) a more punitive penology

As well, a high proportion of federal offenders are serving sentences for violent offences, and there has been a decrease in the rate of federal parole grants.[15] This means that offenders are serving longer periods of time in confinement. Also, at the provincial level, the expansion of alternatives to incarceration such as probation and conditional sentences has resulted in inmate populations with more serious criminal profiles that require more secure facilities. All of these factors have limited the ability of corrections systems to design facilities that provide increased responsibility and more freedom of movement for inmates.

A key unanswered question is whether prison architecture contributes to post-release success among inmates. There have been no evaluative studies to determine whether federal women offenders residing in the smaller regional facilities have lower rates of post-release recidivism than women who served time in and were released from the now-closed Kingston Prison for Women, which was a traditional, penitentiary-style institution. Similarly, although strong criticism has been levelled at the "big box" prisons constructed by provincial corrections systems, there is no evidence that these facilities have contributed to higher rates of reoffending upon release.

The lack of research makes it difficult to determine whether prison design has any impact on the dynamics of life inside correctional institutions as those dynamics relate, for example, to the long-standing problems of drug use and violence among inmates. The highly publicized death of a female offender with an intellectual disability at Grand Valley Institution for Women in 2007 (see Chapter 12) suggests that, while prison design may reflect changes in correctional philosophy, it may actually do little to address the needs of those who live in correctional institutions or the challenges of those who work in them.

CORRECTIONAL INQUIRIES: FACILITATING CHANGE?

At various times, governments have directed commissions of inquiry to examine correctional policy and practice. Some of the more significant of these inquiries are set out in Box 2.5. Note well that these investigations have generally focused on federal corrections, which involve a much smaller number of

BOX 2.5

Commissions and Inquiries into Systems of Corrections

Year	Commission/Inquiry	Focus/Impact
1848–49	Royal Commission of Inquiry (Brown)	Investigated charges of corruption and mismanagement at Kingston Penitentiary; identified the rehabilitation of offenders as the primary purpose of penitentiaries; impact on prison reform uncertain; most accurately viewed as a missed opportunity to rethink the concept of the penitentiary

Year	Commission/Inquiry	Focus/Impact
1891	Report of the Commission Appointed to Enquire into the Prison and Reformatory System of the Province of Ontario	Documented problems with classification, poor physical facilities, and inadequate management of provincial and local institutions; contributed to early reforms in the Ontario correctional system
1936	Royal Commission on the Penal System of Canada (Archambault)[a]	Appointed to investigate federal prisons; report (1938) concluded that the goal of prisons should be not only to protect society by incarcerating offenders but also to reform and rehabilitate offenders; gave impetus to an increasing focus on the development and expansion of vocational and educational training programs
1956	Report of a Committee Appointed to Inquire into the Principles and Practices Followed in the Remission Service of the Department of Justice of Canada (Fauteux)[b]	Recommended adoption of a correctional philosophy centred on treatment, the expansion of probation, and recruitment and training of professional staff
1969	Canadian Committee on Corrections (Ouimet)[c]	Questioned whether offenders could be rehabilitated in prisons; emphasized the importance of community corrections
1973	Task Force on the Release of Inmates (Hugessen)[d]	Examined the procedures for the release of offenders from institutions prior to the completion of their sentence; recommended the creation of five regional parole boards at the federal level and the appointment of part-time board members
1977	Report of the Parliamentary Sub-Committee on the Penitentiary System in Canada (MacGuigan)[e]	Inquiry prompted by riots in federal prisons; numerous recommendations made for improving conditions for staff and inmates
1987	Canadian Sentencing Commission	Examined sentencing and identified the purposes and principles of sentencing; proposed sentencing guidelines and revisions to the maximum and minimum sentence structure

(continued)

Year	Commission/Inquiry	Focus/Impact
1990	Task Force on Federally Sentenced Women (*Creating Choices*)[f]	Examined issues surrounding correctional policies and programs for federal female offenders; recommended the closing of the Kingston Prison for Women, to be replaced by smaller regional facilities for female offenders, including a healing lodge for Aboriginal female offenders (see Chapter 13); recommendations were accepted by the federal government
1996	Commission of Inquiry into Certain Events at the Prison for Women in Kingston (Arbour)[g]	In-depth examination of a critical incident at the Prison for Women, during which female offenders were stripped of clothing by male members of the Institutional Emergency Response Team; recommendations focused on women's corrections, cross-gender staffing in correctional institutions for women, the use of force and Institutional Emergency Response Teams, the needs of Aboriginal women, the operation of segregation units, ways of ensuring the accountability of corrections personnel and adherence to the rule of law, and procedures for handling inmate complaints and grievances
2007	Correctional Service of Canada Review Panel (Sampson)[h]	Comprehensive review of all facets of the CSC's operations, including the availability and effectiveness of rehabilitation and mental health programs, programs for Aboriginal offenders, services and support for crime victims, safety and security issues, the transition of offenders into the community, and physical infrastructure; among the recommendations were that CSC create large, regional correctional facilities

[a] J. Archambault (Chair), Report of the Royal Commission to Investigate the Penal System of Canada (Ottawa: King's Printer, 1938).

[b] G. Fauteux (Chair), Report of the Committee Appointed to Inquire into the Principles and Procedures Followed in the Remission Service of the Department of Justice of Canada (Ottawa: Queen's Printer, 1956).

c R. Ouimet (Chair), Toward Unity: Criminal Justice and Corrections: Report of the Canadian Committee on Corrections (Ottawa: Queen's Printer, 1969).

d J.K. Hugessen (Chair), Task Force on Release of Inmates (Ottawa: Solicitor General of Canada, 1972), http://www.johnhoward.ca/media/(1973)%20HV%209308%20T33%201973%20(Hugessen)%20E.pdf.

e M. MacGuigan, Report to Parliament by the Sub-Committee on the Penitentiary System in Canada (Ottawa: Supply and Services Canada, 1977).

f Task Force on Federally Sentenced Women, Creating Choices: The Report of the Task Force on Federally Sentenced Women (Ottawa. Correctional Service of Canada, 1990), http://www.csc-scc.gc.ca/text/prgrm/fsw/choices/toce-eng.shtml.

g Arbour, the Honourable L. (Commissioner), Commission of Inquiry into Certain Events at the Prison for Women in Kingston (Ottawa: Public Works and Government Services Canada, 1996), http://www.justicebehindthewalls.net/resources/arbour_report/arbour_rpt.htm.

h R. Sampson (Chair), Report of the Correctional Service of Canada Review Panel (Ottawa: Minister of Public Works and Government Services Canada, 2007), http://www.publicsafety.gc.ca/csc-scc/cscrprprt-eng.pdf.

offenders than provincial/territorial corrections. There have been far fewer inquiries in the latter jurisdictions, which face many of the same challenges. The findings of several inquiries will be discussed throughout the text.

The impact of these investigations on federal corrections has been mixed. For example, while the Brown Commission of 1848–49 led to the firing of Kingston's warden, few changes were made to that prison's structure and operations. However, the report *Creating Choices* (1990), produced by the Task Force on Federally Sentenced Women, resulted in a major shift in correctional policy with respect to federal women offenders—specifically, the antiquated Kingston Prison for Women was closed, and several smaller regional facilities were constructed to replace it. In the absence of research studies, it cannot be determined whether this reform has had a significant impact on female offenders, correctional staff, or rates of reoffending (see Chapter 13).

PRIVATE PRISONS: COMING TO A NEIGHBOURHOOD NEAR YOU?

In Chapter 1, it was noted that there has been a trend toward private-sector involvement in corrections. For many years, the United States and the United Kingdom have been contracting with private, for-profit companies to build and operate prisons. As of 2012, the private sector was not involved in correctional facilities in Canada. The Government of Ontario experimented with privatization in 2001, when a private company was contracted to operate a maximum security mega-jail in Penetanguishene under a five-year contract. A subsequent evaluation found that the company had complied with its contractual obligations to the province, maintained the required standards for health care, security, and safety, and in doing so had saved the province around

$23 million in operating expenses. This was in comparison to a mega-jail that had been constructed at the same time and was operated by the province. For reasons still unclear, the private-sector contract was not renewed.[16]

The debate in Canada over private prisons is likely to intensify. The federal government is exploring ways to involve the private sector in corrections and thereby reduce corrections expenditures. The discussion revolves around the following: whether this approach (1) is a faster and cheaper way for corrections systems to add capacity; (2) reduces operating costs; (3) improves the quality of service provided to inmates; (4) reduces rates of reoffending; and (5) relieves government of the responsibility to sanction offenders.

Proponents of private prisons contend that these facilities are more cost-effective than "public" prisons, are more flexible, able to expand physical capacity and programs more quickly than government-operated facilities, and are more accountable to monitoring and review than public prisons. Critics of private prisons argue that these facilities expand the prison–industrial complex, that punishment for profit is unethical, and that any cost savings recorded by private prisons are a result of lower, nonunion wages paid to employees.[17]

Research studies conducted in other jurisdictions, including the United States and England, suggest that the performance of private prisons is much the same as that of public prisons and that there is no conclusive evidence of cost savings.[18] See At Issue 2.3.

THE PRIVATIZATION OF THE PENAL SYSTEM

AT ISSUE

Issue 2.3: The Private Sector

Should there be private-sector involvement in correctional institutions?

Proponents argue that private prisons are (1) more cost-effective than "public" prisons, (2) more accountable to monitoring and review, and (3) more flexible and adaptable. Critics of private prisons counter that (1) "punishment for profit" is unethical, (2) any cost savings are due to cutbacks in services and programs for inmates, and (3) private prisons are part of the prison–industrial complex, which should be curtailed. What are your views?

REFLECTIONS ON CORRECTIONS HISTORY

Systems of corrections undergo constant change, driven by the ideologies of the provincial and federal governments of the day, fiscal crises, pressures exerted by public interest groups, and a variety of other influences. Many of the challenges confronting corrections systems at the beginning of the 21st century were first identified early in the 19th century. These challenges include developing structures to ensure that corrections systems are accountable, finding methods to classify offenders accurately, ensuring humane and safe conditions within institutions, and establishing effective treatment and training programs.

Several of the various commissions of inquiry have resulted in improvements to correctional institutions for both inmates and personnel. Increasingly, prison administrators and corrections staff are being held accountable to the rule of law, and inmates have recourse through grievance procedures and the courts for perceived injustices. The living conditions of inmates have improved dramatically. New regional facilities have been built for federal female offenders; facilities that incorporate elements of Aboriginal culture and spirituality have been established for Aboriginal offenders; and at several minimum and medium security facilities, new architectural designs have allowed inmates to live in apartment-like residences, although this may change now that prison populations are increasing and larger correctional facilities are being built.

However, Canadian prisons continue to be beset by violence. Also, persons who are under supervision, whether in the community and in confinement, are still overwhelmingly from vulnerable groups at the lower strata of society. Corrections systems (and the criminal justice system generally) continue to be populated by an "underclass" on the economic and social margins of society; many of these people are afflicted by mental illness, addiction, homelessness, and poverty.

And, as the discussion in the following chapters will illustrate, the long-ago understood needs of these groups are still often not being met. The broader issue—how and why persons become *involved* in corrections systems in the first place—remains largely unaddressed.

SUMMARY

This chapter focused on the origins and evolution of corrections in Canada. The material highlighted the influence of political and economic developments as well as religious beliefs on the response to criminal offenders. The evolution of institutional corrections from the 1600s to the present was traced, as were the changing philosophies of corrections as reflected in the functions and symbolism of prison architecture. A number of inquiries into federal corrections were examined and found to have had an impact on corrections policy and practice. These results included improving the living conditions of inmates and developing correctional strategies for federal women offenders and federal Aboriginal offenders. Provincial/territorial systems of corrections have received less study, and this has hindered reform in those jurisdictions.

KEY POINTS REVIEW

1. The first Canadian penitentiary was constructed in Kingston, Ontario, in 1835, and within several years, concerns were being raised regarding its effectiveness in punishing and reforming offenders.

2. The conditions in early jails and provincial institutions were generally quite bad.

3. Reforms in Canadian corrections began in the 1930s; following World War II, there was an increased emphasis on treatment.

4. Commissions of inquiry into the operation of federal corrections have had some impact on corrections policy and practice.

5. One way to trace the changing philosophy of corrections and punishment is by examining the architecture of correctional institutions over the past 200 years.

6. Many of the challenges that confront systems of corrections at the beginning of the 21st century were first identified early in the 19th century.

7. There is concern that Canadian corrections is being "Americanized."

8. Ontario's experiment with private-sector involvement in operating prisons was short-lived. A comparative evaluation of government-operated and privately operated correctional institutions produced similar results.

KEY TERM QUESTIONS

1. Compare and contrast the **Pennsylvania model** and the **Auburn model** of prisons.
2. What is **moral architecture**, and how does it help us understand the goals of the first penitentiaries that were built in Canada?
3. What was the **Brown Commission** and why was it important in the study of Canadian corrections?

NOTES

1. R. Baehre, "Origins of the Penitentiary System in Upper Canada," *Ontario History* 69, no. 3 (1977): 185–207.

2. D. Coles, *Nova Scotia Corrections: An Historical Perspective* (Halifax: Corrections Services Division, Province of Nova Scotia, 1979), 8.

3. M. MacGuigan, *Report to Parliament by the Sub-Committee on the Penitentiary System in Canada* (Ottawa: Supply and Services Canada, 1977), 12.

4. M. Olotu, D. Luong, C. MacDonald, M. McKay, S. Heath, N. Allegri, and E. Loree, *Report of the Evaluation of CSC's Community Corrections*, Chapter 1, "Correctional Interventions" (Ottawa: Correctional Service of Canada, 2011), 106, http://www.csc-scc.gc.ca/text/pa/ev-cci-fin/ev-cci-fin-eng.pdf.

5. A. Rajekar and R. Mathilakath, *The Funding Requirement and Impact of the "Truth in Sentencing Act" on the Correctional System in Canada* (Ottawa: Office of the Parliamentary Budget Officer, 2010), 99–100, http://www.pbo-dpb.gc.ca/files/files/Publications/TISA_C-25.pdf.

6. Ibid.

7. Ibid.; Public Safety Canada, Portfolio Corrections Statistics Committee, *Corrections and Conditional Release Statistical Overview: Annual Report 2011* (Ottawa: Public Works and Government Services Canada, 2011), 25, http://www.publicsafety.gc.ca/res/cor/rep/_fl/2011-ccrso-eng.pdf.

8. Public Safety Canada, *Corrections and Conditional Release Statistical Overview*; S. Brennan, "Police-Reported Crime Statistics in Canada, 2011," *Juristat* (Ottawa: Minister of Industry, 2012), http://www.statcan.gc.ca/pub/85-002-x/2012001/article/11692-eng.pdf.

9. K. Makin, "Canadian Crime and American Punishment," *Globe and Mail*, November 27, 2009, http://www.prisonjustice.ca/starkravenarticles/american_punish_1209.html.

10. S. Brennan, "Canadians' Perceptions of Personal Safety and Crime, 2009," *Juristat* (Ottawa: Ministry of Industry, 2011), http://www.statcan.gc.ca/pub/85-002-x/2011001/article/11577-eng.pdf.

11. A. Bain, "Please Recycle: Continuities in Punishment," *International Journal of Law, Crime, and Justice* 39, no. 2 (2011): 121–35.

12. M. McKiernan, "Judge Calls Foul on 'Three Strikes' Law: Superior Court Ruling Declares Reverse Onus Provision Unconstitutional," *Law Time News*, September 24, 2012, http://lawtimesnews.com/201209279332/Headline-News/Judge-calls-foul-on-three-strikes-law.

13. N. Pevsner, *A History of Building Types* (Princeton: Princeton University Press, 1976), 293.

14. P. Hancock and Y. Jewkes, "Architectures of Incarceration: The Spatial Pains of Imprisonment," *Punishment and Society* 13, no. 5 (2011): 611–29.

15. Public Safety Canada, *Corrections and Conditional Release Statistical Overview*, 59, 75.

16. Ontario Ministry of Community Safety and Correctional Services, *Central North Correctional Centre Review and Comparison to Central East Correctional Centre* (Toronto: 2006), http://www.privateci.org/private_pics/CNCC.pdf.

17. E. Schlosser, "The Prison-Industrial Complex," *Atlantic Monthly* 282, no. 6 (1998): 51–77 at 54.

18. B.W. Lundahl, C. Kunz, C. Brownell, N. Harris, and R.V. Fleet, "Prison Privatization: A Meta-Analysis of Cost and Quality of Confinement Indicators," *Research on Social Work Practice* 19, no. 4 (2009): 383–94.

CHAPTER 3
CONTEMPORARY CANADIAN CORRECTIONS

CHAPTER OBJECTIVES

After reading this chapter, you should be able to:
- *Describe the "who" and the "what" of corrections.*
- *Define corrections.*
- *Describe the legislative framework of Canadian corrections.*
- *Outline the structure of contemporary Canadian corrections.*
- *Identify and discuss the challenges confronting corrections systems in the early 21st century.*

This chapter provides an overview of the systems of corrections in Canada and identifies a number of challenges that confront corrections in the early 21st century. The discussion is designed to get you thinking about the different dimensions of corrections and to provide a backdrop for the more detailed discussions throughout the text.

THE MANDATE AND GOALS OF CORRECTIONS

Correctional systems and the other components of the criminal justice system have as their primary mandate the protection of society. However, there is often disagreement over how this goal can best be accomplished. Historically, the correctional "pendulum" has swung back and forth between classical/ conservative approaches to offenders and positivist/liberal ones. In the early 21st century, a more punitive penology has emerged, although the restorative justice model is also visible at various stages of the correctional process.

The persistence of these two views of the goals of corrections—punishment versus treatment—has resulted in what is often referred to as the "split personality" of corrections.

THE "WHO" AND THE "WHAT" OF CORRECTIONS

"Corrections" describes such a wide range of structures and activities that it is often difficult to determine what is being discussed. Many people make the mistake of equating corrections with prisons (and many college and university texts have pictures of prisons or inmates in cells on their covers).

The "Who" of Corrections

Noncarceral
That portion of systems of corrections relating to offenders in noninstitutional settings.

Carceral
That portion of systems of corrections relating to confinement in correctional institutions.

All correctional systems have both **noncarceral** (noninstitutional) and **carceral** (institutional) components. See Table 3.1.

"Community corrections" include alternatives to confinement (e.g., diversion and probation), as well as programs for offenders released from correctional institutions (e.g., who are on parole). Also, both lists in Table 3.1 include Criminal Court judges, because the correctional process actually begins when the sentence is passed (see Chapter 4).

There are more correctional personnel, offenders, and programs in noncarceral corrections, since most convicted persons are not sent to a correctional institution (although most federal correctional personnel work in institutions). Figure 3.1 presents a breakdown of Canada's adult noncarceral

Table 3.1   The "Who" of Noncarceral and Carceral Corrections

Noncarceral	Carceral
Judges	Judges
Probationers	Inmates
NGOs, e.g., John Howard Society	Superintendents and wardens
NGOs, e.g., E. Fry Society	Correctional officers, Institutional Parole Officers
Community counsellors/treatment professionals	Spiritual advisers, e.g., chaplains and Aboriginal Elders
Aboriginal friendship centres	Native prison liaison workers
Community volunteers	Citizen Advisory Committees
Offender's family	Treatment professionals
Parole board members	Community volunteers
Parolees	Offender's family
Parole officers	
Halfway house staff	

Figure 3.1

Average Counts of Adults in Correctional Services, by Type of Admission to Adult Correctional Services, 2010–11

Federal custody

Provincial/territorial custody (sentenced custody, remand, other)

Probation

Conditional sentences

Full parole (federal)

Statutory release

Day parole

Provincial parole

Source: M. Dauvergne, *Adult Correctional Statistics Canada, 2010–2011* (Ottawa: Minister of Industry, 2012). p. 20. Found at: http://www.statcan.gc.ca/pub/85-002-x/2010003/article/11353-eng.pdf.

and carceral populations. Note that around 23 percent of offenders are in some type of custody, whereas 77 percent are under community supervision.

Figure 3.2 presents the average counts of adults in provincial/territorial correctional systems in 2010–11 per 100,000. Note the high rates in Yukon, the Northwest Territories, and Nunavut, which pose unique challenges for these jurisdictions.

Figure 3.2

Average Counts of Adults in Correctional Services, by Jurisdiction, 2010–11

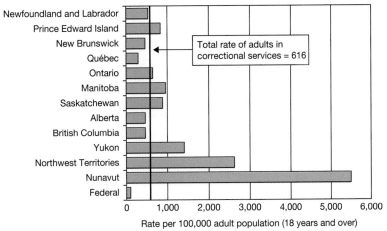

Source: M. Dauvergne, *Adult Correctional Statistics Canada, 2010–2011* (Ottawa: Minister of Industry, 2012). p. 6. Found at: http://www.statcan.gc.ca/pub/85-002-x/2010003/article/11353-eng.pdf.

The "What" of Corrections

The "what" of corrections is somewhat more complicated. Correctional systems can be described in a number of ways, including the following.

Corrections as a Political Enterprise

This reflects the perspective of the critical school, discussed in Chapter 1. Correctional policies and practices are influenced by laws and by the government of the day. An illustration of this is the shift away from a liberal, European-influenced approach to offenders toward a more punitive penology (discussed in Chapter 2).

Corrections as a Philosophy for Responding to Criminal Offenders

Various philosophies of crime and punishment have, at different times, provided the basis for the response to persons designated as criminal. These responses have ranged from the death penalty and corporal (physical) punishments to treatment and rehabilitation.

Corrections as a Subsystem of the Criminal Justice System

Systems of corrections, together with the public, the police, and the criminal courts, are the foundation of the criminal justice system. These components of the criminal justice system are interconnected. For example, patterns of police enforcement and arrest affect the number of cases that Crown counsel must handle; the case screening decisions of Crown counsel then determine the caseloads of criminal courts.

For another example, the sentencing decisions of Criminal Court judges can influence the caseloads of probation officers and determine the number of admissions to correctional institutions, while the decisions of parole boards affect the number of offenders who are incarcerated as well as the caseloads of parole officers. Throughout the criminal justice process, various key decisions affect the likelihood that an offender will end up under the supervision of a correctional authority. The impacts of these decisions are depicted in Figure 3.3.

Figure 3.3 shows that there are four main groups of agencies and organizations whose activities and decisions affect correctional systems: the police (apprehension), the judiciary (sentencing), correctional departments and parole boards (release from custody), and legislative bodies (the framework within which the police, the judiciary, and corrections/parole boards operate).[1]

Figure 3.3

Organizational Impacts on the Adult Correctional System

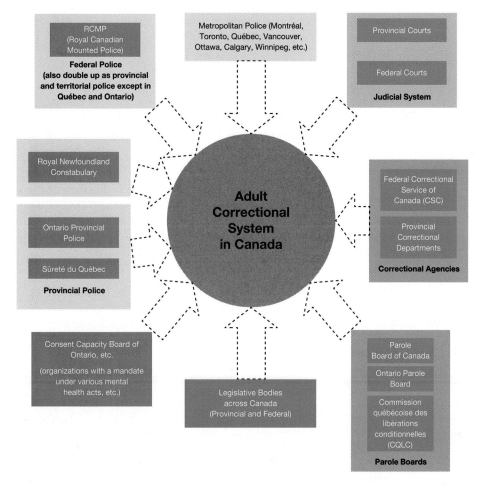

Source: A. Rajeka and R. Mathilakath, *The Funding Requirement and Impact of the "Truth in Sentencing Act" on the Correctional System in Canada.* (Ottawa: Office of the Parliamentary Budget Officer, 2010). Pg. 36. Found at: http://www.parl.gc.ca/PBO-DPB/documents/TISA_C-25.pdf.

Corrections as a Range of Programs Delivered in Community and Institutional Settings

Most convicted offenders are not incarcerated; instead, they complete their sentences under some form of supervision in the community. This includes probation (Chapters 4 and 5) and conditional sentences (Chapter 5). There are also offenders who have been released from custody, either on parole or (for federal offenders) on statutory release (Chapter 11). Correctional systems offer programs and services to the relatively small number of offenders who are sentenced to a period of custody (Chapter 10).

A Definition of Corrections

Combining all of the above dimensions, **corrections** can be defined as the structures, policies, and programs delivered by governments, not-for-profit organizations, and members of the general public to sanction, punish, treat, and supervise, in the community and in correctional institutions, persons convicted of criminal offences.

Corrections
The structures, policies, and programs to punish, treat, and supervise persons convicted of criminal offences.

THE CORRECTIONAL PROCESS

Persons who become involved in the criminal justice system move through a variety of stages, from initial contact with police, through courts, and, if convicted, into corrections. Along the way, many decisions are made by criminal justice personnel and others, all of whom are working in agencies and organizations that have specific mandates. This process is illustrated in Figure 3.4.

The flow of cases through the criminal justice system has been characterized as a sieve or a funnel; in other words, the deeper into the process, the smaller the number of cases. Fewer than 5 percent of incidents reported to the police ultimately result in a prison sentence (see Figure 3.5).

Figure 3.4

The Criminal Justice System

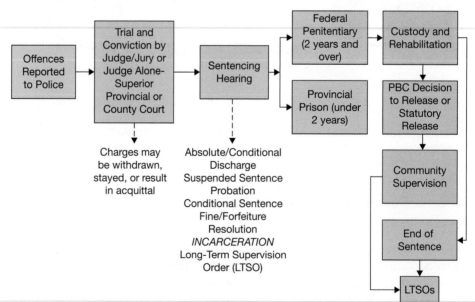

Offenders come from the community

... *and offenders return to the community.*

Source: A Road Map to Strengthening Public Safety, http://www.publicsafety.gc.ca/csc-scc/cscrprprt-eng.pdf. (Correctional Service of Canada, 2007). Reproduced with the permission of the Minister of Public Works and Government Services Canada, 2013.

Figure 3.5

The Criminal Justice Funnel

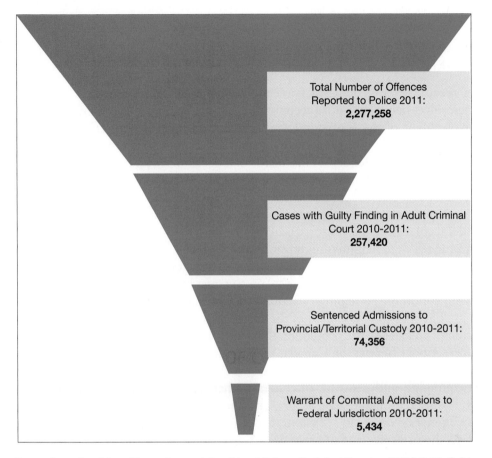

Total Number of Offences
Reported to Police 2011:
2,277,258

Cases with Guilty Finding in Adult Criminal
Court 2010-2011:
257,420

Sentenced Admissions to
Provincial/Territorial Custody 2010-2011:
74,356

Warrant of Committal Admissions to
Federal Jurisdiction 2010-2011:
5,434

Source: Reproduced from "Corrections and Conditional Release Statistical Overview 2012," Public Safety Canada Portfolio Corrections Statistics. Reproduced with the permission of the Minister of Public Works and Government Services Canada, 2012.

CORRECTIONS IN A DEMOCRATIC SOCIETY

Systems of corrections, along with the police, the criminal courts, and the criminal law, are the primary mechanisms by which the state attempts to ensure the safety and security of the general public. In democratic societies, however, there are tensions among these systems of power and authority. Corrections systems are designed to ensure the safety and security of the community; but at the same time, there is a need to ensure that the rights of accused and convicted persons are protected. Under the Canadian Charter of Rights and Freedoms, offenders have all of the same rights as other citizens except for those removed by law or incarceration.

Court decisions and various commissions of inquiry have had a strong impact on correctional policies and procedures and on how offenders are managed. For example, court decisions have placed limits on the use of solitary confinement and strip searches and have also given federal inmates the right to vote.

Increasing Accountability and a Concern with the Rule of Law and Justice

In recent years, systems of corrections and conditional release have found themselves being held more accountable. This has coincided with the increasing involvement of the courts and the Canadian Human Rights Tribunal, which are now imposing on correctional agencies and personnel a **duty to act fairly** when managing offenders. This means that decisions must be fair and equitable and that offenders must have the opportunity to respond to any assessments made by correctional personnel about their conduct and performance. In 2012, for example, a federal judge ordered a review of the inmate grievance system in federal correctional facilities, based on a finding that delays in resolving official grievances were heightening tensions and violence.[2]

Correctional authorities have been the target of civil suits launched by crime victims and are also being taken to court by inmates over issues such as living conditions, disciplinary actions, and various regulations.

The Mission Statement of the Correctional Service of Canada reflects an attempt to balance the protection of society with the rights of offenders: "The Correctional Service of Canada, as part of the criminal justice system and respecting the rule of law, contributes to the protection of society by actively encouraging and assisting offenders to become law-abiding citizens, while exercising reasonable, safe, secure, and humane control." (Note: The "rule of law" generally refers to a "system that attempts to protect the rights of citizens from the arbitrary and abusive use of government power"; http://ebook.law .uiowa.edu/ebook/faqs/what-is-the-rule-of-law.)

THE LEGISLATIVE FRAMEWORK OF CORRECTIONS

Correctional systems operate under a variety of federal and provincial/territorial statutes that establish the authority of correctional officials, set out jurisdiction, and provide the framework within which decisions are made and programs are administered. Among the more significant pieces of legislation are the following:

- The **Canadian Charter of Rights and Freedoms** is the primary law of the land and guarantees fundamental freedoms, legal rights, and equality rights for all citizens of Canada, including those accused of crimes.
- The **Constitution Act (1867)** sets out the respective responsibilities of the federal and provincial governments in many areas, including criminal justice. The federal government operates correctional facilities for offenders who have been sentenced to two years or more.

Duty to act fairly
The obligation of corrections to ensure that offenders are treated fairly by corrections personnel.

Canadian Charter of Rights and Freedoms
The primary law of the land, which guarantees basic rights and freedoms for citizens, including convicted offenders.

Constitution Act (1867)
Legislation that includes provisions that define the responsibilities of the federal and provincial governments with respect to criminal justice.

- The **Criminal Code** is a federal statute that defines most criminal offences, the procedures for prosecuting them, and the penalties that sentencing judges can hand down.
- The **Corrections and Conditional Release Act (CCRA)** is the primary legislation under which the federal system of corrections operates. Sections in this act cover institutional and community corrections, conditional release and detention, and the Office of the Correctional Investigator.
- Provincial legislation includes corrections statutes that set out the framework within which provincial correctional systems operate.
- Finally, there are international agreements and conventions to which the Canadian government is a signatory. These include the United Nations Standard Minimum Rules for the Treatment of Prisoners and the International Covenant on Civil and Political Rights.

The response to offenders by systems of corrections in Canada has sometimes not met international standards.

THE STRUCTURE OF CONTEMPORARY CANADIAN CORRECTIONS

Correctional systems in Canada are operated by the federal and provincial/territorial governments, which together spend just over $4 billion a year on personnel, programs, services, and infrastructure. Most of this money is spent on custodial services.[3]

The Split in Correctional Jurisdiction

A unique feature of Canadian corrections is the **two-year rule**, under which offenders who receive sentences of two years or longer fall under the jurisdiction of the federal government, and offenders receiving sentences of two years less a day are the responsibility of provincial/territorial correctional authorities. The historical record provides no clear explanation for why the two-year rule was established at the time of Confederation in 1867. Observers have offered a number of reasons, including these: (1) the federal government wanted to strengthen its powers; (2) only the federal government had the resources to establish and maintain long-term institutions; and (3) offenders receiving short sentences were seen as in need of guidance, whereas those receiving longer sentences were seen as more serious criminals who had to be separated from the society for longer periods.[4]

This split in jurisdiction has a number of implications for offenders and correctional authorities. On the negative side, the relatively short period of time that offenders are confined in provincial/territorial institutions means there is a high turnover of the population, which makes it difficult to provide treatment programs. As well, there are considerable variations among the provinces and territories in the noncarceral and carceral programs and services

Criminal Code
Federal legislation that sets out the criminal laws of Canada and the procedures for administering justice.

Corrections and Conditional Release Act (CCRA)
The primary legislation under which the federal system of corrections operates.

Two-year rule
The basis for the division of responsibility for convicted offenders between the federal and provincial/territorial governments.

offered. Many offenders spend their entire "careers" in provincial/territorial facilities, while others spend time in both systems. On a more positive note, the two-year rule helps separate more serious offenders, who receive lengthier sentences and, potentially, have greater access to treatment programs, from those who have committed less serious crimes. As well, provincial offenders have access to a wide range of alternatives to incarceration, including probation, conditional sentences, and electronic monitoring.

FEDERAL AND PROVINCIAL/TERRITORIAL SYSTEMS OF CORRECTIONS

The federal system of corrections is operated by the Correctional Service of Canada (CSC), an agency of Public Safety and Emergency Preparedness Canada. The CSC, headquartered in Ottawa, has five regions: Atlantic, Québec, Ontario, Prairie, and Pacific. It operates a variety of facilities, including federal penitentiaries, halfway houses, healing lodges, and treatment centres for Aboriginal offenders, community parole offices, psychiatric hospitals, reception and assessment centres, health care centres, palliative care units, and an addiction research centre. Also, the CSC has partnered with not-for-profit organizations to operate halfway houses across the country.

While the CSC's activities and events involving federal offenders receive more attention from researchers and the media, the large majority (96 percent) of convicted offenders receive sentences that place them under the jurisdiction of provincial/territorial correctional authorities. Just more than half the custodial sentences imposed by the courts are for less than one year.[5] As a result, the larger percentage of offenders in Canada are confined in provincial/territorial facilities.

All of the provinces/territories operate a variety of noncarceral programs and services, including probation, bail supervision, fine options, community service, and diversion programs. Other programs and services include electronic monitoring (most often as a condition of probation or temporary absence), house arrest, intensive supervision probation, temporary absences, and parole. Most of the offenders in provincial/territorial correctional systems are on probation. The provincial/territorial governments also operate correctional facilities and remand centres. Remanded individuals (1) have been charged with an offence, and the court has ordered they be held in custody while awaiting trial, or (2) have been found guilty at trial and are awaiting sentencing.

Provincial/territorial systems of corrections have received little attention from researchers, mainly because of the diversity of programs and services they offer, the relatively short periods that provincial offenders remain in confinement (see Figure 3.6), and the widely held view that provincial/territorial offenders are a less serious threat in terms of their criminal behaviour. This, even though many provincial jails are faced with overcrowding, gang activity, high rates of communicable diseases (including HIV, tuberculosis, and hepatitis C), a lack of inmate safety, and poor working conditions for staff. There is

Figure 3.6

Median Days Spent by Adults in Provincial and Territorial Sentenced Custody, by Province and Territory, 2009–10 and 2010–11

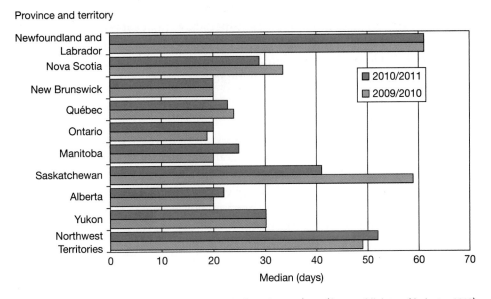

Source: M. Dauvergne, *Adult Correctional Statistics in Canada, 2010/2011*, (Ottawa: Minister of Industry, 2012). Pg. 11. Found at: http://www.statcan.gc.ca/pub/85-002-x/2010001/article/11715-eng.pdf

evidence that offenders in provincial/territorial institutions may not have access to the same level of programs and services, including health care services, as their counterparts in the federal corrections system.[6]

Parole Boards

The Parole Board of Canada (PBC) is a federal agency that operates independently of the CSC and makes final decisions regarding when (most) federal offenders will be released from custody. The PBC's decision making is examined in Chapter 11. Two provinces—Québec and Ontario—operate their own provincial parole boards, with provincial probation officers supervising offenders released on provincial parole. In the other eight provinces, the PBC handles the release of some offenders and CSC parole officers supervise offenders.

Correctional Investigators

The Office of the Correctional Investigator is an independent federal agency whose mandate is (1) to investigate the problems experienced by federal offenders in institutions, or who are under supervision in the community, and (2) to ensure that the CSC meets its obligations to manage offenders in a manner that conforms to the law and that respects the rights of offenders (www.oci-bec.gc.ca).

Video Link
theStar.com:
Interview with
Canada's Prison
Ombudsman
**www.youtube.com/
watch?v=2Xh
_PpJCMpM**

There are also provincial ombudspersons who have the authority to investigate citizen complaints against the decisions and actions of provincial government agencies and employees. Such complaints include those made by offenders under the supervision and control of provincial correctional systems. The findings and recommendations of the correctional investigator and the provincial ombudspersons are only advisory; these offices have no legal power to mandate changes in corrections policy and practice. Note well that, while expenditures on corrections have increased significantly in the past decade, there has not been a corresponding increase in the budgets of correctional investigators.

Citizen's Advisory Committees (CACs) and Correctional Institutions

CACs are composed of local citizens who volunteer their time. Attempts are made to ensure that these committees reflect the ethnic, gender, socioeconomic, and cultural diversity of the community at large. The goals of CACs include these: to promote public knowledge and understanding of corrections; to contribute to the development of correctional facilities and programs; and to increase public participation in the corrections process. They are also meant to serve as impartial observers of the CSC's day-to-day operations. CACs offer advice to CSC managers, meet regularly with correctional staff and management, and serve as liaisons between correctional institutions and the community. There is little evidence that CACs have increased community involvement in, or oversight of, the operations of correctional institutions. This suggests that they may be more symbolic than substantive.

THE PRIVATE, NOT-FOR-PROFIT SECTOR

Private, not-for-profit organizations have long been helping deliver correctional services and programs. The John Howard Society operates a variety of programs, including bail supervision, community assessment and parole supervision, residential halfway housing, victim assistance, victim–offender mediation, and public and legal education. In Calgary, for example, the society operates a substance abuse program, a community conferencing program based on the principles of restorative justice, and a number of counselling, advocacy, referral, and pre-release planning programs for offenders in correctional institutions, as well as a halfway house for special needs offenders (www.johnhoward.ca).

The Elizabeth Fry Society lobbies for reform at all levels of the criminal justice system, with a particular focus on women in conflict with the law. The society advocates for correctional policy reforms and develops and operates its own programs. It played a major role in the closing of Kingston's Prison for Women and its replacement by smaller, regional facilities. The branch in Hamilton, Ontario, operates a community service order program and provides a range of services for female offenders, including counselling and pre-release services (www.elizabethfry.ca).

The Salvation Army has been involved in Canadian corrections since the late 1880s. It provides a range of services and programs, including community service order supervision, family group conferencing, substance abuse counselling, and supervision of offenders in the community (www.salvationarmy.ca).

Across Canada, affiliates of the St. Leonard's Society sponsor a wide range of programs and facilities for offenders. St. Leonard's Community Services London and Region, for example, operates a number of community-based and residential programs. These include an attendance centre program for youth as an alternative to custody, an employment readiness program, and Maison Louise Arbour, a residential centre for women in conflict with the law and for women who have a mental illness (www.stleonards.ca).

There are also Aboriginal not-for-profit organizations that help Aboriginal persons in conflict with the law and that try to address the over-representation of Aboriginal people in the justice system. The Native Counselling Service of Alberta (NCSA) is the oldest of the organizations involved in providing justice-related programs and services for Aboriginal people. The NCSA delivers a variety of institutional and community-based correctional programs and services for Aboriginal offenders, many of these under contract with the CSC (www.ncsa.ca).

Video Links
John Howard
Society
www.johnhoward.ca

Elizabeth Fry
Society
www.elizabethfry.ca

Video Link
Native Counselling
Services of Alberta
www.ncsa.ca

CHALLENGES FOR SYSTEMS OF CORRECTIONS

Correctional systems in the early 21st century face a number of challenges, many of which are discussed throughout the text. These include the following:

Diverse, Marginalized Populations

The men, women, and youth who become involved in the criminal justice system represent various ethnicities as well as specific categories of offenders. Those categories include white-collar, violent, intellectual disabled, long-term, and sex offenders—and, increasingly, elderly offenders.

For many offenders, criminal behaviour is only a symptom: they have other functional problems involving their family, peer group, and/or workplace. Although this is not universally true, many offenders were raised in dysfunctional homes afflicted by alcoholism and violence and were victims of child abuse (physical, sexual, or psychological) or neglect. Many adult offenders have low levels of formal education, few marketable skills, and low self-esteem. A disproportionate number are Aboriginal, and an unknown number of offenders are afflicted with Fetal Alcohol Spectrum Disorder (FASD).

The federal and provincial/territorial governments have developed a variety of programs for vulnerable persons. A number of these initiatives will be discussed throughout the text. They range from Mental Health Courts and Drug Courts (see Chapter 4), which make it possible for offenders to be diverted from the justice system, to specialized post-incarceration programs. The CSC has developed specialized units for mentally ill offenders in several federal institutions, and probation and parole officers have received training to increase the effectiveness of their efforts.

Long-Term Programs and Services for Offenders

The police and criminal courts spend very little time with individual offenders during the criminal justice process. By contrast, corrections must provide programs and services over a longer term, be it in the community or in institutional settings.

Corrections in a Multicultural Society

Canada's multicultural society presents unique challenges for correctional systems. Visible minorities, most of whom live in Canada's major urban areas, now make up just more than 10 percent of the population. There is no evidence that immigrants have higher rates of criminality than people born in Canada; in fact, the rate of offending for immigrants is lower. Many new immigrants speak neither English nor French and come from countries where there is widespread distrust of the criminal justice system. Correctional personnel may struggle with language barriers, especially with older citizens who have English or French as a second language, and they may be challenged to identify, develop, and sustain correctional programs in the community.

Corrections in the Canadian North

Providing correctional services and delivering programs in remote and northern regions of the country is a difficult challenge, given that northern communities typically have the highest rates of crime and serious violent crime in the country. The Northwest Territories, for example, has a crime rate six times greater than the national average, and the rate of sexual assault there is many times greater than in the rest of the country.

Some small northern communities are accessible only by air (or, for a brief part of the year, by sea), which makes it difficult to address the needs of offenders in these regions. Also, many small northern communities do not have full-time probation and parole officers, so justice services must be provided on a "fly-in" or "drive-in" basis. This, even though offenders in these regions may have multiple needs, including alcohol and drug addiction, mental illness, and FASD.[7] Offenders who receive federal sentences or who require specialized treatment may have to be sent hundreds of kilometres from their home community, and follow-up supervision and treatment are often limited or nonexistent.

Similarly, northerners' access to mental health services is often severely limited. In the NWT, for example, there is one psychiatrist for the entire territory and court-ordered psychiatric assessments are conducted in Alberta. For offenders with mental illness or FASD, there may be few alternatives to incarceration. Regarding the lack of resources in Nunavut, one judge remarked that "Nunavut has a psychiatric hospital. It's called BCC [Baffin Correctional Centre]."[8] A study of facilities and services for the mentally ill in the NWT concluded that "the territory's correctional system either fails even to identify prisoners with mental health problems; recognizes them but does nothing; or is simply ineffective when it does try to help. The offenders keep their heads down, their medical, mental, or addiction needs unmet, and wait for their release."[9]

Developing and Implementing Evidence-Based Correctional Policies and Programs

Throughout the text, the term **evidence-based practice** will be used in discussions of all stages of the correctional process. Evidence-based practices include those policies, strategies, and programs that have been shown by evaluation research to be effective in achieving specified objectives. They can be contrasted with tradition-based practices, which develop from the established routines, politics, and philosophies of agencies, organizations, and individuals—and from emotion as well (see Table 3.2). Attempts to implement evidence-based practices have been uneven and are more prevalent in federal corrections.

Evidence-based practice
Policies, strategies, and programs that have been shown by evaluation research to be effective in achieving specified objectives.

Table 3.2   Evidence-Based versus Tradition-Based Practices

	Evidence-Based Practices	Tradition-Based Practices
Purpose	Provide efficient and effective responses to problems	Respond to individual beliefs and desire for revenge
Assumption	Policies and practices should be based on evidence	Policies should be responsive to emotions
Relationship to the goals of the criminal justice system	Practices focus on all goals of the criminal justice system	Focus is mainly on retribution and just deserts
Focus on cost	Cost-effectiveness is central to decision making	Limited focus
The role of the community	Community plays an active role by providing information that can be used to determine effectiveness	Community plays a passive role, with opinions serving as the public's input
Role of leaders	To promote cultural change in the organization	To manage and maintain traditional strategies

(continued)

	Evidence-Based Practices	Tradition-Based Practices
Role of line officers	To implement and set new practices	To maintain status quo
Time orientation	Focus on present and future	Focus on the past
Focus on evaluation	Extensive	Limited
Role of researchers	To evaluate programs to determine effectiveness and recommend changes	To study public attitudes; provide little input to program operations and effectiveness
Definition of success	Quality of program	Quantity of offenders

Source: Adapted from M. DeMichele and B. Payne, *Offender Supervision with Electronic Technology. Community Corrections Resource,* (Washington, D.C.: U.S. Department of Justice, 2009). Pg. 50.

With a few notable exceptions, there is in Canada no well-developed body of empirical knowledge on which to formulate policies and operate programs. What is known about what works and what doesn't work in corrections are presented in various research files throughout the text. See At Issue 3.1.

AT ISSUE

Issue 3.1: Evidence-Based Practices

Should there be legislation that requires systems of corrections to adopt evidence-based practices?

A body of literature is emerging about what works in correctional practice and what does not. Proponents of evidence-based practices argue that corrections policies and programs should be based on what research has shown makes correctional systems more accountable and effective. Critics of this approach counter that correctional professionals are in the best position to determine which policies and programs are most appropriate for their particular jurisdiction and circumstances. What is your view?

Utilizing Risk–Needs–Responsivity Principles in Correctional Interventions

A model that has gained prominence in corrections studies is Risk–Needs–Responsivity (RNR). It is introduced in Chapters 5 and 6 in discussions of alternatives to incarceration and probation. Although RNR has most often been associated with institutional treatment programs, it is now recognized that this model may have validity in community corrections—that is, in providing supervision and programs for offenders who have avoided a custodial sentence and for those released into the community after a period of confinement.[10] Applications of RNR will be described in later chapters. At this juncture, it is enough to summarize the model's basic principles:

- The **risk principle**—correctional interventions have a greater chance of success when they are matched with the offender's level of risk because higher risk offenders benefit more than medium- and low-risk offenders.
- The **need principle**—correctional interventions should target the criminogenic needs (i.e., dynamic risk factors) of offenders, which can include substance abuse, peer relations, and pro-criminal attitudes.
- The **responsivity principle**—correctional interventions should be matched to the learning styles and abilities of individual offenders, with particular emphasis on cognitive-behavioural interventions.

Programs and interventions that utilize RNR have been proven to be more successful than those based on traditional practice.

SUMMARY

This chapter has provided an overview of the "who" and the "what" of the federal and provincial/territorial corrections systems. There was a discussion of the various organizations that are involved in corrections, including the not-for-profit sector, parole boards, corrections investigators, and the community. The materials in this chapter provide the framework for the remainder of the text, which includes more detailed discussions of the different dimensions of corrections. The notion of evidence-based corrections was introduced and contrasted with traditional correctional practice. The principles of RNR were introduced as key to the success of correctional interventions.

KEY POINTS REVIEW

1. Systems of corrections and the other components of the criminal justice system have as their primary mandate the protection of society.
2. Corrections is a philosophy for responding to criminal offenders; it is also a range of programs and services delivered in community and institutional settings.

Risk principle
Correctional interventions are most effective when matched with the offender's level of risk, and higher risk offenders benefit from interventions more than medium- and low-risk offenders.

Need principle
To be effective, correctional interventions must address the criminogenic needs of offenders.

Responsivity principle
Correctional interventions should be matched to the learning styles of individual offenders.

3. Corrections can be defined as the structures, policies, and programs to punish, treat, and supervise persons convicted of criminal offences.

4. In democratic societies, there are tensions between systems of corrections and the need to ensure that the rights of accused and convicted persons are protected.

5. Corrections systems operate under a variety of federal and provincial/territorial statutes that establish the authority of corrections officials, set out jurisdiction, and provide the framework within which decisions are made and programs are administered.

6. The large majority of convicted offenders receive sentences that place them under the jurisdiction of provincial/territorial correctional authorities.

7. Corrections lacks a well-developed body of empirical knowledge on which to formulate policies and operate programs.

8. Corrections systems face a number of challenges, including how to address the needs of a diverse, marginalized population; how to deliver programs and services in the Canadian North; and how to implement evidence-based policies and programs that include the principles of Risk–Needs–Responsivity.

KEY TERM QUESTIONS

1. Describe the components of *noncarceral* and *carceral* corrections.

2. Define *corrections*.

3. In corrections, what is meant by the *duty to act fairly*?

4. Describe the role of each of the following in providing the framework for corrections: the *Canadian Charter of Rights and Freedoms*, the *Constitution Act (1867)*, the *Criminal Code*, and the *Corrections and Conditional Release Act*.

5. What is the *two-year rule*, and what role does it play in corrections?

6. What is *evidence-based practice*?

7. Define the principles of *risk*, *need*, and *responsivity* and note their importance in corrections programming.

NOTES

1. A. Rajeka and R. Mathilakath, *The Funding Requirement and Impact of the "Truth in Sentencing Act" on the Correctional System in Canada* (Ottawa: Parliamentary Budget Office, 2010), 34, http://www.parl.gc.ca/PBO-DPB/documents/TISA_C-25.pdf.

2. D. Quan, "Inmate Complaints Not Addressed Speedily, Judge Ruled," *Ottawa Citizen*, August 8, 2012, http://o.canada.com/2012/08/08/inmate-complaints-not-addressed-speedily-judge-ruled.

3. M. Dauvergne, *Adult Correctional Statistics in Canada, 2010–2011* (Ottawa: Correctional Service of Canada, 2012), http://www.statcan.gc.ca/pub/85-002-x/2012001/article/11715 -eng.pdf.

4. R. Ouimet (Chair), *Toward Unity: Criminal Justice and Corrections: Report of the Canadian Committee on Corrections* (Ottawa: Information Canada, 1969).

5. Public Safety Canada, Corrections Statistics Committee, *Corrections and Conditional Release Statistical Overview* (Ottawa: Public Works and Government Services Canada, 2011), http://www.publicsafety.gc.ca/res/cor/rep/_fl/2011-ccrso-eng.pdf.

6. J.R. Bernier and K. MacLellan, *Health Status and Health Services Use of Female and Male Prisoners in Provincial Jail* (Halifax: Atlantic Centre of Excellence for Women's Health, 2011), http://www.acewh.dal.ca/pdf/prisoner-health2011.pdf.

7. L. Burd, D.K. Fast, J. Conry, and A. Williams, "Fetal Alcohol Spectrum Disorder as a Marker for Increased Risk of Involvement with Correction Systems," *Journal of Psychiatry and Law* 38 (2010): 559–83.

8. K. Murphy, *Mental Health Crisis Overflows into Jail Cells* (2002), http://www.nunatsiaqonline .ca/archives/nunavut020517/news/nunavut/20517_10.html.

9. L. McKeon, "The Prisoner Dilemma," *This Magazine*, June 1, 2010, 8, http://this.org/ magazine/2010/06/01/nwt-prisoners-mental-health.

10. J. Bonta, G. Bourgon, T. Rugge, T.-L. Scott, A.K. Yessine, L. Gutierrez, and J. Li, "An Experimental Demonstration of Training Probation Officers in Evidence-Based Community Supervision," *Criminal Justice and Behavior* 38, no. 11 (2011): 1127–48.

CHAPTER 4

SENTENCING: BEGINNING THE CORRECTIONS PROCESS

CHAPTER OBJECTIVES

After reading this chapter, you should be able to:

- *Describe the purpose, principles, and goals of sentencing and the various sentencing options.*
- *Describe the special sentencing provisions for dangerous and long-term offenders as well as the sanction of judicial determination.*
- *Discuss the effectiveness of sentencing.*
- *Discuss the arguments that surround Section 718.2(e) of the Criminal Code.*
- *Speak to the arguments surrounding the potential expansion of the number of mandatory minimum sentences in the Criminal Code.*
- *Discuss the arguments that surround the use of the death penalty.*
- *Discuss the differences between the principles of the criminal courts and the principles of community circles.*

An often overlooked component of corrections is the sentences that are imposed by judges in the criminal courts. The criminal courts can be viewed as the beginning of the correctional process. It is here that judgments are passed on offenders and that specific sanctions are imposed through sentencing. See Figure 4.1. The decisions made by Criminal Court judges not only determine which system of corrections (federal or provincial/territorial) the offender will enter but also whether the offender will be under supervision and control in the community or be incarcerated. Public opinion surveys over the past three decades have consistently found that 75 percent of Canadians view sentencing as too lenient. There appears to be widespread support for mandatory sentences, albeit with judges retaining some discretion to impose a lesser sentence in exceptional cases.[1]

In recent years, there have been significant changes in sentencing legislation, including abolition of the two-for-one credit for offenders who spend time in remand prior to trial or sentencing and an increase in the number of mandatory minimum sentences.[2]

Figure 4.1

Outline of the Canadian Court System

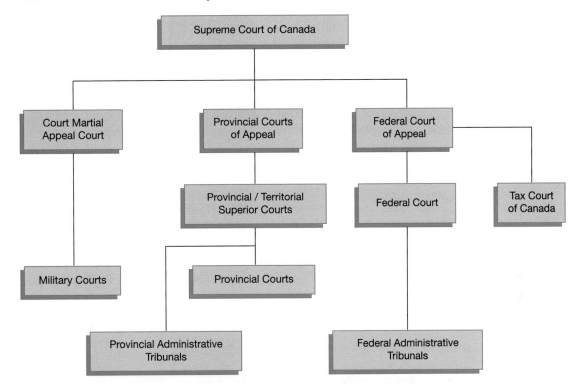

Source: Canada's Court System, http://www.justice.gc.ca/eng/dept-min/pub/ccs-ajc/page3.html. (Justice Canada, 2012). Reproduced with the permission of the Minister of Public Works and Government Services Canada, 2012.

THE PURPOSE AND PRINCIPLES OF SENTENCING

Section 718 of the Criminal Code sets out the purpose and principles of sentencing:

> *The fundamental purpose of sentencing is to contribute, along with crime prevention initiatives, to respect for the law and the maintenance of a just, peaceful and safe society by imposing just sanctions that have one or more of the following objectives:*
>
> *(a)   to denounce the unlawful conduct;*
> *(b)   to deter the offender and other persons from committing offences;*
> *(c)   to separate offenders from society, where necessary;*
> *(d)   to assist in rehabilitating offenders;*
> *(e)   to provide reparations for harm done to victims or to the community; and*
> *(f)   to promote a sense of responsibility in offenders, and acknowledgment of the harm done to victims and to the community.*

The Goals of Sentencing: The Cases of Mr. Smith and Mr. Jones

There are three primary groups of sentencing goals in the criminal courts: utilitarian, retributive, and restorative.[3] The real-life cases of "Mr. Smith" and "Mr. Jones" (not their real names) will be used to illustrate how these sentencing goals are applied. Mr. Smith was a Quebec police chief and swimming coach who was convicted of four counts of sexual assault for fondling two girls aged twelve and thirteen. Mr. Jones, a computer engineer in British Columbia, was convicted of sexual assault for fondling his young stepdaughter over a two-year period. The cases of Mr. Smith and Mr. Jones—neither of whom had a prior criminal record—were widely publicized in their respective communities, and both men eventually lost their jobs.

Utilitarian Goals

Utilitarian sentencing goals focus on the future conduct of Mr. Smith, Mr. Jones, and others who might commit similar offences. These goals focus on protecting the public from future crimes in the following ways:

- by discouraging potential Mr. Smiths and Mr. Joneses from crime (**general deterrence**);
- by discouraging Mr. Smith and Mr. Jones from doing it again (**specific deterrence**);
- by addressing the reasons why Mr. Smith and Mr. Jones did it (*rehabilitation*); and
- by keeping Mr. Smith and Mr. Jones in jail to protect society (*incapacitation*).

General deterrence
An objective of sentencing designed to deter others from engaging in criminal conduct.

Specific deterrence
An objective of sentencing designed to deter the offender from future criminal conduct.

Retributive Goals

The past, rather than the future, is the focus of retributive sentencing goals, which include the following:

- to express society's disapproval of Mr. Smith's and Mr. Jones's behaviour and to validate existing laws (*denunciation*); and
- to make Mr. Smith and Mr. Jones "pay" for their offences, based on the philosophy "an eye for an eye" (*retribution*).

Central to the retributive goals of sentencing is the notion of proportionality—that is, the sentences received by Mr. Smith and Mr. Jones should be proportionate to the gravity of their offences as well as to their degree of responsibility.

Restorative Goals

The most widely used restorative approaches are victim–offender reconciliation programs, circle sentencing, and family group conferencing. Restorative justice is based on the principle that criminal behaviour injures not only the victim but also communities and offenders. Any attempt to resolve the problems that the criminal behaviour has created should, therefore, involve all three parties. Restorative justice approaches also have a utilitarian function in that they are designed to protect the public from future criminal behaviour.

Since the victims in both these cases were children, they would be excluded from any restorative justice forum. However, the victims' families would have the opportunity to discuss the impact of the crimes, and Mr. Smith and Mr. Jones would be held accountable for their criminal behaviour.

What Sentences Did Mr. Smith and Mr. Jones Receive?

The offence of sexual assault carries a maximum penalty of 10 years' imprisonment. Although neither Mr. Smith nor Mr. Jones had a prior criminal record and both had a good job history, the offences they committed were serious and had a significant impact on the victims. One of Mr. Smith's victims suffered long-term emotional and academic problems, while Mr. Jones's former spouse

© Mike Baldwin / Cornered

"They say time is money. I had a very generous judge."

© Mike Baldwin http://www.CartoonStock.com

Concurrent sentences
Sentences that are amalgamated and served simultaneously.

Consecutive sentences
Sentences that run separately and are completed one after the other.

Intermittent sentence
A sentence that is served on a "part-time" basis, generally on weekends.

and children experienced considerable emotional difficulties. The child victims in both cases had been young and vulnerable. Mr. Smith had been an authority figure in the community, and parents trusted him to supervise their children, a trust he violated. Similarly, Mr. Jones violated the trust of his step-daughter and most likely would have continued sexually abusing her had she not informed her mother of his improper behaviour.

Mr. Smith was sentenced to three years' probation (the maximum) and 180 hours of community service work. The Crown appealed the sentence on the grounds that it was too lenient. But the Quebec Court of Appeal upheld the sentence, in part because Mr. Smith had been fired from his job as police chief and so had already experienced a severe sanction. The Appeal Court acknowledged that child abuse typically demands a denunciatory sentence for the protection of society, but noted that each case must be judged on its merits.

Mr. Jones was not so fortunate. He was sentenced to eighteen months' confinement in a provincial correctional facility and three years' probation (the maximum). In explaining the sentence, the presiding judge cited the objectives of denunciation and general and specific deterrence.

SENTENCING OPTIONS

The sentencing options from which Canadian judges may select are set out in Table 4.1. Most of the options provide alternatives to confinement (discussed in greater detail in Chapters 5 and 6). Some of these options may be mixed and matched; for example, the judge may impose a period of probation in conjunction with a sentence of two years less a day for offenders in provincial/territorial systems, or they may impose fines along with probation or a period of confinement.

Sentences imposed in court can be concurrent, consecutive, or intermittent. **Concurrent sentences** received by the offender are merged into one sentence and served simultaneously. Thus, an offender sentenced to two terms of nine months each will serve a nine-month sentence (not an eighteen-month sentence). With **consecutive sentences**, the sentences are served separately: one begins after the other has expired. That is, an offender sentenced to 2 terms of 9 months each will serve 18 months. **Intermittent sentences** are served on a "part-time" basis (generally weekends, from Friday evening until Monday morning) and are generally no more than ninety days in length. Intermittent sentences may pose challenges for provincial/territorial systems of corrections. Many facilities are overcrowded, so it may be difficult to find appropriate accommodations for these individuals.

The Criminal Code states that all sentences are to be concurrent unless the trial judge specifies that they are to be consecutive. By contrast, sentences under the Provincial Offences Act are to be consecutive unless the sentencing judge specifies that they are to run concurrently.

Table 4.1   Sentencing Options

Absolute discharge	The offender is found guilty but technically not convicted and is set free with no criminal record.
Conditional discharge	The offender is found guilty and released upon the condition that he or she comply with the conditions of a probation order. If the offender fails to meet the conditions, he or she may be returned to court to be sentenced on the original charge.
Suspended sentence	The offender is convicted of the offence, but the imposition of the sentence is suspended pending successful completion of a period of probation.
Fine	The offender must pay a specific amount of money within a specified time or face the prospect of imprisonment for fine default.
Intermittent sentence	The offender is sentenced to jail, generally served on weekends, and when not in custody is subject to a probation order with specific conditions. Available only for sentences that do not exceed 90 days.
Probation	The offender is placed under supervision in the community for a specified period of time (maximum three years), must fulfill general conditions, and may be required to adhere to or complete specific conditions (e.g., attend alcohol or drug counselling).
Conditional sentence	The offender receives a term of confinement (less than two years) and is allowed to serve it in the community under the supervision of a probation officer, provided he or she meets certain specified conditions (although the offender is *not* on probation and may be imprisoned for violation of conditions).
Imprisonment	The offender is sentenced to a period of confinement.

Sentencing Aboriginal Offenders

There is a special provision in the Criminal Code (Section 718.2 (e)) for the sentencing of Aboriginal offenders. It is intended to reduce the overrepresentation of Aboriginal people in correctional institutions. It was reaffirmed by the Supreme Court of Canada in **R. v. Gladue** ([1999] 1 S.C.R. 688). In that landmark case, the Court held that where a term of incarceration would normally be imposed, judges must consider the unique circumstances of Aboriginal people.

R. v. Gladue
A decision by the SCC that held that in cases where a term of incarceration would normally be imposed, judges must consider the unique circumstances of Aboriginal people.

Specifically, Section 718.2(e) requires judges to consider (1) the unique systemic or background factors that may have contributed to the criminal behaviour of the Aboriginal person before the court and (2) specific sentencing procedures and sanctions (including restorative justice and traditional healing practices) that may be more appropriate for the individual Aboriginal offender. This includes considering colonialism, the impact of residential schools, and the marginality of Aboriginal people in Canadian society.

Gladue was most recently confirmed by the SCC in *R. v. Ipeelee* (2012 SCC 13, [2012] 1 S.C.R. 433; see Box 4.1). In 2012, the Ontario Court of Appeal ruled that two Aboriginal men arrested for drug smuggling at the U.S. border

BOX 4.1

R. v. Ipeelee

Manasie Ipeelee is an Aboriginal offender with a lengthy record of convictions for violent offences and a history of alcohol and drug abuse. Ipeelee was designated a long-term offender (see below) and was sentenced to 6 years in prison to be followed by a long-term supervision order (which meant that he was to be supervised for 10 years following the expiry of his sentence).

Following his release from confinement, Ipeelee committed a new offence while under the influence of alcohol, breaching a condition of his LTSO. He was then sentenced to three years in prison, less six months time served in remand. Ipeelee appealed this sentence; his appeal was dismissed by the Appeal Court. In a subsequent decision, the SCC held that the trial judge had erred in not applying the principles of *Gladue* in sentencing Ipeelee for the new offence and the violation of the LTSO. More specifically, the SCC majority held that the sentencing judge had failed to consider the potential for rehabilitation or to give sufficient attention to Ipeelee's situation as an Aboriginal offender. In view of this, the SCC ruled that an appropriate sentence would be one year in prison. The dissenting judges expressed the view that there was evidence that Ipeelee posed a risk that could not be adequately managed in the community. An additional point made was that in cases involving long-term offenders and breaches of LTSOs, protection of the community should be paramount and that these circumstances limited the applicability of the *Gladue* principles.

Read the full SCC decision at http://scc.lexum.org/en/2012/2012scc13/2012scc13.html. Do you agree or disagree with the SCC's decision in this case? Which position—that of the majority of justices, or that of the dissenting justices—do you find most persuasive?

Source: R. v. Ipeelee, 2012 SCC 13, [2012] 1 S.C.R. 433

AT ISSUE

Issue 4.1: Sentencing Options

Is Section 718.2(e) a valuable sentencing option or a misguided reform?

Supporters argue that Section 718.2(e) represents enlightened sentencing policy and is only one component of a wider effort to address the overrepresentation of Aboriginal people in the criminal justice system and in correctional institutions. Also, that the section requires only that judges *consider* sanctions other than confinement when sentencing Aboriginal offenders. Critics counter that special sentencing provisions for Aboriginal people discriminate against non-Aboriginal offenders and are based on the faulty assumption that sentencing practices, rather than complex historical and contemporary factors, are the primary reason for the high rates of Aboriginal incarceration.

What other arguments might be made in support of, or in opposition to, Section 718.2(e)? Which of these do you find most persuasive?

Sources: S. Haslip, "Aboriginal Sentencing Reform in Canada: Prospects for Success—Standing Tall with Both Feet Planted Firmly in the Air," *Murdoch University Electronic Journal of Law* 7, no. 1 (2000), http://www.murdoch.edu.au/elaw/isssues/v7n1/haslip71nf.html; P. Stenning, C. LaPrairie, and J.V. Roberts. "Empty Promises: Parliament, the Supreme Court, and the Sentencing of Aboriginal Offenders," *Saskatchewan Law Review* 64, no. 1 (2001): 137-68; M.E. Turpel-Lafond, "Sentencing Within a Restorative Justice Paradigm: Procedural Implications of *R. v. Gladue*," *Criminal Law Quarterly* 43, no. 1 (2000): 34-50.

should not be extradited to the United States, where their Aboriginal heritage would not be considered at sentencing, as required in Canada.[4] See At Issue 4.1.

The involvement of Aboriginal persons in systems of corrections is discussed in Chapter 14; so are policies and programs for Aboriginal offenders. Despite a multitude of laws and initiatives to address the problem, Aboriginal persons continue to be overrepresented in the justice system and in corrections. Indeed, their overrepresentation has steadily increased over the past decade.

Judicial Determination

Section 743.6 of the Criminal Code gives sentencing judges the authority to impose, on some offenders receiving a sentence of imprisonment of two years or more, the requirement that the offender serve half the sentence before being eligible for parole, instead of the typical one-third. The main objectives of this provision—known as **judicial determination**—are to protect the public and to strengthen specific and general deterrence. Aboriginal offenders are overrepresented in the group of offenders receiving judicial determination. Offenders receiving judicial determination are more likely than other offenders to serve their entire sentence in confinement.

Judicial determination
An order by the sentencing judge that the offender serve one-half of his or her sentence before being eligible to apply for parole.

Life Imprisonment

Under the Criminal Code, persons convicted of murder are subject to life imprisonment. This means that the offender is under sentence for life, although he or she may serve this sentence both in prison and upon release on parole in the community. The Criminal Code sets out the minimum number of years that an offender must serve in prison before being eligible to apply for release on parole. The key word is *apply*—there is no guarantee that the parole board will grant a release.

The death penalty was abolished by Parliament in 1976 and replaced with a mandatory life sentence without possibility of parole for 25 years in cases of first-degree murder (although it was retained for a number of military offences, including treason and mutiny). The debate over the death penalty continues, however. See At Issue 4.2.

Dangerous and Long-Term Offenders

Sections 752 and 753 of the Criminal Code set out the procedures and criteria for designating certain offenders as either **dangerous offenders** or **long-term offenders**.

On application by Crown counsel, the judge may designate a dangerous offender as a person who has been convicted of committing a serious personal injury offence (except murder) or a person who has a pattern of serious violent offences, is deemed to present a danger to society and is highly likely to put the community at risk if not imprisoned. The application to designate an offender as dangerous must be made at the time of sentencing. A judge who makes a dangerous offender designation will order that person to serve an indeterminate period of time in prison. These offenders are eligible for a hearing before the PBC every two years after serving seven years from the day they were taken into custody. There has been a steady increase in the number of offenders designated as dangerous.

The long-term offender designation, designed to deal with specific sexual offences, is another option for Crown counsel, particularly where the Crown falls short of the rigid requirements or level of evidence to file a dangerous offender application. As with dangerous offenders, there must be evidence that the offender presents a substantial risk of reoffending by committing a serious personal offence. However, there must also be risk assessment evidence demonstrating that the offender may be effectively managed in the community with appropriate supervision and treatment.

The designation is available only for those offenders who have received a sentence of more than two years. At sentencing, the judge sets the length of the long-term supervision order. This means that at the end of the sentence (which includes confinement and post-release supervision), the long-term supervision order comes into effect. This order requires that the offender be supervised by a parole officer for the remaining period of the order, which may be up to

Dangerous offender
A designation made by the judge after conviction that results in an indeterminate term of imprisonment in a federal correctional institution.

Long-term offender
A designation under Section 752 or 753 of the Criminal Code that requires the offender to spend up to 10 years under supervision following the expiry of his or her sentence.

AT ISSUE

Issue 4.2: The Death Penalty

Should the death penalty be re-instated in Canada?

Proponents for re-instating the death penalty cite a 2012 poll of Canadian adults (*N* = 1,002) which found that 8 percent felt it was always appropriate and that 63 percent felt that the death penalty was appropriate in some cases. Two of the main arguments presented in support of the death penalty are that it permanently removes dangerous offenders from society and that it reaffirms society's right to respond severely to severe violence.[a] Opponents cite research evidence that the death penalty does not serve as a general deterrent to crime, that wrongfully convicted persons have been executed in the United States, that the death penalty is disproportionately used for minority offenders, and that the death penalty is not more cost-effective than life imprisonment, given the lengthy legal and appeal process. What is your opinion of the death penalty? What other arguments could be made in support or opposition to it? Which arguments do you find most persuasive?

[a] Angus-Reid, *Canadians Hold Conflicting Views on the Death Penalty* (2012), http://www.angus-reid.com/polls/44374/canadians-hold-conflicting-views-on-the-death-penalty.

Sources: J.J. Brennan, "Majority of Canadians Support Return of Death Penalty, Poll Finds," *Toronto Star,* February 8, 2012, http://www.thestar.com/printarticle/1127764; S.H. Decker and C.W. Kohfeld, "The Deterrent Effect of Capital Punishment in the Five Most Active Execution States: A Time Series Analysis," *Criminal Justice Review* 15, no. 2 (1990): 173–91; T.V. Kaufman-Osborn, "Critique of Contemporary Death Penalty Abolitionism," *Punishment and Society* 8, no. 3, (2006): 365–83; S.P. Klein, R.A. Berk, and L.J. Hickman, *Race and the Decision to Seek the Death Penalty in Federal Cases: Executive Summary* (Washington: U.S. Department of Justice, 2006), http://www.ncjrs.gov/pdffiles1/nij/grants/214729.pdf.

10 years. The PBC sets the conditions under which the offender will be supervised following the expiration of his or her sentence.

HOW JUDGES DECIDE

Criminal Court judges consider a wide range of factors when determining the sentence to be imposed on a convicted offender. The purposes of sentencing and the various sentencing options available to judges were presented earlier in the chapter. Box 4.2 sets out the additional information that judges may consider in any case. Even with the expansion of the number of offences that carry a mandatory minimum sentence, Canadian judges exercise considerable discretion in sentencing.

To gain an appreciation of the challenges judges face in making sentencing decisions, review the summaries of actual cases presented in Box 4.3 and place yourself in the position of the sentencing judge.

BOX 4.2

Factors Considered in Sentencing

Aggravating circumstances	Facts about an offender and the offence that are considered negative and tend to increase the severity of a sentence, for example violence.
Mitigating circumstances	More positive facts about the offender and the offence that may decrease the severity of a sentence, for example being Aboriginal; being addicted.
Case law precedent	Judges consider sentencing decisions in previous, similar cases. A general principle is that there should be similar sentences in similar cases.
Pre-sentence reports	A PSR, prepared by a probation officer, presents information on the offender's background, present situation, and risk/needs. It also sets out options for sentencing that the judge will consider.
Victim impact statements	These contain information on the harm done to the victim (psychological and physical) as well as the consequences of the victimization.
Psychological assessments	These are completed on offenders and address the mental state and treatment needs of the offender.
Aboriginal offenders	Section 718.2(e) requires judges to consider alternatives to incarceration for Aboriginal offenders.

The purposes of sentencing and the various sentencing options available to judges were presented earlier in this chapter. Note that you can mix and match options—that is, you can sentence the offender to a period of custody in a provincial/territorial correctional facility and, as well, add on a period of probation of up to three years. However, probation cannot be used in conjunction with a sentence of more than two years, for such sentences place the offender under the jurisdiction of federal corrections. Also discussed earlier were the various objectives of sentencing. (Note that as the judge you are not required to accept the recommendations for sentencing of either the Crown or defence counsel.)

While the case summaries in Box 4.3 do not provide all of the materials that a sentencing judge would have access to, such as the PSR, the exercise does provide you with a sense of the challenges faced by sentencing judges.

BOX 4.3

You Be the Judge

Case #1

In October 2008, a 38-year-old off-duty male police officer, who had consumed five beers at a party prior to driving home, collided with a motorcycle, killing its 21-year-old driver. The off-duty police officer left the scene of the accident and walked his children to their nearby family home. He indicated that he consumed two quick shots of vodka to calm his nerves before returning to speak with police officers attending the scene of the accident. The officer subsequently pled not guilty to charges of obstructing justice for having consumed the two vodka shots to cover up his consumption of five beers prior to the collision.

At trial, the officer was found guilty of obstruction of justice and is now before you for sentencing. In your view (i.e., as the judge), the offender does not appear to be remorseful about his actions and does not appear to have taken responsibility for them. At the beginning of the sentence hearing, the offender had voluntarily resigned from his police agency, ending his policing career. The maximum sentence for obstruction of justice, as set out in Section 139(2), is 10 years in prison. The Crown counsel is seeking up to nine months in prison or a conditional sentence of up to eighteen months; defence counsel has asked for a conditional sentence of up to six months. What do you decide, and what is the purpose of your decision?

Case #2

Appearing before you is a 33-year-old woman convicted of 2 counts of manslaughter for killing her young sons (aged 10 months and two-and-a-half years) in the family's bathtub on February 1, 2010. The offender was originally charged with second-degree murder, but due to difficulties proving she had the required intent at the time she killed her children to be convicted of murder, she was ultimately convicted of two counts of the lesser charge of manslaughter. After killing her children, the offender attempted to commit suicide by throwing herself off a highway overpass into oncoming traffic. This was not her first attempt at suicide; the first attempt had been in her teenage years after her father impregnated her.

The offender took responsibility for drowning her children, although she claims she cannot remember what happened the weekend she consumed a bottle of sleeping pills and subsequently drowned her boys. The offender claims that she did not realize her children were dead until her sister informed her that she had drowned them. Doctors suggest this could be a consequence of her drug overdose, the concussion she sustained when she jumped off the overpass, or the trauma of having drowned the boys.

At the time of the offence, the offender was going through a bitter divorce, and the Crown alleges that she drowned her boys as revenge against her husband, who had

(continued)

denied her request to move the boys to her native country, Australia. The defence counsel argues that the offender was severely depressed and suicidal; also, that sleeping pills, alcohol, and (potentially) prescription drugs had clouded her judgment at the time she drowned her children.

Crown counsel argues that a 12-year sentence would be appropriate but recommends that the judge give the offender one and a half times credit for the time she has spent in a psychiatric hospital prior to sentencing. This would result in a nine-year prison term. The defence lawyer argues that the offender is a depressed, suicidal woman who should be allowed to return to her home country as a free woman because she has served approximately two years in custody and because she will continue to pay the price for killing her two young sons due to a mental disorder. He argues that his client deserves to obtain two-for-one credit, which would amount to approximately four and a half years of time already served.

The maximum sentence for manslaughter, as set out in the Criminal Code, is life imprisonment, and there is no minimum punishment in this case. As presiding judge, what sentence would you impose?

Case #3

The offender before you today is an ex-hockey coach who has been charged (in 2010) with sexually assaulting two young boys he coached on a junior hockey team during the 1980s and early 1990s. On December 7, 2011, the offender pleaded guilty to sexually assaulting the two young boys. The offender also pled guilty to sexually assaulting a third victim, but those charges were stayed as a condition of the offender entering a guilty plea to the sexual assault charges against the two other victims. Victim testimony indicates that the hockey coach sexually assaulted the boys hundreds of times, beginning with fondling and groping and escalating to performing oral sex on the victims and offering them money in exchange for sexual acts. He has a previous criminal record for sexually assaulting three young male players in the 1980s and 1990s. In 1997, the offender pled guilty to these charges and was sentenced to three-and-a-half years in prison; however, he served only 18 months of that sentence before being released. He was pardoned by the National Parole Board in 2007 and moved to Mexico.

Crown counsel is seeking a six-year prison term for the offender; the defence counsel is seeking a conditional sentence that would include a curfew, monitoring, and counselling. The maximum sentence for sexual assault proceeded by indictment, as set out in the Criminal Code, is a period of imprisonment for a term not exceeding ten years. As presiding judge, what sentence would you impose?

Record your sentencing decisions and why you selected each particular sentence. Once you have completed all three cases, refer to the end of the chapter to see the actual sentences imposed. Then, for each question, ask yourself these questions and be prepared to discuss your answers: (1) Did my sentence match the sentence of the judge? (2) Was it more lenient or more harsh? (3) Did the judge in the actual case make a good decision?

CIRCLE SENTENCING: A RESTORATIVE JUSTICE APPROACH

Circle sentencing was first developed in several Yukon communities as a collaboration between community residents and territorial justice personnel, primarily RCMP officers and judges from the Territorial Court of Yukon.

In circle sentencing, all of the participants, including the judge, defence lawyer, prosecutor, police officer, victim and family, offender and family, and community residents, sit facing one another in a circle. Through discussions, those in the circle reach a consensus about the best way to dispose of the case, taking into account both the need to protect the community and the rehabilitation and punishment of the offender. Circle sentencing is premised on traditional Aboriginal healing practices and has number of different objectives, which include addressing the needs of communities, victims, the families of victims, and offenders through a process of reconciliation, restitution, and reparation.

At the core of circle sentencing is the idea that the sentence is less important than the process used to arrive at it. Note that the presiding judge has the final word on the sentence to be imposed; also, that the final decision is informed by direct input from the community, the offender, and (often) the victim of the crime.

Table 4.2 compares the formal, adversarial Criminal Court system with the community-based, restorative approach as exemplified by circle sentencing.

Circle sentencing
An approach to sentencing based on the principles of restorative justice.

Video Link
Circle Sentencing Part 1 and Part 2. The use of circle sentencing in New South Wales, Australia.
www.youtube.com/watch?v=GkHuVvquWQ8

Table 4.2   Differences Between Criminal Court and Circle Sentencing Principles

Criminal Courts	Community Circles
View the conflict as the crime	View the crime as a small part of a larger conflict
Hand down sentence to resolve the conflict	View the sentence as a small part of the conflict
Focus on past conduct	Focus on present and future conduct
Take a narrow view of behaviour	Take a broader, holistic view
Avoid concern with social conflict	Focus on social conflict
Result (i.e., the sentence) is most important	Result is least important; the process is most important, as the process shapes the relationships among all parties

Source: Griffiths, 2007. Reprinted by permission of Justice Barry D. Stuart.

Joe Bryska, *The Winnipeg Free Press*, March 27, 1999.
Reprinted with permission.

Healing circle, Aboriginal Ganootamaage Justice Services (Winnipeg).

It is important to note that offenders who have their cases heard in a sentencing circle may still be sent for a period of incarceration. However, a wide range of other sanctions are available, including house arrest, community service, and, for Aboriginal offenders, banishment (generally to a wilderness location).

Circle sentencing is an example of how the principles of restorative justice can be applied within a holistic framework in which justice system personnel share power and authority with community residents. In contrast to the adversarial approach to justice, circle sentencing is designed to rebuild relationships within the community; to address the needs and interests of all parties, including the victim; and to focus on the causes of problems rather than just their symptoms.

Several First Nations communities have established peacemaking circles under the auspices of provincial courts. The Tsuu T'ina First Nations Court in Alberta has a program centred on peacemaking circles.[5] This provincial court has an Aboriginal judge, Crown prosecutor, and court clerks. Adult and youth cases (except those involving homicide and sexual assault) can be referred to peacemaking by the court. To be eligible for referral, the offender must admit responsibility for his or her actions and the victim must agree to participate.

Eligible cases are assigned to a peacemaker, who facilitates a circle healing process involving elders, the victim, the offenders, and others. In the circle, the participants discuss what happened, the impact of the offender's actions, and what should be done. Final agreements may require the offender to provide restitution, attend counselling, and/or to complete a number of community service hours. A final ceremony is held when the offender has completed the provisions in the agreement. A report is sent to the Tsuu T'tina court, where the Crown counsel reviews the case and, if satisfied, drops the charges against the offender. If the charge is not dropped, the report from the peacemaking circle will be submitted to the judge at sentencing.[6] A case heard in a Tsuu T'tina peacekeeping circle is presented in Box 4.4.

BOX 4.4

A Case in the Tsuu T'tina Court

A husband had assaulted his wife. The couple had a history of domestic strife because of drinking and arguments. After the husband was charged, the case was taken into peacemaking. The peacemaking circle enabled the couple to speak openly with each other and to set limits for each other's conduct. The wife was able to tell her husband that she would not let him assault her again. She would call the police if necessary and she would leave the marriage. In the circle, the husband was able to express his frustrations and say to his wife that he would not accept her verbal harassment. The husband was also able to speak about his personal unresolved grief issues. They had children and neither wanted the marriage to break up. The husband undertook to take grief counselling, and the couple agreed to take marriage counselling together. The peacekeeping circle was witness and party to these agreements. After the circle, the husband took counselling. As the counselling progressed, the husband began to feel better about himself and, as a result, the marital relationship has improved.

Source: L.S.T. Mandamin, "Peacemaking and the Tsuu T'ina Court," *Native Law Centre* Vol. 8(1), Pg. 1-4, 2003. Found at: http://www.usask.ca/nativelaw/publications/jah/2003/Peace_Tsuu_Tina_Ct.pdf.

RESTORATIVE/COMMUNITY JUSTICE: THE COLLABORATIVE JUSTICE PROGRAM, OTTAWA–CARLETON JUDICIAL DISTRICT

It is often assumed that programs such as circle sentencing, which involve substantial community participation, are suited only to rural and remote communities with a strong cultural identity and foundation. This assertion is often used to deflect suggestions that justice personnel in suburban and urban areas should explore the potential for restorative justice approaches.

The Collaborative Justice Program is an example of a successful restorative justice initiative in an urban centre. This program indicates that restorative justice approaches need not be restricted to minor offences but can be applied successfully to serious crimes, including crimes of violence, and may be used in conjunction with a period of incarceration. The program is a post-plea, pre-sentence restorative justice initiative.

The Collaborative Justice Program operates in the Ottawa–Carleton judicial district. Its initial aim was to demonstrate how a restorative approach can be used in cases of serious crime to deliver more satisfying justice to victims, the accused, and the community. As well as less serious cases, the program considers cases of serious offending, including robbery, break and enter, assault causing bodily harm, weapons offences, and driving offences that involve death or bodily harm and for which a conviction would normally result in a period of incarceration.

Cases are referred to the program by a variety of sources, which can include the judiciary, judicial pretrials, the Crown or defence counsel, the police, the probation office, and victim services. To be eligible for the program, the accused person must display remorse and be willing to take responsibility for the crime and to work to repair the harm done, and the victim must be interested in participating. A summary of one case is presented in Box 4.5.

BOX 4.5

Possession of Stolen Property and Dangerous Driving: Collaborative Justice Program

The accused, Kyle[a], attempted to receive payment for stolen merchandise at a pawnshop. The police were waiting for him there, and a car chase ensued during which Kyle's vehicle collided with another. Upon arrest, it was discovered that he had possession of several other pieces of stolen property. As a result, Kyle faced numerous serious charges. At the time, he was on parole and had a long criminal record. The Crown's initial sentencing position was 18 to 24 months in jail.

Kyle was in custody when the process began and was dealing with a serious drug addiction, which he "fed" through theft. He had previously served time in both provincial and federal institutions.

There were six victims involved, all of whom were contacted by the program. All agreed to participate. Information was exchanged between parties, and Kyle answered all of their questions. Five victims met with Kyle to talk about what had happened, why it had happened, and what Kyle could do about it. The sixth was kept informed by letter.

Kyle pled guilty to several charges and was released to a residential drug treatment program under strict conditions.

One victim who met with Kyle was a community planner. They agreed that Kyle would write down his crime prevention ideas for inclusion in an article that the planner was writing for a professional journal.

Kyle also met with the four other victims in a Circle Conference. Kyle took responsibility for his offences, apologized to each one, and committed to a reparation plan.

The plan included partial restitution, continued drug treatment, developing a personal plan with short- and long-term goals, and community speaking about drug abuse. The circle participants asked for a three-month delay of the sentencing so that Kyle could complete some elements of the plan. At that time, they reconvened to develop a final collective recommendation to the court.

Kyle was doing well in drug treatment. He sent a letter of apology to the sixth victim and participated in several public speaking opportunities. In view of all this and the Resolution Proposal reached by the program, the Crown attorney and defence counsel joined in recommending a 15-month conditional sentence (a jail sentence, which the offender serves in the community under strict conditions) followed by 2 years' probation. Kyle successfully completed his sentence and continues to do well several years later.

[a] Note that identifying details and names have been changed to protect the confidentiality of the participants.

Source: Collaborative Justice Program.

Despite the critical role played by sentencing in the criminal justice and corrections systems, there are questions about its effectiveness in addressing the needs of offenders and protecting the community. Some of the research on the effectiveness of sentencing is summarized in Research File 4.1.

RESEARCH FILE 4.1

The Effectiveness of Sentencing

Does increasing the severity of punishment have a deterrent effect on offenders? Generally, no. It is the *certainty* of punishment, rather than the severity of punishment, that has the most significant deterrent effect on offenders and others. While persons with a stake in conformity may fear lost opportunities if they are criminally sanctioned, marginal persons who perceive that they have few legitimate opportunities (and who in fact do not have many) may not engage in this calculus.[a]

Is there consistency in sentencing? Not always. With a few exceptions involving mandatory minimum sentences, most offences have only a maximum penalty, and this provides judges with considerable discretion in deciding both the objective of the sentence and the specific penalty. This makes it difficult to predict with any accuracy what type of sentence will be imposed for offences, even though judges are guided by case precedents.

(continued)

Are sentences matched effectively to individual offenders? Often, no. Matching specific sentencing options with the needs and risks of offenders is, at best, an inexact science. Few research studies have examined which types of sentences are most effective—that is, which ones serve as a deterrent and address risk and needs—with specific types of offenders.

Is there continuity from criminal courts to corrections? Not always. Once the offender leaves the courtroom, he or she becomes the responsibility of corrections. Judicial recommendations for placement and treatment programming are not binding on correctional decision makers. (However, this continuity is increased in specialized courts; see Chapter 5.)

Are circle sentencing and peacemaking effective? Potentially. There have been few controlled evaluations of these programs. Most of the literature on circle sentencing is anecdotal, which makes it difficult to develop evidence-based practices and to determine the factors that may facilitate (or hinder) the effective use of this restorative justice strategy. This includes whether the community itself has the capacity to support circle sentencing and whether the rights of the victim will be protected.[b] Concerns have surrounded the use of circle sentencing in cases involving domestic violence, with critics arguing that the power imbalances between the accused and the accuser may result in the revictimization of women.[c] An evaluation of the Tsuu T'ina peacemaking program found that this initiative produced a number of positive outcomes (see Box 4.4).

[a] S.N. Durlauf and D.S. Nagin, "The Deterrent Effect of Punishment," in *Controlling Crime: Strategies and Tradeoffs*, ed. P.J. Cook, J. Ludwig, and J. McCrary, 43–94 (Chicago: University of Chicago Press, 2011).

[b] C.T. Griffiths and R. Hamilton, "Sanctioning and Healing: Restorative Justice in Canadian Aboriginal Communities," in *Restorative Justice: Theory, Practice, and Research*, ed. J. Hudson and B. Galaway (Monsey: Criminal Justice Press, 1996).

[c] A. Cameron, "Sentencing Circles and Intimate Violence: A Canadian Feminist Perspective," *Canadian Journal of Women and the Law* 18, no. 2 (2006): 479–512; A. Shagufta, "Should Restorative Justice Be Used for Cases of Domestic Violence?", *International Journal of Restorative Justice* 6, no. 1 (2010): 1–48.

SUMMARY

This chapter examined the sentencing stage of the corrections process and included a description of the principles and goals underlying sentencing in the criminal courts. Judicial decision making influences whether an offender will enter the federal or provincial/territorial system of corrections; it also determines whether the offender will be under supervision in the community or incarcerated in an institution. The various factors that may influence judicial decision making were discussed, including provisions related to Aboriginal offenders. Judicial discretion and the challenges that judges face when imposing appropriate sanctions were illustrated through the use of actual case summaries. The restorative justice approach of circle sentencing was discussed.

KEY POINTS REVIEW

1. Sentencing in the criminal courts can be identified as the beginning of the correctional process.
2. There are three primary groups of sentencing goals in the criminal courts: utilitarian, retributive, and restorative.
3. Canadian judges have a variety of sentencing options ranging from an absolute discharge to imprisonment.
4. There are special provisions in the Criminal Code relating to the sentencing of Aboriginal offenders.
5. Circle sentencing is a restorative justice approach to sentencing that differs from that of traditional criminal courts.
6. Restorative justice practices can be used in urban, as well as rural and remote areas.
7. It is difficult to determine the effectiveness of sentencing in reducing rates of reoffending.
8. It is questionable whether sentencing assists the offender and protects the community.

KEY TERM QUESTIONS

1. What is meant by *general deterrence* and *specific deterrence* in sentencing?
2. Define and contrast *concurrent sentences*, *consecutive sentences*, and *intermittent sentences*.
3. What is the significance of the *Gladue decision*?
4. What is *judicial determination*, and what are its objectives?
5. Describe the process for designating offenders as *dangerous offenders* and *long-term offenders*.
6. What is *circle sentencing* and how does it differ from traditional criminal courts?

ANSWERS FOR BOX 4.3

Case #1

The now 42-year-old male who committed the offence was RCMP Cpl. Monty Robinson; the victim was 21-year-old Orion Hutchinson. On July 27, 2012, B.C. Supreme Court Judge Janice Dillon sentenced Robinson to a one-year conditional sentence, ordered him pay a $1,000 victim surcharge, and also ordered him to write an apology letter to Hutchinson's family. One month of the one-year conditional sentence will be served at home under house arrest, and a probation officer will supervise the rest of the term, which includes a 9 p.m. curfew. In passing sentence, Judge Dillon noted the aggravating factors, including these: Robinson's behaviour had damaged the reputation of the RCMP; the crime "strikes at the heart of the justice system"; Robinson did not accept responsibility for his actions; and he did not show any remorse. The mitigating factors that contributed toward a rehabilitative rather than a punitive sentence included Robinson's Aboriginal status, medical issues (defence counsel provided evidence that Robinson was an alcoholic), his first-time offender status, and the fact that putting a police officer in jail would mean protective custody. The Crown counsel's office subsequently decided not to appeal the sentence, stating that "an appeal court would likely defer to the sentencing judge, and no judicial error had been identified."[7] The president of the Union of B.C. Indian Chiefs stated that it was inappropriate for the judge to take Robinson's Aboriginal background into account and that the *Gladue* principle should not automatically be applied, but only in cases where the offender had experienced significant trauma when growing up.[8]

At the time of sentencing, the offender was still awaiting perjury charges resulting from the testimony he and three other officers had given subsequent to the 2007 death of Robert Dziekanski at Vancouver International Airport. Dziekanski was a Polish immigrant who was Tasered a number of times during an incident with Constable Robinson and three other RCMP constables.

Case #2

On April 20, 2012, Justice Michelle Crighton of the Court of Queen's Bench convicted Allyson McConnell of two counts of manslaughter for drowning her boys, Jayden and Connor. On June 4, 2012, Justice Crighton imposed a prison sentence of six years for each offence, to be served concurrently, less a two-for-one credit for time served. (Note: the two-for-one provision has subsequently been abolished.) This meant McConnell would be required to spend another 15 months in custody, although she would be eligible for parole release in less than 1 year. Judge Crighton recommended that McConnell serve her sentence at the Alberta Hospital Edmonton, where she had been held since her arrest, until she was ready to be transferred somewhere else. Because McConnell is being held on a mental health warrant, it is possible she may not be released when her sentence is over; doctors will keep her under psychiatric care until they do not consider her a danger to herself or to those around her.

In passing sentence, Judge Crighton indicated that the public interest would be best served if McConnell were both punished and rehabilitated, noting that the sentence would provide McConnell with the opportunity to address her severe psychological issues.

At the time of writing in late 2012, two appeals have been filed in this case. Crown counsel has appealed the manslaughter conviction, believing that McConnell should have been convicted of second-degree murder. The second appeal is of the sentence given to McConnell after being found guilty of two counts of manslaughter; the Crown suggests that the sentence was "demonstrably unfit" and "was not proportionate to the gravity of the offences and the blameworthiness of the offender" (http://www.edmontonjournal.com/news/Alberta+Justice+files+appeal+Allyson+McConnell+child+death+case/6667324/story.html).

Case #3

The former hockey coach was Graham James, and the two victims of the sexual assaults were former NHL player Theoren Fleury and his younger cousin, Todd Holt. On March 20, 2012, Manitoba Provincial Court judge Catherine Carlson sentenced James to two years on each offence, to be served concurrently. This means that Graham will be eligible for parole at the one-third mark of his sentence, after eight months. Judge Carlson also ordered that James provide a DNA sample for the National Sex Offender Registry, have no contact with the victims of his crimes, and conform to his lifetime ban on volunteering in any positions of trust to children.

Judge Carlson identified the following aggravating factors in the case: there were multiple victims; the victims were under 18; James had abused a position of authority and trust; and his "behaviour was predatory and orchestrated to make victims dependent on him" (http://www.cbc.ca/news/canada/manitoba/story/2012/03/19/graham-james-sentence.html). Victim testimony demonstrated the total control James had over his young victims; he had threatened to end their hockey careers if they refused his advances. One mitigating factor considered by Judge Carlson was that James had apparently controlled his impulses and desires, in that he had not reoffended since being released from prison following confinement in the late 1990s for other sexual offences. Furthermore, his guilty plea demonstrated that he had taken responsibility for what he had done and recognized the harm he had caused. Judge Carlson did, however, indicate that these types of offences are every parent and child's worst nightmare; whatever sentence the court imposed, the victims and the public would not consider it satisfactory, for no sentence "will give back to Mr. Holt and Mr. Fleury that which was taken by Mr. James." In passing sentence, Judge Carlson sent a message of denunciation to those who committed these types of offences by imposing a federal term of imprisonment.

As of mid-2013, Crown counsel has appealed James' two-year sentence, suggesting that the judge had made errors in her sentence. In particular, Crown counsel suggests that Judge Carlson "erred in the approach taken in sentencing" James, in part by "over-emphasizing the significance of prior sentences for similar offences" (http://www.cbc.ca/news/canada/manitoba/story/2012/04/12/mb-graham-james-sentence-appeal.html).

NOTES

1. J.V. Roberts, N. Crutcher, and P. Verbrugge, "Public Attitudes to Sentencing in Canada: Exploring Recent Findings," *Canadian Journal of Criminology and Criminal Justice* 49, no. 1 (2007): 153–84.

2. A. Rajekar and R. Mathilakath, *The Funding Requirement and Impact of the "Truth in Sentencing Act" on the Correctional System in Canada* (Ottawa: Office of the Parliamentary Budget Officer, 2010), http://www.parl.gc.ca/PBO-DPB/documents/TISA_C-25.pdf.

3. C.T. Griffiths, *Canadian Criminal Justice: A Primer*, 4th ed. (Toronto: Nelson, 2011).

4. A. Jones, "Court Quashes Extradition Orders Because Men's Aboriginal Status Not Considered," Canadian Press, September 21, 2012.

5. L.S.T. Mandamin, "Peacemaking and the Tsuu T'ina Court," *Native Law Centre* 8, no. 1 (2003): 1–4, http://www.usask.ca/nativelaw/publications/jah/2003/Peace_Tsuu_Tina_Ct.pdf.

6. Ibid.

7. S. McKnight, "Crown Won't Appeal Sentence Against Former Mountie," *Vancouver Sun*, August 25, 2012, A10.

8. R. Mickleburgh, "Native Leader Decries Lenient Sentence for Ex-Mountie," *Globe and Mail*, July 29, 2012.

PART II

CORRECTIONS IN THE COMMUNITY: ALTERNATIVES TO CONFINEMENT

Community corrections refers to programs that are alternatives to confinement and to the supervision of offenders on conditional release from correctional institutions.

The chapters in this part focus on correctional strategies that are designed to serve as alternatives to custody. Chapter 5 considers diversion, probation, intermediate sanctions, and restorative justice programs. In recent years, a number of initiatives have been developed that are designed to divert offenders from the criminal justice system. These include specialized, problem-solving courts and various restorative justice programs. There has also been an expansion of intermediate sanctions, as well as innovations in probation. These programs are under the jurisdiction of provincial/territorial governments, and there is considerable diversity in the specific programs that have been developed.

The majority of offenders who are under supervision in the community are on probation, so various dimensions of probation practice are examined in Chapter 6. This includes the occupation of probation officer, the role and activities of probation officers, and the experiences of probationers. It is often assumed that placing an offender on probation will allow that person to avoid the negative consequences of being incarcerated. The discussion in Chapter 6 reveals, however, that probationers and their families can experience challenges while being supervised in the community.

CHAPTER 5

ALTERNATIVES
TO CONFINEMENT

CHAPTER OBJECTIVES

After reading this chapter, you should be able to:
- *Comment on the concept of "community corrections."*
- *Describe the traditional alternatives to incarceration: diversion and probation.*
- *Compare and contrast traditional criminal courts and problem-solving courts.*
- *Discuss the effectiveness of problem-solving courts.*
- *Discuss the notion of therapeutic justice.*
- *Describe the objectives of intermediate sanctions and the types of programs that have been developed as intermediate sanctions.*
- *Describe how electronic monitoring works.*
- *Discuss conditional sentences as an alternative to incarceration, their use, and the issues that surround conditional sentences in Canada.*
- *Discuss the effectiveness of alternatives to confinement.*

Community corrections includes both alternatives to incarceration (discussed in this chapter and in Chapter 6) and post-release supervision and programs (see Chapter 12). When used as an alternative to confinement, community corrections includes diversion and probation as well as a variety of intermediate sanctions and restorative justice initiatives. Recall from Chapter 4 that most offenders who receive a sentence of supervision remain in the community and that only a very small number of convicted persons are sent to custody. Federal legislation, however, including Bill C-10, has constricted the use of alternative measures and imposed mandatory minimum sentences for offenders convicted of violent and sexual offences.

The search for alternative measures has been driven by the escalating costs of confining offenders in correctional institutions and, to a lesser extent, by research evidence that has called into question the effectiveness of incarceration as a general and specific deterrent (see Chapter 7). Note, however, that the trend toward the use of alternative measures has been accompanied by the increased use of technology to provide surveillance of offenders in the community.

PERSPECTIVE

Ex-Offender

We should be providing offenders with more alternatives than incarceration. I think that what has to be done is that we have to work with our young offenders or our youths a lot earlier, with a lot more emphasis and a lot more money spent in the young offender area. Once a youth has entered an institution, it's going to be very, very difficult to get that person to change their ways, because once he gets in there he is going to be conditioned to the situation that is happening. It's a very negative environment. I know in my situation, I had been a youth in a training school. I was being conditioned to the adult person I would be for the longest time, and I would spend 23 years of my life in institutions. If you put that into dollars and cents, I think it could have been spent a lot better than it was on me. (personal communication with C.T. Griffiths)

DIVERSION

Diversion programs have been a feature of Canadian criminal justice for decades. Offenders can be diverted from the formal criminal justice process at several points. There are diversion programs at the pre-charge, post-charge, and post-sentencing stages.

The objective of all diversion programs is to keep offenders from being processed further into the formal criminal justice system, thereby reducing costs and social stigmatization and helping offenders address the specific factors that led to their offending. Most diversion programs require that offenders acknowledge responsibility for their behaviour and agree to fulfill certain conditions within a specified time. If these conditions are met, the charges are withdrawn and the person is not saddled with a criminal record.

Traditional diversion programs focus on low-risk, first-time offenders; in recent years, however, cases involving more serious offences have been referred to diversion programs. Many diversion programs are centred on the principles of restorative justice (see Chapter 1). A number of restorative justice approaches have as their goal to divert offenders from more extensive involvement in the justice system, including custody. Victim–offender mediation (VOM) programs (often referred to as victim–offender reconciliation [VOR] programs) take a restorative approach in which the victim and the offender are provided with the opportunity to express their feelings and concerns. With the help of a neutral mediator, the offender and the victim resolve the conflict, address the consequences of the offence, and, ultimately, come to understand each other (see Box 5.1 for an example of a

Diversion
Programs designed to keep offenders from being processed further into the formal criminal justice system.

BOX 5.1

The Restorative Resolutions Program, Winnipeg

Restorative Resolutions is an intensive supervision program using VOM to achieve restorative justice. The program is an alternative to incarceration for offenders who are willing to take responsibility for their behaviour and to compensate their victims. Among the services provided are counselling, anger management programs, and intensive supervision. The program is operated by the John Howard Society of Manitoba and staffed by workers trained in probation practices and restorative justice.

A Case Study

A 32-year-old man with a lengthy youth and adult record of assault and break and enter was charged with four new counts of break and enter and theft. The Crown attorney wanted a period of incarceration. Restorative Resolutions staff prepared an alternative plan and recommended that the judge issue a suspended sentence. They also recommended that supervision of the offender be carried out by Restorative Resolutions; that he complete the Interpersonal Communication Skills Course and the Addictions Foundation of Manitoba assessment; that he complete the conditions outlined in the mediation agreement; and that he attend AA regularly and receive literacy training. The judge accepted the plan.

Source: Church Council on Justice and Corrections, *Satisfying Justice: Safe Community Options That Attempt to Repair Harm from Crime and Reduce the Use or Length of Imprisonment.* (Ottawa: Correctional Service of Canada, 1996), 5, http://www.ccjc.ca/wp-content/uploads/2010/11/Satisfying-Justice.pdf.

VOM program). In recent years, VOM and VOR programs have been extended to cases involving crimes of violence and have included incarcerated offenders. Figure 5.1 presents the restorative justice model being used in a program in Nova Scotia.

Net widening
A potential, unanticipated consequence of diversion programs in which persons who would otherwise have been released outright by the police or not charged by Crown counsel are involved in the justice system.

A major concern with diversion program is **net widening**—that is, involving offenders who would otherwise have been released outright by the police or not charged by Crown counsel. Another concern is that diversion programs can be coercive and punitive. Also, there is some ambiguity regarding the notion of "choice" in the operations of diversion programs and whether diversion programs may infringe on the rights of accused persons. A study of the "John School" diversion program in Toronto (a program for men apprehended for soliciting street prostitution) found that it focused disproportionately on offenders of lower socioeconomic status and that criminal charges were withdrawn if offenders waived basic procedural rights in order to gain admission to the program.[1]

Figure 5.1

Adult Restorative Justice—Process Model

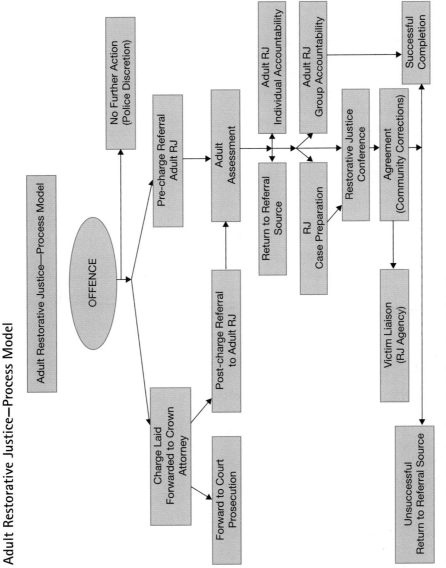

Source: Correctional Services, Nova Scotia Department of Justice.

PROBATION

Probation is the most common strategy for supervising offenders in the community as an alternative to incarceration. There are a number of ways that adult offenders can be placed on probation: (1) as part of a conditional discharge, (2) as a condition of a suspended sentence, (3) as part of an intermittent sentence, (4) as a sentence on its own (the most common), (5) following a prison term of 2 years or less, (6) in conjunction with a conditional sentence, or (7) as a federal offender who has received a sentence of exactly 2 years.

Offenders who receive a conditional discharge, a suspended sentence, or an intermittent sentence *must* be placed on probation. Those receiving a fine, incarceration, or a conditional sentence *may* be placed on probation. When probation follows a term of confinement, probation supervision begins either at the time of release or on the expiration of provincial parole. Probation practice is examined in detail in Chapter 6.

SPECIALIZED, PROBLEM-SOLVING COURTS

In recent years, a number of specialized, **problem-solving courts** have been developed that attempt to divert offenders with special needs from the criminal justice system. These specialized courts include community courts, drug courts, and mental health courts (MHCs).

Drug treatment courts (DTCs) target the needs of addicted persons in conflict with the law; MHCs are quite similar. In Vancouver, the Downtown Community Court focuses on offenders in that city's highly troubled Downtown Eastside; in Toronto, the Integrated Violence Court handles both criminal and family law cases. Toronto also has an Aboriginal community court (see Chapter 14). In these courts, offenders may avoid incarceration by agreeing to abide by specific conditions. In DTCs, for example, the offender may agree to participate in a drug abuse treatment program and to submit to regular drug testing.[2]

The three defining attributes of problem-solving courts are these: (1) they address the underlying problems of offenders, victims, and communities; (2) they involve collaboration among various agencies and disciplines; and (3) they are accountable to the community.[3] These principles are complementary to those of restorative justice (see Chapters 1 and 4). Unlike traditional courts, however, community-based courts have the potential to improve the quality of life in communities, increase residents' familiarity with the court process, and heighten community satisfaction with the response to persons in conflict with the law.[4]

These problem-solving courts abandon adversarial/legalistic approaches in favour of one that centres on treatment and rehabilitation. They develop intervention plans that address behaviours and the circumstances that contributed to them.[5] They are meant to counter the "revolving door" syndrome that affects many offenders and to improve collaboration among justice and social service agencies. Many of the principles of restorative justice are found in the

Table 5.1   Comparison of Traditional Courts and Problem-Solving Courts

Traditional Court	Problem-Solving Court
Adversarial/legalistic	Therapeutic/restorative
Anonymous/impersonal	Personalized
Little collaboration among criminal justice/social service personnel	Collaborative
Offence-focused	Offender-focused
Sanction-focused	Problem-focused
Generic supervision	Individualized supervision
Minimal community involvement	Community involvement, e.g., personal mentors

practices of problem-solving courts. Table 5.1 compares traditional with problem-solving courts.

Specialized problem-solving courts incorporate the concept of **therapeutic justice**, which involves using the law as well as the courts' authority as change agents to promote the health and well-being of offenders, while at the same time ensuring that their legal rights are protected and that justice is done.

Critics of therapeutic justice argue that it blurs the line between treatment and enforcement and that problem-solving courts can be coercive—for example, DTCs require abstinence by drug users instead of taking a harm reduction approach.[6]

There is considerable variation among the problem-solving courts with regard to the types of cases that are handled, their eligibility criteria, the sanctions imposed, the length and type of supervision, and the involvement of justice, social service, and community agencies.[7] Some courts only take offenders who have committed less serious crimes, while others will accept more serious offenders. DTCs in Canada, for example, will accept only those offenders who have committed nonviolent, drug-related offences.[8] As with all diversion programs, offender participation in specialized courts is voluntary. Some courts operate at the pre-plea level, while others require an admission of guilt and the acceptance of responsibility.

These courts establish screening protocols to ensure that only those offenders who are appropriate for the court are selected. Two examples of problem-solving courts and therapeutic justice are MHCs and Yukon's Wellness Court.

Therapeutic justice
The use of the law and the authority of the court as change agents in promoting the health and well-being of offenders.

Diversion of Mentally Ill Persons:
The Mental Health Court

Many persons who come into conflict with the law are suffering from some form of mental illness. The importance of addressing the needs of this population became more urgent with the closing of mental hospitals as part of the philosophy of deinstitutionalization that become popular in the 1970s. One concern is that, in the absence of community-based resources, mentally ill persons will be criminalized.

The barriers to addressing the needs of mentally ill persons in the community have included a lack of coordination between criminal justice and mental health professionals. That is in addition to the problems these persons encounter in securing housing, employment, and services tailored to them. It is generally accepted that the needs of mentally ill offenders are best met within the mental health system rather than the criminal justice system and that treatment, rather than sanctions, is more effective at reducing rates of reoffending. Across North America, a variety of diversion programs have been developed for mentally ill persons who have come into contact with the law. The Community Wellness Court (CWC) in Yukon is profiled in Box 5.2. Its clients include persons with a mental illness.

BOX 5.2

The Yukon Community Wellness Court

The Yukon CWC has been established to address the needs of offenders with alcohol and drug problems, mental health issues, and other underlying issues that may be related to their offending. Participation is voluntary, and offenders must admit guilt. Persons committing sex crimes and serious and violent offences are excluded. The CWC incorporates the principles of therapeutic justice and restorative justice and offers a multifaceted approach designed to reduce reoffending, while at the same time addressing the needs of the victim and the community.

Among the objectives of the CWC are to ensure that offenders assume responsibility for their behaviour, to provide intensive supervision that is culturally relevant, to build partnerships with justice and nonjustice agencies and services and the community, and to use sanctions and incentives to motivate offenders to change.* A key feature of the CWC is that it provides offenders with a support network during and after the program and sentencing.

Figure 5.2 sets out the flow of clients through the CWC; it includes data on offenders processed through the court between June 2007 and May 2011.

The figure illustrates the CWC court process and a parallel program process. The data indicate that 63 of the 91 offenders referred to the program met the eligibility

Figure 5.2

Number of Clients Processed Through the Community Wellness Court (June 2007 to May 2011)

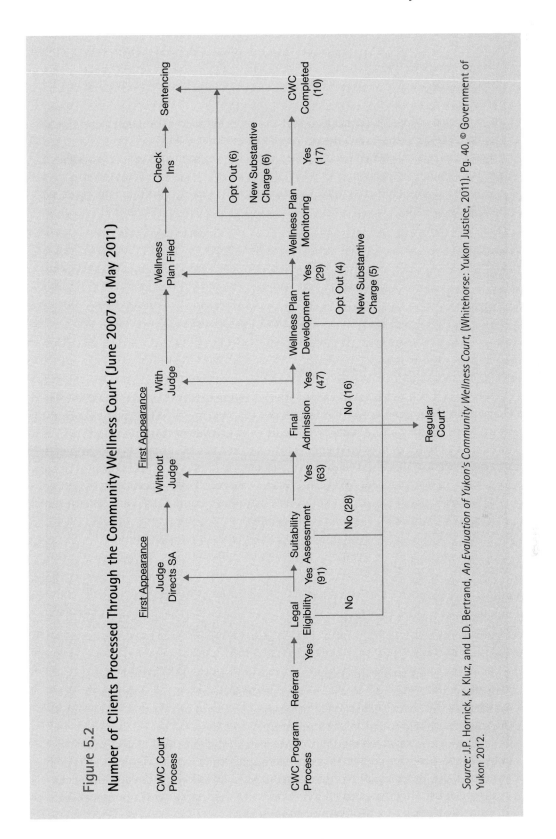

Source: J.P. Hornick, K. Kluz, and L.D. Bertrand, *An Evaluation of Yukon's Community Wellness Court*, (Whitehorse: Yukon Justice, 2011). Pg. 40. © Government of Yukon 2012.

criteria; 47 of them were subsequently admitted to the CWC program. Other offenders were dropped from the program for a variety of reasons, leaving 10 who completed it.

An evaluation of the CWC concluded that the court provided a valuable alternative to traditional criminal courts and met its objectives effectively. Offenders who completed the program felt that generally, it had been very helpful to them and had provided an opportunity for them to change their lives. One concern is that only 10 of the offenders who were initially admitted to the CWC successfully completed the program. However, many of the offenders had previous criminal records and a long history of alcohol/drug abuse or mental illness. This is a challenge faced by all specialized courts.

* J.P. Hornick, K. Kluz, and L.D. Bertrand, *An Evaluation of Yukon's Community Wellness Court* (Whitehorse: Yukon Justice, Pg. 40, 2011). © Government of Yukon 2012. http://www.yukoncourts.ca/pdf/cwc_final _report_05-10-11.pdf.

The Effectiveness of Specialized Courts

There have been few evaluations of specialized courts in Canada; most studies have been conducted in the United States. Comparing the effectiveness of various types of specialty courts is difficult due to wide variations in admission criteria and services provided and in how success is measured.[9] For example, it may be easier to develop measures of success for DTCs (e.g., cessation of drug or alcohol use) than for MHCs. Some observers have questioned whether MHCs allow persons with mental illness who have come into contact with the justice system to queue-jump, that is, gain access to scarce mental health resources at the expense of law-abiding persons with a mental illness.[10]

Ongoing issues with many of the courts include the high rates of noncompliance with the conditions imposed by the courts. One study of the Toronto Drug Treatment program found that 84 percent of those enrolled did not complete the program.[11] Many of these courts have had difficulty attracting Aboriginal men and women.[12] It is not known how heavily these courts are used by visible minorities, nor is it known which factors may facilitate or hinder their effectiveness in a diverse community. The relationship between gender and ethnicity and program completion has not been examined in Canada. Both Canadian and American studies suggest that persons who do not have a stable residence, who have substance abuse issues, and who have a severe mental illness are less likely to complete a program.[13]

Evaluation research would provide greater insights into many factors that may affect program outcomes; for example, they could determine which offenders are most likely to benefit from specialized courts, which interventions are most effective, and which factors are associated with noncompliance or noncompletion of a program of supervision.

Even lacking this research, there is evidence that these courts may be an effective alternative to the traditional criminal justice system. The courts appear to be most effective at reducing reoffending when the principles of risk, needs, and responsivity (RNR) are followed—that is, when offenders are selected who are most suited for the program in terms of their level of risk, their needs, and their motivation and ability to complete the requirements imposed by the courts.[14]

Table 5.2 summarizes the objectives, processes, and effectiveness of specialized courts. Note that much of the research has been conducted in the United States and that studies vary considerably in their design and in the data sets used for the analysis. Caution, then, should be exercised in generalizing these findings. For an excellent summary of community-based alternatives for persons with mental illness in conflict with the law, see Heilbrun and colleagues.[15]

Table 5.2   The Objectives, Process, and Effectiveness of Specialized Courts

Type of Court	Objective/Process	Outcomes
Mental Health Court (MHC)	Reduce the criminalization of the mentally ill; operate at pre- and post-charge stage	Reduced reoffending by 10–75%; can reduce the amount of time offenders spend in custody, increase access to treatment services, and change life circumstances (e.g., homelessness), particularly for persons who complete the program and "graduate"[a]; court personnel perceive that MHCs improve clients' lives, reducing reoffending, reducing Criminal Court workloads, and holding offenders accountable[b]; an evaluation of the Calgary Diversion Program for mentally disordered offenders found high rates of client satisfaction, a significant reduction in charges and court appearances and in the need for acute care services[c]; potentially significant reductions in reoffending
Drug Treatment Court (DTC)	Address alcohol/drug addiction of offenders and reduce reoffending; treatment-oriented approach with specified conditions (e.g., abstinence)	Helps even offenders with lengthy criminal records[d]; offenders who do not complete the program tend to lack family support, have unstable housing, and lack motivation to complete the program[e]; per-client costs are less than in traditional courts[f]; high rates of noncompletion; women and Aboriginals less likely to participate and to complete[g]

(continued)

Type of Court	Objective/Process	Outcomes
Vancouver Downtown Community Court (DCC)	Address the needs of residents in the Downtown Eastside area; reduce crime and recidivism, improve public safety and justice efficiencies[h]	Interim evaluation (2010) revealed that case processing times were longer than in regular provincial court; shorter stays in pretrial detention; higher use of alternative measures and sentencing options; high rates of completion of community service hours; low rates of attendance at recommended information sessions and other referrals (e.g., housing assistance); a higher rate of return to the DCC than in the provincial courts; impact on crime uncertain[i]; impact on reoffending unknown
Domestic Violence Court	Stop the cycle of domestic violence; assist victims, their families, and offenders; reduce revictimization	Cases may be heard more quickly than in traditional court; potential increase in guilty pleas; may reduce Crown stay of proceedings; evaluation of Yukon Domestic Violence Treatment Option found low rates of reassault, effectiveness in dealing with domestic violence cases, but problems connecting with victims[j]

[a] S. Lange, J. Rehm, and S. Popova, "The Effectiveness of Criminal Justice Diversion Initiatives in North America: A Systematic Literature Review," *International Journal of Forensic Mental Health* 10, no. 3 (2011): 200–14; R.D. Schneider, "Mental Health Courts and Diversion Programs: A Global Survey," *International Journal of Law and Psychiatry* 33, no. 4 (2010): 201–6; C. M. Sarteschi, M. G. Vaughn, and K. Kim, "Assessing the Effectiveness of Mental Health Courts: A Quantitative Review," *Journal of Criminal Justice* 39, no. 1 (2011): 12–20.

[b] D.E. McNiel and R.L. Binder, "Stakeholder Views of a Mental Health Court," *International Journal of Law and Psychiatry* 33, no. 4 (2010): 227–35.

[c] C. Mitton, L. Simpson, L. Gardner, F. Barnes, and G. McDougall, "Calgary Diversion Program: A Community-based Alternative to Incarceration for Mentally Ill Offenders," *Journal of Mental Health Policy Economics* 10, no. 3 (2007): 145–51, http://www.ncbi.nlm.nih.gov/pubmed/17890831.

[d] Public Safety Canada, *Toronto Drug Treatment Court Project* (Ottawa: National Crime Prevention Centre, 2007), http://www.publicsafety.gc.ca/prg/cp/bldngevd/_fl/2007-ES-09_e.pdf.

[e] B. Newton-Taylor, L. Gliksman, and J. Patra, "Toronto Drug Treatment Court: Participant Intake Characteristics as Predictors of 'Successful' Program Completion," *Journal of Drug Issues* 39, no. 4 (2009): 965–88.

[f] M.W. Finigan, S.M. Carey, and A. Cox, *Impact of a Mature Drug Court Over 10 Years of Operation: Recidivism and Costs* (Washington, DC: U.S. Department of Justice, National Institute of Justice, 2007), http://www.ncjrs.gov/pdffiles1/nij/grants/219225.pdf.

[g] P. Allard, T. Lyons, and R. Elliott, *Impaired Judgment: Assessing the Appropriateness of Drug Treatment Courts as a Response to Drug Use in Canada* (Toronto: Canadian HIV/AIDS Legal Network, 2011), http://www.aidslaw.ca/publications/interfaces/downloadFile.php?ref=2034.

[h] British Columbia, *Downtown Community Court in Vancouver: Interim Evaluation Report* (Victoria: 2010), http://www.criminaljusticereform.gov.bc.ca/en/reports/pdf/interimevaluation.pdf.

[i] Ibid.

[j] J.P. Hornick, M. Boyes, L. Tutty, and L. White, *The Domestic Violence Treatment Option (DVTO), Whitehorse, Yukon: Final Evaluation Report* (Ottawa: National Crime Prevention Centre, 2005), http://people.ucalgary.ca/~crilf/publications/Final_Outcome_Analysis_Report.pdf.

INTERMEDIATE SANCTIONS

Intermediate sanctions, often referred to as *alternative sanctions* or *community sanctions*, encompass a variety of correctional programs that fall between traditional probation and incarceration, although specific initiatives may include either of these penalties. Intermediate sanctions include fines, community service, day attendance centres, home detention with or without EM, intensive probation supervision, strict discipline camps (boot camps), conditional sentence orders (CSOs), and halfway houses. Intermediate sanctions have two sets of objectives:

- *Offender*-oriented objectives, which include the assurance of real punishment, retribution, and some degree of incapacitation and control of offenders.
- *System*-oriented objectives, which include reducing institutional populations and the costs of corrections, as well as rates of recidivism.[16]

The primary objective of intermediate sanctions is to hold offenders responsible for their behaviour through restrictive and intensive intervention. Treatment and rehabilitation are generally secondary, although usually a component of these sanctions. Studies that have queried offenders about their perceptions of the severity of intermediate sanctions as opposed to incarceration confirm that alternatives to incarceration can be effective at sanctioning and managing.[17]

Electronic Monitoring

A key trend in punishment and corrections noted in Chapter 1 was the increasing surveillance of offenders under supervision in the community. This has been made possible by technologies that allow authorities to track offenders through various forms of EM and global positioning systems (GPSs). These technologies may provide alternatives to confinement and allow the offender to remain in the community. See Figure 5.3.

Electronic monitoring (EM) has been used for provincial/territorial offenders for many years. Bill C-10, passed in 2012, has a provision that allows the CSC and the PBC to require that offenders on TA, work release, parole, statutory release, or long-term supervision wear a monitoring device.

There are "front end" and "back end" EM programs, referring to the stage of the correctional process at which the strategy is used. In some provinces, EM is imposed by the sentencing judge, while in others, such as Ontario, EM is a condition of early release from incarceration, although offenders with a history of sex offences or domestic abuse are not eligible for EM.

Where EM is used in support of an alternative to confinement, its main objective is to ensure public safety while allowing the offender to remain in the community. Generally, only offenders who have been convicted of less serious, nonviolent offences and who have a stable residence and a telephone are eligible to participate in EM programs.

Intermediate sanctions
A wide range of correctional programs that generally fall between probation and incarceration, although specific initiatives may include either of these penalties as well.

Electronic monitoring
A correctional strategy that involves using electronic equipment to ensure that the conditions of supervision are fulfilled.

EM can be "active" or "passive." With active EM systems, the offender wears a transmitter that provides a "continuous signal" as to his or her location; passive systems, by contrast, utilize a computer to call the offender at either random or specified times in order to verify that the offender is where he or she is supposed to be. Increasingly, GPS tracking systems are being used to monitor the location and movements of high-risk offenders, including sex offenders. This follows a pattern in the United States that is likely to accelerate with the move toward decarceration (see Chapter 1).

First-generation EM technology only allows corrections personnel to verify the location of an offender; the more recent GPS technology can track an offender's movements on an ongoing basis. This provides greater protection for crime victims, who can thus be notified if the offender travels outside pre-established boundaries. GPS monitoring makes it possible to determine

Figure 5.3

Global Positioning System Monitoring Components

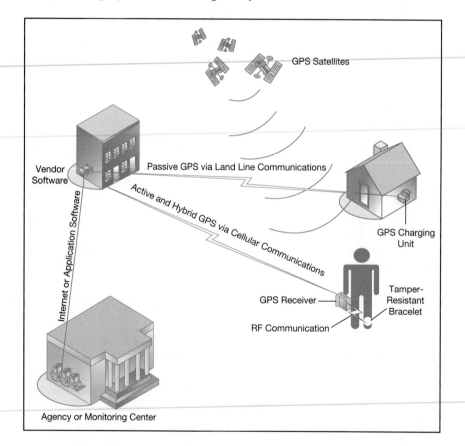

Source: T. Brown, S. McCabe, and C. Wellford, *Global Positioning System (GPS) Technology for Community Supervision: Lessons Learned* (Washington, DC: U.S. Department of Justice, 2007), p.1.3. Found: http://www.ncjrs.gov/pdffiles1/nij/grants/219376.pdf; © 2007 Noblis.

where an offender is at any given moment. In addition, GPS makes it possible to "customize" tracking by specifying the boundaries of an offender's movements and establishing locations where the offender is not permitted (e.g., a sex offender may be prohibited from going near schools and/or playgrounds). A monitoring program can be designed that will alert both the offender and the agency if the offender violates certain area restrictions. The State of California requires all sex offenders to be monitored by GPS.

A number of concerns surround the use of these technologies. GPS tracking systems do not relieve corrections personnel of the task of supervising offenders, given that technology cannot prevent the actual commission of crimes.[18] Also, given that EM and GPS tracking systems are sold to governments by the private sector and in many cases are monitored by private companies, there is a danger that the benefits and effectiveness of this correctional strategy may be exaggerated, thus contributing to an expansion of the prison-industrial complex.

It is likely that in the coming years, advances in technology will allow authorities not only to track offenders but also to control their behaviour. These developments will most certainly be accompanied by considerable debate. See At Issue 5.1.

AT ISSUE

Issue 5.1: Electronic Monitoring

Should electronic monitoring be expanded to include behavioural surveillance of offenders?

It is likely that in the not-too-distant future, technology will be able to track offenders as well as provide surveillance/control of the offender's behaviour. It may soon be possible to monitor heartbeat, brain activity, and other vital signs. When paired with chemical implants, it may soon be possible to monitor—and where required, control—an offender's behaviour. Would you support the use of such technology for these purposes? What arguments could be made for and against this type of surveillance?

Also, if you were convicted of a crime and were offered the opportunity to be placed under a 24-hour GPS tracking system rather than being sent to custody, which would you choose, and why?

Conditional Sentences

Section 742 of the Criminal Code states that a convicted person who would otherwise be incarcerated for less than 2 years can be sentenced to a conditional term of imprisonment, to be served in the community rather than in custody. This is a **conditional sentence**, which requires the offender to fulfill

Conditional sentence
A sentence imposed on an offender who would otherwise be incarcerated for a period of less than two years but whose risk is determined to be manageable in the community.

certain conditions. Failure to comply with the conditions of a conditional sentence order (CSO) results in the offender being returned to court, where the sentencing judge has a variety of options, including sending the offender to prison.

Offenders on conditional sentences are supervised in the community by probation officers; however, *these offenders are not on probation*. The Supreme Court of Canada has delineated the differences between a conditional sentence and probation (*R. v. Proulx* 2000, SCR 61). The main difference is that probation focuses on rehabilitation, whereas a conditional sentence embraces the principles of rehabilitation *and* punitive justice. This means that the conditions attached to a conditional sentence are generally more onerous and more restrictive than the conditions attached to a probation order. The SCC in *Proulx* directed that two factors be taken into account in determining whether a conditional sentence is appropriate: (1) the risk that the offender will reoffend, and (2) the amount of harm the offender would cause in the event of offending again.

All CSOs contain standard, compulsory conditions that are similar to those contained in probation orders. Optional conditions may also be set down and may be added to or reduced by the court over time. These may include abstaining from alcohol or drugs; providing for the support or care of dependents; performing community service work; and/or attending a treatment program.

Noncompliance with the conditions of a CSO can result in the offender being incarcerated. If an allegation is made that a condition has been breached, the offender may have to appear in court to prove that the allegation is false. This is a reverse onus situation; in other words, it is up to the offender to prove that the breach did *not* occur.

Considerable controversy has surrounded conditional sentences since their inception in 1996. They are popular with judges, but there have been concerns about high violation rates and about the misuse of this sentencing option by judges. To address these concerns, Bill C-10, enacted in 2012, prevents judges from imposing a conditional sentence in cases where the offender has been convicted of an offence involving bodily harm, drug trafficking, or the use of a weapon (along with a variety of other offences in which the Crown had proceeded by indictment).

Offenders who are given a CSO and placed under house arrest are often viewed by the media and the general public as having received a "slap on the wrist" and as having escaped the negative experiences of incarceration. Yet adhering to a CSO's requirements, which may include 24-hour house arrest, presents challenges for offenders that are no less intense than those of incarceration. In interviews, offenders on CSOs mention the negative impact on their working lives and on those who are close to them, including their children.[19]

For a summary of the effectiveness of alternatives to confinement, see Research File 5.1.

RESEARCH FILE 5.1

The Effectiveness of Alternatives to Confinement

Does traditional diversion work? Inconclusive. There have been few formal evaluations. It may "widen the net" by focusing on low-risk, first-time offenders. There is no evidence that diversion has any impact on correctional populations; in fact, it may increase the justice system's workload and costs.[a]

Do problem-solving courts work? Potentially. They can be effective at reducing rates of reoffending (see Table 5.1).

Does probation work? Potentially. It can be effective if the principles of RNR are followed (see Chapter 6).

Do electronic supervision and GPS work? Potentially. EM can play a significant role in reducing rates of recidivism, even among more serious offenders, including sex offenders.[b] There is, though, no evidence that EM programs reduce prison admissions or that they are less costly than incarceration. The perception among probation officers and offenders in an American study was that EM had a negative impact on the offender's personal and family relationships and hindered efforts to secure housing and employment.[c] Also, it may increase the workload for probation and parole officers and may cause net widening and raise privacy issues. There is evidence that EM in Canada has not generally been used as a true alternative to confinement.[d]

Do conditional sentences work? Potentially. There are high rates of violations of conditions (up to 40 percent of cases). There are also concerns that despite limitations under Bill C-10, such sentences are being used inappropriately by judges.[e] Research evidence suggests that conditional sentences may be more effective than imprisonment in reducing recidivism.[f]

Do restorative justice alternatives work? They can. There is evidence that some restorative justice programs, such as the Restorative Resolutions program in Winnipeg (see Box 5.1), succeed at reducing rates of reoffending and at addressing the needs of victims, offenders, and communities.[g]

[a] J. Bonta, "Adult Offender Diversion Programs: Research Summary," *Corrections Research and Development* 3, no. 1 (Ottawa: Solicitor General Canada, 1998), http://www.publicsafety.gc.ca/res/cor/sum/_fl/cprs199801-eng.pdf; J. Nuffield, *Diversion Programs for Adults* (Ottawa: Solicitor General Canada, 1997).

[b] W. Bales, K. Mann, T. Blomberg, G. Gaes, K. Barrick, K. Dhungana, and B. McManus, *A Quantitative and Qualitative Assessment of Electronic Monitoring* (Washington: National Institute of Justice, U.S. Department of Justice, 2010), http://www.ncjrs.gov/pdffiles1/nij.grants/230530.pdf; S. Bottos, *An Overview of Electronic Monitoring in Corrections: Issues and Implications* (Ottawa: Correctional Service of Canada, 2007), http://csc-scc.gc.ca/text/rsrch/reports/r182/r182-eng.pdf.

[c] Bales et al., *A Quantitative and Qualitative Assessment.*

(continued)

ᵈ J. Bonta, S. Wallace-Capretta, and J. Rooney, "Can Electronic Monitoring Make a Difference? An Evaluation of Three Canadian Programs," *Crime and Delinquency* 46, no. 1 (2000): 61–75.

ᵉ D. North, "The Catch-22 of Conditional Sentencing," *Criminal Law Quarterly* 44, no. 3 (2001): 342–74.

ᶠ Cf. J. Cid, "Is Imprisonment Criminogenic? A Comparative Study of Recidivism Rates Between Prison and Suspended Prison Sanctions," *European Journal of Criminology* 6, no. 6 (2009): 459–80.

ᵍ Bonta, Wallace-Capretta, and Rooney, "Can Electronic Monitoring Make a Difference?"

SUMMARY

This chapter has provided an overview of the various strategies used by systems of corrections as alternatives to confinement. These include traditional practices such as diversion and probation, as well as more recent innovations such as the electronic surveillance of offenders. Also important has been the development of a variety of problem-solving courts designed to address the needs of specific groups of offenders, including the mentally ill and addicted persons. These courts utilize an approach quite distinct from that of the traditional criminal courts. As well, there are a variety of restorative justice programs that function as alternatives to incarceration. The effectiveness of these alternatives to confinement varies; some hold great promise, while others, such as traditional diversion, while widely used, have been found to be less effective.

KEY POINTS REVIEW

1. When used as an alternative to confinement, community corrections includes diversion, probation, intermediate sanctions, and restorative justice initiatives.

2. Offenders can be diverted from the criminal justice process at several points: pre-charge, post-charge, and post-sentencing.

3. There is concern that traditional diversion programs may "widen the net" and be coercive and punitive.

4. A significant trend in diversion has been the development of problem-solving courts that incorporate therapeutic justice with elements of restorative justice.

5. Problem-solving courts, particularly those that incorporate the principles of RNR, can be an effective alternative to the traditional criminal justice system.

6. Probation is the most widely used strategy for supervising offenders in the community as an alternative to incarceration.

7. Intermediate sanctions, which fall between traditional probation and incarceration, have both offender-oriented objectives and system-oriented objectives.

8. There are significant differences between probation and conditional sentences.

9. Considerable controversy has surrounded the use of conditional sentences, centring on high violation rates and, prior to the enactment of Bill C-10, the use of conditional sentences in cases involving a violent offence.

10. There is evidence that programs that use a restorative justice approach can be at least as successful as incarceration in reducing reoffending and assisting offenders.

KEY TERM QUESTIONS

1. Identify and discuss the objectives of *diversion* programs.

2. What is *net widening* and why is it a concern associated with diversion programs?

3. Describe the correctional strategy of *probation*.

4. Describe the principles and practices of *problem-solving courts* and provide examples of the types of courts in Canada.

5. What is *therapeutic justice* and what role does it play in problem-solving courts?

6. Identify and discuss the objectives of *intermediate sanctions* and provide examples of these types of sanctions.

7. Describe the use of *electronic monitoring*, including the potential role of GPS technology, as a corrections strategy.

8. Compare and contrast *conditional sentence* orders and probation and note the controversy that has surrounded the use of conditional sentence orders in Canada.

NOTES

1. B. Fischer, S. Wortley, C. Webster, and M. Kirst, "The Socio-Legal Dynamics and Implications of Diversion," *Criminology and Criminal Justice* 2, no. 4 (2002): 385–410.

2. J. Weekes, R. Mugford, G. Bourgon, and S. Price, *Drug Treatment Courts: FAQs* (Ottawa: Canadian Centre on Substance Abuse, 2007), http://www.ccsa.ca/2007%20CCSA%20 Documents/ccsa-011348-2007.pdf.

3. R. Porter, M. Rempel, and A. Mansky, *What Makes a Court Problem-Solving? Universal Performance Indicators for Problem-Solving Justice* (Washington, DC: Center for Court Innovation, 2010), http://www.courtinnovation.org/sites/default/files/What_Makes_A_Court_P_S.pdf.

4. R. Saner, *Community Perceptions of Red Hook, Brooklyn: Views of Quality of Life, Safety, and Services* (New York: Center for Court Innovation, 2010), http://www.courtinnovation.org/ sites/default/files/Community_Perceptions.pdf.

5. A.J. Lurigio and J. Snowden, "Putting Therapeutic Jurisprudence into Practice: The Growth, Operations, and Effectiveness of Mental Health Court," *Justice System Journal* 30, no. 2 (2009): 196–218.

6. P. Allard, T. Lyons, and R. Elliott, *Impaired Judgment: Assessing the Appropriateness of Drug Treatment Courts as a Response to Drug Use in Canada* (Toronto: Canadian HIV/AIDS Legal Network, 2011), http://www.aidslaw.ca/publications/interfaces/downloadFile.php?ref=2034.

7. F. Sirotich, "The Criminal Justice Outcomes of Jail Diversion Programs for Persons with Mental Illness: A Review of the Evidence," *Journal of the American Academy of Psychiatry and Law* 37, no. 4 (2009): 461–72.

8. E. Slinger and R. Roesch, "Problem-Solving Courts in Canada: A Review and a Call for Empirically-Based Evaluation Methods," *International Journal of Law and Psychiatry* 33, no. 4 (2010): 258–64 at 260.

9. Lurigio and Snowden, "Putting Therapeutic Jurisprudence into Practice," 207.

10. R. Pierce, "Queue-Jumping? Do Mental Health Courts Privilege Criminal Behavior?," *Journal of Ethics in Mental Health* 3, no. 2 (2008): 1–6.

11. B. Newton-Taylor, L. Gliksman, and J. Patra, "Toronto Drug Treatment Court: Participant Intake Characteristics as Predictors of 'Successful' Program Completion," *Journal of Drug Issues* 39, no. 4 (2009): 965–88.

12. Department of Justice Canada, *Drug Treatment Court Funding Program Summative Evaluation: Final Report* (Ottawa: Evaluation Division, Office of Strategic Planning and Performance Management, 2009), http://www.justice.gc.ca/eng/pi/eval/rep-rap/09/dtcfp-pfttt/dtcfp.pdf.

13. A. Verhaaff, *Individual Factors Predicting Mental Health Court Diversion Outcome*, MA thesis, University of Ontario Institute of Technology, 2011, http://ir.library.dc-uoit.ca/bitstream/10155/164/Verehaaf_Ashley.pdf.

14. L. Gutierrez and G. Bourgon, *Drug Treatment Courts: A Quantitative Review of Study and Treatment Quality* (Ottawa: Public Safety Canada, 2009), http://www.publicsafety.gc.ca/res/cor/rep/_fl/2009-04-dtc-eng.pdf; C.T. Lowenkamp, J. Pealer, P. Smith, and E.J. Latessa, "Adhering to the Risk and Needs Principles: Does It Matter for Supervision-Based Programs?" *Federal Probation* 70, no. 3 (2006): 3–8.

15. K. Heilbrun, D. Dematteo, K. Yasuhara, S. Brooks-Holiday, S. Shah, C. King, A.B. Dicarlo, D. Hamilton, and C. Laduke, "Community-Based Alternatives for Justice-Involved Individuals with Severe Mental Illness: A Review of the Relevant Research," *Criminal Justice and Behavior* 39, no. 4 (2012): 351–419.

16. J. Junger-Tas, *Alternatives to Prison Sentences: Experience and Developments* (New York: Kugler, 1994), 11, 13.

17. J. Petersilia and E.P. Deschenes, "What Punishes? Inmates Rank the Severity of Prison vs. Intermediate Sanctions," *Federal Probation* 58, no. 1 (1994): 308.

18. Ibid.; B.K. Payne, M. DeMichele, and D.M. Button, "Understanding the Electronic Monitoring of Sex Offenders," *Corrections Compendium* 33, no. 1 (2008): 1–5.

19. J.V. Roberts. "Serving Time at Home: The Conditional Sentence of Imprisonment," in *Criminal Justice in Canada: A Reader*, 4th ed., ed. J.V. Roberts and M.G. Gorssman (Toronto: Nelson, 2012), 178–86.

CHAPTER 6
PROBATION PRACTICE

CHAPTER OBJECTIVES

After reading this chapter, you should be able to:
- *Describe the differences between probation and parole.*
- *Discuss the recruitment, training, roles, and responsibilities of probation officers, including the dual role of probation officers in supervising offenders.*
- *Describe the four models of probation practice.*
- *Describe the features of intensive probation supervision.*
- *Describe the "pains" of probation.*
- *Discuss the obstacles to effective probation practice.*
- *Discuss the effectiveness of probation.*

Section 731 of the Criminal Code provides that, in cases in which no minimum penalty is prescribed, the sentencing judge may place the offender on probation. Probation is generally used as an alternative to confinement; however, it can also be used in conjunction with a period of incarceration—including an intermittent sentence, which is generally served in a provincial/territorial facility on weekends. The maximum time that a probation order can be in effect is three years. Probation, which is the most widely used alternative to confinement, differs in significant ways from parole (see Table 6.1). Recall from Chapter 5 that probation is also different from a conditional sentence, although it may be used in conjunction with one.

The proportion of cases receiving a sentence of probation has remained stable over the years (around 45 percent), as has the average length of probation orders (around 15 months).[1]

Probation is popular largely because it is so versatile. The length and conditions of a probation order can be tailored to the individual needs and circumstances of the offender. Intensive probation supervision is often used to manage the risk presented by high-risk offenders. Some of the statutory conditions of a probation order, including to obey the law and keep the peace, are mandatory. However, the sentencing judge may attach further conditions, such as requiring the offender to abstain from drugs and/or alcohol or to attend a treatment program. The frequency of reporting and intensity of supervision may be set by the court or determined by the supervising probation officer.

Table 6.1   Probation versus Parole

Probation	Parole
Imposed by Criminal Court judge	Granted by an administrative tribunal (a parole board)
Available only for provincial/territorial offenders (except those federal offenders who receive a sentence or sentences totalling exactly two years); maximum length is three years	Available to federal and provincial/territorial offenders who are released from custody and supervised by federal parole officers; except in Ontario and Québec, where provincial offenders on parole are supervised by probation officers
May be used in conjunction with a period of confinement in a provincial/territorial institution (and following a sentence of exactly two years in a federal correctional facility)	A form of conditional release from confinement in a provincial/territorial/federal correctional facility
Breach of condition can be a charge under the Criminal Code that requires evidence for conviction of Breach of Probation; additional conditions may be imposed and the term of probation extended; incarceration rarely imposed	Breach of condition may result in suspension or revocation; conditions may be added or offender returned to custody
Requires offender to abide by general conditions (e.g., obey the law and keep the peace) and perhaps specific conditions tailored to the offender's individual case (e.g., abstain from alcohol)	Requires offender to abide by general conditions and perhaps also specific conditions

Note that offenders who receive a period of custody to be followed by supervised probation (which would follow the completion of parole if this were granted) present a different risk/needs profile than offenders who have been placed on probation as an alternative to confinement.

Probation conditions must be reasonable, and ideally, they are designed with an eye to preventing the offender from committing further crimes. During the period of supervision, the probation officer may ask the sentencing judge to increase, decrease, or eliminate additional conditions or to reduce (but not lengthen) the total period of the probation order.

An adult probationer who, without a reasonable excuse, fails or refuses to comply with a condition, or who commits a new offence, *may* be charged with breach of probation. A breach of probation is an elective (or hybrid) offence and carries a maximum penalty of two years' imprisonment if proceeded with by indictment.

MODELS OF PROBATION PRACTICE

How probation officers carry out their responsibilities will reflect one or more models of practice. At least four such models have been identified, each of which has a purpose and characteristics that affect how probation is implemented. The four models are set out in Table 6.2.

Table 6.2   Probation and the Practice Models

Practice Model	Purpose and Characteristics	Examples of How This Applies to Probation
Due process	Criminal justice is "for" justice, which should shape practice and procedure	Fair, consistent, and scrupulous determination of punishment; court's orders are implemented in a principled manner respecting the rights of offenders; accessible and effective complaints procedures
Crime control	Criminal justice practice should reduce crime	Crime reduction and public protection are prominent objectives; probation's outcomes and successes are assessed through reduced reconviction; contemporary priority of public protection through assessment and management of risk
Treatment	Broadly encompassing all modes of intervention that seek to change the offender's behaviour other than principally through fear or physical restraint	Rigorous assessment of risk and offending-related need; interventions follow from assessment; principles of risk, need, and responsivity; effectiveness gauged in terms of reduced reconviction or associated indicators
Restorative justice	Emphasis on making amends	Restorative approaches; mediation, conferencing; unpaid work/community payback as making amends; increasing victim awareness

Source: R. Canton, *Probation: Working with Offenders,* (New York: Routledge, 2011). Pg. 10.

RECRUITMENT AND TRAINING OF PROBATION OFFICERS

As noted earlier, probation falls under the authority of the provinces/territories. Each jurisdiction has developed its own procedures and standards for recruiting and training probation officers. Most often there is pre-employment training, during which potential applicants must complete a number of courses (many of which are offered online), often at their own expense, before being eligible to apply for a position as a probation officer.

Most jurisdictions also offer ongoing in-service training courses for probation officers. These focus on the supervision of special populations (such as sex offenders and the mentally disordered) and the use of assessment instruments.

ROLE AND RESPONSIBILITIES OF PROBATION OFFICERS

The activities of probation officers largely involve assessing clients with respect to their needs and the risks they pose; providing individualized case management with the objective of reducing criminal behaviour; and supervising offenders on probation as well as persons who have been released on bail while awaiting trial. In Québec and Ontario, probation officers supervise offenders who have been released on provincial parole; in the other provinces and territories, these offenders are supervised by federal parole officers. Some probation officers supervise offenders involved in diversion programs (i.e., who have been diverted from the criminal justice system). The myriad activities of probation officers are listed in Table 6.3.

Table 6.3   The Activities of Probation Officers

Officer of the Court

Preparing pre-sentence reports (PSRs); attending court proceedings; applying to change conditions of probation orders; writing progress reports; consulting with Crown counsel

Investigation	**Assessment**
Preparing pre-sentence reports; preparing community assessments (for provincial parole boards in Ontario and Québec); preparing case files	Risk assessment and case management planning (e.g., interviewing clients and collateral contacts); making evidence-based assessments of offender; determining appropriate interventions to address risk and need areas

Counselling	**Service Coordination**
Conducting initial interviews; motivational interviewing; challenging difficult client attitudes and behaviours; individual supervision; group	Collaborating with police and social services; identifying educational, vocational, and employment goals; providing treatment opportunities;

Counselling

counselling; facilitating core programs (in provinces where POs play this role) such as Respectful Relationships, Substance Abuse Management, Violence Prevention, Sex Offender Maintenance

Service Coordination

assisting with locating housing; addressing family, financial, and other issues

Surveillance/Enforcement

Monitoring compliance with conditions of probation; monitoring compliance with conditions of provincial parole (in Ontario and Québec); conducting home visits; documenting violations; preparing violation reports and recommendations; preparing violation reports for provincial parolees (in Ontario and Québec)

Source: Adapted from J. B. Stinchcomb, *Corrections: Foundations for the Future,* (New York: Routledge, 2011). Pg. 92.

Probation officers help prepare PSRs on adult offenders who have been convicted. The PSR contains a wealth of information on the offender's background and offence history, as well as victim impact information and assessments completed by treatment professionals. For Aboriginal offenders, there are special considerations that the PSR must address. For example, it must include information on the offender's background and community, as well as on available community-based programs and services, including restorative justice programs such as sentencing circles and elder-assisted interventions (see Figure 6.1).

No information can be included in the PSR that was not presented in court, and the PSR's summary cannot include any information that is not contained in the body of the report. In many provinces, as a matter of policy, probation officers are proscribed from making sentencing recommendations to the judge, although the PSR will generally set out available community and institutional programs for the judge to consider in determining the sentence. Where probation officers do make sentencing recommendations, they are generally accepted.[2]

Pre-sentence report (PSR)
A document prepared by the probation officer for the sentencing judge that contains information on the convicted offender, including sociobiographical information, offence history, victim impact, and risk assessments.

TYPES OF SUPERVISION ORDERS

Probation officers are responsible for a variety of supervision orders. These are set out in Box 6.1.

ASSESSMENT OF OFFENDER RISK AND NEEDS

Effective case management requires that the risks and needs of offenders be identified so that the appropriate level of supervision can be determined (i.e., more intensive supervision for higher risk/needs offenders and less

Figure 6.1

Components of the Pre-sentence Report

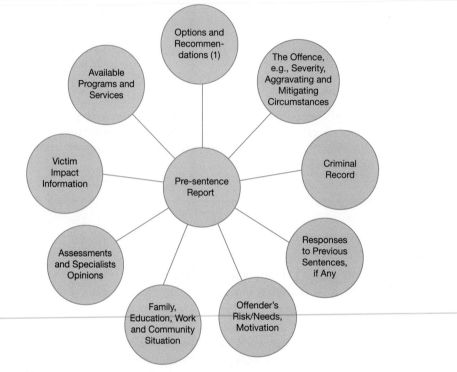

(1) In some jurisdictions probation officers can make recommendations
to the sentencing judge.

BOX 6.1

Types of Supervision Orders

Type of Order	Maximum Custody	Maximum Community
Conditional Discharge or Suspended Sentence	None	3 years
Fine plus Probation	None	3 years
Conditional Sentence plus Probation	None	3 years
Probation	None	3 years
Intermittent Prison plus Probation	90 days	3 years
Prison plus Probation	2 years less a day (provincial) Exactly 2 years (federal)	3 years 3 years
Section 810 Recognizance	None	12 months

supervision for lower risk/needs offenders). This process also identifies services to address the needs of offenders.[3]

As noted earlier, in the new Canadian penology of the early twenty-first century, there is a focus on the surveillance and control of offenders. This has affected probation practice. Risk management and protection of the public are now core features of probation supervision.[4] A number of observers have documented the shift toward "managerial" probation—a shift that has often been made at the expense of treatment and rehabilitation.[5] This is reflected in the use of various instruments for classifying offenders and assessing the risk they pose.[6]

A core component of the probation officer's work is completing assessments, which are designed to identify the offender's needs, to evaluate risk, and to help formulate plans of supervision. These assessments are used not only during the case management process but also at parole hearings, where provincial parole boards determine whether to grant conditional release to offenders in custody (see Chapter 9).

Two of the more common instruments are the Level of Service Inventory-Revised (LSI-R) and the Level of Service/Case Management Inventory (LS/CMI); these are used for adult offenders. The LSI-R is a 54-item, interview-driven assessment that measures risk factors in relation to a number of areas, including criminal history, education/employment, financial status, and drug problems. The LS/CMI measures risk and need factors, taking basically the same approach. In Saskatchewan, probation officers use the Saskatchewan Primary Risk Assessment instrument for case and risk management.

The Youth Level of Service/Case Management Inventory (YLS/CMI) has a number of subscales designed to assess major risk factors. These subscales touch on prior and current offences, peer relations, substance abuse, and personality/behaviour. Each of these dimensions is scored, and the result is a risk estimate, ranging from Low to Very High.

There are also assessment instruments for specific groups of offenders, including sex offenders (Sex Offender Risk Assessment [SORA]) and offenders convicted of spousal assault (Spousal Assault Risk Assessment [SARA]).

The scores developed through these assessment instruments allow probation officers to target specific risk/needs areas and to devise case management and supervision plans. All of these instruments have been effective in identifying needs and in predicting the likelihood of reoffending. Research studies have found that these instruments are valid for both genders and different ethnicities.[7] Some observers have questioned the objectivity of risk assessment instruments such as the LSI-R, arguing that probation officers exercise considerable discretion when conducting these assessments and developing plans of supervision.[8]

It has also been argued that the role of probation officers has become more restricted and rule-bound. This points to efforts to standardize probation practices and to hold probation officers accountable for adhering to evidence-based practice standards.[9] The use of risk assessment instruments as the basis for case management also allows probation officers to "externalize responsibility" for their decisions and to avoid criticism if an offender reoffends.[10]

Risk assessment instruments are now a core component of probation practice; even so, there is evidence that individual probation officers continue to exercise considerable discretion in their supervisory practices. A study conducted in an open-custody facility for young offenders found that the staff employed a variety of strategies to subvert the results of risk assessments; they also applied their experience and subjective assessments when constructing and implementing case management plans.[11]

THE DUAL ROLE OF PROBATION OFFICERS

Probation officers play a dual role: they provide assistance and support for offenders and at the same time they enforce the conditions of probation orders. In carrying out the assistance and support role, the probation officer may help the offender address issues that have contributed to the offence and identify resources in the community such as alcohol and drug treatment programs, education upgrading courses, and mental health services. However, the probation officer must at the same time ensure compliance with the general and specific conditions of the probation order. For offenders who are less cooperative, an approach based on control may be effective; for offenders who are motivated to change, the probation officer can provide encouragement, support, and assistance. Probation officers have the discretion to tailor their style of supervision to the needs and risk of the individual probationer. See At Issue 6.1.

It is often difficult for probation officers to handle both roles, and this can be a barrier to effective case management. For example, a probationer with a history of drug addiction who has relapsed and started "using" again (or who never ceased using drugs) may want to ask his or her probation officer for help finding a treatment program. However, that person could trigger a charge of breach of probation by disclosing the illegal drug use to the probation officer.

AT ISSUE

Issue 6.1: Probation Officers' Discretion

How much discretion should probation officers have in supervising offenders?

In recent years, the emergence of evidence-based practices and predictive risk assessment instruments has reduced the broad discretion traditionally exercised by probation officers. Proponents argue that this has helped standardize probation practices and increase effectiveness. Critics counter that probation officers should be able to use professional discretion and adapt their supervisory practices to the requirements of individual offenders. What is your view on this?

PERSPECTIVE

Probation Officer

I think it is our responsibility to try to help individuals and to identify the issues that they have so they can begin working on themselves. For the offenders on my caseload, I try to help them with basic needs, such as food, shelter, employment training, and core programming that will help them develop their self-confidence and address their issues. It is important to have empathy and to understand the client's needs while also having realistic expectations of them. I try to see that the conditions of the probation order are followed while at the same time respecting the person. (personal communication with C.T. Griffiths).

On the other hand, failing to disclose the drug relapse could result in the commission of further criminal acts to support the addiction.

A probation officer who becomes aware that the probationer is not adhering to the conditions of the probation order often has considerable discretion in deciding whether to revoke probation. This decision making may be affected by a number of factors, including the organization in which the probation officer works, the individual style of the officer, and the severity of the violation.[12]

SUPERVISION

Over the past decade there has been a strong shift in the role and orientation of probation officers toward control and surveillance.[13] This shift has been due in large measure to increasing caseloads, the focus on risk assessment in order to ensure accountability and reduce liability, and the increasing number of higher risk categories of offenders—such as sex offenders and assaultive male offenders—who are receiving sentences of probation.

This new focus on risk management may be placing pressure on probation officers to abandon efforts to build therapeutic relationships with probationers centered on RNR, in favour of a more enforcement-oriented approach centred on adherence to the conditions of probation.

To be effective, a probation officer must, to the greatest extent possible, balance enforcement with treatment and balance a client-centred approach with organizational requirements (e.g., completing assessments and other paperwork).[14] Successfully implementing RNR-based probation practice requires organizational and policy changes as well as a commitment by both management and probation staff.[15] An example of an innovative evidence-based approach to probation supervision is presented in Box 6.2.

BOX 6.2

The Application of RNR to Probation Practice: The STICS Initiative

In an attempt to introduce evidence-based practices into the probation supervision of offenders, the Strategic Training Initiative in Community Corrections (STICS) was delivered to a sample of probation officers in B.C., Saskatchewan, and P.E.I. (the experimental group). The STICS program focuses on the principles of RNR and teaches probation officers ways to utilize those principles when supervising probationers, with particular attention to criminogenic factors such as relationships with peers and criminal thinking patterns. A comparative group of probation officers in these provinces did not receive the STICS training (the control group); this allowed for an assessment of the effectiveness of the approach.

In a subsequent analysis of audiotapes recorded during client sessions conducted by probation officers from the experimental and control groups, it was found that the officers trained in STICS altered their traditional supervisory practices and incorporated the need principle into their interactions with probationers. This included spending more time discussing criminogenic factors with their clients and less time on noncriminogenic topics such as the conditions of probation. A review of the audiotaped sessions also revealed that the probation officers who had participated in the STICS program evidenced better skills in developing relationships with their clients and used more cognitive-behavioural intervention techniques in client sessions.[a] This approach contributed to lower rates of reoffending among probationers who were supervised by officers who had completed the STICS training.

The STICS initiative demonstrated that focusing on changing probationers' cognitive processes, including their attitudes, thinking, and perceptions of self, was as important, if not more important, than providing general assistance. On a more general level, the STICS project demonstrated that it is possible to move from the conceptual level (the principles of RNR) to practice.[b]

[a] J. Bonta, G. Bourgon, T. Rugge, T-L. Scott, A.K. Yessine, L. Gutierrez, and J. Li, "An Experimental Demonstration of Training Probation Officers in Evidence-Based Community Supervision," *Criminal Justice and Behavior* 38, no. 11 (2011): 1127–48 at 1144.

[b] G. Bourgon, L. Gutierrez, and J. Ashton, *From Case Management to Change Agent: The Evolution of "What Works" in Community Supervision* (Ottawa: Public Safety Canada, 2012), http://www.publicsafety.gc.ca/res/cor/rep/_fl/2012-01-cmca-eng.pdf.

Key elements of successful probation supervision include establishing and maintaining rapport, considering the risk/needs of the offender, and adjusting the balance between control and assistance as required. The efforts of the probation officer will be enhanced if probationers are able to speak openly about their issues and challenges, while at the same time understanding what is expected of them. Probation officers have identified interpersonal communication and interviewing skills, knowledge of community resources, and the ability to cope with the offender's emotions as required core competencies for effective supervision.[16] When the probation officer can focus on addressing the problems the probationer is experiencing, there is often a reduction in reoffending.[17]

An evidence-based practice that many probation officers follow is **motivational interviewing (MI).** This approach uses empathy and other nonconfrontational strategies to improve the relationship between the probation officer and the offender and to strengthen the offender's motivation to change.[18]

Through the use of MI, the probation officer facilitates a client-centred conversation that empowers the probationer to make positive changes in his or her life.[19] The evidence is mixed as to whether MI lowers rates of reoffending; however, it is viewed as a central component of an RNR approach to probation supervision.[20]

Many probation offices now have specialized supervision units composed of specially trained officers for offenders convicted of spousal assault, sex offences, and other specific types of crime. Studies suggest that specially trained probation officers are less likely to be punitive in responding to violations of a probation order, perhaps because of their more in-depth understanding of the cognitive thinking patterns and behaviours of specific groups of offenders.[21]

Questions have been raised as to whether probation officers who supervise sex offenders, domestic violence offenders, and other high-risk probationers have received the required training.[22] The effectiveness of these specialized probation officers at reducing reoffending among high-risk probationers is uncertain, and so is the extent to which these probation officers utilize evidence-based supervision strategies.

Key to PO–offender relationships is **continuity of supervision.** Offenders who are supervised by many different probation officers during their probation period are at a higher risk to reoffend. One study ($N = 5{,}134$) found that offenders who were supervised by just one probation officer while on probation were nearly 60 percent more likely to complete their probation sentence successfully.[23] Continuity of supervision is an understudied area in corrections and may apply, as well, to both judges and probation officers in the problem-solving courts discussed in Chapter 5.

Little is known about the impact of gender in probation supervision. For example, we know little about the challenges that women face when working with certain groups of offenders (e.g., male sex offenders), or how female probation officers cope with offenders' gender stereotypes. In one study, female probation officers described how their male probationers often attempted to manipulate the supervisory relationship to undermine the officer's authority. Techniques ranged from flirting to physical and psychological intimidation.[24] Similarly,

Motivational interviewing (MI)
An interview technique used by probation officers designed to empower offenders to change their attitudes and behaviour.

Continuity of supervision
The requirement that, to be effective, offenders be supervised by the same probation officer during their term of probation.

female probation officers may experience a heightened sense of vulnerability and, for officers who are mothers, a heightened sense of risk. It can be anticipated that visible and cultural minority probation officers may also experience unique challenges in carrying out their roles, although this remains to be explored.

PROGRAMS FOR PROBATIONERS

Provincial/territorial systems of corrections and not-for-profit organizations offer probationers a variety of programs and services. In B.C., officers are actively involved in several programs for their probationers. These include Violence Prevention, Substance Abuse Management, Respectful Relationships, Living Skills, Cognitive Skills, and Educational Upgrading, as well as a program for sex offenders. The components of the Violence Prevention Program are set out in Box 6.3.

BOX 6.3

Violence Prevention Program (VPP)

Rationale	Offenders learn to differentiate between violence and anger
	Offenders explore sources of anger
	Offenders identify nonviolent ways to express and resolve anger
	Participants learn about their cycle of violence
	Participants develop self-management techniques to behave in a healthy manner
Objectives	Practice stress management skills
	Identify positive communication skills
	Learn problem-solving skills
Trained facilitators	Correctional staff in correctional centres
	Correctional staff in community corrections offices
Targeted population	Offenders assessed as medium or high risk to reoffend
	Offenders convicted of domestic violence attend Respectful Relationship (RR), not VPP
Duration	Ten 150-minute sessions
	Recommended participation: one to two sessions/week

These programs are offered by community corrections offices throughout the province and are available for both probationers and provincial parolees. Participation is generally stipulated on the offender's probation order, although the programs also accept persons other than probationers.

INTENSIVE SUPERVISION PROBATION

Intensive supervision probation (ISP) is meant to be an intermediate sanction between traditional probation practice—which generally involves minimal supervision—and incarceration. ISP programs entail increased surveillance of probationers, various treatment interventions, efforts to ensure that offenders are employed, and reduced caseloads for probation officers. In Canada, ISP is used primarily with youth offenders.

Offenders in ISP programs are monitored closely and rigorous conditions are imposed on them, such as multiple weekly reporting, strict enforcement of the probation order's mandatory and optional conditions, and the requirement that offenders secure and maintain employment. ISP is more suited to offenders who pose a greater risk to reoffend. A premise of these programs is that they can help reduce the number of prison admissions, cut operational costs, and protect the public, while providing increased supervision of more serious offenders.

Intensive supervision probation (ISP)
An intermediate sanction (between the minimal supervision of traditional probation and incarceration) that generally includes reduced caseloads for probation officers, increased surveillance, treatment interventions, and efforts to ensure that probationers are employed.

THE EXPERIENCE OF PROBATIONERS

Few studies have examined the experiences of persons on probation. There is some evidence that many probationers believe that their sentence served as a deterrent and that being on probation was beneficial.[25] A survey ($N = 1,121$) conducted in B.C. found that probationers had a positive overall experience of probation (81 percent); that most of them (90.5 percent) felt their probation officer treated them fairly; and that they did not have difficulty accessing programs (91.3 percent). Similarly, most of the probationers surveyed (63.5 percent) indicated that they were involved in their supervision plan.

With respect to continuity of supervision, most of the respondents had only one (48 percent) or two (32 percent) different probation officers in the course of their sentence/supervision.[26] Overall client satisfaction did not vary with the gender or Aboriginal status of the probationer, nor did it with the region of the province in which they resided.

Despite these findings from B.C., there is evidence that some offenders experience **pains of probation**. Depending on the specific conditions attached to the probation order, these pains may include loss of autonomy, having to change daily routines, the stigma associated with probation, and possible difficulties with employment. The pains experienced by inmates in correctional institutions are often physical; by contrast, those associated with probation tend to be economic and emotional.[27] Intensive supervision programs may place restrictions on the probationer, who as a result may view probation negatively.

Pains of probation
The emotional and economic challenges that probationers may experience while under probation supervision in the community.

American researchers found that some offenders rate being on probation as more punitive than a short-term prison sentence.[28] Offenders' perceptions of probation may be partly a function of their past experiences of prison and probation: offenders who have been incarcerated in the past may not find confinement as punitive as close supervision in the community.

CHALLENGES IN PROBATION PRACTICE

The perspectives and experiences of correctional officers have been studied extensively; little attention has been paid to those of probation officers. What studies have been done have found that the most satisfying part of a probation officer's job is working with offenders, and that the least satisfying part is the ever increasing burden of administrative duties, including paperwork and dealing with agency management.[29]

The Stress Levels of Probation Officers

Studies have found that probation officers face higher stress levels than the general population. Female probation officers may have higher levels of stress than their male counterparts, because of the issues noted earlier regarding their supervision of male probationers.[30]

Probation Officer Safety

An issue that has recently emerged is officer safety: there is evidence that incidents involving probation officers are vastly underreported. Many probation officers do not conduct visits to the homes of their probationers. Often this is because they don't have enough time or because they worry for their safety. Still other officers believe that home visits are an intrusion on probationers and their families (personal communication with C.T. Griffiths).

Difficulties in Accessing Resources and Services for High-Need Clients

I have a client on my caseload who called 9-1-1 hundreds of times one weekend. He is mentally disabled, but forensic services will not do an assessment on him until his alcohol addiction problems have first been addressed. (probation officer, personal communication with C.T. Griffiths)

Probation officers often struggle to access services for their clients, especially probationers who face mental impairments, addictions, or other challenges.

Heavy Workloads

The duties of probation officers have continued to expand and now include providing bail supervision for adult criminal courts; preparing PSRs for sentencing courts; supervising offenders on conditional release orders; and liaising with social services, the police, and the courts.

High Caseloads

Probation officers in many jurisdictions have experienced increases in their caseloads, some of which are in the 100+ range per officer. In Ontario probation officers have the highest average caseload of 66.5 clients per officer. In British Columbia, the average caseload is 64 clients per officer, an increase of 28 percent since 2005–06.[31] The impact of caseload size on the quality of supervision provided and on rates of violations of probation orders and reoffending, however, is unknown. In the absence of evidence-based treatment, reduced caseloads may not improve the effectiveness of probation.

A Lack of PO–Offender Contact and Intervention

Depending on other commitments and responsibilities, probation officers may have only one contact per month with individual offenders on their caseloads. Contact may be by telephone, and when the officer does meet with the offender, the session may be short. When probation services shift to more of a managerial approach, focusing on risk assessments, and away from client-centred practice, it may be even more difficult for probation officers to find adequate time for their clients.

Increasing Needs and Risks of Probationers

In the past, the typical probationer had been convicted of a nonviolent property offence and did not have an extensive criminal history. In recent years, there has been an increase in the needs and risk levels of offenders placed on probation and in the numbers of offenders who are mentally disordered or who have been convicted of sex-related crimes and crimes of violence. Today, more probationers have been convicted of a violent crime and many probationers have been assessed as being high risk.[32]

The Need to Provide Probation Services in Remote and Northern Regions

Unique challenges are involved in providing effective probation services in remote and northern areas of the country. For example, community resources are absent, and it is difficult to recruit and retain probation officers. These difficulties are particularly acute given the high rates of crime and violence that afflict many northern and remote communities (see Box 6.4).

Supervising a Diverse Clientele

An unstudied dimension of probation practice in Canada is the challenge presented by factors such as language, culture, religion, and ethnicity. Most probation officers in Canada are Caucasian, yet these officers carry out their tasks in a diverse society. English- or French-speaking probation officers can

BOX 6.4

Probation in the Remote North

There are unique challenges in probation practice in northern and remote communities. These communities often lack the capacity to provide programs for probationers, especially those who are high-risk violent offenders or sex offenders and those suffering from a mental illness, addiction issues, and/or FASD. Concerns have been raised regarding whether probation is overused or being used inappropriately and whether probation orders protect communities. Also, programs and services for probationers are severely lacking, and, in some communities, so is adequate supervision.

Concerns about the effectiveness of probation were reflected in the comments of an Inuit woman who had been the victim of violence in one of the communities:

> *He was charged with assault. Then, a few weeks later, he was in JP court and he got six months probation. I thought it was going to be ok because after the JP court he said he would quit beating me up. But after one month he started again. That was against his probation. He'd go see his probation officer every month and when he still had six or eight months to go, he quit going. Nobody said anything and nothing happened. He was still drinking when he was on probation. It's just a lot of words, no action.*[a]

Circuit Court judges, who hold court in northern and remote communities, may be reluctant to sentence offenders to custody in correctional institutions that may be hundreds of kilometres from the offender's home community.

[a] Griffiths, C.T., E. Zellerer, D.S. Wood, and G. Sville. 1995. *Crime, Law, and Justice Among Inuit in the Baffin Region, N.W.T., Canada.* Burnaby, B.C.: Criminology Research Centre, Simon Fraser University.

expect to encounter difficulties when supervising newly arrived Canadians, who may have limited language skills; similarly, cultural differences may impede the development of therapeutic relationships with probationers as well as with community partners. Research in the United States found that probationers who were supervised by an officer of their own race had more positive perceptions of that officer.[33] This question has not yet been explored in Canada.

Research File 6.1 sets out what is known about the effectiveness of probation. Community corrections agencies often do not gather the information required to determine the effectiveness of probation practices.[34] Few of the more common programs for probationers, including those operated by private contractors, have been evaluated.

RESEARCH FILE 6.1

The Effectiveness of Probation

Does probation supervision reduce reoffending? Potentially. There is no evidence that traditional probation practices reduce reoffending.[a] This is for a variety of reasons, including the lack of training of probation officers in strategies that may improve probation outcomes, in particular the absence of the principles of RNR in probation practice. It also depends to some extent on the criminality of the group being studied. Many probationers who have committed less serious crimes successfully complete; less positive results are reported for offenders with lengthy criminal records and who have additional issues, such as addiction and mental illness.[b]

Does ISP Work? Yes. These programs can manage risk while providing probationers with access to treatment. ISP may be more cost-effective than incarceration and produce better outcomes.[c]

For which offenders is probation most effective? Research studies suggest that probation is most effective for offenders who are in a stable personal relationship, are employed, have higher levels of education, and do not have an extensive criminal record. Specialized supervision units can be effective in increasing offender accountability and reducing rates of reoffending; they also have a positive impact on victim satisfaction.[d]

Do risk assessment instruments such as the LSI-R and LS/CMI improve probation outcomes? Potentially. Although these instruments are an important component of case management and are effective at identifying the risks and needs of offenders, there is some evidence that probation officers still exercise considerable discretion in the supervision of offenders.

Do the principles of RNR improve the effectiveness of probation? There is growing evidence that incorporating RNR into probation practice improves the quality of supervision as well as case outcomes.[e] A study ($N = 192$) of youth probationers in Saskatchewan found that case management centred on the "needs principle" and on the criminogenic needs of youth resulted in lower rates of reoffending.[f] The results of the STICS initiative are promising.

Do collaborative partnerships between probation and other agencies, including police services, improve probation outcomes? Collaboration may improve information sharing and the quality of supervision, but it is uncertain whether this results in more effective probation outcomes and reduced reoffending. Concerns have been expressed that probation–police partnerships may blur the roles and mission of the two agencies, with probation officers abandoning their treatment and assistance role for one of enforcement and control.[g] This role distortion may be resisted by some probation officers, who see their primary role as addressing the offender's needs. It may also increase the role ambiguity of probation officers as they attempt to balance the enforcement and assistance roles discussed above.[h]

What factors may compromise successful probation outcomes? The effectiveness of probation may be compromised by low program completion rates by offenders. A random sample of 60 offenders on probation in B.C. found that only 35 percent of offenders with a condition on their probation order to complete a treatment program did so.[i] (See a PPT on this investigation at www.bcauditor.com/pubs/report10/bc-community-corrections-cccp.) The reasons why probationers fail to complete mandated programs are many, but they certainly include a lack of access to programs and weak motivation. Furthermore, the guiding principle of RNR that program efforts should focus on high-risk probationers may prove to be unworkable if these offenders have needs that exceed the capacity of community-based programs.[j] In such cases, programs for low and medium-risk probationers may be more effective.

It is important that the supervision strategies the officer employs match the needs and risk of the individual offender. However, there is often a disconnect between the risk assessment and the intervention plan developed by the supervising probation officer.[k] Probation agencies may also lack the capacity to assess effectiveness, determine gaps in program delivery, and ensure that probationers receive the interventions identified as required by the risk assessment.

[a] J. Bonta, G. Bourgon, T. Rugge, T-L. Scott, A.K. Yessine, L. Gutierrez, and J. Li, "An Experimental Demonstration of Training Probation Officers in Evidence-Based Community Supervision," *Criminal Justice and Behavior* 38, no. 11 (2011): 1127–48 at 1129.

[b] M. DeLisi and P.J. Conis, *American Corrections: Theory, Research, Policy, and Practice*, 2nd ed. (Burlington: Jones and Bartlett Learning, 2013), 248.

[c] Ibid., 251.

[d] A.R. Klein, D. Wilson, A.H. Crowe, and M. DeMichele, *Evaluation of the Rhode Island Probation Specialized Domestic Violence Supervision Unit* (Washington: U.S. Department of Justice, 2008), http://www.ncjrs.gov/pdffiles1/nij/grants/222912.pdf.

[e] J. Bonta, G. Bourgon, T. Rugge, T-L. Scott, A.K. Yessine, L. Gutierrez, and J. Li, "An Experimental demonstration of Training Probation officers in Evidence-Based Community Supervision," *Criminal Justice and Behaviour* 38, no. 11 (2011):1127–48.

[f] D. Luong and J.S. Wormith, "Applying Risk/Need Assessment to Probation Practice and Its Impact on the Recidivism of Young Offenders," *Criminal Justice and Behavior* 38, no. 12 (2011): 1177–99 at 1197.

[g] B. Kim, J. Gerber, and D.R. Beto, "Listening to Law Enforcement Officers: The Promises and Problems of Police–Adult Probation Partnerships," *Journal of Criminal Justice* 38, no. 4 (2010): 625–32.

[h] D. Murphy and F. Lutze, "Police–Probation Partnerships: Professional Identity and the Sharing of Coercive Power," *Journal of Criminal Justice* 37, no. 1 (2009): 65–76.

[i] B.C. Office of the Auditor General, *Effectiveness of BC Community Corrections* (Victoria: 2011), http://www.bcauditor.com/pubs/2011/report10/bc-community-corrections-cccp.

[j] D.A.S. Pearson, C. McDougall, M. Kanaan, R.A. Bowles, and D.J. Torgerson, "Reducing Criminal Recidivism: Evaluation of Citizenship: An Evidence-Based Probation Supervision Process," *Journal of Experimental Criminology* 7, no. 1 (2011): 73–102.

[k] J. Bonta, T. Rugge, B. Sedo, and R. Coles, *Case Management in Manitoba Probation*, 27–28 (Ottawa: Public Safety Canada, 2004), http://www.publicsafety.gc.ca/res/cor/rep/_fl/2004-01-cse-mana-eng.pdf; B.C. Office of the Auditor General, *Effectiveness of BC Community Corrections*.

SUMMARY

This chapter has considered various aspects of probation practice. Probation differs in significant ways from parole, which is discussed later in the text. Probation is used for offenders who are under the jurisdiction of provincial/territorial systems of correction. It may be used as an alternative to incarceration or in conjunction with a period of time in confinement. Probation officers are involved in a range of activities, including preparing PSRs, conducting risk and needs assessments, and supervising offenders. Probation officers confront a number of challenges in carrying out their mandate. The application of the principles of RNR holds considerable promise in probation practice.

KEY POINTS REVIEW

1. Probation officers have a variety of roles and responsibilities, including preparing pre-sentence reports, assessing offender risk and needs, and providing supervision and assistance.
2. There are significant differences between probation and parole.
3. Continuity of supervision—that is, maintaining the same probation officer—is key to effective probation practice.
4. Probation officers play a dual role: they provide assistance and support for offenders, and they enforce the conditions of the probation order.
5. The role of probation officers has shifted; it now focuses more on control and surveillance.
6. Probationers may experience economic and emotional challenges while on probation.
7. There are a number of challenges in probation practice, including officer stress, safety, heavy workloads and high caseloads, limited PO–client interaction, and the increasing risk/needs levels of offenders on probation.
8. Providing probation services in rural and remote regions is a particular challenge.
9. Probation appears to be most effective with offenders who are employed, have stable family relationships, and do not have an extensive criminal record.
10. The supervision strategies used by probation officers must match the needs and risk of the individual offender; that is, the principles of RNR must be followed.

KEY TERM QUESTIONS

1. What is a *pre-sentence report (PSR)* and what role does it play in sentencing?
2. Describe how *motivational interviewing* is used in probation supervision.

3. What is meant by ***continuity of supervision*** in probation and why is it important in probation practice?

4. What are the features of ***intensive probation supervision***?

5. What are the ***pains of probation*** and how might these affect probation practice?

NOTES

1. M. Marth, "Adult Criminal Court Statistics, 2006/2007," *Juristat* 28, no. 5 (Ottawa: Minister of Industry, 2008), http://www.statcan.gc.ca/pub/85-002-x/2008005/article/10567-eng.htm.

2. J. Bonta, G. Bourgon, R. Jesseman, and A.K. Yessine, *Presentence Reports in Canada* (Ottawa: Public Safety Canada, 2005), http://www.publicsafety.gc.ca/res/cor/rep/_fl/2005-03-presntnce-eng.pdf.

3. J. Bonta, T. Rugge, B. Sedo, and R. Coles, *Case Management in Manitoba Probation* (Ottawa: Public Safety and Emergency Preparedness Canada, 2004), http://www.publicsafety.gc.ca/res/cor/rep/_fl/2004-01-cse-mana-eng.pdf.

4. G. Robinson, "Exploring Risk Management in Probation Practice," *Punishment and Society* 4, no. 1 (2002): 5–25.

5. G. Bourgon, L. Gutierrez, and J. Ashton, *From Case Management to Change Agent: The Evolution of "What Works" in Community Supervision* (Ottawa: Public Safety Canada, 2012), http://www.publicsafety.gc.ca/res/cor/rep/_fl/2012-01-cmca-eng.pdf.

6. L.A. Gould, M. Pate, and M. Sarver, "Risk and Revocation in Community Corrections: The Role of Gender," *Journal of Community and Criminal Justice* 58, no. 3 (2011): 250–64.

7. C.S. Schwalbe, "A Meta-Analysis of Juvenile Justice Risk Assessment Instruments," *Criminal Justice and Behavior* 35, no. 11 (2008): 1367–81.

8. K. Bullock, "The Construction and Interpretation of Risk Management Technologies in Contemporary Probation Practice," *British Journal of Criminology* 51, no. 1 (2011): 120–35.

9. Ibid.

10. D. Ballucci, "Subverting and Negotiating Risk Assessment: A Case Study of the LSI in a Canadian Youth Custody Facility," *Canadian Journal of Criminology and Criminal Justice* 54, no. 2 (2012): 203–28 at 205.

11. Ibid.

12. J.J. Krebs, M. Jones, and J.M. Jolley, "Discretionary Decision Making by Probation and Parole Officers: The Role of Extralegal Variables as Predictors of Responses to Technical Violations," *Journal of Contemporary Criminal Justice* 25, no. 4 (2009): 424–41.

13. R. Burnett, and F. McNeill, "The Place of the Officer–Offender Relationship in Assisting Offenders to Desist from Crime," *Probation Journal* 52, no. 3 (2005): 221–42.

14. J. Matthews, "'People First: Probation Officer Perspectives on Probation Work'—A Practitioner's Response," *Probation Journal* 56, no. 1 (2009): 61–67.

15. D.A. Andrews, "The Impact of Nonprogrammatic Factors on Criminal Justice Interventions," *Legal and Criminological Psychology* 16, no. 1 (2011): 1–23.

16. D. Bracken, "Skills and Knowledge for Contemporary Probation Practice," *Probation Journal* 50, no. 2 (2003): 101–14.

17. J. Bonta, T. Rugge, T.-L. Scott, G. Bourgon, and A.K. Yessine, "Exploring the Black Box of Community Supervision," *Journal of Offender Rehabilitation* 47, no. 3 (2008): 248–70.

18. M. McMurran, "Motivational Interviewing with Offenders: A Systematic Review," *Legal and Criminological Psychology* 14, no. 1 (2009): 83–100.

19. J. Paul and L. Feuerbach, "A Changing Role: Perspectives from Two Officers," *Federal Probation* 72, no. 2 (2008): 77–79.

20. D.A. Andrews, "The Impact of Nonprogrammatic Factors on Criminal Justice Interventions," *Legal and Criminological Psychology* 16, no.1 (2011): 1–23.

21. J. Louden, J.L. Skeem, J. Camp, and E. Christensen, "Supervising Probationers with Mental Disorder: How Do Agencies Respond to Violations?", *Criminal Justice and Behavior* 35, no. 7 (2008): 832–47.

22. B.C. Office of the Auditor General, *Effectiveness of BC Community Corrections* (Victoria: 2011), http://www.bcauditor.com/pubs/2011/report10/bc-community-corrections-cccp.

23. J. Clark-Miller and K.D. Stevens, "Effective Supervision Strategies: Do Frequent Changes of Supervision Officers Affect Probationer Outcomes?", *Federal Probation* 75, no. 3 (2011): 11–18.

24. M. Petrillo, "Power Struggle: Gender Issues for Female Probation Officers in the Supervision of High Risk Offenders," *Probation Journal* 54, no. 4 (2007): 394–406.

25. B.K. Applegate, H.P. Smith, A.H. Sitren, and N.F. Springer, "From the Inside: The Meaning of Probation to Probationers," *Criminal Justice Review* 34, no. 1 (2009): 80–95.

26. R.A. Malatest and Associates Ltd., *BC Community Corrections Client Survey Research: Client Satisfaction—Community Corrections Services* (Victoria: B.C. Ministry of Public Safety and Solicitor General, 2008).

27. I. Durnescu, "Pains of Probation: Effective Practice and Human Rights," *International Journal of Offender Therapy and Comparative Criminology* 55, no. 4 (2011): 530–45.

28. B.M. Crouch, "Is Incarceration Really Worse? Analysis of Offender's Preferences for Prison Over Probation," *Justice Quarterly* 10, no. 1 (1993): 67–88; J. Petersilia and S. Turner, "Intensive Probation and Parole," in *Crime and Justice: A Review of the Research*, ed. M. Tonry, 281–335 (Chicago: University of Chicago Press, 1993).

29. J. Annison, T. Eadie, and C. Knight, "People First: Probation Officer Perspectives on Probation Work," *Probation Journal* 55, no. 3 (2008): 259–71; J. Matthews, "'People First: Probation Officer Perspectives on Probation Work' – A Practitioner's Response," *Probation Journal* 56, no. 1 (2009): 61–67.

30. C. Simmons, J.K. Cochran, and W.R. Blount, "The Effects of Job-Related Stress and Job Satisfaction on Probation Officers' Inclination to Quit," *American Journal of Criminal Justice* 21, no. 2 (2007): 213–29; R.N. Slate, T.L. Wells, and W.W. Johnson, "State Probation Officer Stress and Perceptions of Participation in Workplace Decision Making." *Crime and Delinquency* 49, no. 4 (2003): 519–41.

31. B.C. Auditor General, *Effectiveness of BC Community Corrections*. 19.

32. L. Landry and M. Sinha, "Adult Correctional Services in Canada, 2005/2006," *Juristat*, 28 no.6 (Ottawa: Minister of Industry, 2008), http://www.statcan.gc.ca/pub/85-002-x/2008006/article/10593-eng.htm.

33. N.F. Springer, B.K. Applegate, H.P. Smith, and A.H. Sitren, "Exploring the Determinants of Probationers' Perceptions of Their Supervising Officers," *Journal of Offender Rehabilitation* 48, no. 3 (2009): 210–27.

34. B.C. Auditor General, *Effectiveness of BC Community Corrections*.

PART III

INCARCERATION

The discussion of the origins and evolution of punishment and corrections in Chapter 2 revealed that the use of incarceration for punishment is a relatively recent development. A review of Canadian correctional history found that the difficulties surrounding prisons emerged very soon after Canada opened its first penitentiary in 1835. Many of these difficulties have yet to be overcome; corrections officials and inmates are still struggling to build institutional environments that promote positive change, protect the community, and reduce reoffending.

The dynamics that develop in correctional institutions are complex and present challenges for administrators, correctional officers, treatment staff, and the inmates themselves. Chapter 7 examines the attributes of correctional institutions and the complexities of operating and managing these facilities; Chapter 8 explores the experiences of correctional officers (COs) and the important role they play in the daily life of institutions.

But it is the lives of the inmates themselves that have received the most attention from scholars and in the popular media. Chapter 9 examines life in custody for inmates, the relationships among them, and the various strategies they use to survive in custody. Chapter 10 explores the strategies and interventions used by systems of corrections to classify, manage, and address the risk and needs of inmates. The discussion reveals that while a number of programs hold promise, there are many obstacles to effective treatment in correctional institutions.

CHAPTER 7

CORRECTIONAL INSTITUTIONS

CHAPTER OBJECTIVES

After reading this chapter, you should be able to:
- *Identify the types of correctional institutions.*
- *Discuss the structure, operations, and management of institutions.*
- *Identify and discuss the attributes of the modern prison.*
- *Identify and discuss the challenges of operating and managing correctional institutions.*
- *Describe the various prevention and interdiction strategies used by correctional systems to prevent the spread of HIV/AIDS and infectious diseases, as well as the issues that surround harm reduction efforts.*
- *Discuss the effectiveness of incarceration.*

For 150 years, correctional institutions (as they are now called) have been a core component of the response to criminal offenders. These facilities have endured despite ongoing challenges, many of which emerged within the walls of Canada's first penitentiary in the 1830s—overcrowding, the lack of classification, and inmate safety, among others. Only a small percentage (around 5 percent) of convicted offenders are sentenced to a period of custody. Generally speaking, correctional facilities house those offenders who present the highest risks and have the greatest needs.

TYPES OF CORRECTIONAL INSTITUTIONS

The federal and provincial/territorial governments operate a wide variety of facilities. These include correctional institutions and correctional centres that house sentenced offenders; jails and detention centres for short-term offenders who are awaiting sentencing; remand centres for accused persons awaiting trial; and correctional camps, treatment centres, and community residences that house lower risk inmates in a minimum security setting as well as those on conditional release.

Security Levels

Federal correctional facilities have three security levels:

- **Minimum security institutions** generally have no perimeter fencing and allow unrestricted inmate movement, except at night.
- **Medium security institutions** are surrounded by high-security perimeter fencing and place some restrictions on inmate movements.
- **Maximum security institutions** have highly controlled environments and high-security perimeter fencing, and strictly control and monitor inmates' movements through video surveillance.

Canada has a one **Special Handling Unit (SHU)** located in Ste-Anne-des-Plaines, Québec for inmates who present such a high level of risk both to staff and to other inmates that they cannot be housed even in maximum security facilities. There are also **multilevel institutions**, which contain more than one of the above security levels. Within the same institution, there may be distinct inmate populations that, for security and safety reasons, cannot be allowed to commingle. Finally, the CSC operates a number of regional health centres, which house violent offenders and offer treatment programs that focus on violence and anger management.

The provinces and territories operate facilities with various levels of security, though there are no uniform designations. These jurisdictions make more extensive use of maximum security institutions than the federal CSC, mainly because they are responsible for housing persons who are on remand awaiting trial or sentencing. These individuals present a broad range of security risks, and in the absence of time to assess individual offenders, all are detained in maximum security. Provincial correctional systems also operate treatment facilities for special populations, such as sex offenders.

SECURITY

All correctional facilities have two types of security: (1) **static**, which includes things such as perimeter fencing, video surveillance, and alarms, as well as fixed security posts staffed by correctional officers (COs), and (2) **dynamic**, which includes ongoing interactions (beyond observation) between COs and inmates. This includes working with and speaking with inmates, making suggestions, providing information, and being generally proactive.

THE ATTRIBUTES OF CORRECTIONAL INSTITUTIONS

Correctional institutions are impacted by both their internal and external environments (Figure 7.1). These features determine the daily challenges that confront correctional managers as well as the patterns of interaction among

Minimum security institutions
Federal correctional facilities that generally have no perimeter fencing and allow unrestricted inmate movement except at night.

Medium security institutions
Federal correctional facilities that have a less highly controlled institutional environment than maximum security institutions and in which the inmates have more freedom of movement.

Maximum security institutions
Federal correctional institutions with a highly controlled institutional environment.

Special Handling Unit (SHU)
A federal correctional facility that houses inmates who pose such a high risk to inmates and staff that they cannot be confined in maximum security institutions.

Multilevel institutions
Federal correctional institutions that contain one or more security levels (minimum, medium, and maximum) in the same facility or on the same grounds.

Figure 7.1

The External and Internal Environments of a Correctional Institution

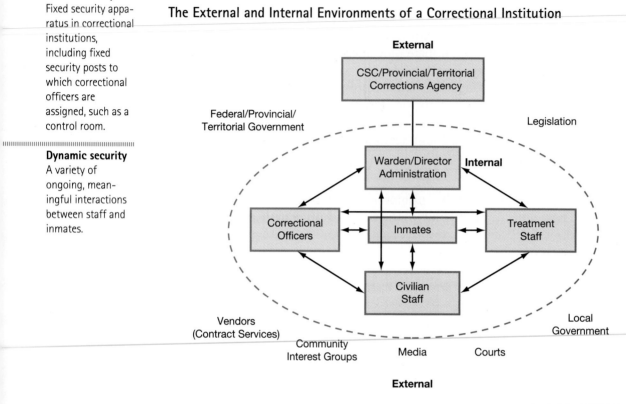

Static security
Fixed security apparatus in correctional institutions, including fixed security posts to which correctional officers are assigned, such as a control room.

Dynamic security
A variety of ongoing, meaningful interactions between staff and inmates.

the various groups who live and work inside correctional facilities. Three of the more significant features are described below:

Prisons Are Asked to Pursue Conflicting Goals

The primary goal of correctional institutions is to protect society by housing offenders who pose a serious risk to the community. But these same institutions are also expected to prepare offenders for eventual release into the community as law-abiding and contributing members of society. These two goals underscore the split personality of corrections.

Prisons Are Political and Public Institutions

The impact of social, political, and economic forces on Canadian prison systems was discussed in Chapter 2. Those forces continue to determine the goals of incarceration and the extent to which those goals are achieved. Politicians, legislatures, and bureaucrats exercise considerable control over how correctional institutions are operated, the goals they are asked to pursue, and the resources that are made available to corrections personnel. For example, it is anticipated that recent federal legislation (see Chapter 2) will have a significant impact on correctional institutions by increasing prison populations, because offenders will be serving longer periods of time under mandatory minimum sentences. These are part of the external environment.

Prisons Are Total Institutions

More than four decades ago, the sociologist Erving Goffman introduced the concept of the prison as a **total institution**, that is, "a place of residence and work where a large number of like-situated individuals, cut off from the wider society for an appreciable period of time, together lead an enclosed, formally administered round of life."[1] Goffman outlined the principal attributes of life inside total institutions (which, for him, also included mental hospitals and military installations). They included the fact that all aspects of life are conducted in the same place; also, the activities of persons with similar status (inmates, in the case of prisons) are tightly scheduled and controlled by an administrative hierarchy.[2] Compare this regimen with the one set out in Box 2.2 on page 26. For many inmates, little has changed over the past century, though in minimum security facilities, the daily regimen is less structured.

In modern correctional institutions, this control has been extended by advanced technologies that allow ever-larger numbers of inmates to be housed, monitored, and controlled by fewer staff. While high-tech institutions are less expensive to operate, the end result may be *higher* costs because of disturbances and riots by inmates as well as increased rates of recidivism when inmates are released from these facilities. The reduced contact in high-surveillance institutions may also have significant implications for treatment interventions (see Chapter 10) and for positive interactions between COs and inmates (see Chapter 8). High-tech regimens may heighten the pains of imprisonment, reduce staff–inmate contact and communication, and increase the stress levels and isolation of COs.[3]

While all correctional institutions are total institutions, some are more "total" than others. That is, they vary in terms of their security classification, affiliation (federal/provincial/territorial), size, management style, inmate characteristics, and other factors that affect the dynamics of institutional life. To reflect this variability, a **continuum of correctional institutions** can be constructed, based on the extent to which individual institutions reflect Goffman's description. At one end of such a continuum would be minimum security and community correctional facilities; at the other end would be maximum security facilities. Clearly, the dynamics of life inside institutions at either end of the continuum will be considerably different. And even institutions at the same security level have their own "personalities," which are a function of their history, the attitudes and behaviour of administrators and staff, the attributes of the inmate population, and other, less tangible factors.

Institutional Management Models

Leadership has a powerful impact on the quality of life for staff and inmates inside correctional institutions and may have a direct impact on levels of violence and misconduct among the inmates.[4] Recall from the discussion of

Total institution
Correctional institutions, mental hospitals, and other facilities characterized by a highly structured environment in which all movements of the inmates/patients are controlled 24 hours a day by staff.

Continuum of correctional institutions
The differences in institutional environments among correctional institutions located at either end of the security spectrum—minimum to maximum.

Canadian correctional history in Chapter 2 that an 1848–49 investigation into the Kingston Penitentiary centred on the warden, Henry Smith. Fast forward to 2010, when a government report about a riot at the Central Nova Scotia Correctional Facility described "veteran guards shaken by filthy prison cells, chaotic behavior of inmates and lack of leadership for staff."[5]

In federal facilities for men at the maximum and medium security levels, the management model includes an Assistant Warden, Operations, and an Assistant Warden, Interventions. Each of these wardens is responsible for a variety of personnel. The Assistant Warden, Operations, oversees the activities of several correctional managers: Scheduling and Deployment, Operations, and Desk/Sector; the latter two managers supervise the CO1s and CO2s. The Assistant Warden, Interventions, oversees assessments, intervention programs, and chaplains and psychologists. The same person is also responsible for sentence management officers and the Aboriginal Liaison Officer.

Unit Management Model

The supervisory arrangement in many provincial/territorial correctional institutions.

Many provincial/territorial institutions are structured around the **Unit Management Model** (also often referred to as the Living Unit Model). Under this model, each unit in the institution has a manager, who reports to a deputy warden and supervises the unit's COs, classification officers, and support staff. The unit manager's responsibilities include security, case management, programming, and health and safety. One group of COs works directly with the inmates; the other group provides static security.

Provincial and territorial institutions have found it a challenge to develop effective management models. This has had a significant impact on the role of COs and on quality of interactions with inmates (see Chapter 8).

PERSPECTIVE

Deputy Warden, Federal Correctional Institution

The long-term inmates are more manageable than short-term inmates. They understand they are going to have to get along with other inmates and the staff. The long-term guys are the ones that end up being on the inmate committees and taking a more balanced view of things. It's the short-term guys that are the most difficult to manage. They are part of the 20 percent of the inmates in the prison who are difficult to manage, and it's this group that causes all of the problems. It's the quiet guys that are there, doing their own time, working their way through the programs, getting out on parole and not coming back—those are the guys you don't even remember and that's the vast majority of guys. (personal communication with C.T. Griffiths).

THE CHALLENGES OF OPERATING AND MANAGING CORRECTIONAL INSTITUTIONS

Meeting the Requirements of Legislation and Policy

The legal framework within which correctional systems operate has become increasingly complex. Senior correctional personnel must stay abreast of changes in law and policy and ensure that the operations of the institution and the activities of its staff comply with those laws and policies. The violent confrontation that occurred between women offenders and correctional staff at the Kingston Prison for Women (now closed) in 1994 occurred because the staff and administration did not follow the rule of law and administrative policies. This incident is discussed in Chapter 13. Institutions are also subject to periodic external audits to ensure that they are following proper administrative and fiscal procedures.

Increasing Accountability and the Rule of Law and Justice

There has been an increase in the accountability of systems of corrections and conditional release. This has coincided with the increasing involvement of the courts, which are now imposing on correctional agencies and personnel a duty to act fairly in managing offenders and to ensure that decision making is fair and equitable.

More and more crime victims are filing civil suits against correctional authorities. Also, millions of dollars have been paid out by correctional systems to settle lawsuits filed by inmates over a range of issues, from violations of regulations to unsafe living conditions. There have also been civil suits filed by the parents of inmates who have been severely injured or killed by another inmate. In 2011, the parents of Jeremy Phillips filed an $11 million suit (later settled out of court for an undisclosed sum) against the CSC alleging negligence after their son was murdered by a serial killer with whom he had been double-bunked.[6] The coroner's jury in the Phillips case recommended that serial killers be housed in separate, single cells. Note that the recommendations of coroner's juries are not binding on correctional services.

Managing Staff

Wardens and other senior correctional administrators often spend as much time on staff issues as they do on the inmates. The smooth functioning of an institution requires good morale and a shared sense of purpose among staff, including COs and program staff. A failure of leadership can result in a poor working environment that, if nothing is done, can lead to incidents and disruptions.

Conditions in Correctional Institutions

> *The first was the deplorable physical condition of the penitentiary. The cleanliness or lack of it is horrendous. There is a build up of dirt and grime throughout the Penitentiary ... It appeared that the interior of the Penitentiary had not*

been painted for years as there were areas where the paint was literally peeling off the walls and ceilings … Washrooms were filthy and staff often had to resort to cleaning them on their own. While some cells had been renovated, others had been plastered at some point and had gaping holes in the walls.[7]

A description of a Canadian prison in the 1800s? No—that quote comes from a provincial report dated 2008 on a provincial penitentiary in Nova Scotia that was built in 1903. Remember the Kingston Penitentiary, Canada's first prison? It will finally close in 2014. The physical condition of a correctional facility can have a significant impact on relations among inmates and between inmates and staff.[8] In a potentially precedent-setting case, a Québec judge in 2012 reduced an offender's sentence from 53 to 44 months after calling a provincial correctional facility "unhygienic" and commenting, "There are rats and vermin (in the jail)." The judge also cited gang activity and the high rate of drug use in the prison as imposing unnecessarily severe punishment on offenders there.[9]

The Growth in Remand Populations

An important trend in Canadian corrections has been the sharp increase in the number of persons on remand and in the length of time they spend on remand. This population often outnumbers those in sentenced custody.[10] Nearly one-quarter of those on remand are in prison for offences against the administration of justice—for example, breach of probation or bail conditions, or failure to appear in court.[11] Because offenders on remand are housed in provincial/territorial institutions, the increase in their numbers is straining resources and leading to overcrowding. (Facilities in B.C. and Manitoba are presently as high as 200 percent overcapacity.)

All prisoners on remand are held in maximum security facilities, regardless of the alleged offence and their criminal record, and have minimal access to programs and services. Remand populations include persons charged with violent offences but also persons with mental health and addiction problems. This presents challenges to correctional staff, whose role is generally limited to custody-type activities. It has been argued that the conditions faced by persons in remand violate international human rights standards, which require that those on remand who have not been convicted of a crime be held in conditions better than those for sentenced offenders.[12] According to one ex-offender who spent time in the Calgary Remand Centre, conditions in these facilities can be horrible:

I have been to CRC twice. The staff treat you like animals. Remand is a place where you go before you are convicted. Needless to say, if you are in remand, you are still innocent until proven guilty. Not in CRC. In CRC you are guilty until proven innocent. You are belittled, and battered by staff. You are stuck in conditions that the SPCA wouldn't allow animals to be placed in.

In 2010, in an attempt to reduce remand populations, the federal government enacted Bill C-25, which reduced "credit for time served" from two days' credit for every day served to one day's credit. There had been concern that defence lawyers were stretching out the justice process in order to secure time served credit for their clients at sentencing.

The Changing Offender Profile

More and more federal offenders are being classified as maximum security at admission, and a higher proportion of them are serving a sentence for a violent offence. Although most of the offenders committed to provincial/territorial institutions have been convicted of nonviolent offences, these populations pose challenges as well. For example, inmates in this group have high rates of alcohol and drug abuse and unstable work histories. Inmates in both jurisdictions have high rates of communicable diseases, including HIV/AIDS, tuberculosis, and hepatitis B and C. An inquiry in Saskatchewan found that provincial correctional facilities were sorely lacking in programs to address inmates' substance abuse, weak job skills, and family/marital problems.[13]

Inmates in custody are likely to be single and poorly educated and to have a variety of treatment needs. Over 90 percent have been assessed as requiring treatment for substance abuse. Almost 90 percent of inmates in federal custody have treatment needs in the personal/emotional domain.[14] There are also groups of offenders who require special attention. These include the following:

Elderly Inmates

Elderly inmates are a growing segment of the incarcerated population: just under 20 percent of federal inmates (a 50 percent increase in the past decade) and 30 percent of federal offenders under supervision in the community are more than 50 years old.[15] These offenders are more likely to have been convicted of more serious violent offences or sexual offences, although many of their cases involve "cold cases" or "historical" crimes, which makes them a lower risk to the community.

Chronic illnesses, disabilities, hearing and vision loss, incontinence, mental disorientation, and Alzheimer's disease require special attention and resources. Older inmates—especially those serving their first prison term—may have difficulty adjusting to the prison regimen and may also be susceptible to psychological and physical victimization by younger inmates.[16]

Most correctional facilities were not designed to address the needs of elderly offenders. It has been suggested that separate correctional facilities be constructed for elderly inmates, although given the trend toward "big box" institutions, this is not likely to happen.

The Mentally Ill

The number of offenders entering correctional institutions with mental health issues is growing: in 2009, 18 percent of provincial inmates in Ontario had a psychiatric disorder, and it is estimated that 35 percent of federal inmates have a mental impairment that requires treatment.[17] There are much higher rates of mental health disorders such as schizophrenia, major depression, and bipolar disorder among carceral and noncarceral populations than among the general population. In the absence of community services and facilities, correctional institutions have become the "asylums of the 21st century."[18]

The CSC has made slow progress on addressing the mental health needs of offenders. A 2010 report found that although the CSC had launched a Mental Health Strategy six years earlier, it still had no comprehensive plan.[19] The death of Ashley Smith in a federal women's correctional centre has helped spotlight deficiencies in the system's response to mentally ill persons who become involved in the justice and corrections systems (see Chapter 13).

Provincial and territorial governments have only recently begun to develop strategies for managing mentally ill offenders. Generally, there has been an absence of screening and assessment for identifying mental health issues.[20]

In Nova Scotia, the development of a provincial mental health and addictions strategy was precipitated by the death of Howard Hyde in the Central Nova Scotia Correctional Facility, where he had been remanded while awaiting a court appearance. Hyde had lived for many years with severe, chronic schizophrenia and was being held following arrest on a charge of domestic assault. Physicians who had examined him had assumed that he would be sent for a psychiatric assessment (he wasn't). A judicial inquiry into his death documented his involvement with medical and corrections personnel and made a number of recommendations. For example, it called for a provincial mental health strategy to ensure continuity of care between the mental health and criminal justice systems.[21]

Correctional managers find it a challenge to provide treatment programs for inmates with mental health issues. Inmates with a mental illness may have difficulty following institutional rules, may be highly susceptible to victimization by other inmates, and may lack access to treatment programs, especially in provincial/territorial correctional facilities.[22]

The challenges are especially acute in provincial/territorial institutions, given the short periods of confinement and the lack of program resources. The Québec Ombudsman investigated the conditions facing mentally ill offenders in detention and found that they had lengthier records of probation and detention than other inmates. Newly committed inmates were being evaluated for suicide risk, but otherwise, there was no screening for mental health problems. In addition, personnel in the detention facilities received little support in managing these offenders, who had difficulty accessing psychological and psychiatric services.[23] In Ontario, it was found that offenders with a mental illness were more likely to face discipline than to receive treatment and that this had a significant impact on their opportunities for conditional release and their ultimate success in the community.[24]

An example of how some provinces are attempting to address the special needs of mentally ill offenders is the St. Lawrence Valley Correctional and Treatment Centre in Ontario. In this joint initiative, the Ministries of Corrections and Community Services provide correctional staff, and Royal Ottawa Hospital provides doctors, nurses, and treatment programs. The hundred-bed facility offers treatment in a secure setting.

Offenders with Fetal Alcohol Spectrum Disorder

Fetal Alcohol Spectrum Disorder (FASD) is a consequence of a woman drinking alcohol while pregnant and often results in irreversible brain damage to the fetus. The defining symptoms of persons suffering from FASD include impulsive violence and an inability to control aggressive, harmful behaviour.[25] Persons with FASD tend not to learn from their mistakes and do not connect "cause and effect." They also tend to be egocentric, to minimize the impact of their actions on others, and to blame their victims.[26]

Research studies have established a link between FASD and youth delinquency and adult crime.[27] Persons with FASD are at heightened risk of alcohol and substance abuse, repeated inappropriate sexual behaviour, and involvement in the criminal justice system.[28]

It is likely that a high number of offenders have FASD, yet systems of corrections have only recently begun to develop screening protocols.[29] To diagnose FASD requires multidisciplinary teams of medical professionals, and these are not present in Canadian correctional institutions. A study in Manitoba at Stony Mountain Institution found that inmates there were 10 times more likely than the general population to have FASD. Nearly all of the offenders diagnosed with FASD had poor problem recognition abilities and were unaware of the consequences of their actions; all were described as having poor stress management and conflict resolution skills.[30] Another study assessed federal inmates at intake ($N = 91$) over an 18-month period and diagnosed 10 percent of them with FASD.[31]

Individuals afflicted with FASD may have only a limited ability to benefit from correctional treatment programming designed to alter their attitudes and behaviour.[32] They may also be subject to victimization and manipulation by other inmates. Inmates with FASD require special programming while in custody and extensive support when they are released into the community.

Overcrowding

Overcrowding has plagued correctional institutions since the Kingston Penitentiary was constructed in 1835. Today, many Canadian prisons are beyond 100 percent capacity—for example, Saskatchewan facilities are operating at twice their capacity.[33] Some federal prisons are double-bunking

Fetal Alcohol Spectrum Disorder (FASD)
A condition of mental impairment due to the birth mother drinking alcohol while pregnant.

Video Link
FASD in a Correctional Population (PowerPoint)
events.online broadcasting.com/ fas/090707/ppts/ correctional.ppt

inmates in segregation cells.[34] Changes in judicial sentencing patterns, the increase in the number of long-term inmates, the growing reluctance of parole boards to release offenders into the community, and the absence of new facilities contribute to overcrowding. In provincial/territorial institutions, overcrowding is also related to increases in the number of offenders on remand.

Overcrowding can affect daily prison life by heightening tensions among inmates and between inmates and COs; it can also compromise security and overburden treatment programs.[35] And it can lead to double-bunking—two offenders being confined to a cell designed for one. In 2012, 17 percent of federal offenders were double-bunked. The increase in double-bunking has corresponded with a 36 percent increase in violent incidents in federal institutions involving staff and inmates.[36] However, studies on the relationship between overcrowding and inmate–staff assaults have generated mixed results, suggesting that much depends on the prison management, the "mix" of inmates, and the competence of the correctional staff, among other factors.[37]

Double-bunking violates the UN's Minimal Standards for Prisoners; it also places inmates at risk. In recent years, several inmates have been murdered by their cellmates.

A major concern is that recent federal legislation may worsen overcrowding in correctional facilities by increasing the number of mandatory minimum sentences. If that happens, it will only add to the challenges facing correctional administrators.

Inmate Gangs

Yet another challenge facing prison administrators is the growing prevalence of inmate gangs that are based on communities and import their affiliations and tactics into correctional institutions. Estimates are that one in six federal inmates is affiliated with a known gang or with organized crime.[38] There seems to have been an increase in gang activity in many provincial and federal institutions, especially in the Prairie provinces. This is partly a result of legislative and enforcement efforts that have targeted gangs in communities. There has been exponential growth in Aboriginal gangs in urban and rural areas of the Prairie provinces. Aboriginal youth are especially susceptible to gangs' recruiting efforts—a consequence of poverty as well as disenfranchisement from family, school, and community.

Among the most notorious gangs in the Prairie provinces are the Alberta Warriors, Indian Posse, Redd Alert, Native Syndicate, and Manitoba Warriors. Other gangs include the Asian Crazy Dragons in Alberta, the U.N. and Red Scorpion gangs in B.C., and the multinational Hells Angels. Within correctional institutions, gangs involve themselves in a variety of activities, including smuggling, drug dealing, and extortion. Gang members often resort to assault and intimidation in order to secure and maintain power and influence within the prison. Conflicts between gang members within institutions are a major cause of riots and disruptions.

Video Link
16 x 9: Behind
Bars: Overcrowded
Prisons in Canada
**www.youtube
.com/watch?v=
2mDOof6H6cc**

The following is a posting by a member of the Garden City Renegades in Manitoba, putting down other gangs (Garden City is a First Nations Reserve): "Garden Hill Renegades and STP Soldiers in a rise together, holding down Island Lake. Down with Manitoba Warriors. Fuck the krazies and locolz, and who the hell are the wpg krazies? They are just hairspray-drinking rubies (sic) from the rez, wannabe fukks" (www.insideprison.com). For a look inside the culture of Aboriginal gangs, visit the video links provided on this page.

Ensuring Inmate Safety

The accountability of corrections officials extends to ensuring the safety of inmates in their charge—an onerous task, especially in federal maximum security institutions. Wardens have little say in how many inmates are sent to their facility, the types of inmates they receive, and when inmates will leave their institution via transfer, conditional release, or statutory release. They are, however, responsible for the safety and security of the inmates once they have arrived.

Recent years have seen a number of high-profile incidents within prisons, some of them involving inmates murdered by fellow inmates. This has increased the pressure on the CSC to ensure that its policies and procedures protect inmates.

Protective custody (PC ' . section of the prison that holds inmates who are at risk in the gene— ppulation. Variously, it houses inmates who have snitched out or testif— gainst other inmates, inmates who have drug debts or other outstandi— ligations, and inmates convicted of sexual crimes such as rape and c' molestation. It is possible for inmates who feel themselves to be at ris' check themselves in" to PC.

Canadian courts have become more active in addressing inmates' rights, which include the right to serve time in a safe and secure environment. The federal government is being sued more and more frequently by inmates who have been victimized while serving their time.

Preventing Disorder and Disturbances

A number of factors influence the level of order or disorder in an institution, including the composition of the inmate population; the behaviour of COs; the prison's physical design; and the management style of prison administrators. The presence of inmates from rival gangs and tensions between ethnic groups can spark inmate-on-inmate attacks. As noted earlier, overcrowding can generate strained relationships within a correctional facility. Inmates who are confined in institutions that have a higher proportion of violent offenders are more likely to become involved in misconduct; inmates who have work responsibilities inside the facility may be less likely to violate regulations. This suggests that there are specific measures that correctional managers can take to reduce the levels of prison misconduct.[39]

Video Links

code red diss
**www.youtube
.com/watch?v=
0lFqwiJ9OJA**

12 Block Code Red
**www.youtube
.com/watch?v=
AbQHjmn6yJQ**

represent your set
(AW-SW-MW)
**www.youtube
.com/watch?v=
AOuDYdVDE9Q**

Manitoba Warriors
**www.youtube
.com/watch?v=
gRU_0SBUneY**

Gang Violence in
Winnipeg's Prison
**www.youtube
.com/watch?
v=3D7_O5PkICl**

Protective custody
A section of the prison that holds inmates who are at risk in the general inmate population.

Involuntary segregation can be used to control inmates who are disruptive and who pose a threat to staff or other inmates. As noted, inmates who fear for their personal safety can have themselves placed in segregation. Male inmates in segregation—voluntary or not—tend to have long criminal histories, high-risk/needs ratings, and low reintegration potential. These inmates are likely to have difficulty adjusting to life in the institution and to be deeply entrenched in the inmate subculture. Female inmates in involuntary segregation tend to be Aboriginal and to have lengthy criminal records.[40]

Considerable controversy surrounds the use of segregation (historically referred to as "solitary confinement"). The negative consequences of that regimen include confusion, disorientation, and depression.[41] Of particular concern is the use of segregation for mentally ill offenders.[42] There have been several high-profile deaths of inmates in segregation, including that of Ashley Smith, discussed in Chapter 13.

HEALTH ISSUES AND INFECTIOUS DISEASES

Correctional systems face challenges providing short- and long-term health care, dispensing medication, and developing policies to combat high-risk behaviours.

HIV/AIDS and Other Infectious Diseases

Perhaps the most critical challenge facing correctional authorities is the spread of communicable diseases, including HIV/AIDS, tuberculosis, and hepatitis B and C.[43] There are alarmingly high rates of infection among Canadian inmates. Estimates are that the rate of HIV/AIDS infection in federal prisons is 10 times higher than in the general population; for Aboriginal offenders, the rate is even higher. It is a serious concern that these rates are continuing to rise. Moreover, these figures are based on cases *known* to correctional authorities; many offenders may not have disclosed their medical condition, may not be aware that they are infected, or refuse to be tested. This places other inmates and correctional staff at risk in the institution, as well as in communities and families when the offender is released from custody.

There are also high rates of infection among provincial/territorial inmates, with those rates especially high among Aboriginal offenders incarcerated in provincial facilities in the three Prairie provinces. As many as 75 percent of the women in the Edmonton Prison for Women are known to be HIV-positive, compared to less than 1 percent of the Canadian population.[44]

High-Risk Behaviour

High rates of HIV/AIDS are a result of high-risk behaviours before and during incarceration. Though the HIV virus can be transmitted via anal intercourse between inmates, the most frequent route of infection is the sharing of

HIV-contaminated needles and syringes. HIV and other blood-borne diseases such as hepatitis B and C are also transmitted by the pens, pencils, and wire instruments that inmates use for body piercing and tattooing. In addition to this, many offenders are already infected by the time they enter systems of corrections. The incarceration of offenders who are injection drug users has contributed to an increase in HIV transmission.[45] As one female ex-offender recalled:

> *I would say about 80 percent of the women in the prison were using drugs. 35 percent would have to do sexual favors for drugs. And 25-50 percent of the women would be injecting drugs. To inject, we would use used needles from the nurse's office, which we stole. Anywhere from 10 to 15 people would share one needle over a months' time … I also got a tattoo. I know the needle for my tattoo had been used a lot; I don't know where it came from or who had used it. Back then, we were not allowed to bleach, so we never used it to clean our needles. We were aware of getting hepatitis C and HIV from sharing needles, but we didn't care. Being in there, we felt our lives sucked so it didn't matter anyway.*[46]

Woman formerly incarcerated in the Prison for Women in Kingston, Ontario. *Women in Prison, HIV and Hepatitis C,* (Canadian HIV/AIDS Legal Network, 2012). Pg. 1.

Prevention Strategies

Systems of corrections have developed a number of **prevention strategies** in their efforts to prevent and reduce high-risk behaviours among inmates and to reduce levels of infection. For example, the CSC provides inmates with condoms, lubricants, dental dams, and bleach kits for needles (though not needles). In several federal institutions, inmates have been trained as peer health counsellors to educate others on how to reduce the risk of infection. The federal government has also expanded its methadone maintenance program for heroin-addicted offenders. Provincial/territorial systems of correction have undertaken similar efforts, though there is considerable variation in the harm reduction resources provided to inmates. The challenges are considerable, given the higher turnover of inmates in the latter system and the short periods of confinement.

The Canadian Human Rights Commission has expressed concern that the absence of needle exchange programs is denying inmates harm reduction strategies that are available to the outside community.[47] In 2012, a federal inmate launched a lawsuit against the federal government for failing to provide clean needles to inmates in correctional institutions. The argument presented was that this was a violation of the right to life, liberty, and security of the person as set out in the Charter of Rights and Freedoms, besides denying the right to health care.[48] See At Issue 7.1.

Research studies have found that in those countries that provide clean needles and syringes to inmates, those programs do not lead to increased drug use. They do, however, increase referrals to drug treatment programs. But they have *not* increased the risk to COs from inmates using needles and syringes as

Prevention strategies
Efforts to prevent and reduce high-risk behaviour among inmates and to reduce the levels of infection of HIV/AIDS and other infectious diseases.

weapons.[49] However, it is not yet clear whether providing condoms and bleach kits reduces either the risk or the level of infection among inmate populations.

An in-depth study of the actions taken on HIV/AIDS found considerable variation in the initiatives undertaken by Canada's systems of corrections. Federal institutions have developed intensive support units (ISUs) that can be accessed by inmates who have substance abuse issues as well as by inmates who wish to reside in a "drug-free" environment. Preliminary evaluations indicate that these units have strong support both from the inmates who utilize them and from correctional staff, although the long-term effectiveness of these units on both drug use and recidivism is uncertain.[50] The CSC also has health education programs to educate inmates about the risks of hepatitis C virus (HCV) and HIV; these programs seem to have succeeded in reducing high-risk behaviour, such as sharing needles and injecting with a dirty needle.[51]

AT ISSUE

Issue 7.1: Harm Reduction Programs

Should governments initiate/expand harm reduction programs in prisons?

Proponents of harm reduction programs argue that needle exchanges and related measures reflect the reality that drugs are widely available to inmates; in their view, inmates should be provided with clean needles to help reduce infection rates. Also, it is cheaper to implement strategies to prevent HIV infection than to treat persons who have become infected. The costs of HIV treatment are estimated to be $29,000 per year.[52] Opponents of such programs counter that harm reduction measures encourage drug use and the violation of institutional regulations and the law, and that needles can be used as weapons against corrections staff.

To what extent should the government be involved in harm reduction initiatives, such as providing condoms and bleach kits, and how can such initiatives be reconciled with the requirement to enforce institutional regulations against drug use and sexual relationships between inmates? Should clean needles and syringes be provided?

For a time, in an effort to reduce rates of infection, tattoo parlours were established in several federal institutions. The program involved one prisoner tattoo artist in each institution trained in infectious disease prevention and supervised by a member of the correctional staff. An evaluation found that the program was cost-effective, especially in relation to the costs of treating infectious diseases, and that it had the potential to reduce disease transmission among inmates and to increase health and safety for the inmates, the corrections staff, and the community.[53] The Conservative government cancelled the program in 2006, saying it was a waste of taxpayers' money and had not been proven effective.

Interdiction Strategies

The general public would be surprised to learn how prevalent illegal drugs are in correctional institutions. The CSC uses a number of **interdiction strategies** to reduce the use of illegal drugs and other high-risk behaviours, such as tattooing. These strategies include frequent searches, a urinalysis program, drug-sniffing dogs, video surveillance, and ion scanners that can detect drug residue on visitors' clothing and on the clothes of inmates returning from absences in the community.

The effectiveness of interdiction strategies is uncertain. One concern is that the various drug detection strategies may lead to an *increase* in hard drug use in institutions, because drugs such as marijuana and hashish remain in the bloodstream for many days, whereas heroin stays in the body's system for around 48 hours. This makes the chances of being caught by a random urinalysis test higher for those inmates who use "soft" drugs. While mandatory drug testing may reduce levels of marijuana use in prisons, there is no evidence that these programs reduce the use of opioids such as heroin.[54]

Interdiction strategies
Efforts to reduce the use of illegal drugs and other high-risk behaviours in order to prevent HIV/AIDS and other infectious diseases.

THE EFFECTIVENESS OF INCARCERATION

I don't think that punishment works with a lot of these guys. Most of them have grown up in terrible social environments and were abused mentally and physically. Pushing them around and mistreating them is what they expect. It's when you treat them differently, with respect, while making them responsible. That often impacts their behaviour because they are not expecting it. If you model prosocial behaviour with a lot of these guys, you can change the way they think and act.

Deputy warden, federal institution, personal communication with C.T. Griffiths

A number of questions surround the use of incarceration as a response to criminal offenders. Several of these are discussed in Research File 7.1.

RESEARCH FILE 7.1

The Effectiveness of Incarceration

Does incarceration reduce reoffending? It depends. The research evidence suggests that prisons should not be used with the expectation of reducing reoffending and that the excessive use of incarceration as a sanction can have substantial cost implications as well as increase criminal behaviour among some offenders.[a] Individuals sent to prison may be further marginalized and socially and economically stigmatized.[b]

(continued)

The threat of custody is unlikely to deter "state-raised" offenders. However, some research suggests that incarceration can be effective in interrupting the crime trajectory of individual offenders and result in reduced offending upon release. This seems to depend on the criminal history and age of the offender: offenders with lengthy criminal records may continue offending upon release; older inmates with a criminal history are less likely to reoffend.[c]

Can incarceration increase offending? Potentially. Sentencing to custody persons with little or no prior involvement in crime and the justice system may result in increased criminality when they return to the community, particularly if they are confined in higher security institutions.[d] There is some evidence that, all things being equal, inmates housed in higher levels of security and in harsh conditions are more likely to reoffend upon release.[e]

Is incarceration more effective in reducing reoffending than community supervision? Maybe not. There is evidence that offenders who spend their time under supervision in the community have lower rates of reoffending than offenders released from correctional institutions, even considering the types of offences committed.[f]

How does incarceration compare to community supervision in terms of cost? It's more expensive. Imprisonment is much more costly than supervision in the community and may not make the community safer or increase the potential of offenders to return to the community as law-abiding citizens.

Can prisons, generally, be considered change agents? Generally speaking, no. But it is difficult to measure the impact, positive or negative, that confinement may have on the individual offender, and particularly on offenders who do not have a lengthy history of incarceration in youth and adult facilities. Some offenders, especially those who are "state-raised," may view correctional institutions as "home" and as providing safe sanctuary from a hectic outside world. For many of these offenders, surviving in the outside, free community often poses far greater challenges than doing time in prison (state-raised offenders are discussed in Chapter 9).[g]

Do all offenders view prison negatively? No. "State-raised" offenders and offenders with lengthy criminal histories may not be deterred by a sentence of confinement and may find it preferable to nonincarcerative options such as probation or intermediate sanctions.[h] Ironically, rather than serving as a deterrent to future criminal behaviour, the correctional institution may mark a significant improvement over the quality of life in the offender's community and home environment. Offenders who are unemployed, who have no family and no permanent living address, who are drug addicted, and/or who are living with a medical conditions such as HIV/AIDS or hepatitis C may view confinement as a way to get three meals a day and a bed (often referred to as "three hots and a cot"), a paid job, and plenty of rest.

In the words of one inmate incarcerated in a provincial correctional facility: "A lot of the guys who come in here are drug sick. They had served their sentence, or been granted parole, went back out on the street, and got right back into the drug life. They come back, get well, put on a few pounds, and they are ready to go out and start it all over again" (personal communication with C.T. Griffiths). Offenders from remote communities may view a trip out to a correctional institution as a welcome break from boredom and isolation.[i] Recall from the discussion in Chapters 5 and 6 that alternatives to incarceration, including CSOs, EM, and probation, may impose "pains" on offenders and their families.

[a] F.T. Cullen, C.L. Jonson, and D.S. Nagin, "Prisons Do Not Reduce Recidivism: The High Cost of Ignoring Science," *Prison Journal* 91, no. 3 (2011): 48–65.

[b] S.N. Durlauf and D.S. Nagin, "The Deterrent Effect of Punishment," in *Controlling Crime: Strategies and Tradeoffs*, ed. P.J. Cook, J. Ludwig, and J. McCrary, 43–94 (Chicago: University of Chicago Press, 2011).

[c] A.S. Bhati and A.R. Piquero, "Estimating the Impact of Incarceration on Subsequent Offending Trajectories: Deterrent, Criminogenic, or Null Effect?," *Journal of Criminal Law and Criminology* 98, no. 1 (2008): 207–54.

[d] S.D. Bushway and R. Paternoster, "The Impact of Prison on Crime," in *Do Prisons Make Us Safer? The Benefits and Costs of the Prison Boom*, ed. S. Raphael and M.A. Stoll, 119–50 (New York: Sage, 2009).

[e] M.K. Chen and J.M. Shapiro, "Do Harsher Prison Conditions Reduce Recidivism? A Discontinuity-Based Approach," *American Law and Economics Review* 9, no. 1 (2007): 1–29.

[f] J. Cid, "Is Imprisonment Criminogenic? A Comparative Study of Recidivism Rates Between Prison and Suspended Sentence Sanctions," *European Journal of Criminology* 6, no. 6 (2009): 459–80.

[g] Cullen et al., "Prisons Do Not Reduce Recidivism."

[h] D.C. May, and P.B. Wood, "What Influences Offenders' Willingness to Serve Alternative Sanctions?," *Prison Journal* 85, no. 2 (2005): 145–67.

[i] C.T. Griffiths, E. Zellerer, D.S. Wood, and G. Saville, *Crime, Law, and Justice Among Inuit in the Baffin Region, N.W.T., Canada* (Burnaby: Criminology Research Centre, Simon Fraser University, 1995).

SUMMARY

Correctional institutions have endured since the first prison was built in Kingston in the early 1800s. The task of these facilities is to house offenders to protect the community while preparing them for life outside the walls. Among the challenges in operating and managing correctional institutions are these: meeting the requirements of legislation and policy, ensuring adherence to the rule of law, and dealing with changing and diverse inmate populations. Conditions inside correctional institutions, including overcrowding and the presence of inmate gangs, often make it difficult to ensure inmate safety. Correctional authorities use a variety of prevention and interdiction strategies in an attempt to reduce the spread of communicable diseases in the inmate population. For many offenders, including state-raised offenders, incarceration may not reduce reoffending.

KEY POINTS REVIEW

1. Only a very small percentage of convicted offenders are incarcerated in correctional institutions.
2. A wide variety of correctional facilities are operated by the federal government and provincial/territorial governments.
3. The dynamics inside correctional institutions are impacted by the internal and external environments.
4. Operating correctional institutions has a number of inherent challenges, including these, among others: meeting the requirements of legislation and policy, managing staff, addressing overcrowding, combating inmate gangs, ensuring inmate safety, and meeting the needs of special inmate groups.
5. Correctional authorities have developed a number of prevention and interdiction strategies in an attempt to reduce the transmission of HIV/AIDS and other infectious diseases.
6. Incarceration should not be used with the expectation that reoffending will be reduced.

KEY TERM QUESTIONS

1. Describe the attributes of the *minimum, medium*, and *maximum security facilities* and the *multilevel institutions* and *Special Handling Unit,* operated by the federal Correctional Service of Canada.
2. Compare and contrast *static security* and *dynamic security*.
3. Why are prisons viewed as *total institutions*?
4. What is the *continuum of correctional institutions* and how does this concept assist our understanding of life inside prisons?
5. Describe the *unit management model* in correctional institutions.
6. What are some of the challenges that inmates with *FASD* experience while incarcerated?
7. What is *protective custody* and how is it used in correctional institutions?
8. Discuss the *prevention strategies* and *interdiction strategies* that correctional systems have implemented in their efforts to reduce the rates of HIV/AIDS and other infectious diseases inside correctional institutions.

NOTES

1. E. Goffman, *Asylums: Essays on the Social Situation of Mental Patients and Other Inmates* (Garden City: Doubleday, 1961).

2. Ibid., 6.

3. P. Hancock and Y. Jewkes, "Architectures of Incarceration: The Spatial Pains of Imprisonment," *Punishment and Society* 13, no. 5 (2011): 611–29.

4. W. W. Franklin, C. A. Franklin, and T. C. Pratt, "Examining the Empirical Relationship Between Prison Crowding and Inmate Misconduct: A Meta-Analysis of Conflicting Research Results," *Journal of Criminal Justice* 34, no. 4 (2006): 401–12.

5. CBC News, "N.S. Prison Report Describes Filthy Conditions," December 7, 2010.

6. G. Hamilton, "Natural Born Killer," National Post, November 30, 2011, A3.

7. S. Poirier (Chair), *Decades of Darkness: Moving Towards the Light. A Review of the Prison System in Newfoundland and Labrador* (St. John's: Ministry of Justice, 2008), 17, http://www.justice.gov.nl.ca/AC_Report.pdf.

8. D. M. Bierie, "Is Tougher Better? The Impact of Physical Prison Conditions on Inmate Violence," *International Journal of Offender Therapy and Comparative Criminology* 56, no. 3 (2012): 338–55; Franklin, Franklin, and Pratt, "Examining the Empirical Relationship."

9. QMI Agency, "'Unhygienic' Prison Conditions Leads to Less Time for Prisoner," *Canoe Network*, October 12, 2012, http://cnews.canoe.ca/CNEWS/Canada/2012.120.13/pf-20280551.html.

10. L. Porter and D. Calverley, "Trends in the Use of Remand in Canada," *Juristat* (Ottawa: Ministry of Industry, 2011), http://www.statcan.gc.ca/pub/85-002-x/2011001/article/11440-eng.pdf.

11. D. Calverley, "Adult Correctional Services in Canada, 2008–2009," *Juristat* 30, no. 3 (Ottawa: Statistics Canada, 2010), http://www.statcan.gc.ca/pub/85-002-x/2010003/article/11353-eng.htm.

12. Standing Committee on Prison Conditions in Ontario, *Remand in Ontario: Second Report to the Board* (Toronto: John Howard Society, 2007), 9, http://www.johnhoward.on.ca/pdfs/remand_in_ontario_2.pdf.

13. M. Dauvergne, *Adult Correctional Statistics in Canada, 2010–2011*, (Ottawa: Minister of Industry, 2012), 12, http://www.statcan.gc.ca/pub/85-002-x/2012001/article/11715-eng.pdf.

14. Calverley, "Adult Correctional Services in Canada, 2008–2009."

15. Office of the Correctional Investigator, *Annual Report, 2010–2011* (Ottawa: 2011), http://www.oci-bec.gc.ca/rpt/annrpt/annrpt20102011-eng.aspx.

16. Ibid., 22.

17. K. Makin, "Senator Fights for Mentally Ill in Prison," *Globe and Mail*, November 19, 2010, A9; idem, "To Heal and Protect: Mental Illness and the Justice System," *Globe and Mail*, January 21, 2011.

18. Mental Health Commission of Canada, *Changing Directions, Changing Lives: The Mental Health Strategy for Canada* (Calgary: 2012), 60, http://strategy-mentalhealthcommission.ca/pdf/strategy-images-en.pdf.

19. John Service Consulting, *Under Warrant: A Review of the Implementation of the Correctional Service of Canada's 'Mental Health Strategy* (Ottawa: Office of the Correctional Investigator of Canada, 2010), 3, http://www.oci-bec.gc.ca/rpt/oth-aut/oth-aut20100923-eng.aspx.

20. Schizophrenia Society of Ontario, *Provincial Correctional Response to Individuals with Mental Illnesses in Ontario: A Review of Literature* (Toronto: 2012), http://cefso.ca/wwdnews/uploads/Provincial_Corrections_Literature_Review_Final_March_2012.pdf.

21. The Honourable A. S. Derrick, *In the Matter of a Fatality Inquiry Regarding the Death of Howard Hyde, Halifax, Nova Scotia* (Halifax: Department of Justice, 2010), http://www.courts.ns.ca/hyde_inquiry/hyde_inquiry_report.pdf; Province of Nova Scotia, *Building*

Bridges: Improving Care in Custody for People Living with Mental Illness (Halifax: 2010), http://www.gov.ns.ca/just/global_docs/Building_Bridges_Hyde_Report.pdf.

22. K. Adams and J. Ferrandino, "Managing Mentally Ill Inmates in Prisons," *Criminal Justice and Behavior* 35, no. 8 (2008): 913–27; C. L. Blitz, N. Wolff, and J. Shi, "Physical Victimization in Prison: The Role of Mental Illness," *International Journal of Law and Psychiatry* 31, no. 5 (2008): 385–403.

23. Le Protectuer du Citoyen, *Report by the Québec Ombudsman: Toward Services That Are Better Adjusted to Detainees with Mental Disorders* (Québec City: 2011), http://www.protecteurducitoyen .qc.ca/fileadmin/medi/as/pdf/rapports_speciaux/10-05-11_Rapport_sante_mentale _FINAL_EN.pdf.

24. Schizophrenia Society of Ontario, *Provincial Correctional Response.*

25. L. Burd, "Fetal Alcohol Syndrome," *Addiction Biology* 9, no. 2 (2006): 115–18; L. M. Caley, C. Kramer, and L. K. Robinson, "Fetal Alcohol Syndrome Disorder," *Journal of School Nursing* 21, no. 3 (2005): 139–46.

26. D. K. Fast and J. Conry, "The Challenge of Fetal Alcohol Syndrome in the Criminal Legal System," *Addiction Biology* 9, no. 2 (2006): 161–6 at 162.

27. F. J. Boland, R. Burrill, M. Duwyn, and J, Karp, *Fetal Alcohol Syndrome: Implications for Correctional Service* (Ottawa: Correctional Service of Canada, 1998); Fast and Conry, "The Challenge of Fetal Alcohol Syndrome." http://www.csc-scc.gc.ca/text/rsrch/reports/r71/ r71_e.pdf.

28. A. P. Streissguth, F. L. Brookstein, H. M. Barr, P. D. Sampson, K. O'Malley, and J. K. Young, "Risk Factors for Adverse Outcomes in Fetal Alcohol Syndrome and Fetal Alcohol Effects," *Developmental Behavioral Pediatrics* 25, no. 4 (2004): 228–38.

29. L. Burd, D. K. Fast, J. Conry, and A. Williams, "Fetal Alcohol Spectrum Disorder as a Marker for Increased Risk of Involvement with Correction Systems," *Journal of Psychiatry and Law* 38, no. 4 (2010): 559–83.

30. P. MacPherson and A. E. Chudley, *FASD in a Correctional Population: Preliminary Results from an Incidence Study* (Montague: Addictions Research Centre, 2007).

31. P. H. MacPherson, A. E. Chudley, and B. A. Grant, *Fetal Alcohol Spectrum Disorder (FASD) in a Correctional Population: Prevalance, Screening, and Characteristics* (Ottawa: Correctional Service of Canada, 2011), http://www.csc-scc.gc.ca/text/rsrch/smmrs/rg/rg-r247/rg -r247-eng.shtml.

32. F. J. Boland, R. Burrill, M. Duwyn, and J, Karp, *Fetal Alcohol Syndrome: Implications for Correctional Service* (Ottawa: Correctional Service of Canada, 2011).

33. K. B. Carlson, "Prison Ground Break," *National Post*, September 24, 2011, A4.

34. PASAN, "Prison Double-Bunking Used in Segregation Cells," *Cell Count* 64 (2011–12), 7, http://www.pasan.org/Cell_Count/Issue_64.pdf.

35. Office of the Correctional Investigator, *Annual Report, 2009–2010 (Ottawa*: 2010), http:// www.oci-bec.gc.ca/rpt/annrpt20092010-eng.aspx.

36. A. M. Paperny, "As Prisons Close, Complaints of Overcrowding Rise," *Globe and Mail*, June 18, 2012.

37. Franklin, Franklin, and Pratt, "Examining the Empirical Relationship"; K. F. Lahm, "Inmate Assaults on Prison Staff: A Multilevel Examination of an Overlooked Form of Prison Violence," *Prison Journal* 89, no. 2 (2009): 131–50.

38. R. Sampson (Chair), *Report of the Correctional Service of Canada Review Panel: A Roadmap to Strengthening Public Safety* (Ottawa: Minister of Public Works and Government Services Canada, 2007), http://www.publicsafety.gc.ca/csc-scc/cscrprprt-eng.pdf.

39. M. Solinas-Saunders and M. J. Stacer, "Prison Resources and Physical/Verbal Assault in Prison: A Comparison of Male and Female Inmates," *Victims and Offenders* 7, no. 3 (2012):, 279–311.

40. S. Bottos, *Profile of Offenders in Administrative Segregation: A Review of the Literature* (Ottawa: Correctional Service of Canada, 2008), 4, http://www.csc-scc.gc.ca/text/rsrch/briefs/b39/b39-eng.pdf.

41. Office of the Correctional Investigator, *Annual Report, 2009–2010* (Ottawa: 2010), 6, http://www.oci-bec.gc.ca/rpt/annrpt20092010-eng.aspx.

42. Ibid.

43. R. Jurgens, M. Novak, and M. Day, "HIV and Incarceration: Prisons and Detention," *Journal of the International AIDS Society* 14, no. 1 (2011): 26–42.

44. R. Lines, 2002. *Action on HIV/AIDS in Prisons: Too Little, Too Late—A Report Card* (Montreal: Canadian HIV/AIDS Legal Network, 2002), http://www.aidslaw.ca/publications/interfaces/downloadFile.php?ref=179.

45. D. Werb, T. Kerr, W. Small, K. Li, and J. Montaner, "HIV Risks Associated with the Incarceration Among Injection Drug Users: Implications for Prison-Based Public Health Strategies," *Journal of Public Health* 30, no. 2 (2008): 126–32.

46. Canadian HIV/AIDS Legal Network, *Women in Prison, HIV, and Hepatitis C* (Toronto: 2012), 1, http://www.aidslaw.ca/publications/interfaces/downloadFile.php?ref=2008.

47. Canadian Human Rights Commission, *Protecting Their Rights: A Systematic Review of Human Rights in Correctional Services for Federally Sentenced Women* (Ottawa: 2003), 3, http://www.publications.gc.ca/collections/collection_2008.chrc-ccdp/HR-21-69-20003E.pdf.

48. A. Mehler-Paperny, "Prison Inmate Takes Ottawa to Court Over Access to Clean Needles," *Globe and Mail*, September 25, 2012.

49. Ibid., 3.

50. R. Jurgens, A. Ball, and A. Verster, "Interventions to Reduce HIV Transmission Related to Injecting Drug Use in Prison," *Lancet Infectious Diseases* 9, no. 1 (2009): 57–66; D.D. Varis, "Intensive Support Units for Federal Inmates: A Descriptive Review," *Forum on Corrections Research* 13, no. 3 (2001), http://www.csc-scc.gc.ca/text/pblct/forum/e133/e133m-eng.shtml.

51. D. Zakaria, J. M. Thompson, and F. Borgatta, *The Relationship Between Knowledge of HIV and HCV, Health Education, and Risk and Harm-Reducing Behaviours Among Canadian Federal Inmates* (Ottawa: Correctional Service of Canada, 2010), http://www.csc-scc.gc.ca/text/rsrch/reports/r195/r195-eng.shtml.

52. S. Chu and K. Peddle, *Under the Skin: A People's Case for Prison Needle and Syringe Programs* (Toronto: Canadian HIV/AIDS Legal Network, 2009), http://www.aidslaw.ca/publications/interfaces/downloadFile.php?ref=1990.

53. M. Nafekh, *Evaluation Report: Correctional Service of Canada's Safer Tattooing Practices Pilot Initiative* (Ottawa: Correctional Service of Canada, 2009), http://www.csc-scc.gc.ca/text/pa/ev-tattooing-394-2-39/index-eng.shtml.

54. Jurgens et al., "Interventions to Reduce HIV Transmission."

CHAPTER 8

WORKING INSIDE: THE EXPERIENCE OF CORRECTIONAL OFFICERS

CHAPTER OBJECTIVES

After reading this chapter, you should be able to:
- *Discuss the roles and responsibilities of correctional officers (COs).*
- *Discuss the arrangements for the recruitment and training of COs.*
- *Describe the normative code that exists among COs.*
- *Examine the relationships between COs and inmates.*
- *Describe the attitudes and orientations that COs have toward inmates and toward the organizations in which they work.*
- *Describe the accommodative relationships that develop between COs and inmates and the roles that COs can play in these relationships.*
- *Speak to the decision making of COs and the exercise of discretion.*
- *Discuss the relationships between COs and treatment staff and administration.*
- *Identify and discuss the sources of stress for COs.*

The responsibilities of correctional officers (COs) have grown more complex in recent years and also more challenging. Their duties centre on providing static and dynamic security and include carrying out motorized and foot patrols, staffing control posts, counting and escorting offenders, searching for contraband, enforcing institutional regulations, and providing emergency response. COs mediate conflicts, control inmate movement within the facility, admit and process new arrivals, and serve as information and referral sources for inmates. In many institutions, COs play an active role in case management. In some provincial institutions, they help provide core programming to inmates. In general terms, they have four main tasks: (1) security: providing surveillance inside the prison, (2) service: looking after inmate needs, (3) helping inmates adjust to life inside, and (4) helping inmates prepare to reenter the community.

In federal institutions, CO1 officers are responsible for dynamic and static security, establishing working relationships with inmates and other staff, and supporting case management. The CO1's priority is security. CO2s, by contrast, focus on case management and on facilitating and encouraging inmate participation in programs. In provincial/territorial institutions, the role of COs is more multifaceted.

ROLES AND RESPONSIBILITIES

COs play a pivotal role in correctional institutions. It is COs who have the most daily contact with the inmates. Although systems of corrections make extensive use of advanced technology, such as video surveillance and various warning devices (static security), COs are the primary mechanism by which institutional policies and regulations are implemented and by which the inmates are controlled (dynamic security). COs are also a key part of efforts to rehabilitate offenders.

The authority of COs in prisons is both legal and moral. With respect to legal authority, COs do not have the power to discipline inmates, but in enforcing the institution's policies and regulations, they are able to initiate the punishment process. Equally important is their moral authority, which is based on establishing functional relationships with the inmates.

The desirable attributes of COs, as identified by correctional managers, COs, and the inmates themselves, include these: setting consistent boundaries, communicating well, showing moral integrity, exercising power and authority fairly, understanding the challenges faced by inmates, and being optimistic in a difficult environment.[1]

RECRUITMENT AND TRAINING

Correctional Service of Canada

At the federal level, each of the CSC's five regions (Atlantic, Quebec, Ontario, Prairies, Pacific) recruits, selects, assesses, and hires its own COs according to national standards. Those who are seeking an entry-level CO position must apply to the region where they want to work (www.jobs.gc.ca). Applicants are screened for experience and education and must provide the following documentation: a driver's licence, proof of citizenship, and automated external defibrillator (AED), cardiopulmonary resuscitation (CPR), and First Aid certification. They must pass a general aptitude test, the Bona Fide Occupational Requirements (BFOR) for COs, and a set of medical and physical standards, including the Correctional Officer Physical Abilities Test (COPAT).

This is followed by an in-depth interview that focuses on the applicant's background and personal integrity. The CSC has dropped the requirement that applicants have a university degree; it now requires only a high school diploma or high school equivalency. The CSC pre-employment questionnaire is posted at www.csc-scc.gc.ca/text/carinf/crnl/pre-employ-quest-eng.shtml.

Video Link
B.C. Corrections –
COPAT
**www.youtube
.com/watch?v=
ZClqSilC-s8**

Successful applicants are required to complete the Correctional Training Program, which has four phases:

Phase 1: Four- to eight-week online learning modules that include law and policy.

Phase 2: Two to four weeks of workbook assignments

Phase 3: Eight-week training program at the Regional Staff College, focusing on the development of skill sets, including interpersonal and communication skills, security procedures and strategies, self-defence, firearms, and interviewing techniques.

Phase 4: On-the-job training, during which new officers are deployed to institutions in the region and their skills are assessed over a two-week period. After building up seniority, officers may request a transfer to another institution.

The CSC has developed a special process for selecting and training staff to work in institutions for federally sentenced women. Specific criteria are used to identify personnel who are sensitive to women's issues, their life histories, and their unique needs. Besides the training provided to all new COs, staff selected to work in women's facilities must complete a "women-centred training" course. That course has a number of modules covering areas such as these: women's criminality and its links to personal history, self-injury, and suicide; same-sex relationships; cultural sensitivity; and dealing effectively with lifers.[2]

One of the most ambitious studies of Canadian COs examined how the attitudes of officers changed between the training phase and the field. It was found that new recruits held positive views about correctional work generally and about the idea of rehabilitation and that these attitudes persisted after one year on the job. After starting the job, however, officers experienced stress associated with shift work, threats to their safety, the lack of challenges in their work, and COs' low degree of decision-making autonomy.[3]

Provincial/Territorial Training

There are no national standards for recruiting and training COs for provincial/territorial systems of corrections. Each province and territory has its own procedures, standards, and training courses, some of which are more thorough than others. A review of training in Nova Scotia, for example, found gaps in training for front line staff and no centralized capacity to monitor training requirements.[4] Many recruits to provincial corrections are trained using some combination of initial and on-the-job training. They must generally complete a multistage process that includes (among other things) a physical activities test, a background check, and a medical exam. Increasingly, potential recruits are required to pay the costs of their own training. Some jurisdictions offer pre-employment courses through community colleges.

In most jurisdictions, someone who is interested in a career as a CO can enroll in a certificate course offered by a community college or justice training centre. These courses may enhance an applicant's chances of being hired, but they do not guarantee a successful application.

GOING INSIDE: THE SOCIALIZATION OF NEW CORRECTIONAL OFFICERS

A number of challenges confront new COs, not the least of which is a lack of knowledge of what it will be like working inside a prison. A new CO probably has not visited a correctional institution in any capacity before being hired. Indeed, most new COs have been exposed to prison life solely through movies and sensational media reports.

If they are to exercise discretion properly and carry out their tasks effectively, new COs must learn the subtle nonverbal cues that will help them "read" individual inmates. They must also become familiar with the intricacies of the inmate social system, the methods they use to distribute drugs and other contraband, and other inmate activities such as gambling, strong-arming, and debt collection. Inmates will "test" new COs to determine how they will exercise their discretion and authority. Adapting to prison life, learning how it works, and developing strategies to cope with its pressures and demands is much the same process for COs as for the inmates themselves.[5]

Another challenge confronting new COs is gaining acceptance from coworkers. New officers must demonstrate their solidarity through their actions. There is often a "probationary" period during which the neophyte must prove that he or she can be trusted and can perform the job.

Video Link
North Fraser Pretrial Centre (B.C.)
www.youtube .com/watch?v= yvJfowXlgTc

PERSPECTIVE

Deputy Warden

When you step into the world of the prison for the first time [as a CO], the thing that always stays with you is the sound of the door clanging behind you. When I first went to work as a correctional officer, everything inside seemed to be in chaos. You wonder what the heck is going on. It takes a few months to get in tune with the place. After you've been there awhile you get to know who the major players are, how different correctional officers approach situations. You develop a rapport with the inmates and begin developing relationships with them. I've always said that being a correctional officer is an art … to know how to balance the authority you have with the realities of life inside. (personal communication with C. T. Griffiths)

PATTERNS OF RELATIONSHIPS AMONG COS

It has long been assumed that COs, much like police officers, have developed an occupational subculture. The foundations for the **normative code of behaviour** among COs are said to include the following: always assisting another officer who is in real or potential danger; not becoming overly friendly with the inmates; and deferring to the experience of veteran officers.[6] This is similar to the code among inmates (see Chapter 9).

Normative code of behaviour
The behavioural rules that guide interaction and contribute to solidarity among correctional officers.

Among the factors that have been identified as contributing to solidarity among COs are these: the ever-present potential for injury on the job; the hostility directed toward COs by inmates; the often conflicting demands made on COs, largely as a consequence of shifting correctional philosophies; a work environment where rewards and recognition are few and far between; and the reliance of officers on one another.[7] The resulting normative code of behaviour provides a mechanism for COs to cope with the demands of both inmates and the prison administration.

On closer examination, however, the subculture of COs seems not to be monolithic. Indeed, COs as a work group may be as fragmented as the inmates are. Line-level security personnel build friendship networks, which may be gender based or centred on shared experiences, such as completing a university degree. The extent to which COs exhibit solidarity depends on a number of factors, including the security level of the institution; the age, gender, and backgrounds of the officers; the relations between officers and the administration; and other factors that are less tangible, including the extent to which the COs in any one institution perceive that they are threatened by the inmates or by administrative policies.

In fact, for many COs it is their *colleagues*, not the inmates, who are the main source of job-related stress. COs who gossip among themselves, who share information with inmates, and who are perceived as too authoritarian are potential sources of stress for line-level personnel. Conflict may also arise when certain officers are viewed as "slackers"—for example, because they sleep during graveyard shifts and fail to make their rounds at the appointed times.

A TYPOLOGY OF COS

Attempts have been made to categorize COs based on their attitudes toward the inmates, their coworkers, their occupation, and the institutional environment. Such efforts are fraught with difficulty, since it is unlikely that any single officer will exhibit all of the attitudinal and behavioural features of one particular type. But these attempts do sensitize us to the fact that not all COs think and act the same way.

Individual COs can be placed on a continuum based on how they exercise their discretionary authority. At one end are those who are rigid and who attempt to enforce all the rules at all times; at the other are officers who do little or no rule enforcement. This latter group may include officers who are close to retirement. In the middle are officers who are consistent in their decision making and straightforward with inmates, who do not make arbitrary decisions, and who temper their authority with common sense and a respect for the law. These officers have good judgment and communication skills, are able to mediate potentially explosive behavioural situations, and are good judges of character.[8]

Box 8.1 presents a typology developed from a study of COs in several prisons in the United States. It is likely that a similar typology could be constructed for Canadian COs.

BOX 8.1

A Typology of Correctional Officers

To develop her typology, Mary Ann Farkas surveyed a sample of officers (*N* = 79) and classified their responses according to their orientation toward the following: rule enforcement (RE); negotiation or exchange in working with inmates (NE); norms of mutual obligations toward colleagues (MO); desire or interest in human service delivery (HS).

	RE	NE	MO	HS
Rule enforcer	Rule-bound, inflexible in discipline; mandate is custody and control; enforces rules to maintain order and teach discipline	Unwilling to negotiate or exchange to secure inmate compliance	Norms of mutual obligation with other officers are strong	No interest in human service; avoids contact with inmates
Hard liner	Subtype of the rule enforcer; hard, inflexible with rules; power-hungry; rules enforced to punish and show authority	At times abusive and aggressive toward inmates; extremely negative attitude toward inmates	Identifies strongly with officers who share negative views of inmates	Resents having to provide services to inmates
People worker	Older, more experienced; relies on verbal skills and common sense	Comfortable style in working with inmates; flexible in rule enforcement; secures inmate compliance through interpersonal communication and personalized relations; problem solver	More focused on conflict resolution than on maintaining authority of fellow officers	Enjoys challenge of working with inmates

(continued)

	RE	NE	MO	HS
Synthetic officer	Synthesis of rule enforcer and people worker; follows rules closely but attempts to consider the circumstances in dealing with inmates	Response to inmates is highly situational; firm but fair	Supports other officers	Attempts to treat inmates fairly while not being taken advantage of
Loner	Strictly enforces rules to avoid being criticized; often a minority or female officer	Conforms strictly to rules and regulations to provide validation to inmates and fellow officers and to avoid making mistakes; unwilling to negotiate for inmate compliance	Feels need to continually "prove" his or her worth to co-workers and management; alienated from other officers	Wary of inmates, mistrustful; prefer to work posts away from inmates (and other officers)

Source: M.A. Farkas, "A Typology of Correctional Officers," *International Journal of Offender Therapy and Comparative Criminology, 44,* 4 (2000): 431–49.

Research studies have provided some insights into the orientations and attitudes of COs. Note well that this includes Canadian and American studies and that the Canadian materials relate to federal COs. There is little information on provincial/territorial COs. Some of the insights from these studies are outlined below.

Attitudes toward inmates. COs may view inmates as manipulative, as not being interested in rehabilitation, and as having too much power, which places officers' safety at risk.[9]

Factors affecting CO attitudes toward inmates. Older COs, COs in minimum security facilities, and COs in the Pacific Region of Canada (British Columbia) tend to hold more favourable attitudes toward offenders and to be more supportive of rehabilitation efforts.[10]

Job satisfaction and commitment to the organization. COs who are empathetic, nonpunitive, and supportive of rehabilitation programs are more committed to their work and more satisfied with the work they perform; they also experience less stress on the job. COs often score lower than other institutional staff on perceptions of staff empowerment, staff recognition, and fair treatment of employees, as well as on overall job satisfaction. COs with higher levels of education report high levels of job dissatisfaction.[11] COs in generation X (born between 1965 and 1980) and Y (born between 1981 and the present) are more likely to be dissatisfied with their work than older COs.[12]

Generational differences and commitment to the organization. Officers from generations X and Y may have different expectations of their work and expect to work in an environment that is participatory rather than top-down.[13] A deputy warden in a federal prison complained that "there is no loyalty and commitment from many in the new generation of officers ... If they want Christmas off, they'll take it off, regardless of whether they are scheduled to work ... It's a very me-focused bunch" (personal communication with C.T. Griffiths). COs who have higher levels of commitment to the organization are more supportive of rehabilitation for inmates.[14]

CO–INMATE RELATIONSHIPS AND PATTERNS OF ACCOMMODATION

Even though a core principle among COs is "never trust an inmate," the exigencies of daily life inside institutions generate unique pressures for COs and inmates to develop accommodative relationships. For inmates, this helps reduce the pains of imprisonment; for COs, it ensures daily stability and order.

Relations with inmates are generally not a source of stress for COs, though the officers realize they are outnumbered by the inmates and that peace and order in the institution require the inmates' cooperation. Inmates and COs have a mutual interest in ensuring that order and routine are maintained in the institution. An unstable environment characterized by disruptions and unpredictable events increases stress levels for both inmates and COs and places everyone at risk.[15]

The specific patterns of interaction that develop between COs and inmates depend on a variety of factors, including the individual CO, the size of the inmate population, the security level of the facility, and the policies and management style of the senior administration. The advent of the high-tech prison with its increased surveillance and restricted inmate movement will reduce dynamic security and increase static security so that COs have less frequent contact with inmates.

Generally, inmates serving life sentences (25-year minimums) are the easiest group to deal with. By contrast, many younger offenders (often referred to as "new school inmates"), because they have a "get high today, the hell with tomorrow" attitude, are a source of instability in the institution for both COs and other inmates. Ironically, then, even though conditions in correctional institutions have improved, life has become more unpredictable for COs and other staff. Figure 8.1 illustrates the "push-pull" nature of interactions between COs and inmates and the factors that may come into play.

Instability and lack of routine in correctional institutions may be in part a result of the erosion of the "inmate code" (see Chapter 9). That erosion has brought about changes in how inmates relate to one another. Not so long ago, some inmates functioned as "elder statesmen," exerting control over the units and helping keep peace and stability in the institution as a whole. Today, in the words of one CO, "it's all intimidation, and brute force, and who has the most

Figure 8.1

Dynamics of the CO–Inmate Relationship

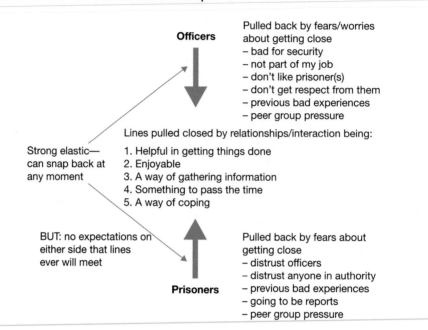

Source: A. Liebling, D. Price, and G. Shefer, *The Prison Officer, 2nd ed.*, (New York: Willan Publishing, 2011). Pg. 113.

drugs to sell."[16] This attitudinal shift among inmates was noted by a correctional staff member in a Saskatchewan provincial institution: "Before, there were tough guys [inmates] and you [the inmate] knew to stay away from them. There was a code. Now everyone gets beat on."[17]

The Agendas of COs

Custodial agenda
The activities of correctional officers that centre on control and enforcement of regulations.

Studies have revealed that COs can have one of two agendas: custodial or correctional. The **custodial agenda** of COs centres on control and the enforcement of regulations. Historically, this agenda included the excessive use of force against inmates, although these types of incidents have decreased in recent years. According to some observers, the prison environment itself, with its features of a total institution, contributes to many of the problems that arise between COs and inmates.[18]

Correctional agenda
The activities of correctional officers as change agents using their authority to help inmates cope with the problems of living in confinement.

By contrast, the **correctional agenda** involves COs functioning as change agents by referring inmates to programs and other resources, by helping them resolve problems and personal crises related to their incarceration, and by serving as intermediaries between the inmate and the institutional bureaucracy.[19] COs have considerable discretion to help inmates and ease the difficulties they encounter so often in their daily lives.

Officers who develop a rapport with inmates beyond the basic "keeper and the kept" level are generally more effective at maintaining order in the units. A positive relationship with inmates may also increase the amount of information that "snitches" or "information providers" pass along to officers, as well as encourage inmates to tell officers about problems that are developing in the unit. It seems that generally speaking, most inmates "get along" with COs.

The institution's management model can have a significant impact on CO–inmate interactions. A review of correctional institutions in Newfoundland and Labrador found that they followed a paramilitary model wherein the COs focused on rule enforcement. These officers had little interaction with the inmates.[20] See At Issue 8.1.

AT ISSUE

Issue 8.1: Correctional Officer Respect for Inmates

What should systems of corrections do to ensure that inmates are treated with respect?

In 2013, the results of an internal survey conducted by the CSC revealed the following finding: "Apparently social values around respect toward offenders have not been encouraged within CSC to the same extent as values of respect toward the organization and co-workers—leaving this aspect to each individual's discretion." Responses to the survey also indicated that corrections staff felt that they did not receive sufficient training in how to support and assist inmates.

What might be the implications of these findings and what measures could be taken to address this issue?

Source: W. Campbell, "Prison Guards Lack 'Common Understanding' on Basic Respect for Inmates: Survey," *The Canadian Press.* March 31, 2013.

Exercising Authority: COs' Discretion and Decision Making

COs have considerable discretion in carrying out their daily activities and in determining when and how they will enforce the institution's rules and regulations. Officers are well aware that full enforcement of all institutional regulations at all times would make life unbearable both for themselves and for the inmates. A former CO recalled that a general principle was this: "Read the book, but don't throw the book. Do not go prescriptively into any situation."[21]

COs also know that there are limits to the use of incident reports as a means to secure inmate compliance. Thus, they may resort to "informal punishments" such as refusing or "forgetting" to provide certain services for the inmate (e.g., "misplacing" an inmate's paperwork).[22]

THE EXERCISE AND ABUSE OF POWER

COs exert various types of power in the institution. These include *coercive power* (rule enforcement, disciplinary charges, and searches), *reward power* (awarding certain inmates privileges, providing favourable reports), *legitimate power* (the officer's formal authority), *exchange power* (the informal system of rewards, underenforcement of regulations), and *expert* or *"professional" power* (the use of expertise to resolve conflicts).[23]

Following is an exchange between a female ex-offender and a CO from Nova Institution for Women, a federal institution, on the website insideprison.com:

> Female ex-offender: *I really don't have anything good to say about this place. I believe the guards are rude and enjoy controlling the inmates, and the women are treated poorly. If they put themselves in our situation for once and gave us some empathy they would probably get more respect from inmates.*

> Correctional officer: *I really don't think you understand what it is like to be a guard, either. Think about just one person having to run a unit that is overcrowded with inmates who have no respect and treat you like crap all day. You would realize how much of a thankless job it really is … So I'm guessing the only piece of advice to someone who doesn't like the way they are being treated in jail would be to not break the law.*

The low visibility of daily life inside correctional institutions, combined with the broad discretion exercised by COs, may lead to situations where COs abuse their authority and sometimes even violate the law. Visible minority inmates, in particular, may perceive that COs are abusing their discretionary powers. Research in Ontario provincial institutions found a widespread perception among black inmates that they were being punished more often and more severely, for less cause, than white inmates. Black inmates also felt more vulnerable to physical violence by COs. Support for these views was provided by some of the COs interviewed by Gittens and Cole in their study of racism in the Ontario criminal justice system.[24]

Use of Force

Use of Force Management Model
The framework that guides the use of force by correctional officers.

COs in all jurisdictions follow a **Use of Force Management Model** (see Figure 8.2). That model provides for a variety of responses depending on the circumstances. In general terms, COs are permitted to use only the level of force required to carry out their duties. The use of force in correctional institutions can easily generate controversy, because of the low visibility of CO interactions with inmates. Unlike police officers on the street, COs do not need to worry about their decisions and the ensuing actions being recorded by multiple smart phone cameras.

More and more attention is being paid to the use of force by COs. This is for several reasons, including greater accountability and oversight and a number of recent high-profile incidents. Statistics on use-of-force incidents are often sketchy or, in the case of many provincial/territorial institutions, non-existent.[25]

Statistics suggest that the number of CO–inmate incidents has increased, but that increase may be due to more stringent reporting requirements: incidents that in the past would not have been recorded now *must* be recorded. There was a time when COs were not required to report all physical contacts with inmates. The findings from a study of use-of-force incidents in Canadian institutions is presented in Research File 8.1.

Figure 8.2

Use of Force Management Model

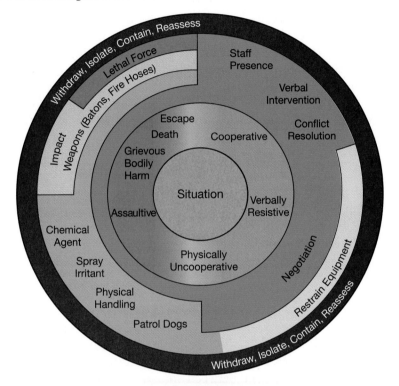

Source: Reproduced from *A Review of Use of Force in Three Types of Correctional Facilities*, Correctional Service Canada. Reproduced with the permission of the Minister of Public Works and Government Services Canada, 2012.

RESEARCH FILE 8.1

A Use-of-Force Study

A study of use-of-force incidents ($N = 185$) in Canadian federal treatment centres and men's and women's institutions found that force was most commonly used in situations where inmates had refused a direct order from a CO or were acting in a threatening or aggressive manner toward a CO. Over 90 percent of the time, the type of force used in the three types of institutions was a verbal order; in most instances, the incident involved a high-risk, high-needs offender serving a sentence of under 5 years for a violent offence. No major injuries were sustained by inmates or COs in the incidents; the minor injuries were scratches and bruises. No complaints of excessive use of force in the incidents ($N = 14/185$; <1 percent) were substantiated. The most common procedural violation by correctional staff was that documentation was not fully completed.[26]

In correctional institutions, CEDs—conducted energy devices, more commonly known as Tasers—are considered an intermediate weapon in the Use of Force Management Model, in the same category as pepper spray and physical restraints. Concerns have been raised about the use of Tasers to control inmates, especially those with a mental impairment. Correctional authorities justify the use of CEDs on the grounds that violence toward staff is increasing, that gangs are becoming more dominant among inmates, and that remand populations are expanding, especially in provincial facilities.[27] It is worth noting that COs have access to a wider variety of control options than police officers; they also have a better idea of whom they are dealing with—that is, they may have extensive knowledge of the inmates and their behaviour.[28]

Increasingly, COs are being held civilly and criminally liable for their actions. In a number of incidents, COs have been fired following riots or inmate deaths. In 2007, for example, three COs and their supervisor at the Grand Valley Institution for Women in Kitchener, Ontario, were charged with criminal negligence causing death in the suicide of 19-year-old Ashley Smith (see Chapter 13). The charges were subsequently dropped due to non-disclosure of documents by the CSC.

ETHICS, PROFESSIONALISM, AND CORRUPTION

Little attention has been paid to ethics and professionalism among COs (i.e., far less than among police). Because of the "closed" nature of correctional institutions and the frequent contact between inmates and COs, there are many opportunities for officers to be compromised. Corrupt conduct can range from minor violations of regulations to criminal acts such as theft, trafficking in contraband, smuggling items into the institution, having sexual relations with inmates, covering up incidents in the institution, and the misuse of authority (including taking gratuities from inmates). Misconduct can involve individual officers or groups.[29] Corrupt COs have sometimes joined forces with organized criminal groups such as Hells Angels. COs have also been dismissed for violating regulations; some have even been convicted of criminal offences.

Among the recent incidents: a provincial CO in British Columbia was sentenced to 3 years in prison for helping an inmate escape. Soon after that, another CO in the same facility was sentenced to 4 years in prison for trafficking drugs, after being caught on a surveillance camera passing drugs to an inmate. A federal CO was fired for having an inappropriate sexual relationship with an inmate.

RELATIONSHIPS WITH THE PRISON ADMINISTRATION

Research on COs' orientation and attitudes has revealed that a key source of stress and alienation is the relationship between COs and the prison administration. Administrators may be viewed with distrust and cynicism, as being distant from the everyday realities of the prison, and as being overly concerned about fiscal and administrative issues that have little relevance to line-level officers. COs are especially critical of administrators who fail to provide clear and consistent operational policies.

RELATIONSHIPS WITH TREATMENT STAFF

Many COs hold a dim view of rehabilitation programs, believing that they are a waste of time and money. The COs' view that few inmates have the ability, resources, and motivation to make significant changes in their attitude and behaviour may limit their potential to be effective change agents. There is also the perception that many inmates become involved in treatment programs primarily to improve their chances of release on parole, rather than for self-improvement.

In federal facilities, officers at the CO2 level are involved in case management; in provincial/territorial facilities, most COs have little input into case management and indeed often find themselves at odds with case managers. This conflict is in part a consequence of the different roles that COs and case management officers play in the institution: the primary role of many COs is security, whereas case managers are charged with developing, implementing, and monitoring the offender's plan of treatment.

SOURCES OF STRESS FOR COs

There is considerable evidence that COs experience high levels of stress and burnout.[30] This may have a significant impact on COs' lack of support for treatment programs, the amount of sick leave they take, and their degree of support for management, as well as on how they interact with the inmates.[31] A survey of provincial COs in British Columbia ($N = 205$) found that the majority had been exposed to blood (90 percent), feces, spit, and urine (75 percent), and inmate threats to their personal safety (66 percent); also, 20 percent of them had witnessed the death of an inmate.[32] More than 90 percent of the officers surveyed stated that their work had become more stressful in recent years. Major causes of this stress were overcrowding and understaffing.[33]

Threats to Personal Security

Concerns about personal security are a leading cause of stress among COs.[34] There has been an increase in inmate assaults on COs in federal institutions.[35] Many COs feel that the institution's policies and procedures are inadequate to ensure their personal security. Among the safety concerns of COs is the danger of exposure to inmates who are infected with HIV/AIDS, hepatitis, and tuberculosis. There is no mandatory testing of inmates for HIV/AIDS, and as a matter of policy, COs are not told which inmates are HIV-positive. This means that officers must assume that every inmate with whom they have contact is infected with a communicable disease. As first responders to incidents that occur in the institution, COs may be exposed to the blood and bodily fluids of infected inmates.[36]

Lack of Support and Respect

COs may feel that senior managers, the media, and the general public neither understand nor respect their profession. This view is reflected in the words of one officer: "We are asked to work in an environment that imposes a heavy personal toll on us, and we get no recognition for it. We do not feel valued by management, and we certainly are not valued by either the inmates or the general public. We're the only ones who understand the difficult environment."[37] There is some evidence however, that COs underestimate the public's regard for them. In a survey in Alberta (N = 1200), the large majority of respondents (85 percent) said they respected correctional centre staff for the work they do.[38]

A related source of frustration for COs is the absence of communication with and support from management, which too often develops policies without consulting front line workers. Uncertainty among officers as to their roles, lack of direction and guidance, and unreasonable expectations of senior management are significant stressors.[39]

The Emphasis on Inmate Rights

A key trend in corrections has been an increasing focus on accountability, the rule of law, and the rights of inmates under the Canadian Charter of Rights and Freedoms. This may lead to COs feeling that the new emphasis on inmate rights has come at the expense of their own rights. Some officers perceive that the inmates are now running the institutions. In the words of one CO: "No two ways about it, we can do nothing to them now. Absolutely nothing. At one point, at least we had the threat of being able to lock them up and charge them, or some type of control. Now you tell them you are going to charge them—they laugh at you."[40]

Multiple Tasks

The duties of federal COs may include not only patrolling, conducting searches, and intervening in inmate disturbances, but also issuing permits and passes, performing casework and reclassification, briefing volunteers, visitors, and professionals, escorting inmates within the institution, transferring and processing inmates, and answering the telephone. In short, in addition to the requirement to provide security, COs are being called on to play the multiple roles of "nurse, psychologist, parole officer, administrator, police, criminologist, fireman, and teacher."[41] Owing to resource constraints, this multitasking may be even more prevalent among COs in provincial/territorial institutions.

A source of considerable stress is the conflicting demands of casework and security. In the words of one CO:

> *A difficulty is handling the two philosophies of corrections right now, which is security and rehabilitation. Having a caseload and security. The caseload … it's hard to be a guard and hug him in the morning and them mace him in the afternoon because he's been a bad person. Don't laugh, it happens.*[42]

Inadequate Training

A common complaint among COs is that the training they receive is insufficient for the variety of tasks they are required to perform. As a consequence, a considerable amount of learning occurs "on the job." A review of training for federal COs found that training needs and requirements have not kept pace with the increased knowledge and skills required of COs.[43] Given the broad range of tasks that COs perform, it is likely that experience on the job will remain a key feature of the position.

The Impact on Personal Life

Many COs find it difficult to separate their work life from their personal life. At the same time, many of them are unwilling or unable to talk about their work experiences with people outside the profession. In the words of one CO:

> *[The job] screws up your relationships. You limit the friends that you've got. How many people are you going to talk to about [it], other than a cop or an ambulance driver, what kind of mayhem you went through that day … It's indescribable.*[44]

Shift Work

COs generally work rotating shifts. For federal officers, the most common schedule is 12-hour shifts on a 2-day, 2-night, 5-days-off rotation. Shift work often results in loss of sleep and a disruption of the circadian rhythm (or biological clock), which controls the body's sleep, wake, and arousal periods. Disruptions of the circadian rhythm result in a feeling similar to jet lag: fatigue, nausea, irritability, and loss of appetite. Shift workers may be more prone to poor performance, accidents, and health problems.[45]

Shift work can also affect a CO's private life and make the management of family and other personal relationships more difficult. It may limit the opportunities for officers to interact with their children during non-school hours and to participate in community activities. A survey of federal CO1s and CO2s ($N = 2000$) found that over 70 percent of officers at each level felt that shift work had a negative or very negative impact on their family life. The level of job satisfaction was lower (and stress higher) among those who reported highly negative impacts of shift work on family relations.[46] A study of Ontario COs ($N = 102$) found that officers who switched from an 8-hour to a 12-hour workday and compressed work week had higher levels of absenteeism than other officers.[47]

The Impact of Prison Conditions

An increase in prison populations has coincided with overcrowding and double-bunking and a rise in violent incidents.[48] These conditions may increase the stress levels of COs and result in an increased number of sick days taken as well as alcohol and substance abuse.[49]

There is some evidence that stress levels among COs are related to the specific correctional environment in which the officer is employed. Maximum security institutions, as well as the more "secure" medium security facilities, may be more tense environments with, it follows, greater potential for violence both between inmates and against COs by inmates.

The Impact of Critical Incidents

In the course of their careers, COs may be exposed to a wide variety of critical incidents, including disturbances and riots, hostage takings, inmate murder, inmate self-mutilation and suicide, threats to the officer's safety, and injury to the officer. These incidents may result in symptoms associated with **post-traumatic stress disorder (PTSD)**, an extreme form of critical incident stress, the symptoms of which include nightmares, hypervigilance, intrusive thoughts, and other forms of psychological distress.[50] In its most extreme forms, such as are found among combat veterans, sufferers experience flashbacks during which they relive the trauma as if they were there.

A study of federal COs in Ontario ($N = 122$) found that 95 percent had experienced severe impacts on their personal life, including sleep disturbances, nightmares, and exaggerated startle response (i.e., hypervigilance). Only 40 percent of the officers had sought professional help for their problems.[51] A survey of corrections employees in Saskatchewan ($N = 271$) found that nearly 80 percent of those surveyed had experienced a traumatic event in their work and that 25 percent reported PTSD symptoms. These levels are comparable to those experienced by combat veterans and emergency service personnel.[52]

The results of surveys highlight the need for correctional systems to develop policies for critical incident stress management centred on **critical incident stress debriefing (CISD)**. This technique involves on-scene debriefing of the CO by a trained intervenor after a critical incident has occurred; "defusing" by a mental health professional or trained peer, during which the symptoms of stress are identified and strategies for stress management are provided; a formal critical incident stress debriefing; and, if required, a follow-up critical incident stress debriefing. The objective of CISD is to protect and support the CO, while imparting information and strategies that will help the officer cope with any symptoms of critical incident stress that might later arise.

COs also have access to employee assistance programs, which provide financial support and legal assistance as well as help with substance abuse, mental and physical health, and family- and work-related issues. The culture of COs may be a barrier to accessing these sources of assistance. Much like police officers, COs may view any disclosure of stress as "emotional weakness." This has led officers to deny that corrections work has had any impact on their well-being.[53]

Video Link
Shocking Video Released of Canadian Prison Riot
www.youtube.com/watch?v=YLLdJJJA6QwY

Post-traumatic stress disorder (PTSD)

An extreme form of critical incident stress that includes nightmares, hypervigilance, intrusive thoughts, and other forms of psychological distress.

Critical incident stress debriefing (CISD)

A procedure for assisting COs following a critical incident.

COPING WITH STRESS

Although COs experience a considerable amount of stress working in institutions, the evidence suggests that most officers have developed effective coping mechanisms and are generally satisfied with their work. Strategies for coping with stress include reducing on-the-job involvement and not talking about work after hours.[54]

In contrast to the stereotype of COs that has developed largely as a result of American studies, Canadian researchers found that officers did not drink to excess, spent a large portion of their off-duty time with their families, and did not limit their socializing to activities with other officers. Another indication that most COs have adequate coping skills is that officers, as a group, report more or less the same alcohol consumption patterns as the general population.[55] For many officers, interpersonal relationships (i.e., having someone to talk to about problems on the job) are an important source of support in coping with the stresses of the job.[56]

Systems of corrections can reduce the stress levels among COs through better recruitment and training, by utilizing realistic performance reviews, and by ensuring that correctional administrators maintain open lines of communication with COs and provide opportunities for professional development.[57] In institutions where COs perceive that there is a positive work environment, including the ability to make recommendations to improve the operations of the facility, there may be lower levels of stress.[58] See At Issue 8.1.

FEMALE COs

In the recent past, women in correctional facilities were confined to clerical and noncustodial positions. In many institutions, especially provincial and territorial ones, female COs are still far outnumbered by male COs.[59] Women encountered strong resistance from men when they were first hired as COs. Female COs work in a largely male-dominated environment that has traditionally valued toughness and physicality over communication skills and tact. They were (and often still are) perceived by male coworkers and supervisors as lacking the mental and physical toughness to survive the rigours of institutional life, to control inmates when required, and to back up male officers in crisis situations. In addition, male COs may believe that women are more prone to being victimized and manipulated by inmates.[60] There is also the issue of the privacy of male inmates, especially in relation to frisks and strip searches. In *Conway v. Canada* (1993) 2 SCR 872, however, the Supreme Court of Canada reaffirmed the right of women to be employed as COs in male institutions.

Research studies have found that the resistance—indeed, sometimes outright hostility—of male officers tends to diminish as women demonstrate their abilities. Research on the experiences of female COs in the United States has revealed that female officers have a positive impact on the management of inmates in maximum security institutions, that they are less likely than their male counterparts to be assaulted by inmates, and that they are less confrontational and often better able to defuse explosive situations.[61]

Internal surveys conducted by the CSC have found a high incidence of sexual harassment, discrimination, and abuse of authority in many federal institutions. Female COs have been called "100-pound weaklings," have had threatening notes left on the windshields of their cars, and have been harassed and embarrassed by male coworkers in the presence of inmates.[62] Many of these surveys, however, are at least a decade old. In the absence of more up-to-date research, it is difficult to determine whether female COs continue to confront these challenges.

THE ROLE OF CORRECTIONAL OFFICER UNIONS

The role that CO unions play in correctional policy at the federal and provincial/territorial levels in Canada has remained largely unexamined. Unions in the United States have lobbied effectively for changes in laws relating to mandatory minimum sentences. These same unions may be impeding the shift away from mass incarceration as a result of their lobbying for more correctional facilities and for restrictions on the movements of high-risk offenders.[63]

In Canada, the Union of Canadian Correctional Officers (UCCO; www.ucco-sacc.csn.qc.ca) advocates on behalf of federal COs. Among the issues the UCCO has addressed are inmate attacks on COs with bodily fluids and the impact of Bill C-10. The UCCO was pleased that Bill C-10 contained provisions making it a disciplinary infraction to assault others with bodily fluids. But at the same time, the UCCO has opposed many of the bill's provisions, contending that by worsening overcrowding, they will increase the number of inmate-on-inmate attacks as well as inmate assaults on COs. They also have concerns about the bill's impact on mentally ill inmates.

SUMMARY

The discussion in this chapter has centred on the pivotal role that COs play in institutions. Most of the published literature in Canada focuses on federal COs; little is known about provincial/territorial COs. New COs must become socialized into daily life in the institution and must gain acceptance from coworkers as well as learn the intricacies of the inmate social system. COs have considerable discretion in carrying out their tasks, and the exercise and abuse of power are important considerations. COs experience a variety of stressors in their work that may negatively affect their professional and personal lives.

KEY POINTS REVIEW

1. The responsibilities of COs have become more complex and challenging in recent years.
2. While training for federal COs is standardized and involves online and in-class sessions, there are no nationwide standards for recruiting and training provincial/territorial COs.
3. COs have the most extensive contact with inmates and are in the position to act as change agents in assisting inmates.
4. Among the challenges confronting new COs is learning the subtle, nonverbal cues that will help them interact with inmates and gain the acceptance of their coworkers.
5. COs vary in how they exercise their discretionary authority, in their attitudes toward inmates, and in their level of commitment to the organization.
6. COs develop accommodative relationships with inmates that are characterized by "push–pull" interactions.
7. The authority of COs is both legal and moral, and they use several different types of power to carry out their role in the institution.
8. Research studies have found that some COs are more rule and enforcement oriented, while others rely on communication skills and common sense to solve problems.
9. COs may have strained relationships with correctional administrators, and may hold a dim view of treatment programs.
10. Among the sources of stress for COs are threats to their personal security, a perceived lack of support and respect from corrections officials and the general public, the impact of the job on their personal lives, and critical incidents.
11. Historically, women COs have experienced high levels of sexual harassment and discrimination.

KEY TERM QUESTIONS

1. What is the *normative code of behaviour* of COs, and what factors may mitigate against officer solidarity?
2. Compare and contrast the *custodial agenda* with the *correctional agenda* of COs.
3. Briefly describe the *Use of Force Management Model* for COs.
4. What is *post-traumatic stress disorder* (PTSD) and why is it a potential source of stress for COs?
5. Describe *critical incident stress debriefing* (CISD) and its objectives.

NOTES

1. A. Liebling, D. Price, and G. Shefer, *The Prison Officer* (New York, NY: Willan, 2011).

2. T. Lajeunesse, C. Jefferson, J. Nuffield, and D. Majury, *The Cross Gender Monitoring Project: Third and Final Report* (Ottawa: Correctional Service of Canada, 2000), http://www.csc-scc.gc.ca/text/prgrm/fsw/gender3/toc-eng.shtml.

3. P. Bensimon, *Correctional Officer Recruits During the Training Period: An Examination* (Ottawa: Correctional Service of Canada, 2005), http://www.csc-scc.gc.ca/text/rsrch/reports/r165/r165-eng.shtml; *Correctional Officers and Their First Year: An Empirical Investigation* (Ottawa: Correctional Service of Canada, 2005), http://www.csc-scc.gc.ca/text/rsrch/reports/r179/r179-eng.shtml.

4. Deloitte & Touche, *Report on Nova Scotia's Adult Correctional Facilities* (Halifax: Department of Justice, 2008), http://www.gov.ns.ca/just/global_docs/Deloitte%20Report%20-%20NS%20Correctional%20Facilities%20Nov08.pdf.

5. M. Welch, *Corrections: A Critical Approach*, 3rd ed. (New York, NY: Routledge, 2011).

6. M. A. Farkas, "The Normative Code Among Correctional Officers: An Exploration of Components and Functions," *Journal of Crime and Justice* 20, no. 1 (1997): 23–36; K. Kauffman, *Prison Officers and Their World* (Cambridge, MA: Harvard University Press, 1988).

7. E. L Grossi and B. L. Berg, "Stress and Job Dissatisfaction Among Correctional Officers: An Unexpected Finding," *International Journal of Offender Therapy and Comparative Criminology* 35, no. 1 (1991): 73–81.

8. M. A. Farkas, "A Typology of Correctional Officers," *International Journal of Offender Therapy and Comparative Criminology* 44, no. 4 (2000): 431–49.

9. J. T. Whitehead and C. A. Lindquist, "Determinants of Correctional Officers' Professional Orientation," *Justice Quarterly* 6, no. 1 (1989): 69–87.

10. M. E. Antonio and J. L. Young, "The Effects of Tenure on Staff Apathy and Treatment Orientation: A Comparison of Respondent Characteristics and Environmental Factors," *American Journal of Criminal Justice* 36, no. 1 (2011): 1–16; N. C. Jurik, "Individual and Organizational Determinants of Correctional Officer Attitudes Toward Inmates," *Criminology* 23, no. 3 (1985): 523–39; M. Larivière and D. Robinson, *Attitudes of Federal Correctional Officers Towards Offenders* (Ottawa: Research Division, Correctional Service of Canada, 1996).

11. E. Grossi, T. Keil, and G. Vito, "Surviving 'the Joint': Mitigating Factors of Correctional Officer Stress," *Journal of Crime and Justice*, 19, no. 2 (1996): 103–20; N. L. Hogan, E. G. Lambert, M. Jenkins, and S. Wambold, "Impact of Occupational Stressors on Correctional Staff Organizational Commitment: A Preliminary Study," *Journal of Contemporary Criminal Justice* 22, no. 1 (2006): 44–62; E. G. Lambert, N. L. Hogan, and M. L. Griffin, "Being the Good Soldier: Organizational Citizenship Behavior and Commitment Among Correctional Staff," *Criminal Justice and Behavior* 35, no. 1 (2008): 56–68.

12. K. A. Cheeseman and R. A. Downey, "Talking 'Bout My Generation: The Effect of 'Generation' on Correctional Employee Perceptions of Work Stress and Job Satisfaction," *Prison Journal* 92, no. 1 (2011): 24–44.

13. C. K. Patterson, "The Impact of Generational Diversity in the Workplace," *Diversity Factor* 15, no. 3 (2007): 17–22.

14. E. Lambert, N. L. Hogan, I. Altheimer, S. Jiang, and M. T. Stevenson, "The Relationship Between Burnout and Support for Punishment and Treatment: A Preliminary Examination," *International Journal of Offender Therapy and Comparative Criminology* 54, no. 6 (2010): 1004–22.

15. S. Tait, "A Typology of Prison Officer Approaches to Care," *European Journal of Criminology* 8, no. 6 (2011): 440–54.

16. M. Harris, *Con Game: The Truth About Canada's Prisons* (Toronto: McClelland and Stewart, 2002), 48.

17. Ombudsman Saskatchewan, *My Brother's Keeper: A Review of Electronic Control Devices in Saskatchewan Correctional Centres Housing Male Inmates* (Regina: 2008), 23, http://www.ombudsman.sk.ca/uploads/document/files/my-brothers-keeper-en.pdf.

18. Kauffman, *Prison Officers and Their World*, 264–65.

19. R. Johnson, *Hard Time: Understanding and Reforming the Prison* (Belmont: Wadsworth, 1996), 229–41.

20. S. Poirier (Chairperson), *Decades of Darkness: Moving Towards the Light: A Review of the Prison System in Newfoundland and Labrador* (St. John's: Ministry of Justice, 2008), 12, http://www.justice.gov.nl.ca/AC_Report.pdf.

21. J. M. Yates, *Line Screw: My Twelve Riotous Years Working Behind Bars in Some of Canada's Toughest Jails* (Toronto: McClelland & Stewart, 1993), 115.

22. Union of Canadian Correctional Officers, *Towards a Policy for Canada's Penitentiaries: The Evolution of Canada's Prison System and the Transformation of the Correctional Officer's Role (1950–2002)* (Montreal: 2002), 123, http://www.ucco-sacc.csn.qc.ca/Documents/UCCO-SACC/National/documents/Research/Towards%20a%20Policy%20for%20Canada_s%20Penitentiaries.pdf.

23. Liebling, Price, and Shefer, *The Prison Officer*, 134.

24. M. Gittens and D. Cole (Co-Chairs), *Report of the Commission on Systemic Racism in the Ontario Criminal Justice System: A Community Summary* (Toronto: Queen's Printer, 1995), http://openlibrary.org/books/OL582562M/Report_of_the_Commission_on_Systemic_Racism_in_the_Ontario_Criminal_Justice_System.

25. Ombudsman Saskatchewan, *My Brother's Keeper*, 24.

26. S. Varrette and K. Archambault, *A Review of Use of Force in Three Types of Correctional Facilities* (Ottawa: Correctional Service of Canada, 2011), http://www.csc-scc.gc.ca/text/rsrch/reports/r236/r236-eng.shtml.

27. Ombudsman Saskatchewan, *My Brother's Keeper*, 23.

28. Ibid.

29. T. E. Barnhart, *Deviance and Corruption* (2010), http://www.corrections.com/articles/23579-deviance-and-corruption; M. C. Braswell, B. R. McCarthy, and B. J. McCarthy, *Justice, Crime, and Ethics*, 7th ed. (Cincinnati: Anderson Publishing, 2012).

30. G. Keinan and A. Malach-Pines, "Stress and Burnout Among Prison Personnel: Sources, Outcomes, and Intervention Strategies," *Criminal Justice and Behavior* 34, no. 3 (2007): 380–98.

31. Lambert et al., "The Relationship Between Burnout and Support."

32. N. Boyd, *Abnormal Working Conditions: Correctional Officers in British Columbia, 2011* (Burnaby: B.C. Government Employees Union, 2011), http://www.bcgeu.ca/sites/default/files/FINAL%20Boyd-Report-2011.pdf.

33. Ibid.

34. W. Millson, "Predictors of Work Stress Among Correctional Officers," *Forum on Corrections Research* 14, no. 1 (2002): 45–7, http://www.csc-scc.gc.ca/text/pblct/forum/e141/141l_e.pdf.

35. M. Brosnahan, "Record-High Prison Numbers Sparking Violence," *CBC News*, August 27, 2012.

36. L. F. Alarid, "Risk Factors for Potential Occupational Exposure to HIV: A Study of Correctional Officers," *Journal of Criminal Justice* 37, no. 2 (2009): 114–22.

37. Joint Committee on Federal Correctional Officers, *Joint Committee Report on Federal Correctional Officers* (Ottawa: Public Service Alliance of Canada, Treasury Board Secretariat, and Correctional Service of Canada, 2000), 54, http://dsp-psd.pwgsc.gc.ca/Collection/BT43-102-2000E.pdf.

38. Alberta Solicitor General and Public Security, *Survey of Albertans* (Edmonton: 2011), http://www.solgps.alberta.ca/Publications1/Survey%20of%20Albertans/2011%20Survey%20of%20Albertans.pdf.

39. Hogan et al., "Impact of Occupational Stressors."

40. Harris, *Con Game*, 49.

41. Environics Research Group, *Focus Group Report to the Joint Committee of the Public Service Alliance of Canada, Treasury Board, and Correctional Service of Canada on the Jobs and Working Environment of Federal Correctional Officers and RCMP Officers* (Ottawa: Public Service Alliance of Canada, Treasury Board, and the Correctional Service of Canada, 2000), 7, http://www.publications.gc.ca/collections/Collection/BT43-102-2000E.pdf.

42. Treasury Board of Canada Secretariat, *Joint Committee Report on Federal Correctional Officers: A Comparison of the Duties, Working Conditions, and Compensation Levels of Federal Correctional Officers, Uniformed RCMP Officers and Selected Provincial Correctional Officers*, 2000.

43. Joint Committee, *Report*, 84.

44. In Environics Research Group, *Focus Group Report*, 15.

45. D. X. Swenson, D. Waseleski, and R. Hartl, "Shift Work and Correctional Officers: Effects and Strategies for Adjustment," *Journal of Correctional Health Care* 14, no. 4 (2008): 299–310.

46. B. Grant, "The Impact of Working Rotating Shifts on the Family Life of Correctional Staff," *Forum on Corrections Research* 7, no. 2 (1995): 40–42.

47. R. A. Venne, "The Impact of the Compressed Work Week on Absenteeism: The Case of Ontario Prison Guards on a Twelve Hour Shift," *Industrial Relations* 52, no. 2 (1997): 382–400.

48. Office of the Correctional Investigator, *Annual Report, 2010-2011* (Ottawa: 2011), http://www.oci-bec.gc.ca/rpt/pdf/annrpt/annrpt20102011-eng.pdf.

49. D. M. Biere, "The Impact of Prison Conditions on Staff Well Being," *International Journal of Offender Therapy and Comparative Criminology* 56, no. 1 (2010): 81–95.

50. L. Rosine, "Critical Incident Stress and Its Management in Corrections," in *Forensic Psychology—Policy and Practice in Corrections*, eds., T. A. Leis, L. L. Motiuk, and J. R. P. Ogloff (Ottawa: Correctional Service of Canada, 1995), 213–26.

51. L. Rosine, "Exposure to Critical Incidents: What Are the Effects on Canadian Correctional Officers?", *Forum on Corrections Research* 4, no. 1 (1992): 31–37.

52. B. L. Stadnyk, "PTSD in Corrections Employees in Saskatchewan," MA thesis, University of Regina, 2003, http://rpnascom.jumpstartdev.com/sites/default/files/PTSDInCorrections.pdf.

53. P. M. Fisher, *The Road Back to Wellness: Stress, Burnout, and Trauma in Corrections* (Victoria: Spectrum, 2000).

54. W. B. Schaufeli and M. C. W. Peeters,. "Job Stress and Burnout Among Correctional Officers: A Literature Review," *International Journal of Stress Management* 7, no. 1 (2000): 19–44.

55. R. W. Holden, L. W. Swenson, G. K. Jarvis, R. L. Campbell, D. R. Lagace, and B. J. Backs, "A Survey of Drinking Behaviors of Canadian Correctional Officers," *Psychological Reports* 76 (1995): 651–55; G.V. Hughes and E. Zamble, "A Profile of Canadian Correctional Workers," *International Journal of Offender Therapy and Comparative Criminology* 37, no. 2 (1993): 99–113.

56. P. Finn, *Addressing Correctional Officer Stress: Programs and Strategies* (Washington, DC: Office of Justice Programs, U.S. Department of Justice, 2000), http://www.ncjrs.gov/pdffiles1/nij/183474.pdf.

57. Schaufeli and Peeters, "Job Stress and Burnout Among Correctional Officers."

58. F. S. Taxman and J. A. Gordon, "Do Fairness and Equity Matter? An Examination of Organizational Justice Among Correctional Officers in Adult Prisons," *Criminal Justice and Behavior* 36, no. 7 (2009): 695–711.

59. Poirier, "Decades of Darkness."

60. R. Lawrence and S. Mahan, "Women Corrections Officers in Men's Prisons: Acceptance and Perceived Job Performance," *Women and Criminal Justice* 9, no. 3 (1998): 63–86.

61. Cheeseman and Downey, "Talking 'Bout My Generation"; J. R. Rowan, 1996. "Who Is Safer in Male Maximum Security Prisons?" *Corrections Today*, April 1, 1996, http://www.thefreelibrary.com/Who+is+safer+in+male+maximum+security+prisons%3f-a018339824.

62. Price-Waterhouse, *CSC All Staff Survey: Final Report* (Ottawa: Correctional Service of Canada, 1994).

63. J. Page, "Prison Officer Unions and the Perpetuation of the Penal Status Quo," *Criminology and Public Policy* 10, no. 3 (2011): 735–70.

CHAPTER 9

DOING TIME: THE EXPERIENCE OF INMATES

CHAPTER OBJECTIVES

After reading this chapter, you should be able to:

- *Provide a general profile of inmate populations.*
- *Discuss the experience of inmates entering and living inside correctional institutions.*
- *Discuss the inmate social system, the inmate code, and the extent to which these are operative in correctional institutions.*
- *Describe how inmates attempt to cope with incarceration.*
- *Describe the challenges that confront offenders serving long-term sentences.*
- *Discuss the patterns of violence and exploitation among inmates and the strategies that inmates use to reduce their risk of being victimized.*
- *Describe the challenges that confront the inmate family.*
- *Discuss the inmate grievance system and the work of provincial ombudspersons and the Office of the Correctional Investigator.*
- *Discuss the issues surrounding self-injurious behaviour and suicide among inmates in correctional institutions.*
- *Comment on the issues that arise relating to inmate rights in prison.*

Is prison a warehouse for beastly humans, or one that turns humans into beasts? I say why choose? Whether people come to Canada's high-priced school of crime as animals, or devolve while on campus, the result is the same: behaviours not even Mother Nature could imagine.

Canadian federal offender doing a life sentence for murder,
http://theincarceratedinkwell.org

A GENERAL PROFILE OF INMATE POPULATIONS

Offenders confined in correctional institutions tend to be male, young, single, poorly educated, and marginally skilled. They are disproportionately Aboriginal and Black and are likely to have lived unstable lives. Many were raised in dysfunctional families. Their problem-solving skills are minimal. Most of them are serving time in provincial/territorial institutions, and more than half of their sentences are for less than one month.[1]

Many inmates were homeless or underhoused prior to their incarceration.[2] A large percentage have a lengthy criminal history. Their treatment needs are high: many of them suffer from alcohol and/or drug addiction, and many have a mental impairment or other affliction such as FASD.

Generally speaking, female offenders share with their male counterparts a marginalized background of poverty, alcohol and/or drug dependency, limited education, and minimal employment skills. In addition, female offenders may have suffered sexual and physical abuse and may be responsible for children or stepchildren (see Chapter 13).

These offenders often have few connections to "mainstream" Canadian society. In this way, they are very similar to their predecessors in previous centuries. They have needs and present risks that place significant demands on systems of corrections, and especially on provincial/territorial institutions, which tend to have fewer resources than their federal counterparts and must attempt to respond in a highly compressed time frame.

Figure 9.1 presents a breakdown of the federal prison population in 2011. Note the high percentages of Aboriginal and Black offenders in relation to their percentages in the Canadian population (Aboriginals 4 percent; Black 2.5 percent).

Figure 9.1

Federal Incarcerated Population by Aboriginal and Race, April 10, 2011

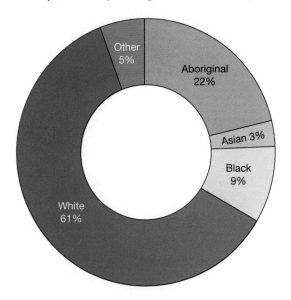

Source: Performance Monitoring Report, 2010/2011, http://pbc-clcc.gc.ca/rprts/pmr/pmr_2010_2011/index-eng.shtml, (Parole Board of Canada, 2012). Reproduced with the permission of the Minister of Public Works and Government Services Canada, 2013.

GOING INSIDE

> *I remember the day that I came in; the first time I went to the cafeteria and I could feel a hundred sets of eyes on me. I could see everybody wondering who you are, what you're in for, how long you're doing.*[3]

The specific impact that entry into prison has on the individual offender depends on a variety of factors, including his or her personality, offence history, and previous incarcerations. First-time offenders may experience severe culture shock, whereas offenders with long criminal histories and previous confinements are likely to be relatively unaffected. For these inmates, the experience of confinement is well known, as are many of the correctional officers (COs) and inmates in the facility. Indeed, returning to prison may be more of a homecoming than a banishment. For the uninitiated inmate, however, adjusting to prison life can be stressful and frightening.

Regardless of background, the individual on entering the prison is materially and psychologically stripped down. This involves a series of **status degradation ceremonies**, which include the issuing of prison clothing, the assignment of an identification number, the loss of most personal possessions, and the end of unhindered communication with the outside community.[4] These are the mechanisms by which the offender is moved from the community, with its attendant freedoms, to the world of the prison, with its rules, regulations, informal economy, and social system.

It can be argued that many of those who are entering correctional institutions have already had their "status" degraded, through a life of poverty, addiction, mental health problems, and dysfunctional environments. Degradation is closely associated with marginalization, and the above-noted profile of offenders suggests that it is persons from vulnerable groups who are most likely to end up incarcerated.

In Box 9.1, a former inmate, who served nearly 20 years inside youth and adult correctional institutions, describes entering Kingston Penitentiary for the first time at age 18.

Status degradation ceremonies
The processing of offenders into correctional institutions whereby the offender is psychologically and materially stripped of possessions that identify him or her as a member of the "free society."

BOX 9.1

A Young Inmate Enters the Prison

The judge said to me that I was a danger to the community and that I would be sentenced to three years in Kingston Penitentiary. I was transferred to the Don Jail (in Toronto) and placed on a range where people were going to the penitentiary. A lot of stories were told to me there about what happens to young kids going into the big house, because when I was a kid I was always told that, "Robert, some day you are going to the big house," and now it was becoming a reality. I was going to the big house, and I was very scared, especially after hearing all these stories, right? And the thing is, I was told that as long as you fight, you won't have a problem.

So I went to Kingston [Penitentiary], and we got through the two clanging doors you have to go to to get into it off King Street. You go through the first door, and "Clang!" Then, you are waiting between the two doors to go into the prison. When I look back in retrospect, I feel that if I had been given a chance at that point to get out, to go back and maybe be in a home or something like that, then maybe I would not have to go through the rest of the life that I would go through. I was really scared at that time, but it seems like once you go through the second clanging door, you start to lose a lot of that fear and you turn that fear into hate and anger.

Source: Personal communication with C.T. Griffiths.

All incoming inmates are provided with a copy of the institution's regulations and with an orientation; but beyond that, each inmate is left to his or her own devices (and wits) when it comes to adjusting to life inside and to developing a survival strategy. Below is part of the advice one inmate gave another who had just arrived at Millhaven, a federal facility in Ontario:

> *Drugs and alcohol are everywhere and I urge you to avoid that trip. Ninety percent of all killings revolve around the dope scene … Don't accept anything from anyone, because you don't want to put yourself in a position where you'll have to repay the favor. Nothing is free. It's in your best interest to avoid cliques. You'll be spending a lot of time on your own—it's much safer that way … Don't encourage conversation with anyone. Be brief and polite … Don't promise anyone anything … Stay quiet and mind your own business.[5]*

Unfortunately, though systems of corrections have perfected the mechanisms for transforming citizens into inmates, there are no "status restoration" ceremonies at the end of confinement that might convert them back into citizens. Chapter 12 explores the consequences of this for the reintegration of offenders released from correctional institutions.

LIVING INSIDE

> *The cells are filthy. The walls are pocked with the carcasses of dead flies. During the day, the roaches visit, at night the mice. The door and door frames to the cells are solid steel, and every time they close, steel against steel, the sound is deafening. It seems as if there is a contest among the guards to determine who can make the doors bang loudest on closing. A constant reminder, if you need one, of where you are and the role you have to play.[6]*

The Pains of Imprisonment

> *If I come out at fifty-six, as a thirty-one-year-old, after twenty-five years in prison, I'll be the same mental age as my children. How do you deal with that?*

Assuming that I make it through this sentence, if I'm fortunate enough to, and I pray that I am, I don't want to die any more than any other person, I like living just as much as anybody else and if I make it through, I still wouldn't see my children. I would make a point of not seeing them. It's far better for them to have me not interfere with their life in any way, shape, or form.[7]

A core concept in understanding the carceral experience is the **pains of imprisonment**. In *Society of Captives*, his classic study of a maximum security prison, Gresham Sykes identified a number of deprivations that inmates experience. These included the loss of liberty, loss of access to goods and services, and loss of access to heterosexual relationships, as well as the loss of personal autonomy and personal security.[8]

Of all the pains of imprisonment, the loss of liberty is perhaps the most devastating for most offenders, especially when we consider that our society places a high premium on citizens' rights and freedoms. In prison, inmates must find ways to cope with the loneliness, boredom, and hopelessness associated with the loss of freedom. Although Canada's correctional systems operate family visit programs, many inmates are not visited by anyone. An inmate may go for years without receiving a letter, much less a personal visit. The pains of imprisonment may be especially acute for Aboriginal inmates, who are often incarcerated hundreds or even thousands of kilometres from their home community (see Chapter 14).

The pains of imprisonment are also brought about by correctional policies and practices. Pains and insecurities are associated with indeterminate sentences, which leave inmates uncertain when they will be released from confinement and what the conditions will be. The inconsistent application of institutional regulations by COs, risk assessments that categorize inmates and that result in loss of personal integrity, and the dangers associated with institutional decisions, all contribute to insecurity in individual inmates.[9] In newer correctional institutions, the use of high-tech surveillance has made the experience of incarceration "'deeper' and more burdensome … less directly oppressive, but more gripping—*lighter but tighter*."[10]

THE INMATE SOCIAL SYSTEM

Every correctional institution has an inmate social system, often referred to as the *inmate subculture*. For decades, criminologists have attempted to determine the origins, components, and functions of the inmate social system. These efforts have provided insights into prison life and the experience of incarceration. Two explanations have long been offered for the evolution of inmate social systems: the **deprivation theory**, which holds that the inmate social system exists to provide inmates with access to illicit goods and services; and the **importation theory**, which holds that the attitudes and behaviours that characterize the inmate social system are imported into the institution by offenders who had criminal careers on the outside.[11] Research studies have found that both theories are useful for understanding the origins of these systems.

Pains of imprisonment
The deprivations experienced by inmates confined in correctional institutions, including the loss of autonomy, privacy, security, and freedom of movement and association.

Video Link
theStar.com: A Canadian Prisoner's Perspective
www.youtube .com/watch?v= 8yXO4wh46vM

Video Links
Kingston Pen: Secrets and Lies
www.cbc.ca/ fifth/2012–2013/ 2012/09/kingston-pen-secrets-and-lies.html

Tales from Kingston Pen
www.cbc.ca/ doczone/episode/ tales-from-the-kingston-penn .html

Deprivation theory
An explanation which holds that the inmate social system develops as a consequence of inmates' attempts to mitigate the pains of imprisonment.

A number of other concepts can help us understand the inmate social system. One of these is **prisonization**, defined as the process whereby inmates become socialized into the norms, values, and culture of the prison.[12] This is not a uniform process; those inmates with extensive carceral experience are likely to already have developed antisocial, criminally oriented attitudes and behaviours. Offenders are said to be **institutionalized** when they have become prisonized to such a degree that they are unable to function in the outside, free community. Many of these persons are **state-raised offenders**—that is, they have spent most of their youth and adult lives confined in correctional institutions.

The longer an inmate is confined, the more difficult it may be for that person to retain prosocial attitudes and behaviours, especially when confined with offenders with even more hardened criminal orientations.

A major challenge confronting correctional systems is preventing offenders from becoming so immersed in the prison's culture that the efforts of correctional staff to promote positive values and behaviours cannot succeed. Another challenge is how to "unprisonize" inmates as they move closer to their release date. Unfortunately, many of the attitudes and values that become embedded in inmate social systems are antithetical to those of the outside, law-abiding community.

The Inmate Code

Another core component of the inmate social system is the **inmate code**, defined as a set of rules governing interactions with other inmates and with institutional staff.[13] These rules include "do your own time" (i.e., mind your own business), "don't exploit other inmates," and "don't weaken."[14]

A number of **social (or argot) roles** are associated with the inmate social system. These roles are based on the inmate's friendship networks, sentence length, current and previous offences, degree of at least verbal support for the inmate code, and participation in illegal activities such as gambling and drug distribution.

For example, "square johns" exhibit prosocial behaviour and a positive attitude toward staff and the administration. "Right guys," by contrast, are

---

Importation theory
An explanation which holds that the inmate social system develops as a consequence of pre-prison attitudes and behaviours that are brought by inmates into the institution.

Prisonization
The process by which inmates become socialized into the norms, values, and culture of the prison.

Institutionalized
Inmates who have become prisonized to such a degree that they are unable to function in the outside, free community.

State-raised offenders
Inmates who have spent most of their youth and adult lives confined in correctional institutions.

Inmate code
A set of behavioural rules that govern interactions among inmates and with institutional staff.

PERSPECTIVE

Inmate

A lot of people here blame the external world for their troubles: they're not big enough to accept the fact that they are responsible for their own situations. There's guys here that I can deal with on a one-to-one basis, guys that understand what I'm going through, guys that you can talk to, eh. And oh, there's people you can associate with and people you can't associate with, people you can trust, people you can't trust. (in P.J. Murphy and L. Johnsen, *Life 25: Interviews with Prisoners Serving Life Sentences* [Vancouver: New Star, 1997], 60)

Social (or argot) roles
Roles that inmates assume based on their friendship networks, sentence length, and other factors related to their criminal history and activities in the institution.

antisocial and have a negative attitude toward authority. "Snitches" ("rats" or "squealers") play a risky game of providing correctional staff with information about other inmates and their activities.[15] That these types of roles exist in inmate populations is strong evidence that the inmate code is not the defining feature of inmate behaviour. In fact, inmate relations are characterized by considerable fear, intimidation, violence, and manipulation; how much this is so depends on the "vibe" of the particular correctional institution and the types of offenders housed in it.

A related feature of inmate society is its specialized vocabulary: a "bit" is the inmate's sentence (e.g., a five-year "bit"); a "beef" is the crime committed; a "fish" is a new inmate; and a "goof" is an inmate who behaves inappropriately in the institution—for example, who violates the inmate-imposed prohibition against whistling anywhere in the facility. Most inmates pay at least lip service to the code, but even when they do, an inmate's greatest source of danger is other inmates. It can be anticipated that adherence to the code is more prevalent in high-security institutions, where inmates are likely to be prison veterans with more entrenched criminal attitudes and behaviours. Contributing to the lack of loyalty and solidarity among inmates is the rat (or snitch) system, by which inmates improve their own position and prospects with COs and the administration at the expense of fellow inmates.

One inmate described doing your own time as follows:

> *It means keep yourself separate from everything and everybody. Don't comment, interfere, or accept favours. Understand that you are "fresh meat" and need to learn the way of the joint. You have to deal with the "Vikings" (slobs, applied to both guards and cons), "booty bandits" (someone looking for ass to fuck), and the "boss," "hook," "grey suit" or "cookie" (all terms for prisons officials of various ranks) without "jeffing" (sucking up) to the staff. You have to deal with other cons who want you as a "punk" or a "fuck boy." Anybody can be carrying a "shank" (home-made knife) made out of a toothbrush and a razor blade or a piece of sharpened steel. Probably the more innocent someone looks, the more you have to worry.*[16]

Inmates and correctional staff distinguish between "convicts" and "inmates" (or "new school kids"). The latter are perceived as not respecting the traditional inmate social system. As a deputy warden in a federal correctional facility stated: "These 'new school kids' think nothing of going into another inmate's cell in groups of four or five and punching out the inmate and taking his TV. That would never happen in the past, and it makes life in the institution much more unpredictable than in previous years" (personal communication with C.T. Griffiths).

Status and Power Among Inmates

The days when one inmate "boss" controlled an entire population in an institution are over. That said, there is still a hierarchy of status and power among inmates, with higher status being accorded to inmates who are serving life sentences, who are intelligent and are able to articulate the concerns and issues of the inmate population, and whose pre-prison status and activities are well known and admired. Other inmates exercise power based on gang affiliation, their ability to control illicit goods and services within the institution (including drugs and gambling), and their sheer physical strength.[17]

Generally speaking, inmates convicted of sex offences, transgendered inmates, inmates who have been tagged as snitches (rats) by other inmates, and those with gambling or drug debts are all vulnerable to physical and perhaps sexual abuse. These inmates may be placed in protective custody (PC) for their protection. Then there are other inmates who, because of their personality, offence, or physical weakness, have little or no power and influence. Inmates confined for sexual offences, especially against children, have low status in most institutional populations and may be subject to victimization.

A defining feature of life in contemporary correctional institutions is that inmates tend to group themselves into niches or friendship networks. These networks may be based on associations formed during previous incarcerations or in the outside community (e.g., gangs); on shared ethnicity or culture (e.g., Black or Aboriginal groups); or on length of sentence (e.g., lifers). It is the friendship group, rather than the inmate population as a whole, that provides the individual inmate with security and support and that is the recipient of the inmate's loyalty. The result is an inmate population characterized by pluralism rather than by uniformity of thought and action.

Parting Thoughts on the Inmate Social System

It is likely that the most highly developed inmate social systems are in federal facilities, which house offenders with more extensive criminal records for longer periods of time. The more rapid turnover of inmates in provincial/territorial institutions would seem to work against the development of inmate social systems. On the other hand, many provincial/territorial inmates have been incarcerated in the past and may be well schooled in the various facets of doing time. While some type of social system always develops among inmates, there are variations in the specific form that system takes—for example, in the extent to which an inmate code takes hold, and how powerful social roles are.

Despite the improvements in correctional institutions, incarceration is still a painful experience. The pains of imprisonment ensure that the inmate social system will remain a prominent feature of prisons—indeed, it may become even stronger in the new corrections model of the early 21st century. One issue to consider is whether there are ways to alter the dynamics in correctional institutions in such a way that inmates and staff are safe and positive changes can occur.

The principles of restorative justice would seem to provide a framework for creating more positive environments in correctional facilities, improving interactions between staff and inmates, and, potentially, reducing rates of reoffending. See Box 9.2.

BOX 9.2

Restorative Justice in Prison

To explore this potential, the CSC conducted a pilot project that involved creating a living unit in Grande Cache Institution, a minimum security federal institution for male offenders in Alberta, centred on the principles of restorative justice. The restorative justice unit (RJU) was designed to facilitate collaborative problem solving among the inmates and with staff and included inmate mediators to resolve conflicts and to facilitate positive interactions in the unit. An evaluation of the program found that while both staff and inmates felt that the program had created a more positive, respectful environment in the living unit, there was no impact on rates of reoffending upon release from the institution. One reason for this was the lack of continuity (throughcare) between the institution and the community; this left the offenders without supports that would have strengthened the skill sets learned in the RJU program.

Source: T. R. Petrellis, *The Restorative Justice Living Unit at Grand Cache Institution: Exploring the Application of Restorative Justice in a Correctional Environment* (Ottawa: Correctional Service of Canada, 2008), http://www.csc-scc.gc.ca/text/rsrch/reports/r189/r189-eng.shtml.

COPING WITH CONFINEMENT

While incarcerated, inmates spend considerable energy trying to reduce the pains of imprisonment. They often become involved in obtaining, distributing, and/or using illicit goods and services, including drugs and other contraband. Consensual sexual relationships may be entered into. Participation in the underground economy is not without risk, however. For example, inmates who incur gambling debts may risk being physically harmed or may be pressured to have family members smuggle drugs and contraband into the prison. To protect themselves, these inmates may request placement in a protective custody unit, where their freedom of movement in the institution and access to programs are severely curtailed.

Drugs and Contraband

> *Illicit drugs and alcohol are the central driving force in the lives of inmates: they not only supply ways of escaping the deadening routine of doing time but also confer currency, collateral, and power on their dealers. Just as on the street, substance abuse in prison leads to violence and further crime.*[18]

In most Canadian correctional facilities, drugs are as freely available as they are on the street. Inmates use drugs or alcohol to cope with their environment, forget their problems, or just relax. Many offenders become addicted to drugs while in confinement.

The smuggling networks in correctional facilities are extensive and sophisticated. Organized gangs play a major role in importing and distributing drugs, especially in federal institutions. Drugs in prison—their distribution and use—are commonly associated with intimidation, extortion, and staff corruption. Moreover, violence and victimization among inmates are often the result of nonpayment for illicit drugs. This presents a risk to the safety and security of both inmates and staff. Of particular concern is "homebrew," a concoction made by inmates with ingredients (bread, fruit, or vegetables) stolen from the kitchen or dining hall. Most illicit drugs in prison have the effect of "downing out" inmates; by contrast, homebrew consumption can precipitate violence.

The problem of illicit drugs and contraband inside prisons might seem surprising at first glance, given the strict regimen of correctional institutions, the various static and dynamic security arrangements, and the multitude of drug interdiction strategies. The latter include metal detectors, ion scanners, nonintrusive searches of all visitors, drug-sniffing dogs, cell searches and physical searches of inmates, and, at the federal level, a national random-urinalysis program that tests the urine samples of 5 percent of the inmate population each month. In reality, however, it is almost impossible for correctional staff to eliminate the flow of drugs and contraband. There is extensive contact between inmates and outside visitors; offenders leave institutions on temporary absences and day parole; and inmate labour is used in a variety of noninstitutional settings, including community service, forestry work, and firefighting.

Drugs enter the prison in a variety of ways: tennis balls or dead birds can be tossed over the fence; visitors and sometimes corrections staff can walk them in. In Box 9.3, a CO in a correctional facility in Manitoba describes how drugs were moved into the prison, transferred to an inmate, and taken into the living unit. In this particular case, a family member had placed the contraband in a condom and inserted it into a body cavity on visiting day and then removed it in the washroom in the visitors' area. The description picks up at that point.

BOX 9.3

Condoms, Coke Machines, and Contraband

One of the tricks they used—we have a Coke machine in there, did at that time, a pop machine. A girl would go up and buy a drink. She would put the money in and she would deposit the drugs in the little opening where the pop would come out. She'd put the condom of drugs in there. She'd buy a drink, take the drink, and leave. The person who was now going to get the drugs, it's usually a kid, first timer, we'd never suspect he was a drug carrier. He would go and buy a drink, along with the condom of drugs and he'd take them back to the location. He would do that for fear of being badly beaten if he didn't agree to it.

(continued)

The only people really chosen at random for a strip search at the end of visiting are known drug users, guys who are really bad characters, guys who are giving staff a lot of problems. We would strip-search them. A young kid, that's the first time into the building, that's the guy the inmates would get to carry their drugs back, because we wouldn't suspect him ... He would insert the drugs in his rectum. Quite often we'd search and we'd find the rear of their pants would be sliced and their underwear would be sliced and they would be sitting right at the table. As rude and crude as that sounds, that's the culture we're dealing with. And this may be a well-educated, blond-hair, blue-eyed kid. But he was going to do it or he was going to get a terrible licking when he got back to his range. So, he took the risk and did it.

Source: The Honourable E. N. (Ted) Hughes (Chair), *Report of the Independent Review of the Circumstances Surrounding the April 25–26, 1996 Riot at the Headingley Correctional Institution* (Winnipeg: Ministry of Justice, Province of Manitoba, 1996), 49. Reprinted by permission of Manitoba Justice.

Sexual Gratification

Inmates who have been deprived of heterosexual relationships still seek sexual gratification. Masturbation and consensual sexual relations with another inmate are the two most common types of sexual activity in correctional institutions. Consensual sex, while technically homosexual, is an adaptation to a unique circumstance; inmates revert to heterosexual sexual activity when they return to the community. The extent to which prison authorities should tolerate sexual relations between inmates is a topic of ongoing discussion.

Little is known about how gay, lesbian, bi-sexual, and trans-gendered (GLBT) inmates adapt to confinement and how their attempts at sexual gratification are viewed and responded to by heterosexual inmates. A less common means of sexual release, which is also a manifestation of power and control in the inmate social system, is the rape of an inmate (see below).

Mature Coping

Mature coping
A positive approach taken by inmates to adjust to life inside correctional institutions.

Inmates encounter many opportunities to participate in illegal activities during their confinement but may choose instead to mitigate the pains of imprisonment through more constructive means. **Mature coping** is a positive approach to adapting to life inside. Inmates who take this route avoid using violence and deception in addressing problems, are altruistic in their relationships with other inmates, and use their time in confinement for positive growth through participation in treatment programs.[19]

There are obstacles to mature coping: the prison regimen may not encourage independent judgment, other inmates may seek to disrupt the prison environment, and inmates who try to cope maturely may find themselves victimized by others.

DOING LIFE

Picture yourself falling into a tunnel, totally dark, and it's going to take you twenty-five years to walk out ... one step at a time.[20]

Reprinted by permission of Manitoba Justice.

The death penalty was abolished by Parliament in 1976 (though it has been retained for certain military offences, including treason and mutiny) and replaced by a mandatory life sentence without possibility of parole for 25 years in cases of first-degree murder. Under the Criminal Code, persons convicted of murder are subject to life imprisonment. This means that the offender is under sentence for life, although he or she may serve this sentence both in prison and upon release on parole in the community. The Criminal Code sets out the minimum number of years that an offender must serve in prison before being eligible to apply for release on parole. The key word is *apply*—there is no guarantee that the parole board will grant a release. An offender serving life offered the following observation:

I've been in for two and a half years, just about going on three years. Seems like forever already. It's hard to remember what it's like out there. So many things can happen in three years. It's a terrible transition period; it's a terrible thing to go through. Especially when you don't see a light at the end of the tunnel anywhere. You're just stuck here and you're herded into your cell every few hours for a count. You feel like cattle. You get a feeling like you're helpless. Herd you in, lock the door. They count you like diamonds and treat you like shit.[21]

Long-term sentences pose challenges not only to correctional systems with regard to housing and programming but also to individual inmates. It is highly unlikely that most long-term offenders will be able to sustain their pre-prison relationships, especially if relations with a spouse and/or children were already unstable.

Long-term confinement may not produce the predicted negative impacts on inmates, but neither does it promote positive changes. Most inmates seem to eventually adjust to life in prison, but this may make it more difficult for them to survive in the outside, free community on release. Ironically, those inmates who adjust well to the highly structured environment of a correctional institution may be the ones who encounter the most difficulties upon release.

PRISON AS "HOME": THE STATE-RAISED OFFENDER

Those who happen not to be in prison at the moment tend to think of themselves as free. Those who were locked behind bars early in their lives and have become "institutionalized" feel free only when in jail. These people have no talent or disposition for filing tax returns, remembering Aunt

Flossie's birthday, obeying the speed limit, or attending the P.T.A. Being told by people like me when to rise, when to eat, when to change their clothes, suits them just fine. Just as it's hard for people on the outside to understand how anyone can love being in prison, the "institutionalized" cannot understand how anyone can love mowing the lawn, joining the Rotary Club, or running for office.[22]

Some offenders have spent most of their youth and adult lives in correctional institutions. These state-raised offenders have experienced only limited periods of freedom in the community and may have neither the social skills nor the ability to function outside the total institutional world of the prison. Many of them are frightened at the prospect of having to cope with the fast pace of modern life. For the state-raised offender, the prison provides security, friends, room and board, and a predictable routine; none of these are guaranteed in the outside community. The prison, not the community, is their home. State-raised offenders present challenges to systems of corrections, especially when these offenders reenter the community.

VIOLENCE AND EXPLOITATION AMONG INMATES

For inmates in many correctional institutions, the potential for violence and exploitation is a fact of daily life, although only a small percentage of inmates are a threat to others.

Male inmates in Canadian federal institutions are more likely to be murdered than males in the outside, free community. Toughness is a central feature of inmate identity, and inmates may use extreme violence for self-protection, to achieve and maintain power and status, and to retaliate against snitches. Though COs are sometimes the source of brutality inflicted on inmates, other inmates present the greatest danger to their safety. Not all inmates, however, are at equal risk of being victimized. The degree to which an inmate is vulnerable to attack and exploitation by other inmates depends in large measure on his or her status, power, and friendship network. Inmates with a mental health disability and lower functioning may be especially vulnerable to exploitation.

Weak and vulnerable inmates may be coerced to provide sexual services, to pay money or goods for protection, to repay loans or favours at high interest, or to persuade family members to bring drugs into the institution. In contrast to the physical aggression that characterizes life inside institutions for male offenders, in women's facilities such aggression appears to be more indirect and to take the form of verbal bullying, threats, ostracism, intimidation, and gossip.[23] Research studies suggest that aggressive inmates commit more assaults in prisons that are overcrowded and in which there is a high percentage of younger inmates (under the age of 25).[24] Also, there seem to be higher levels of inmate victimization by other inmates in maximum security institutions.[25]

CP PHOTO/Paul Chiasson

Federal CO in Québec shows a display of homemade weapons seized from inmates.

The level of violence in correctional institutions is a function of many factors, including living conditions, the actions of COs and administrators, the demographics of the inmate population (e.g., age), overcrowding, and competition among inmate gangs for turf. Some of these factors are related to one another—for example, overcrowding may increase inmate misconduct if there are a large number of younger inmates who are having difficulty adjusting to prison life.[26] There may also be conflicts between gang-affiliated inmates. At Joyceville Institution, a federal facility in Ontario, it is estimated that one in ten inmates is affiliated with a gang. This creates challenges for prison administrators to keep "incompatibles" separate from one another in order to prevent gang-precipitated violence.

Inmates convicted of more serious crimes such as murder do not account for a disproportionate share of prison violence or involvement in misconduct in the institution.[27] Inmates who are in debt in the prison economy, who lend money to other inmates, or who lack sufficient resources to obtain illicit goods and services are more likely to be victimized by other inmates. "Similar to the free world, those who are poor are more likely to be victimized."[28] Prison assaults are disproportionately committed by younger inmates and in institutions that are overcrowded.[29] Often, violent incidents occur because of gambling debts, conflict over the drug market inside the institution, or previous on-the-street relationships. Or, the inmate who was assaulted was a snitch.

Many inmates live in constant fear for their safety. Among the more fearful are the older adults and inmates who lack strong friendship networks. Given the patterns of violence in prison, this fear is most likely justified. Issues related to inmate safety have come to the attention of the courts. In 2004, the Supreme Court of Canada acquitted a former inmate on a charge of possessing a dangerous weapon. Jason Kerr had stabbed another inmate to death with a homemade knife. The court found that Kerr had been carrying the knife for self-defence after he was threatened with harm by the victim and that possession of the weapon did not endanger the public (*R v. Kerr*, 2004 SCC 44).

Sexual Coercion and Rape

Sexual coercion and rape are two brutal realities of prison life, yet there is very little information about the perpetrators and victims of this type of violence or about its prevalence in Canadian institutions. The reluctance of inmate victims to report victimization, combined with the assumption among many correctional observers that most inmate sexual activity is consensual, has hindered an understanding of this important area of institutional corrections.[30] More attention has been given to this topic in the United States (e.g., the website of Stop Prisoner Rape at http://www.spr.org).

Perpetrators use a variety of tactics to coerce sex, including inflicting direct physical harm or threatening to do so, intimidating the target physically, and applying persuasion. An inmate may succeed in taking another inmate as his "punk"—an exploitative relationship that nevertheless provides a measure of security and protection for the weaker inmate. Depending on the circumstances, such as whether there are multiple perpetrators, the target can often prevent the attack by avoiding the perpetrators, consistently refusing, using defensive threats, fighting, or launching a pre-emptive attack.[31]

> *He was always winking, blowing kisses and always trying to talk me into letting him give me a blow job. Until one day when he grabbed ahold of my penis and said I want you. Up until then I let it ride but after dinner that night I caught him by the tennis court where no guards could be and I smiled and said so you want me and when he said yes I plant my foot upside his jaw and left him laying on the ground and that put an end to it.[32]*

There are, however, a number of factors that mitigate against inmates sexually assaulting even weaker inmates in the prison, including the threat of being investigated by prison authorities, the possibility of disciplinary sanctions, and potential criminal and civil charges.

FAILING TO COPE WITH CONFINEMENT: SELF-INJURIOUS BEHAVIOUR AND SUICIDE

The pains of imprisonment, combined with the challenges faced by individual inmates, may lead to **self-injurious behaviour (SIB)** and, in some cases, to suicide. Only in recent years have correctional systems paid attention to these issues. SIB refers to any deliberate action that involves bodily harm or disfigurement; it includes head banging and skin cutting.[33] Female offenders are at higher risk of SIB as a way to cope with isolation, distress, and emotional pain.[34] Aboriginal offenders account for 45 percent of all self-harm incidents in federal prisons.[35]

There have been no definitive studies of SIB; it is known, however, that rates of SIB are higher among inmates than in the general population and much higher (est. 23 percent) among women inmates. Those with mental health issues and childhood trauma are at a high risk of SIB. For many inmates, especially women, SIB appears to be a method of coping with negative emotions.[36]

The CSC has a number of initiatives designed to reduce the incidence of SIB. These include health assessments at intake, policies for managing inmates who are deemed at risk, and various behavioural interventions.[37]

The most frequent causes of inmate death are natural ones, followed by drug or alcohol abuse, accident, and suicide.[38] The prison suicide rate is more than twice that of the general Canadian population. Male inmates are more at risk of suicide; female offenders are more likely to engage in SIB. Most inmates who commit suicide (most often by hanging) were serving a longer sentence, or suffered from a psychological disorder, or had a history of violence.[39] The risk of suicide may be higher for women who are placed in segregation (see Chapter 13).

In recent years, correctional systems have been developing screening protocols to identify inmates at risk of suicide. To reduce the incidence of suicide and self-harm, the CSC has implemented inmate peer support programs in all maximum and medium security institutions. The Samaritans program, which operates in several federal facilities, is a peer support program through which a community-based organization provides suicide prevention training for inmate peer counsellors.

> **Self-injurious behavior (SIB)**
> Deliberate self-inflicted bodily harm or disfigurement.

> Video Link
> Corrections Investigator Raises Alarm Bells Over Prisoner Self-Harm
> **aptn.ca/pages/ news/2012/10/24/ corrections –investigator-raises –alarm-bells-over –prisoner-self-harm**

INMATE FAMILIES

Discussions of corrections often overlook the fact that many inmates are fathers or mothers, husbands or wives. Little attention has been given to the dynamics and needs of inmate families, either during the inmate's confinement or following release. This is surprising, given that nearly half of offenders in confinement were married at the time of admission and that most have children or stepchildren. Furthermore, inmate mothers are likely to be sole caregivers for their children (see Chapter 13).

Correctional systems were not designed to consider the needs of inmate families, and family members may feel isolated and neglected by correctional authorities.[40] Also, the families of inmates may be stigmatized and marginalized in the community.[41] This societal indifference increases the challenges faced by the families of inmates. In the words of an inmate spouse: "David, my son, he was afraid of people knowing about his step-dad because they, you know, parents wouldn't let their kids play with him and those kind of things. That was very very difficult."[42]

Other concerns relate to finances, housing, isolation from the community, and fears related to the offender's return to the community.[43] The partners of offenders may experience trauma, shame, isolation, and depression.[44] The CSC has a family visit program that provides an opportunity for married and common law partners to spend time alone in a separate facility on the grounds of the institution. Not all inmates qualify for these visits, and even when the inmate is eligible for a family visit, the spouse or partner may be unable to travel to the institution, because of the distance involved or financial or other personal reasons. Research suggests that family visit programs have a positive impact on the inmate's family life, reduce institutional misconduct, and lower rates of reoffending.[45] There is evidence that inmates in correctional institutions located far from home are more likely to violate prison regulations than offenders confined closer to home.[46]

Video Link
The Devil You Know
**www.cbc.ca/
fifth/2010–2011/
thedevilyouknow**

Children whose parents are incarcerated can suffer from emotional, behavioural, and academic problems; their type and severity vary with the child's age, gender, and length of separation from the parents.[47] The symptoms can mirror those evidenced by children who have experienced the death of a parent. The children of inmates may feel responsible for their parents' incarceration, be embarrassed among their peers, and worry that they may be sent to prison one day. This is the collateral damage of a punitive penology that results in more offenders being sent to prison and more crime in the next generation. Inmates who had parents who were incarcerated (second-generation prisoners) may exhibit more anger and violent behaviour as well as higher levels of misconduct.[48] In Canada, it is estimated that the children of federal inmates are two to four times more likely to have conflict with the law as compared to other children.[49]

For the inmate, the loss of regular family contact is one of the pains of imprisonment. A number of factors hinder efforts to maintain and strengthen the family ties of incarcerated offenders, including limited visiting hours, poor visiting facilities, the obstacles imposed by geographic distance, and the difficulties of maintaining family ties over the course of a long-term sentence. To address this issue, the State of New York has launched a program that allows inmates to "meet" with their families via videoconference twice a month. It anticipates expanding this program to a number of correctional facilities.[50]

Most correctional institutions also host volunteer programs that provide inmates an opportunity to interact with residents from the outside community. These programs are often sponsored by service organizations and religious groups and can have a number of benefits for the inmates, staff, and the volunteers who participate.[51]

The failure of correctional systems to address the needs of inmate families has undermined the potential for the inmate's partner and family to play a positive role in reintegrating the offender back into the community upon release.[52]

INMATE GRIEVANCES AND COMPLAINTS

The CCRA sets out the procedures for ensuring that official grievances filed by federal inmates are dealt with in a fair, equitable, and timely manner. Inmates must make every attempt to resolve their grievances through the internal grievance procedure in the institution before filing a written complaint with the Correctional Investigator. Similar grievance procedures and requirements are in place for inmates in provincial/territorial institutions. A Federal Court judge ruled in 2012 that the CSC was not responding to official inmate grievances in a timely manner and ordered a high-level review of the grievance system. This investigation may result in significant changes in the grievance process.

Thousands of complaints and grievances are filed every year by inmates in Canadian correctional facilities. The most common complaints received by the federal Correctional Investigator relate to healthcare, institutional transfers, and the use of administrative segregation.[53] A very small proportion (as little as 5 percent) of the inmate population is responsible for nearly 70 percent of the complaints and grievances that are filed (see At Issue 9.1). In an attempt to address this situation, a provision in Bill C-10, enacted in 2012, made it a disciplinary offence for an inmate to knowingly make a false claim for compensation from the Crown. The danger is that this will deter inmates with legitimate complaints from exercising their rights.

The Office of the Correctional Investigator investigates issues related to federal offenders; provincial ombudspersons focus on provincial cases. Following is a case investigated and resolved by the Ontario Ombudsman:

> *An inmate called the Ombudsman because he was eligible for parole in one week and he was afraid his request for a parole hearing would not be submitted on time. His Institutional Liaison Officer had not met with him to begin the process, which takes four to six weeks. Ombudsman staff discovered that delays in processing parole hearing requests were routine at the institution. As a result of the Ombudsman's inquiries, the responsible manager was directed to clear up the backlog to ensure that inmates were given the opportunity for parole hearings before their parole eligibility dates. Additional staff were hired and two senior probation and parole officers were assigned to work with the Institutional Liaison Officer to help improve their performance.*[54]

Video Links

Surviving Supermax
**www.youtube
.com/watch?v=
tQNGrb3xUWo**

The Prisons Video Trust: Families of Prisoners
**www.youtube.com/
watch?v=
R_QFU7Au5mo**

The Trials and Tribulations of Prison Visits
**www.youtube.com/
watch?v=
6U9CHs6eEOM**

AT ISSUE

Issue 9.1: Inmate Grievances

Are inmate grievance procedures being abused?

Thousands of complaints and official grievances are filed by inmates every year. In 2012, the Federal Court of Canada ordered a high-level review of the grievance system, citing lengthy delays in resolving inmate grievances. At the same time, statistics indicate that a relatively small number of inmates are responsible for a majority of the complaints and grievances. Bill C-10 contains a provision designed to reduce the number of false claims for compensation. Supporters of the need for reform in the grievance system argue that the CSC (in this case) must adhere to the duty to act fairly. Opponents contend that existing procedures are sufficient but are being abused by a small number of litigious inmates. What is your view on this issue?

SUMMARY

The discussion in this chapter has centred on the experiences of offenders who are sentenced to a period of custody. Offenders in correctional institutions tend to be from the margins of society and to have limited education and skill sets. On entering the institution, the offender must develop strategies for coping with life inside. Inmates face a number of challenges, including the pains of imprisonment, learning their way around the inmate social system, and avoiding abuse and exploitation. It is likely that this process is easier for state-raised offenders who have spent much of their youth and adult life in custody. Generally speaking, systems of corrections have given little attention to the needs of inmates' families, and this has made it difficult for inmates to maintain their relationships with spouses, partners, and children. There are procedures by which inmates can file grievances and complaints, and the federal Office of the Correctional Investigator and provincial ombudspersons are involved in investigating inmate grievances as well.

KEY POINTS REVIEW

1. Persons confined in correctional institutions tend to have low levels of education, limited employment skills, and addiction issues, and are disproportionately Aboriginal or Black.

2. The specific impact that entry into prison has on an individual offender varies with a number of factors, including personality, offence history, and previous incarcerations.

3. A major challenge confronting correctional systems is to prevent offenders from becoming institutionalized, which is an obstacle to change.

4. While most inmates pay lip service to the inmate code, it appears that it is no longer the behavioural guide that it was in the past.

5. Inmates spend a considerable part of their time attempting to reduce the pains of imprisonment and protecting themselves inside the prison.

6. The degree to which an inmate is vulnerable to attack and exploitation by other inmates depends in large measure on his or her status, power, and friendship networks.

7. There is no empirical evidence that long-term confinement leads to mental and physical deterioration in inmates or to an impairment of coping abilities, although it may affect the inmate's ability to reenter the community.

8. Rates of self-injurious behaviour (SIB) are higher among inmates than in the general population and are much higher for women offenders.

9. Little attention has been paid to the dynamics and needs of inmate families.

10. Correctional systems have formal inmate grievance procedures. They also have ombudspersons who may investigate inmate complaints.

KEY TERM QUESTIONS

1. Define and discuss the importance of the following concepts for the study of corrections and life inside correctional institutions: (1) *status degradation ceremonies*; (2) *pains of imprisonment*; and (3) *state-raised offenders*.

2. Discuss the attributes of the *inmate subculture/inmate social system* and then discuss what is known about its existence in correctional institutions.

3. Describe and contrast the *importation theory* of the inmate social system and the *deprivation theory* of the inmate social system.

4. Discuss the concept of *prisonization* and describe what is meant when it is said that an inmate has become *institutionalized*.

5. Identify the tenets of the *inmate code* and discuss whether the code still exists among inmates in correctional institutions.

6. What role do *niches* (of inmates) and *social* (or *argot*) *roles* play inside correctional institutions?

7. Describe what is meant by **mature coping** by inmates, identify the components of mature coping, and note the obstacles that inmates may encounter in their efforts to engage in this practice.

8. Why is it important to understand **self-injurious behaviour** (SIB) among inmates?

NOTES

1. Public Safety Canada, Corrections Statistics Committee, *Corrections and Conditional Release Statistical Overview* (Ottawa: Public Works and Government Services Canada, 2010), http://www.publicsafety.gc.ca/res/cor/rep/_fl/2010-ccrso-eng.pdf.

2. John Howard Society of Toronto, *Homeless and Jailed: Jailed and Homeless* (Toronto: 2010), http://media.thestar.topscms.com/acrobat/ef/6e/a2fdc45d452d8cc6e23535371b07.pdf.

3. P.J. Murphy and L. Johnsen, *Life 25: Interviews with Prisoners Serving Life Sentences* (Vancouver: New Star, 1997), 41.

4. R. A. Cloward, "Social Control in the Prison," in *Prison Within Society: A Reader in Penology*, ed. L. Hazelrigg, 78–112 (Garden City: Doubleday, 1969).

5. R. Dube, *The Haven: A True Story of Life in the Hole* (Toronto: HarperCollins, 2002), 238–39.

6. Inmate's description of life in the reception centre at Millhaven Institution, Ontario, in F. A. W. Ault, "Imprisoned by an Uncaring Public," *Globe and Mail*, April 21, 1997, A14.

7. In Murphy and Johnsen, *Life 25*, 79.

8. G. M. Sykes, *Society of Captives—A Study of a Maximum Security Institution* (Princeton: Princeton University Press, 1958).

9. B. Crewe, "Depth, Weight, Tightness: Revisiting the Pains of Imprisonment," *Punishment and Society* 13, no. 5 (2011): 509–29.

10. Ibid., 524.

11. J. Irwin and D. R. Cressey, "Thieves, Convicts, and the Inmate Culture," *Social Problems* 10, no. 1 (1962): 142–55.

12. D. Clemmer, *The Prison Community* (Boston: Christopher, 1940).

13. G. M. Sykes and S. L. Messinger, "The Inmate Social System," in *Theoretical Studies in the Social Organization of the Prison*, ed. R. A. Cloward, D. R. Cressey, G. H. Grosser, R. McCleery, L. E. Ohlin, G. M. Sykes, and S. L. Messinger (New York: Social Science Research Council, 1960), 5–19.

14. M. Welch, *Corrections: A Critical Approach*, 3rd ed. (New York: Routledge, 2011), 137.

15. Ibid., 137–38.

16. S. Thompson, *Letters from Prison: Felons Write About the Struggle for Life and Sanity Behind Bars* (New York: HarperCollins, 2002), 15–16.

17. P. L. Faulkner and W. R. Faulkner, "Effects of Organizational Change on Inmate Status and the Inmate Code of Conduct," *Journal of Crime and Criminal Justice* 20, no. 1 (1997): 55–72.

18. M. Harris, *Con Game: The Truth About Canada's Prisons* (Toronto: McClelland and Stewart, 2002), 185.

19. R. Johnson, *Hard Time: Understanding and Reforming the Prison* (Belmont: Wadsworth, 1996).

20. Lifer, in Murphy and L. Johnsen, *Life 25*, 43.

21. Ibid., 30.

22. Former CO, in J. M. Yates, *Line Screw: My Twelve Riotous Years Working Behind Bars in Some of Canada's Toughest Jails* (Toronto: McClelland and Stewart, 1993), 313.

23. J. Ireland and J. Archer, "Descriptive Analysis of Bullying in Male and Female Adult Prisoners," *Journal of Community and Applied Social Psychology* 6 (1996): 35–47.

24. K. F. Lahm, "Inmate-On-Inmate Assault: A Multilevel Examination of Prison Violence," *Criminal Justice and Behavior* 35, no. 1 (2008): 120–37.

25. D. M. Perez, A. R. Gover, K. M. Tennyson, and S. D. Santos, "Individual and Institutional Characteristics Related to Inmate Victimization," *International Journal of Offender Therapy and Comparative Criminology* 54, no. 3 (2010): 378–94.

26. W. W. Franklin, C. A. Franklin, and T. C. Pratt, "Examining the Empirical Relationship Between Prison Crowding and Inmate Misconduct: A Meta-Analysis of Conflicting Research Results," *Journal of Criminal Justice* 34, no. 4 (2006): 401–12.

27. J. Sorensen and M. D. Cunningham, "Conviction Offense and Prison Violence: A Comparative Study of Murderers and Other Offenders," *Crime and Delinquency* 56, no. 1 (2011): 103–25.

28. J. Copes, G. E. Higgins, R. Tewksbury, and D. A. Dabney, "Participation in the Prison Economy and Likelihood of Physical Victimization," *Victims and Offenders* 6, no. 1 (2011): 1–18.

29. Lahm, "Inmate-On-Inmate Assault."

30. T. R. Jones and T. C. Pratt, "The Prevalence of Sexual Violence in Prison," *International Journal of Offender Therapy and Comparative Criminology* 52, no. 3 (2008): 280–95.

31. I. O'Donnell, "Prison Rape in Context," *British Journal of Criminology* 44, no. 2 (2004): 241–55.

32. C. Struckman-Johnson, D. Struckman-Johnson, L. Rucker, K. Bumby, and S. Donaldson, "Sexual Coercion Reported by Men and Women in Prison," *Journal of Sex Research* 33, no. 1 (1996): 67–76 at 73.

33. J. Power and S. L. Brown, *Self-Injurious Behaviour: A Review of the Literature and Implications for Corrections* (Ottawa: Correctional Service of Canada, 2010), 1, http://www.csc-scc.gc.ca/text/rsrch/reports/r216/r216-eng.shtml.

34. C. A. Dell and T. Beauchamp, "Self-Harm Among Criminalized Women," Fact Sheet, Canadian Centre on Substance Abuse, 2006, http://www.ccsa.ca/2006%20CCSA%20Documents/ccsa-011338-2006-e.pdf.

35. Office of the Correctional Investigator, *Annual Report, 2011–2012* (Ottawa: 2012), 36, http://www.oci-bec.gc.ca/rpt/annrpt/annrpt20112012-eng.aspx.

36. J. Power and S. L. Brown, *Self-Injurious Behaviour: A Review of the Literature and Implications for Corrections* (Ottawa: Correctional Service of Canada, 2010.), 1, http://www.csc-scc.gc.ca/text/rsrch/reports/r216/r216-eng.shtml.

37. A. Usher, J. Power, and G. Wilton, *Assessment, Intervention, and Prevention of Self-Injurious Behaviour in Correctional Environments* (Ottawa: Correctional Service of Canada, 2010), http://www.csc-scc.gc.ca/text/rsrch/reports/r220/r220-eng.shtml.

38. Office of the Correctional Investigator, *Annual Report, 2011–2012*, 21.

39. J. Power and D. L. Riley, *A Comparative Review of Suicide and Self-Injury Investigative Reports in a Canadian Federal Correctional Population* (Ottawa: Correctional Service of Canada, 2010), http://www.csc-scc.gc.ca/text/rsrch/reports/r221/r221-eng.shtml.

40. R. Light and B. Campbell, "Prisoners' Families: Still Forgotten Victims?," *Journal of Social Welfare and Family Law* 28, nos. 3–4 (2006): 297–308.

41. S. Hannem, "Stigma and Marginality: Gendered Experiences of Families of Male Prisons in Canada," in *Critical Criminology in Canada: New Voices, New Directions*, ed. A. Doyle and D. Moore, 183–217 (Vancouver: UBC Press, 2011).

42. Ibid., 2002.

43. D. Braman, *Doing Time on the Outside: Incarceration and Family Life in Urban America* (Ann Arbor: University of Michigan Press, 2007).

44. Light and Campbell, "Prisoners' Families"; S. Moroney, *Through the Glass* (Toronto: Doubleday Canada, 2011).

45. D. Derkzen, R. Gobeil, and J. Gileno, *Visitation and Post-Release Outcome Among Federally Sentenced Offenders* (Ottawa: Correctional Service of Canada, 2009), http://www.csc-scc .gc.ca/text/rsrch/reports/r205/r205-eng.shtml.

46. M. Solinas-Saunders and M. J. Stacer, "Prison Resources and Physical/Verbal Assault in Prison: A Comparison of Male and Female Inmates," *Victims and Offenders* 7, no. 3 (2012): 279–311.

47. R. C. Johnson, "Ever-Increasing Levels of Parental Incarceration and the Consequences for Children," in *Do Prisons Make Us Safer? The Benefits and Costs of the Prison Boom*, ed. S. Raphael and M. A. Stoll, 177–206 (New York: Sage, 2009); J. Murray, "The Cycle of Punishment: Social Exclusion of Prisoners and Their Children," *Criminology and Criminal Justice* 7, no. 1 (2010): 55–81.

48. C. M. Novero, A. B. Loper, and J. I. Warren, "Second-Generation Prisoners: Adjustment Patterns for Inmates with a History of Parental Incarceration," *Criminal Justice and Behavior* 38, no. 8 (2011): 761–78.

49. L. Withers and J. Folsom, *Incarcerated Fathers: A Descriptive Analysis* (Ottawa: Correctional Service of Canada, 2007), http://www.csc-scc.gc.ca/text/rsrch/reports/r186/r186-eng.pdf.

50. O. Yaniv, "Videoconference Prison Visit Programs Set to Quadruple in Size This Fall." *New York Daily News*, August 28, 2012.

51. H. E. Duncan and S. Balbar, "Evaluation of a Visitation Program at a Canadian Penitentiary," *Prison Journal* 88, no. 2 (2008): 300–27.

52. J. Christian, J. Mellow, and S. Thomas, "Social and Economic Implications of Family Connections to Prisoners," *Journal of Criminal Justice* 34, no. 4 (2006): 443–52.

53. Public Safety Canada,. "Corrections and Conditional Release Statistical Overview," 31.

54. Ombudsman Ontario, *Annual Report, 2010–2011* (Toronto: 2011), 62, http://www .ombudsman.on.ca/Investigations/Selected-Cases/2011/Counting-the-days.aspx.

CHAPTER 10

CLASSIFICATION, CASE MANAGEMENT, AND TREATMENT

CHAPTER OBJECTIVES

After reading this chapter, you should be able to:
- *Discuss the process of classification and risk assessment.*
- *Discuss the tools and techniques used in classifying inmates.*
- *Describe the goals of the case management process.*
- *Describe CSC's Integrated Correctional Program Model.*
- *Identify and discuss the principles of effective correctional treatment.*
- *Discuss what is known about the effectiveness of various types of correctional treatment programs.*
- *Discuss the difficulties that surround attempts to assess the effectiveness of correctional treatment programs.*
- *Identify and discuss the potential obstacles to effective correctional treatment.*
- *Discuss the issues that surround the question as to whether prison inmates should have the right to refuse treatment.*

There are three major trends in offender classification and treatment: (1) the increasing use of sophisticated risk/needs assessment instruments; (2) the increasing domination of treatment research, policy, and programs by a psychological perspective—in particular, a cognitive–behavioural approach; and (3) differentiated treatment approaches for women, Aboriginals, and specific categories of offenders such as sex offenders.

CLASSIFICATION AND RISK ASSESSMENT

Classification is the process by which inmates are subdivided into groups based on a variety of factors. In each region of the Correctional Service of Canada (CSC), there are reception centres where offenders spend a period of time after sentencing. Classification is used to determine the appropriate

Classification
Using various assessment instruments to categorize inmates in order to determine the appropriate security level and programs.

custody and security level, program placement, and assignment to housing units within the institution.

Classification involves gathering documentation on the offender from a variety of sources, including the family, corrections, the courts, the police, and the victim. Then, at the reception centre, the inmate is evaluated for health, mental health, security concerns, and suicide risk. Also, a risk and needs assessment is conducted. During the initial classification process, the factors considered in determining the inmate's security level include the seriousness of the offence, outstanding charges, the offender's social, criminal, and (where available) young offender history, potential for violence, and any physical or mental illness.

On the basis of all these, an institutional placement is decided on and programming recommendations are made. The classification of offenders, with a strong emphasis on risk and needs, is a core component of correctional treatment.

There is considerable variation in the quality of classification across the country and even between the federal and provincial systems within the same jurisdiction. Federal inmates in Newfoundland and Laborador, for example, gave that province's classification process high marks; inmates in the provincial system, however, viewed it as inadequate.[1]

Early in a federal inmate's sentence, a reintegration potential rating is established, based on information gleaned from a number of risk assessment instruments as well as various static and dynamic risk factors. This rating places the individual inmate in one of three categories: high, medium, or low reintegration potential. Most inmates with high reintegration potential will not require core programming. The existence of this category reflects the concern that some inmates are being steered into programs unnecessarily, which is a waste of their time and the system's resources.

Assessment continues throughout the offender's sentence, from intake through incarceration and release from custody and up to sentence expiry. Inmates are reclassified periodically in the course of their confinement based on their progress and performance in treatment programs and work assignments and on their behaviour in the institution. Both at the initial classification stage and in later classification decisions, correctional personnel consider security and risk concerns as well as the inmate's abilities and program needs. The assessment process for federal offenders is set out in Figure 10.1.

Offenders have a variety of criminogenic needs that must be addressed both within the institution and later in the community. These relate variously to education, mental health, social networks, employment, accommodation, drugs and alcohol, attitudes, and cognitive skills. All of these criminogenic needs are *dynamic* in the sense that they are amenable to change. All have been found to be important in reducing the likelihood of reoffending.[2]

Figure 10.1

Offender Intake Assessment Process

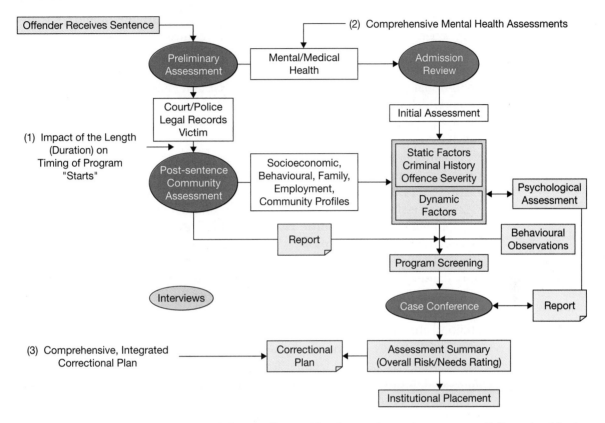

Source: A Road Map to Strengthening Public Safety. http://www.publicsafety.gc.ca/csc-scc/cscrprprt-eng.pdf. (Correctional Service of Canada, 2007). Reproduced with the permission of the Minister of Public Works and Government Services Canada, 2013.

Classification Tools and Techniques

The classification procedures applied by Canadian systems of corrections generally involve psychological, personality, and behavioural inventories. At the federal level, the procedure is referred to as the Offender Intake Assessment (OIA), during which extensive information on the offender's criminal history and patterns is gathered.

The provinces and territories vary considerably with regard to their capacity to conduct classification. A review of Nova Scotia corrections, for example, found that there was no system in place to assess the risk that an offender might pose while incarcerated.[3]

Risk and Needs Profiles of Offenders

Risk assessment and risk management are the mantras of contemporary corrections, and the assessment of risk is central to classification and case management. Risk assessments are designed to identify those offenders who are most likely to reoffend upon release from the institution if no treatment intervention occurs.[4] Risk analysis is used to determine which facility the offender should be confined in or moved to; to identify the offender's treatment needs; to identify those offenders who require higher levels of support, intervention, and supervision upon release; and to assist in release decisions. Since an inmate's criminal history is strongly related to success (or failure) on conditional release, the assessment of both risk and needs improves predictions about which offenders will recidivate. The risk determination, then, involves combining static criminal history information with dynamic (or criminogenic need) factors. This determination plays a role in decisions to release offenders from confinement (see Chapter 11). Risk assessments are also used to assign offenders to a specific level of security, to inform program decisions, as information for release authorities, and to determine supervision requirements.[5]

In assessing the degree of risk posed by an offender, corrections personnel generally consider both **static risk factors** and **dynamic risk factors**. Static risk factors include the offender's criminal history (including prior convictions), the seriousness of prior offences, and whether the offender has successfully completed previous periods of supervision in the community. Dynamic risk factors focus on those attributes of the offender that can be altered through intervention; they include addiction issues, attitude and motivation, cognitive abilities, and education and job skills. As is not the case with static factors, it is possible to change dynamic factors—for the better or, if not addressed, for the worse. Many risk/needs factors are **criminogenic**—that is, if they are not addressed, future criminal behaviour may occur.

All correctional personnel, from institutional staff to parole board members to parole officers, have access to theoretically or empirically based assessment instruments and tools. These instruments provide them with information with which to develop effective management and treatment plans; they also reduce the liability and culpability of personnel should the offender later commits serious crimes in the community.

Box 10.1 describes several of the more common risk assessment instruments used by the CSC, as well as one used in the Province of Ontario for provincial offenders. Many of these instruments can also be used by community corrections personnel, including probation officers and parole officers.

Presumably, these instruments have replaced what has been referred to as "structured professional judgement" (more traditionally, "discretion"). However, corrections personnel can subvert the objective results of risk assessments by exercising discretion.[6] Considerable controversy has surrounded the risk assessment and classification of women offenders (see Chapter 13).

Research studies have identified eight factors that reliably predict involvement in criminality: (1) lack of attachment to family/marital supports, (2) school/employment problems, (3) lack of prosocial leisure or recreation activities, (4) antisocial peers, (5) antisocial attitudes, (6) antisocial personality, (7) substance abuse, and (8) history of antisocial behaviour.[7]

Static risk factors
Attributes of the offender that predict the likelihood of recidivism and that are not amenable to change, including criminal history, prior convictions, seriousness of prior offences, and performance on previous conditional releases.

Dynamic risk factors
Attributes of the offender that can be altered through intervention, including level of education, employment skills, addiction issues, and cognitive thinking abilities.

Criminogenic risk factors
Risk/needs factors that contribute to a person's propensity to commit criminal offences, including substance abuse problems and the acceptance of antisocial values. See also dynamic risk factors.

BOX 10.1

Selected Risk Assessment Instruments

OIA—Revised	Information is gathered at intake on the offender's criminal history and from post-sentence community assessment; measured are static and dynamic risk factors, as well as the offender's accountability, motivation, and responsivity; information is entered into the Offender Management System
Custody Rating Scale	Determines the *initial* risk and classification level of male offenders; used to make an initial placement of new inmates; includes information on offence, sentence length, history of disciplinary infractions, and indicators of social stability
Security Reclassification Scale (SRS for men) (SRS–W for women)	A multipoint scale used to inform decisions on the inmate's security level; includes information on the inmate's behaviour in the institution and participation and progress in treatment programs
Statistical Information on Recidivism Scale Revised	A 15-item scale used to estimate the probability of an offender reoffending within 3 years of release from custody; includes age and criminal history; not administered to women or Aboriginal offenders[a]
STATIC-99/ STATIC-2002	Designed to estimate the probability of sexual and violent recidivism among men who have been convicted of at least one sexual offence against a child or nonconsenting adult; includes items on general criminal history and information specific to the sex offence
Level of Service Inventory—Ontario Revision	Standardized interview relating to the offender, including offence history, substance abuse, and employment history; used in Ontario and several other provinces
LS/CMI	A risk assessment and case management tool; assesses the risk and need factors of offenders; scales cover criminal history, family/marital, alcohol/drug issues, pro-criminal attitudes/orientation, and barriers to release, among others; used in several provinces

(continued)

Spousal Assault Risk Assessment (SARA)	Twenty-item set of risk factors used to predict the risk of future violent offending among men convicted of spousal assault
Psychopathy Check List	Twenty-item scale used to predict recidivism and violent reoffending

^a M. Nafekh and L.L. Motiuk, *The Statistical Information on Recidivism—Revised 1 (SIR-R1) Scale: A Psychometric Examination.* (Ottawa: Correctional Service of Canada, 2002). Found at: http:publications. gc.ca/collections/collection_2010/scc-csc/P583-3-126-eng.pdf.

Figure 10.2 presents data on the rehabilitative needs of offenders admitted to correctional facilities in Saskatchewan in 2010–11. The majority of offenders had five of the six rehabilitative needs. Note the high percentage of offenders with substance abuse issues and social interaction deficits among this population.[8]

Figure 10.2

Adults in Sentenced Custody, by Type of Rehabilitative Need, Saskatchewan, 2010–11

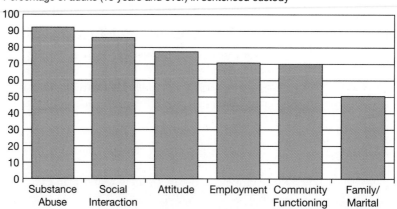

Source: M. Dauvergne, *Adult Correctional Services in Canada, 2010/2011.* (Ottawa: Minister of Industry, 2012). Pg. 13. Found at: http://www.statcan.gc.ca/pub/85-002-x/2012001/article/11715-eng.pdf.

Case management
The process by which the needs and abilities of offenders are matched with correctional programs and services.

CASE MANAGEMENT

Correctional **case management** is the process by which the needs and abilities of offenders are matched with correctional programs and services. The primary goals of case management are (1) to enable systematic monitoring of the offender during all phases of confinement, (2) to balance the need for rehabilitation with community protection, (3) to prepare the inmate for successful reintegration into the community, and (4) to contribute to the effective supervision of the offender in the community. Box 10.2 provides an overview of the case management process. Note that case management is carried out both during the inmate's confinement and after release from the institution.

Because most of the offenders in provincial/territorial correctional systems spend a very short time in confinement, the case management that does occur tends to focus on release planning. For many of these inmates, there is little or no case planning or access to treatment programs. In federal institutions, by contrast, case management generally involves a much longer time frame. Regular reviews are conducted during which program requirements are identified and decisions are made about transferring inmates from one institution to another and, eventually, releasing them.

In federal institutions, a key role in case management is played by institutional parole officers (IPOs), who have the primary responsibility for case management and who work on teams that include COs, psychologists, and the offender, among others. Their duties include the following: assessing offender needs as well as behaviours or attitudes that have contributed to their criminal behaviour; developing intervention plans to address those

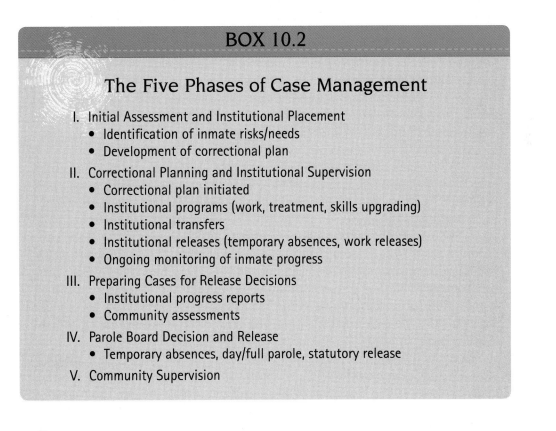

BOX 10.2

The Five Phases of Case Management

I. Initial Assessment and Institutional Placement
   - Identification of inmate risks/needs
   - Development of correctional plan

II. Correctional Planning and Institutional Supervision
   - Correctional plan initiated
   - Institutional programs (work, treatment, skills upgrading)
   - Institutional transfers
   - Institutional releases (temporary absences, work releases)
   - Ongoing monitoring of inmate progress

III. Preparing Cases for Release Decisions
   - Institutional progress reports
   - Community assessments

IV. Parole Board Decision and Release
   - Temporary absences, day/full parole, statutory release

V. Community Supervision

attitudes and behaviours; and helping offenders undertake and complete their intervention plans. The IPOs also make recommendations concerning offender transfers, temporary absences, and other forms of conditional release, including parole. In many institutions, IPOs spend most of their time completing paperwork rather than supervising and counselling inmates; this may make it harder for them to help offenders.

The Correctional Plan

Correctional plan
A key component of the case management process that determines the offender's initial institution placement, specific treatment or training opportunities, and preparation for release.

At the core of case management is the **correctional plan**. One of these is developed for most inmates, the exceptions being those who are serving short sentences. This plan determines the offender's initial institution placement, specific treatment and training opportunities, and release plan.

The correctional plan is based on the risk/needs profile of the inmate and is used to guide all decisions made about the inmate. The plan identifies program needs, based in part on the dynamic factors discussed above. For example, if substance abuse is a contributing factor to the inmate's pattern of criminality, then the offender should be referred to a substance abuse program. The correctional plan also sets out benchmarks, including parole eligibility dates and likely program entrance dates.

INSTITUTIONAL TREATMENT PROGRAMS

The programs most frequently offered in correctional institutions address substance abuse, family violence, and anger management. Also offered are GED (high school equivalency) courses and various vocational programs. Still other programs target specific groups of offenders, such as sex offenders. Some programs are facilitated by outside groups such as AA and Narcotics Anonymous. And there are specific programs for female offenders (see Chapter 13) and Aboriginal offenders (see Chapter 14).

Provincial/territorial institutions vary considerably in the programs they offer. The short time that most offenders spend in these institutions makes it difficult to address alcohol, drug, and mental health issues or to develop specialized programs (e.g., for offenders with FASD). Overcrowding often limits inmate access to programs, with the consequence that many offenders leave the institution without completing a full course of treatment. Although many provincial/territorial programs are modelled on the CSCs, severe time constraints require authorities to compress the program time lines, and this may compromise program integrity. The maintenance of program integrity has been found to be associated with reduced rates of reoffending among inmate participants.[9]

It is valid to ask whether treatment is a priority for correctional authorities. The CSC, for example, spends less on correctional programming than on staff overtime—about 2 percent of its multibillion-dollar budget. Programs for inmates in provincial/territorial facilities are often limited and are the first item to be reduced in times of fiscal restraint.[10] This despite the fact that offenders in custody are generally higher risk and have more needs than those under supervision in the community.

The CSC Integrated Correctional Program Model

The CSC has developed the **Integrated Correctional Program Model (ICPM)**, which consists of three distinct programs: (1) a Multi-Target program, (2) a sex offender program, and (3) an Aboriginal-specific program. The ICPM integrates best practices from programs that had previously been offered separately, including anger management, cognitive skills, and violent offender programs.[11] The ICPM includes the most effective components of these programs while continuing to target the dynamic risk factors of offenders through social-learning, cognitive–behavioural, and structured behavioural practices.[12]

The ICPM model is informed by the Good Lives Model, a strengths-based approach that reflects the importance of providing positive, goal-oriented correctional interventions to increase an offender's motivation to engage in programming and behavioural change.[13] Each program stream allows the CSC to address the specific risks and needs of offender populations and to provide treatment in an integrated, holistic manner. The CSC has included other components in the ICPM, including these: a "Program Primer," an "Extended Primer," a "Motivation Module," a "Community Program," and "Institutional and Community Maintenance."

The ICPM is an interdisciplinary approach to correctional programming that brings together counsellors, COs, Aboriginal elders, and parole officers, among others. These teams oversee the inmate's correctional plan and strive to ensure a "continuum of care" ("throughcare") from the institution to the community. This approach has been found to increase the success of offenders in the community and is especially important for those offenders with special needs, such as a mental health disability.[14] Examples of this program at work include community parole officers meeting with institution staff to provide information on the resources that are available for inmates newly released into the community and meetings between parole officers and inmates to discuss issues surrounding supervision in the community.[15]

Reflecting what is known about the risk principle, the ICPM is delivered according to the offender's likelihood of reoffending. Higher risk offenders participate in high-intensity programs that involve 100 two-hour sessions, whereas lower risk offenders receive moderate-intensity programs that involve 50 two-hour sessions. These hours do not reflect the number of additional hours that offenders may spend in the Primer and Maintenance components of ICPM. The Multi-Target Program–High Intensity, for example, is designed for high-risk offenders. It contains five modules and is centred on the Good Lives model and the principles of RNR. There are 100 sessions, delivered to

Integrated Correctional Program Model (ICPM)
An interdisciplinary approach to correctional programming operated by the CSC.

groups no larger than 12 inmates. There are modules on relationships, clear thinking, living a healthy lifestyle, conflict resolution skills, and the challenges of self-management.

The ICPM also attempts to provide inmates with more timely access to treatment programs, to deliver interventions in a more effective manner, to increase the rates of program completion, and to decrease the rates of readmission for new convictions.

As of mid-2013, the ICPM had been implemented in a number of men's institutions in several regions of the country. Preliminary results indicate that inmates under this model experience shorter wait times to access programs and have higher completion rates. Also, Aboriginal inmates have significantly higher rates of program completion and access their first program earlier in their sentence—within six months of admission.[16]

Treating High–Risk Offenders: Sex Offender Treatment Programs

The treatment of sex offenders has become a focal point of correctional systems, in large measure because of growing public and political concern about this group of offenders and their growing numbers in institutional populations.

Sex offenders are difficult to treat, especially those classified as high risk. Their patterns of deviance are often deeply entrenched. Furthermore, to a greater extent than other offender groups, sex offenders tend to deny having committed an offence, to minimize the impact of the crime on the victim(s), and to attribute their behaviour to the actions and wishes of the victim(s). Sex offenders may not be motivated to participate in treatment programs and to engage in the self-change.[17]

As a group, and in contrast to the general inmate population, sex offenders tend to represent a broad spectrum of society: educated professionals, skilled tradespeople, and persons who, except for their sexual deviance, may live stable lives. This may present challenges for treatment staff, who will be wary of being manipulated.

Most treatment interventions for sex offenders take a multidisciplinary approach that involves psychiatrists, psychometrists, social workers, physicians, nurses, chaplains, recreational staff, and volunteers. These programs are designed to reduce the likelihood that sex offenders will recidivate upon release from the institution. Programs focus on identifying the nature and pattern of the offender's behaviour and on providing skills in self-management and self-control. Many treatment programs for sex offenders take a cognitive–behavioural approach and emphasize relapse prevention. This involves having sex offenders become aware of the thoughts, feelings, and behaviour that are related to their offending. In this way, they learn to identify the "triggers" for their sex offending and to develop strategies for managing these triggers. For some sex offenders, this may include not being alone in the company of a minor or being near schools and playgrounds.

PERSPECTIVE

Sex Offender Treatment Therapist

In discussing treatment, I will always separate out sex offenders in terms of the dynamics of offending and treatment intervention. Sex offenders are the ones who have the greatest difficulty taking responsibility for what they have done. Groups are a good way to get to them. When you facilitate a group of sex offenders, there is a certain dynamic that goes on. A sex offender might say that the only reason that they fondled the five-year-old is because they were drunk; another sex offender across the room will say, "I wasn't drunk when I fondled my victim." Sex offenders in the group have an understanding of behaviour that I will never have. With sex offenders, the biggest strength of the group was their being able to help each other accept responsibility for their behaviour. Sometimes it would get very intense in the groups and the language would be very colourful. They would get into each other's faces and say, "You are lying to yourself. You can lie to us, but don't lie to yourself." (personal communication with C.T. Griffiths)

Community Involvement in Institutional Programs

Community volunteers are involved in a wide range of activities in Canadian institutions. Many volunteers represent community service clubs and various religious organizations; others work one-on-one with inmates both during confinement and following release. The most active programs of this type are M2 (Man to Man) and W2 (Woman to Woman). In these programs, a citizen from the community is matched with an offender. Across the country, college and university students are actively involved in institutional programs.

COMMUNITY SERVICE PROJECTS AND ACTIVITIES

The media's focus on the more sensational events in corrections, such as escapes, riots, and heinous crimes committed by offenders under supervision in the community, tends to obscure the extensive involvement of inmate populations in community service projects. These activities benefit various groups of community residents; at the same time, they provide an outlet for the energies and talents of inmates and engage them in community-focused endeavours. Participation in community projects may help inmates develop prosocial attitudes and behaviours. In some of these projects, inmates contribute to children's charities.

THE PRINCIPLES OF EFFECTIVE CORRECTIONAL TREATMENT

To be effective, correctional treatment programs must (1) be based on empirically supported models of correctional change, (2) incorporate the principles of risk–needs–responsivity (RNR), (3) focus on the dynamic risk factors associated with the offender's criminal behaviour, (4) be monitored, evaluated, and accredited, and (5) be implemented by well-trained, dedicated program staff.[18]

Recall that the risk principle holds that treatment interventions have a greater chance of success when they are matched with the risk level of the offender. Higher levels of service are reserved for higher risk inmates; lower risk inmates do not require the same level of service to benefit from treatment interventions and may, in fact, be negatively affected by intensive service delivery. Among the risk factors that have been identified are antisocial attitudes, values, beliefs, rationalizations, and cognitive–emotional states (such as anger, resentment, defiance, and despair); a lack of problem-solving and self-management skills; and impulsiveness.[19] Note that this list includes both static and dynamic risk factors. Treatment programs have little impact on reoffending among low-risk offenders. Higher risk inmates benefit from treatment programs that focus on criminogenic factors.[20]

The needs principle holds that to be effective, treatment interventions must address the criminogenic needs of inmates, including alcohol or substance abuse, relations with peers, and attitudes toward and experiences with employment.

Finally, the responsivity principle holds that treatment interventions must be matched to the learning styles and abilities of individual inmates. This presents challenges to correctional systems, for many offenders have disabilities that present obstacles to learning. The responsivity principle is associated with the notion of **differential treatment effectiveness**: that not all programs will work with all offenders.

Differential treatment effectiveness
The requirement that, to be effective, treatment interventions be multifaceted and matched to the specific needs of individual offenders.

CREATING THE CONDITIONS FOR EFFECTIVE CORRECTIONAL TREATMENT

Corrections personnel must create conditions that increase the potential effectiveness of treatment programs. In any prison population, there is considerable variability regarding how inmates adapt to confinement and how closely they adhere to institutional rules and display an interest in participating in prosocial activities and programs. One challenge confronting correctional administrators is how to accommodate those inmates who are interested in making positive changes, while at the same time controlling the more negative influences of those inmates who are engaged in illicit and disruptive behaviour. Similarly, correctional staff may be challenged to remain optimistic when high-risk offenders who are disruptive and unmotivated to change are given priority access to treatment programs.[21]

The relations between prison staff (including COs) and inmates are an important factor in correctional treatment. It is important that COs and other staff support the efforts of treatment personnel in their daily interactions with the inmates.

The inmate is a key component of the treatment process. For any program to have a significant impact, the offender must be amenable to treatment.

Among the inmates in any institutional population, there is a **differential amenability to treatment**. In other words, not all inmates are receptive to treatment. This can be for a variety of reasons, including mental deficiency or learning disability, a deeply rooted attitudinal and behavioural pattern centred on a criminal lifestyle, an extensive history of confinement in institutions, and/ or a general lack of interest in making the effort to change.

Many offenders are in a state of denial about the offence for which they have been convicted, and this frame of mind may make effective treatment intervention more difficult. In the words of one treatment professional:

> *Embarrassment and shame are two major issues you have to deal with. And denial. And wanting to blame others: "It's not really my fault. If I hadn't been dating Joe, this would never have happened." Accepting responsibility for what they did, and the fact that they made choices to deal drugs, or whatever, is important. Yes they were involved in prostitution. Yes they were abused and addicted. But that does not give them permission to hurt somebody, to do a home invasion.*

Personal communication with D. Murdoch

Inmates who are receptive to treatment may struggle to alter deeply engrained attitudes and behaviour. An Aboriginal programs officer related how he conducted his violence prevention groups for federal Aboriginal offenders:

> *I give a lot of examples to the guys in my group: the rent's due, your girlfriend's telling you to find a job; she's telling you the diapers are low; the baby needs food. Are you going to do what you did before? Or are you going to find a new way to move forward? You need to tell me what it is about the way of moving forward that is healthy and that's not going to harm anybody.*

Personal communication with D. Murdoch

These challenges are illustrated in Box 10.3, in the responses of one inmate in a "Trigger Thought Exercise" in a violence prevention program.

Differential amenability to treatment
The notion that, for a variety of reasons, not all inmates are receptive to treatment, and/or, that they require interventions tailored to meet their specific needs, abilities, and interests.

BOX 10.3

An Inmate's Responses in a Violence Prevention Program

Trigger Thought Exercise

Instructions: Read each example. If you were the person in the example, what would you be thinking? Write down your response. What thoughts would go through your mind?

(continued)

Example 1: You are driving down the highway and are cut off by another driver. You slam on your brakes to avoid hitting him. If this were you, what would you be thinking?

Response: "What an asshole."

Example 2: The guy next to you bumps into you in a line-up. He looks at you and says, "Hey Buster, watch out." If this were you, what would you be thinking?

Response: "What a fucking loser. It's his fault."

Example 3: Your ex-spouse/partner promises to drop your children off for a visit, but doesn't show up again. If this were you, what would you be thinking?

Response: "Fucking bitch. She did it on purpose."

Example 4: You are financially desperate and have applied for income assistance. Your financial assistance worker sets a meeting up for you in two weeks. When the date comes, you are told that you do not qualify for income assistance. What would you be thinking?

Response: "This is bullshit. I'm being put into a situation where I can't win."

Example 5: Your next-door neighbor leaves a note on your door saying if you are noisy at night again, she's calling the police. If this were you, what would you be thinking?

Response: "Fucking rat."

Source: Anonymous.

In this exercise, the inmates in the VPP are being taught to recognize their triggers for violence. The approach reflects the reality that many offenders have few coping skills or alternative methods for resolving stressful situations they become involved in and may have few nonviolent conflict resolution skills.

Inmates in provincial/territorial institutions may have difficulty accessing programs in a timely manner, and they are often released from custody before completing their programs. Provincial inmates often identify a lack of programming as a major issue.[22] Access to and completion of treatment programs may be especially problematic for sex offenders, who may be released before they have completed a multimonth treatment program.

MEASURING THE EFFECTIVENESS OF CORRECTIONAL TREATMENT

The traditional approach for determining success has been **recidivism rates**—that is, the number of offenders who, once released from confinement, are returned to prison either for a technical violation of their parole or statutory release or for the commission of a new offence.

Recidivism rates
The number of offenders released from confinement who, once released from confinement, are returned to prison.

Using recidivism rates as a measure of success prevents an assessment of the "relative" improvement in the offender. For example, an offender who previously committed serious crimes and is subsequently returned to confinement for a relatively minor offence could be viewed as a "relative success" rather than as a failure. Or if that inmate succeeds, it may have been for reasons unrelated to the treatment intervention. There are many reasons why an individual might cease violating the law, including the efforts of a supportive family and/or spouse, success in securing stable employment, maturation, and the availability of programs and services in the community. On the other hand, the offender may have returned to criminal activity without being detected.

The success or failure of an offender upon release may also turn on the level and type of supervision he or she receives on the outside. Among parole officers, there are a variety of supervision styles, ranging from officers who have a more punitive orientation to those who focus on providing services and assistance (see Chapter 12).

POTENTIAL OBSTACLES TO EFFECTIVE CORRECTIONAL TREATMENT

The emphasis should be put on programming and rehabilitation ... Here for the most part it is warehousing. It's like you are put on a shelf.[23]

Inmate in a provincial institution

There are a number of potential obstacles to the delivery of effective treatment programs in correctional institutions.

Punishment versus Treatment

The principal mandate of correctional institutions—to securely confine offenders—often undermines the objectives of treatment programs. Recall from Chapter 7 that a defining attribute of correctional institutions is that they are public and political entities. This means that the availability of treatment resources may be restricted by politicians, legislatures, and community interest groups. Attempts to introduce innovative, evidence-based correctional interventions may be hindered by penal populism and punitive penology (see Chapters 1 and 2).

Doing Time and Doing Treatment

The dynamics of life inside the institution may hinder an inmate's efforts to participate in treatment programs. As Chapter 9 revealed, inmates are confronted with a variety of pains of imprisonment, as well as with the need to develop coping and survival strategies for doing time. Though inmate adherence to the convict code has eroded in recent years, the inmate social system, with its attendant illicit goods and services, and the violence and coercion that exist in many institutions, may be a major obstacle to treatment within the system.

Inmates who must expend a considerable portion of their time and energy coping with confinement and avoiding victimization may find it difficult to pursue self-change through participation in treatment programs. They may also be intimidated by other inmates not to participate in correctional programming (personal communication with a deputy warden, federal correctional institutions). Ironically, one of the biggest obstacles to the delivery of effective correctional treatment may be the institution itself and the dynamics of life inside correctional institutions.[24]

The Expectations of Rehabilitation

Rehabilitation is a value-laden process in which a key question is this: just what is correctional intervention attempting to accomplish?[25] The answers to that question may include the following: to develop in the offender prosocial attitudes and behaviour; to address the issues associated with criminal behaviour; to stabilize and strengthen inmates' personal lives and relationships; or—the most common measure—to prevent reoffending.

The challenges facing offenders who want to significantly alter their attitudes and behaviour should not be underestimated. Many offenders have grown up in marginalized, dysfunctional circumstances, with little contact with law-abiding citizens. Often they have few if any noncriminal friends. They may suffer from addiction, mental health disability, or FASD and have limited skills. The expectation that participation in a compressed treatment program in a provincial/territorial institution will begin to address what are often long-standing difficulties is unrealistic, especially in the absence of follow-up programs and services in the community.

The challenges for offenders may be compounded by treatment staff who bring to their work professional and middle-class values that influence the decisions they make about offenders. The chasm between treatment professionals as the providers of service, and offenders as clients of that service, may hinder the development of positive therapist–offender relationships and compromise the effectiveness of interventions.[26] Conversely, treatment professionals may be labouring under legislation and correctional policies that reflect a punitive penology.

Inmate Access to Programs

The challenges of providing treatment programs in provincial/territorial institutions are especially acute, given that periods of confinement average less than one month. There is a shortage of programs in many of these institutions, and existing programs must be delivered within an extremely compressed time frame.[27] Yet offenders in these facilities face many of the same problems as federal inmates, including low levels of education, anger management problems, a propensity to violence, mental disabilities, FASD, and substance abuse problems. It is unlikely that an offender with a long-standing drug addiction is going to even begin to address this issue during a six-week program inside the institution. Even federal offenders may face a very short time line for completing programs so that evidence of treatment success can be presented to the parole board as part of the inmate's application for conditional release. The federal ICPM, discussed earlier, was designed specifically to provide inmates with timely access to programs.

There is **differential treatment availability** in correctional institutions. This results in situations where, for example, a high-risk sex offender receives one year of treatment in a specialized program in one CSC region, while a sex offender in another region completes only a six-month nonresidential program. The newly minted ICPM is designed to increase inmate access to programs in federal institutions.

For provincial/territorial offenders, the use of probation, either as an alternative to confinement or following a period of confinement, may hold the most promise for effective treatment interventions (see Chapter 5). There are unique challenges in delivering effective treatment programs for female offenders (see Chapter 13) and Aboriginal offenders (see Chapter 14).

Differential treatment availability
The recognition that, within systems of corrections, not all inmates have equal access to treatment programs.

Low Rates of Inmate Participation and Program Completion

Although the classification process can determine the programming needs of inmates, many offenders either never enroll in programs or fail to complete the ones that have been recommended. Noncompletion rates appear to be higher among Aboriginal inmates, higher risk inmates, and inmates with less education.[28] Only about 50 percent of federal inmates who have a treatment component in their correctional plan actually participate in a treatment program.[29] A large study of federal offenders ($N = 24,315$) found that between 35 and 50 percent of the offenders did not complete assigned programs prior to their release. Reasons for noncompletion included transfers, the limited capacity of programs, and short sentences.[30]

Program Fidelity, Program Drift, and Therapeutic Integrity

A key factor in the development of effective correctional treatment programs is program implementation.[31] Correctional authorities must ensure that there is **program fidelity**—that is, that the treatment program is delivered in the way it was originally designed.

Program fidelity can be assured by providing a clear program manual as well as appropriate training and supervision to treatment staff. This is closely related to the principle of program integrity noted earlier.

Program fidelity may be compromised in institutions where COs are involved in facilitating core treatment programs, as has occurred in some provincial institutions. One can imagine the challenges of having a CO facilitate a treatment group of offenders, which requires the inmates to speak openly and honestly about their issues. There is also the issue of **program drift,** where for a variety of reasons, including lack of qualified staff and effective

Program fidelity
The extent to which a treatment program is delivered in accordance with the original program design.

Program drift
The extent to which a treatment program as delivered has moved away from the original design, with a potential impact on program effectiveness.

administrative oversight, a treatment initiative moves away from its original design and objectives. This compromises the integrity and potential effectiveness of the intervention.

Closely associated with this is the **therapeutic integrity** of programs. This concept underscores the importance of treatment staff having adequate training, appropriate skill sets, and competent supervision.[32]

Therapeutic integrity
The importance of the training, skill sets, and supervision of treatment staff for the effectiveness of correctional treatment programs.

The Importance of Throughcare

A long-standing challenge for correctional systems has been to ensure continuity between treatment interventions in institutional settings and those in the community following release. This is the concept of **throughcare**. Studies have found that the effectiveness of institution-based treatment programs is enhanced when there is a "seamless" transition to community-based treatment when the offender is released from confinement (see Chapter 11).[33] For provincial/territorial offenders who are not released on parole, there are generally no programs and services provided unless the offender has a term of probation to complete.

Throughcare
The notion that there should be continuity between institutional treatment programs and community-based services for offenders.

The absence of resources, a lack of communication between institutional treatment personnel and their community-based counterparts, and the loss of eligibility to participate in community-based programs on warrant expiry (end of sentence) all contribute to the lack of treatment continuity. Throughcare is especially problematic in cases where Aboriginal and Inuit offenders return to their remote northern communities. As well, continuity of care is a problem once the offender's sentence has expired. Except for offenders on long-term supervision orders, corrections authorities do not have the authority to provide services beyond the end of an offender's sentence. There may also be problems in jurisdiction: a federal offender, for example, may experience challenges in accessing provincial healthcare.[34]

THE ETHICS OF CORRECTIONAL TREATMENT

In the past, inmates had no power to resist the sanctions imposed on them, and a wide variety of punishments have been inflicted on inmates under the guise of treatment. At one time, these punishments included electroshock "therapy," which psychiatrists administered to many inmates without their consent until the 1980s. Throughout the 1960s and 1970s, prison inmates were used as subjects in a variety of experiments conducted by drug companies, federal agencies, and universities. Inmates were also used as subjects in a variety of experiments, this included studies of the effects of LSD. The inmates in this series of studies did provide "consent"; the issue is whether a captive person is able to provide informed consent.

The Canadian Charter of Rights and Freedoms guarantees all persons the right to life, liberty, and security of the person—rights that would most likely be violated by any provision of mandatory treatment.[35] The CCRA states that inmates must provide informed consent, both at the outset and during treatment, and that they have the right to refuse treatment or to withdraw from a treatment program at any time. Research suggests that mandated (coerced) participation in treatment programs is ineffective at reducing reoffending.[36] See At Issue 10.1.

AT ISSUE

Issue 10.1: Refusal of Treatment

Should prison inmates have the right to refuse treatment?

Consider the following scenario: An inmate convicted of a sex offence is sentenced to 15 years in prison. During confinement, he refuses to participate in treatment programs. As a consequence, he does not receive any form of conditional release, is denied statutory release after having served two-thirds of the sentence, and serves his entire sentence in prison. On his warrant expiry date, he is released, untreated, from the correctional institution, at high risk of reoffending. What is your view on the right of inmates to refuse treatment?

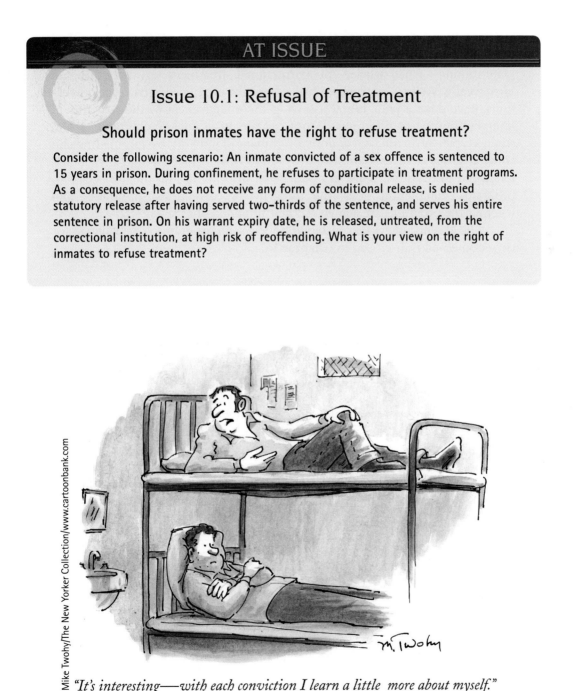

Mike Twohy/The New Yorker Collection/www.cartoonbank.com

"It's interesting—with each conviction I learn a little more about myself."

DOES CORRECTIONAL TREATMENT WORK?

Since the introduction of treatment programs into correctional institutions in the 1950s, there has been an ongoing debate over their effectiveness. The debate has involved politicians, community interest groups, correctional scholars, and senior and line-level corrections personnel.

What Works in Correctional Treatment?

Determining "what works" in correctional treatment is very difficult. Historically, systems of corrections, especially provincial/territorial corrections, have done a poor job at assessing the effectiveness of their treatment interventions. Most programs do not contain an evaluative component, and studies typically do not use random assignment of inmates to experimental and control groups. Investigations have found that, especially in provincial/territorial institutions, there is a paucity of information on inmate access to programs, completion rates, the integrity of correctional programs, and whether the programs are achieving their intended objectives.[37]

The absence of evidenced-based policies and programs is a challenge for corrections and is discussed in Chapter 16.

"Nothing Works" versus "Some Things Work": The Legacy of Robert Martinson

No discussion of the effectiveness of correctional treatment would be complete without mention of Robert Martinson, a scholar who nearly 40 years ago conducted a survey of more than 200 treatment programs and concluded that, with a few exceptions, none of them had an impact on reoffending (1974). Although scholarly research, historically, had little impact on correctional policy, this finding was seized on by politicians and used as a premise to not vigorously develop and support treatment programs. No mind that Martinson, on the basis of further analysis, recanted his original conclusion (1979).[38]

In the past two decades, researchers (led by Canadians) have conducted in-depth studies of treatment effectiveness. This research has made significant contributions to the scholarly literature and had an impact on correctional policy and practice. There is conclusive evidence that effective correctional interventions are (1) based on empirically supported models of behavioural change; (2) based on RNR; (3) focused on the dynamic (i.e., changeable) factors related to criminal behaviour; (4) geared to the learning style of the offender; (5) monitored, evaluated, and accredited; and (6) implemented by well-trained, dedicated program staff.[39]

A number of scholars have argued that the "nothing works" mantra still prevails despite evidence to the contrary.[40] A review of some of what we know about the effectiveness of correctional treatment interventions is presented in Research File 10.1.

RESEARCH FILE 10.1

The Effectiveness of Correctional Treatment Interventions

Do correctional treatment programs work? They can. The general consensus among researchers is that some programs work to reduce reoffending for some offenders; and that treatment programs are more likely than criminal sanctions to reduce recidivism; that effective treatment programs follow the principles of risk and need; and that treatment programs using a cognitive–behavioural approach have considerable promise.[a] If the principles of RNR are adhered to, reductions in recidivism can range from 10 to 40 percent.

Significant reductions in reoffending are possible if key factors are targeted, including criminal attitudes, criminal peer groups, and the attitudes and behaviours associated with antisocial personalities.[b] Inmates who complete treatment programs have higher success rates in terms of successful reintegration than offenders who do not acknowledge their level of risk.[c] In the words of one scholar, "offenders are good judges of their need for treatment."[d] The preliminary results from the federal ICPM are encouraging.

Do correctional programs successfully address the risk and needs of offenders? Perhaps not. A large study of federal offenders ($N = 24,315$) on conditional release between 2005 and 2010 found little change in their risk levels (93.5 percent no change) or in their needs (88.2 percent no change) from intake to release from custody. This suggests that whatever programming these offenders received while incarcerated did not alter their risk or needs ratings.[e]

Do adult basic education and vocational/work programs reduce reoffending? They can. Participation in prison education programs can reduce rates of reoffending. The effectiveness of education programs could be improved if there was more continuity between prison education and post-release follow-up and support.[f]

Participation in vocational and work programs can reduce levels of misconduct in the institution, increase the likelihood that the offender will find employment when released, and increase the chances of success in the community.[g] A key requirement is "throughcare"—continuity between the institutional program and programs and services in the community (discussed in Chapter 12).

Do cognitive skills programs work? Results are mixed. Some studies have found that these programs can increase critical reasoning skills, the capacity for optional thinking, and interpersonal problem solving, as well as reduce rates of recidivism. These programs may be effective for offenders under supervision in the community.[h]

Do programs for offenders with mental health issues work? Potentially. An evaluation of the CSC Mental Health Strategy, which was designed to provide a continuum of care from the institution to the community, found that offenders who had access to mental health specialists were less likely to have their conditional release revoked or suspended.[i] Challenges to providing effective interventions for this population

(continued)

include a lack of institutional resources and the fact that inmates with mental health issues are more likely to be held in segregation, limiting their access to programs.[j]

Do treatment programs for special populations of federal offenders work? Some appear to. There is evidence that programs for violent offenders, sex offenders, and inmates with substance abuse issues can succeed in reducing reoffending.[k] Federal inmates who reside in "drug-free" Intensive Supervision Unit (ISU) programs are less likely to be returned to custody than other offenders and are less likely to be returned to custody for a new offence.[l] Participation in drug treatment programs can reduce rates of reoffending upon release, as can multistage residential programs that provide a bridge between the prison and the community.[m]

Do sex offender treatment programs work? Some do. Some interventions do appear to reduce reoffending among certain groups of sex offenders. Part of the problem in determining the effectiveness of programs is the wide variety of offenders who are classified as "sex offenders." Offenders who participate in treatment programs generally have lower rates of reoffending than those in comparison groups who received no intervention (in one meta-analysis of 23 studies [$N = 6,746$ offenders], 11 *v.* 19 percent).[n] Programs for sex offenders based on the principles of RNR are the most effective at reducing reoffending; cognitive–behavioural interventions that focus on dysfunctional thoughts and feelings have also had some success.[o]

Do treatment programs in provincial/territorial institutions work? Unknown. Even though most offenders in confinement are in these facilities, program evaluations are virtually nonexistent.

Are risk assessment instruments effective at predicting future reoffending? Generally, yes. Research studies have validated the effectiveness of risk assessment instruments, including the LSI-OR and the Static-99R/Static-2002R.[p]

Does effective correctional treatment save money? Yes. A CSC evaluation of programs in federal institutions found the following returns on a per-dollar investment: $1 of correctional programming = return of $1 to $8; $1 of sex offender programming = return of $6.59; and $1 of substance abuse programming = return of $2.69. Note that "returns" here refers to cost savings associated with achieved correctional outcomes (i.e., offenders are supervised in the community and do not reoffend). In addition, the "cost of participating in institutional employment programs = $779 in terms of good correctional outcomes vs. offenders not participating in institutional employment programs in terms of poor correctional outcomes = $15,662."[q]

[a] J. Bonta, *Offender Rehabilitation: From Research to Practice* (Ottawa: Department of the Solicitor General of Canada, 1997), http://www.publicsafety.gc.ca/res/cor/rep//_fl/199701-eng.aspx; L.W. Sherman, D. Gottfredson, D. MacKenzie, J. Eck, P. Reuter, and S. Bushway, *Preventing Crime: What Works, What Doesn't, What's Promising* (Washington: Office of Justice Programs, U.S. Department of Justice, 1997), http://www.ncjrs.gov/works; P. Smith, P. Gendreau, and K. Swartz, "Validating the Principles of Effective Intervention: A Systematic Review of the Contributions of Meta-Analysis in the Field of Corrections," *Victims and Offenders* 4, no. 2 (2009): 148–69.

[b] J. Bonta and D.A. Andrews, "Viewing Offender Assessment and Treatment Through the Lens of the Risk-Need–Responsivity Model," in *Offender Supervision: New Directions in Theory, Research, and Practice*, ed. F. McNeil, P. Raynor, and C. Trotter, 19–40 (New York: Willan, 2010).

c M. Nafekh, N. Allegri, A. Fabisiak, D. Batten, Y. Stys, H. Lie, et al., *Evaluation Report: Correctional Service Canada's Correctional Programs* (Ottawa: Correctional Service of Canada, 2009), http://www.csc-scc .gc.ca/text/pa/cop-prog/cp-eval-eng.shtml; C.T. Griffiths, Y. Dandurand, and D. Murdoch, *The Social Reintegration of Offenders and Crime Prevention* (Ottawa: National Crime Prevention Centre, Public Safety Canada, 2007), http://www.publicsafety.gc.ca/res/_fl/soc-reint-eng.pdf

d J.S. Levenson, "'But I Didn't Do It!': Ethical Treatment of Sex Offenders in Denial," *Sexual Abuse: A Journal of Research and Treatment* 23, no. 3 (2011): 346–64.

e M. Olotu, D. Luong, C. MacDonald, M. Mckay, S. Heath, N. Allegri, and E. Loree, *Report of the Evaluation of CSC's Community Corrections*, Chapter 1, "Correctional Interventions" (Ottawa: Correctional Service of Canada, 2011), 48, http://www.csc-scc.gc.ca/text/pa/ev-cci-fine/ev-cci-fin-eng.pdf, *Report*, 48.

f J.H. Esperian, "The Effect of Prison Education on Recidivism," *Journal of Correctional Education* 61, no. 4 (2010): 34; John Howard Society of Alberta, *Inmate Education* (Edmonton: 2002), http://www `.johnhoward.ab.ca/pub/respaper/educa02.htm.

g C.A. Gillis, L.L. Motiuk, and R. Belcourt, *Prison Work Program (Corcan): Impact on Post-Release Employment and Recidivism* (Ottawa: Correctional Service of Canada, 1998), http://www.csc-scc.gc.ca/text/rsrch/ reports/r69/r69_e.pdf.

h D. Robinson, *The Impact of Cognitive Skills Training on Post-Release Recidivism Among Canadian Federal Offenders* (Ottawa: Correctional Service of Canada, 1995), http://www.csc-scvc.gc.ca/text/rsrch/reports/ r41/r41e-eng.shtml; J. Vennard, D. Sugg, and C. Hedderman, "Changing Offenders' Attitudes and Behaviour: What Works?," Home Office Research Study 171 (London: Home Office Research and Statistics Directorate, 1997), http://www.unisa.edu.au/hawkeinstitute/sprg/documents/what-works.pdf.

i N. Allegri, K. Delveux, D. Loung, H. Li, T. Jensen, D. Batten, K. Barney, E. Loree, and M. Henighan, *Evaluation Report: Community Mental Health Initiative* (Ottawa: Correctional Service of Canada, 2008), http://www .csc-scc.gc.ca/text/pa/ev-cmhi-394-2-51/cmhi-eng.pdf.

j M. Olotu, D. Luong, C. MacDonald, M. Mckay, S. Heath, N. Allegri, and E. Loree, *Report of the Evaluation of CSC's Community Corrections*, Chapter 1, "Correctional Interventions" (Ottawa: Correctional Service of Canada, 2011), 48, http://www.csc-scc.gc.ca/text/pa/ev-cci-fine/ev-cci-fin-eng.pdf, *Report*, 66.

k S. Belenko, C. Foltz, M.A. Lang, and H-E. Sung. 2004. "Recidivism Among High-Risk Drug Felons: A Longitudinal Analysiss Following Residential Treatment," *Journal of Rehabilitation* 40 no. 1–2: 105–32; A. Gordon and T. Nicholaichuk, "Applying the Risk Principle to Sex Offender Treatment," *Forum on Corrections Research* 8, no. 2 (1996): 36–38; F. Cortoni, K. Nunes, and M. Latendresse, *An Examination of the Effectiveness of the Violence Prevention Program* (Ottawa: Correctional Service of Canada, 2006), http://www.csc-scc.gc.ca/text/rsrch/reports/r178/r178_e.pdf.

l D.D. Varis, D. Lefebvre, and B.A. Grant, "Intensive Support Units for Federal Offenders with Substance Abuse Problems: An Impact Analysis," *Forum on Corrections Research* 18, no. 1 (2006), http://www.csc -scc.gc.ca/text/pblct/forum/e181/e181g-eng.shtml.

m J.A. Inciardi, S.S. Martin, and C.A. Butzin, "Five-Year Outcomes of Therapeutic Community Treatment of Drug-Involved Offenders After Release from Prison," *Crime and Delinquency* 50, no. 1 (2004): 88–108; B. Pelissier, W. Rhodes, W. Saylor, G. Gaes, S. Camp, S. Vanyur, and S. Wallace; TIRAD Drug Treatment Evaluation Project, *Final Report of Three-Year Outcomes: Part 1* (Washington: Federal Bureau of Prisons, 2008), http://www.bop.gov/news/PDFs/TRIAD/TRIAD_pref.pdf; N. Allegri, K. Delveux, D. Loung, H. Li, T. Jensen, D. Batten, K. Barney, E. Loree, and M. Henighan, *Evaluation Report: Community Mental Health Initiative* (Ottawa: Correctional Service of Canada, 2008), http://www.csc-scc.gc.ca/text/pa/ev -cmhi-394-2-51/cmhi-eng.pdf.

(continued)

n R.K. Hanson and M.T. Bussiere, "Predicting Relapse: A Meta-Analysis of Sexual Offender Recidivism Studies," *Journal of Consulting and Clinical Psychology* 66, no. 2 (1998): 348–62; F. Losel and M. Schmucker, "The Effectiveness of Treatment for Sexual Offenders: A Comprehensive Meta-Analysis," *Journal of Experimental Criminology* 1, no. 1 (2005): 117–46.

o F. Cortoni and K.L. Nunes, *Assessing the Effectiveness of the National Sexual Offender Program* (Ottawa: Correctional Service of Canada, 2007), http://www.csc-scc.gc.ca/text/rsrch/reports/r183/r183-eng.shtml; P. Corabian, M. Ospina, and C. Harstall, *Treatment for Convicted Adult Male Sex Offenders* (Edmonton: Institute of Health Economics, 2010), http://www.sexual-offender-treatment.org/93.html; R.K. Hanson, G. Bourgon, L. Helmus, and S. Hodgson, *A Meta-analysis of the Effectiveness of Treatment for Sexual Offenders: Risk, Need, Responsivity* (Ottawa: Public Safety Canada, 2009), http://www.publicsafety.gc.ca/res/cor/rep/_fl/2009-01-trt-so-eng.pdf.

p Cf. K.M. Babchishin, R.K. Hanson, and L. Helmus, *The RRASOR, Static-99R, and Static-2002R All Add Incrementally to the Prediction of Recidivism Among Sex Offenders* (Ottawa: Public Safety Canada, 2011), http://www.publicsafety.gc.ca/res/cor/rep/2011-02-aipraso-eng.aspx; R. Hanson and K.E. Morton-Bourgon, "The Accuracy of Recidivism Risk Assessments for Sexual Offenders: A Meta-Analysis of 188 Prediction Studies," *Psychological Assessment* 21, no. 1 (2009): 1–21; S.M. Hogg, "The Level of Service Inventory (Ontario Revision) Scale Validation for Gender and Ethnicity: Addressing Reliability and Predictive Validity," MA thesis, 2011, University of Saskatchewan, Saskatoon, http://ecommons.usask.ca/bitstream/handle/10388/etd-04112011-085608/Hogg_MA_Thesis.pdf?sequence=1; C.M. Langton, "Actuarial Assessment of Risk for Reoffense Among Adult Sex Offenders: Evaluating the Predictive Accuracy of the Static-2002 and Five Other Instruments," *Criminal Justice and Behavior* 34, no. 1 (2007): 37–59.

q M. Olotu, D. Luong, C. MacDonald, M. Mckay, S. Heath, N. Allegri, and E. Loree, *Report of the Evaluation of CSC's Community Corrections*, Chapter 1, "Correctional Interventions" (Ottawa: Correctional Service of Canada, 2011), 48, http://www.csc-scc.gc.ca/text/pa/ev-cci-fine/ev-cci-fin-eng.pdf, *Report*, 106.

SUMMARY

This chapter has focused on the strategies and programs in correctional institutions that are designed to assess and address the risk and needs of offenders. There is a question as to whether incarceration is effective in addressing the identified risk and needs of offenders during the period from intake to release. To be effective, correctional interventions must adhere to the principles of risk, need, and responsivity and must overcome a number of obstacles, including the dynamics of life inside correctional institutions, the limited skill sets of inmates, and the challenges of providing inmates with timely access to programs. The issue as to "what works" in correctional treatment is complex, although there is evidence that some programs work with some offenders and that there are successful interventions with specific groups of offenders.

KEY POINTS REVIEW

1. Three major trends in offender classification and treatment are the increasing use of risk assessment instruments, the use of psychological approaches to treatment, and the development of differentiated treatment approaches for women, Aboriginals, and specific categories of offenders.

2. The assessment of risk is a key component of classification and case management.

3. Among the requirements of successful treatment programs is adherence to the principles of risk, needs, and responsivity.

4. As a group, sex offenders are difficult to treat, particularly those classified as high risk.

5. Recidivism rates are an inadequate measure of the effectiveness of correctional treatment programs.

6. The conditions required for effective correctional treatment include supportive COs and staff, the matching of inmates' needs/amenability to programs, and continuity of treatment from the institution to the community.

7. Among the potential obstacles to effective correctional treatment are the conflicts between punishment and treatment; the dynamics of life inside prisons; unrealistic expectations of offenders with respect to changes in attitudes and behaviour; inmate access to programs; low rates of inmate participation and completion; an absence of therapeutic integrity; and the lack of continuity between prison treatment programs and community treatment programs.

8. Inmates must provide informed consent at the outset and during treatment and may refuse or withdraw from participation in treatment programs.

9. The general consensus among corrections researchers is that some programs work to reduce reoffending among some offenders and that higher risk inmates are more likely to benefit from correctional treatment than low-risk inmates.

10. There is some question as to whether incarceration and institutional programs are effective in reducing the risk/needs levels of offenders.

KEY TERM QUESTIONS

1. Define *classification* and its role in corrections.

2. Compare and contrast *static risk factors* and *need* (or *dynamic*) *risk factors*, and note the role of each type of factor in the classification process.

3. What are *criminogenic risk factors*?

4. Define and discuss the goals of correctional *case management*.

5. What is the *correctional plan* and what role does it play in correctional treatment?

6. Describe the approach and components of the *CSC Integrated Correctional Program Model (ICPM)*.

7. What is meant by (1) *differential treatment effectiveness* and (2) *differential amenability to treatment*, and how does each of these notions contribute to our understanding of correctional treatment for inmates?

8. What are the issues that surround the use of *recidivism rates* as a measure of the success of correctional treatment programs, and what alternatives have been suggested that may more accurately reflect treatment success?

9. What is meant by *differential treatment availability*?

10. Define these concepts—*program fidelity, program drift, therapeutic integrity*, and *throughcare*—and discuss why these concepts are important in the study of correctional treatment.

NOTES

1. S. Poirier (Chair), *Decades of Darkness, Moving Towards the Light: A Review of the Prison System in Newfoundland and Labrador* (St. John's: Government of Newfoundland and Labrador, 2008), 27, http://www.cbc.ca/news/pdf/nl-corrections-report-20081208.pdf2008.

2. G. Harper and C. Chitty, *The Impact of Corrections on Re-Offending: A Review of What Works*, Home Office Research Study 291 (London: Development and Statistics Directorate, Home Office, 2005), http://www.homeoffice.gov.uk/rds/pdfs04/hors291.pdf.

3. Deloitte & Touche, *Report on Nova Scotia's Adult Correctional Facilities* (Halifax: Department of Justice,2008),92,http://www.gov.ns.ca/just/global_docs/Deloitte%20Report%20%-20NS%20Correctional%20Facilities%20Nov08.pdf.

4. G. Taylor, "Implementing Risk and Needs Classification in the Correctional Service of Canada," *Forum on Corrections Research* 9, no. 1 (1997): 32–35.

5. L. Motiuk, *Risk Assessment in Corrections*, paper presented to the Canadian Criminal Justice Association Congress, October 2009, 5, http://www.ccja-acjp.ca/cong2009/en/presentations_en.html.

6. D. Ballucci, "Subverting and Negotiating Risk Assessment: A Case Study of the LSI in a Canadian Youth Custody Facility," *Canadian Journal of Criminology and Criminal Justice* 54, no. 2 (2012): 203–28.

7. D.A. Andrews and J. Bonta, *The Psychology of Criminal Conduct*, 5th ed. (New Providence: Matthew Benders, 2010).

8. M. Dauvergne, *Adult Correctional Services in Canada, 2010–2011* (Ottawa: Minister of Industry, 2012), 12, http://www.statcan.gc.ca/pub/85-002-x/2012001/article/11715-eng.pdf.

9. C.T. Lowenkamp, E.J. Latessa, and P. Smith, "Does Correctional Program Quality Really Matter? The Impact of Adhering to the Principles of Effective Intervention," *Criminology and Public Policy* 5, no. 3 (2006): 575–94.

10. Office of the Correctional Investigator Canada, *Annual Report, 2010–2011* (Ottawa: Office of the Correctional Investigator Canada, 2011), 32, http://www.oci-bec.gc.ca/rpt/annrpt/annrpt20102011-eng.pdf.

11. John Howard Society, "CSC-Integrated Correctional Program Model," *The Bridge*, Spring 2010, http://www.jhslmbc.ca/images/2010Spring.pdf.

12. John Howard Society of the Lower Mainland of British Columbia, *CSC—Integrated Correctional Program Model* (Vancouver: John Howard Society of the Lower Mainland of British Columbia, 2010), http://www.jhslmbc.ca/images/2010Spring.pdf.

13. T. Ward and S. Maruna, *Rehabilitation: Beyond the Risk Paradigm* (New York: Routledge, 2007).

14. C.T. Griffiths, Y. Dandurand, and D. Murdoch, *The Social Reintegration of Offenders and Crime Prevention* (Ottawa: National Crime Prevention Centre, Public Safety Canada, 2007), http://www.publicsafety.gc.ca/res/cp/res/soc-reint-eng.aspx.

15. M. Zbar, "Transformation Update: It's All About Integration," *Let's Talk* 34, no. 1 (2009), http://www.csc-scc.gc.ca/text/pblct/lt-en/2009/34-1/16-eng.shtml.

16. Correctional Service of Canada, *Departmental Performance Report, 2010-2011* (Ottawa: 2011), http://www.tbs-sct.gc.ca/dpr-rmr/2010-2011/inst/pen/pen-eng.pdf.

17. K.L. Nunes, R.K. Hanson, P. Firestone, H.M. Moulden, D.M. Greenberg, and J.M. Bradford, "Denial Predicts Recidivism for Some Sexual Offenders," *Sexual Abuse: A Journal of Research and Treatment* 19, no. 2 (2007): 91–105.

18. Andrews and Bonta, *The Psychology of Criminal Conduct*; J. Bonta and D.A. Andrews, *Risk–Need–Responsivity Model for Offender Assessment and Rehabilitation* (Ottawa: Public Safety Canada, 2007), http://www.publicsafety.gc.ca/res/cor/rep/risk_need_200706-eng.aspx; Office of the Correctional Investigator, *Annual Report*, 44.

19. D. Andrews, "The Psychology of Criminal Conduct and Effective Treatment," in *What Works: Reoffending—Guidelines from Research and Practice*, ed. J. McGuire, 35–62 (Chichester: Wiley, 1995); D.A. Andrews and J. Bonta, *The Psychology of Criminal Conduct*, 5th ed. (New Providence: Matthew Benders, 2010).

20. P. Smith and P. Gendreau, "The Relationship Between Program Participation, Institutional Misconduct, and Recidivism Among Federally Sentenced Adult Male Offenders," *Forum on Corrections Research* 19, no. 1 (2007), http://www.csc-scc.gc.ca/text/pblct/forum/Vol19No1/v19n1-chap2-eng.pdf.

21. J.S. Wormith, "Principles of Effective Correctional Treatment: Musing of a Former Clinician and Administrator," *Forum on Corrections Research* 19, no. 1 (2007), http://www.csc-scc.gc.ca/text/pblct/forum/Vol19No1/v19n1a-eng.shtml.

22. S. Poirier, (Chairperson), *Decades of Darkness, Moving Towards the Light: A Review of the Prison System in Newfoundland and Labrador* (St. John's: Ministry of Justice, 2008), http://www.justice.gov.nl.ca/AC_Report.pdf.

23. T. Carlson, *Judging the Prisons of Newfoundland and Labrador: The Perspectives of Inmates and Ex-Inmates*, 135–188, in S. Poirier, *Decades of Darkness*, 149.

24. A. Day and T. Ward, "Offender Rehabilitation as a Value-Laden Process," *International Journal of Offender Therapy and Comparative Criminology* 54, no. 3 (2010): 289–306.

25. Ibid.

26. Ibid.

27. Carlson, in ibid., 195.

28. K.L. Nunes and F. Cortoni, *The Heterogeneity of Treatment Non-Completers* (Ottawa: Correctional Service of Canada, 2006), http://www.csc-scc.gc.ca/text/rsrch/reports/r176/r176_e.pdf; J.S. Wormith and M.E. Olver, "Offender Treatment Attrition and Its Relationship with Risk, Responsivity, and Recidivism," *Criminal Justice and Behavior* 29, no. 4 (2002): 447–71.

29. Correctional Investigator, *Annual Report, 2010–2011*, 32.

30. D. Luong, C. MacDonald, M. McKay, M. Olotu, S. Heath, N. Allegri, and E. Loree, *Report of the Evaluation of CSC's Community Corrections. Chapter 1: Correctional Interventions* (Ottawa: Correctional Service of Canada, 2011), 52, http://www.csc-scc.gc.ca/text/pa/ev-cci-fin/index-eng.shtml.

31. P. Gendreau, C. Goggin, and P. Smith, "The Forgotten Issue in Effective Correctional Treatment: Program Implementation," *International Journal of Offender Therapy and Comparative Criminology* 43, no. 2 (1999): 180–87; C.T. Lowenkamp, E.J. Latessa, and P. Smith, "Does Correctional Program Quality Really Matter? The Impact of Adhering to the Principles of Effective Intervention," *Criminology and Public Policy* 5, no. 3 (2006): 575–94.

32. P. Smith, P. Gendreau, and K. Swartz, "Validating the Principles of Effective Intervention: A Systematic Review of the Contributions of Meta-Analysis in the Field of Corrections," *Victims and Offenders* 4, no. 2 (2009): 148–69.

33. A.L. Solomon, K.D. Johnson, J. Travis, and E.C. McBride, *From Prison to Work: The Employment Dimensions of Prisoner Reentry* (Washington: Justice Policy Center, Urban Institute, 2004), http://www.urban.org/UploadedPDF/411097_From_Prison_to_Work.pdf.

34. D. Luong, C. MacDonald, M. McKay, M. Olotu, S. Heath, N. Allegri, and E. Loree, *Report of the Evaluation of CSC's Community Corrections. Chapter 1: Correctional Interventions* (Ottawa: Correctional Service of Canada, 2011), 52, http://www.csc-scc.gc.ca/text/pa/ev-cci-fin/index-eng.shtml.

35. C. McKinnon, "The Legal Right of Offenders to Refuse Treatment," *Forum on Corrections Research* 7, no. 3 (1995): 43–47.

36. K.K. Parhar, J.S. Wormith, D.M. Derkzen, and A.M. Beauregard, "Offender Coercion in Treatment: A Meta-Analysis of Effectiveness," *Criminal Justice and Behavior* 35, no. 9 (2008): 1109–35.

37. Office of the Auditor General of Ontario, *Annual Report, 2008* (Toronto: Office of the Auditor General of Ontario, 2008), http://www.auditor.on.ca/en/reports_2008_en.htm.

38. R.M. Martinson, "What Works? Questions and Answers About Prison Reform," *Public Interest* 35 (1974): 22–54; idem, "New Findings, New Views: A Note of Caution Regarding Sentencing Reform," *Hofstra Law Review* 7 (1979): 243–58.

39. Adapted from Office of the Correctional Investigator, *Annual Report, 2010–2011*, 33.

40. P. Smith, P. Gendreau, and K. Swartz, "Validating the Principles of Effective Intervention: A Systematic Review of the Contributions of Meta-Analysis in the Field of Corrections," *Victims and Offenders* 4, no. 2 (2009): 148–69.

PART IV

RETURNING TO THE COMMUNITY: RELEASE AND REENTRY

One of the most important decisions in the criminal justice system is when to release an offender from custody and what conditions will be attached to the release. Chapter 11 discusses the purpose and principles of conditional release, the various release options available to offenders, and the various issues that surround the decision making of parole boards. The decision to release an inmate from custody is often more art than science, and there is significant pressure on parole boards to balance the interests of the offender with the protection of the community.

Chapter 12 examines reintegration and the challenges that offenders experience when reentering the community. Like their probation officer counterparts, parole officers must balance the dual roles of providing assistance and maintaining surveillance. There are special challenges in supervising high-needs/high-risk special offenders on parole. Many offenders returning to the community were marginal before their incarceration and will experience considerable difficulties finding their way in the absence of supports and services. Adjustment to life in the outside community may be made even more challenging by negative responses from community residents and the media. Restorative justice approaches, including circles of support and accountability, are evidence that the community can be mobilized in proactive ways to help offenders and reduce their risk of reoffending.

CHAPTER 11

RELEASE FROM INCARCERATION

CHAPTER OBJECTIVES

After reading this chapter, you should be able to:
- *Discuss the purpose and principles of conditional release.*
- *Identify the types of conditional release.*
- *Discuss the release options for provincial/territorial and federal inmates.*
- *Define statutory release and the detainment practice known as detention during the period of statutory release.*
- *Discuss the changing face of conditional release in Canada.*
- *Describe the issues surrounding crime victims and conditional release.*
- *Describe the dynamics of parole board decision making and the issues that surround it.*

It was noted in the opening pages of this text that nearly everyone who is sent to a correctional institution will eventually be released. Most inmates are released sooner rather than later in their sentence. It is the small percentage of offenders who receive sentences of two years or more who present the greatest challenges. This chapter examines the decisions surrounding the timing and conditions of conditional release.

THE ORIGINS OF EARLY RELEASE

The practice of releasing offenders before the end of their sentence—today called *conditional release*—originated in the days when English convicts were transported to penal colonies in Australia. For centuries, the only avenue for early release had been to petition the king or queen for a Royal Prerogative of Mercy. That is, the monarch could grant a pardon or remission for humanitarian reasons or because the severity of the sentence far exceeded the severity of the crime.

The work of 19th-century penal reformers such as Alexander Maconochie was rooted in the observation that the harsh and brutalizing conditions in prisons did little to encourage convicts to be good citizens and, in fact, did much to ensure that they would become hardened criminals.

Maconochie was the superintendent of Norfolk Island (off the coast of Australia), a penal colony where offenders thought to be incorrigible and irredeemable were sent. He developed a "mark system" whereby a day's labour earned the offender 10 marks, and 10 marks shortened the sentence by 1 day. A day's rations and supplies cost between 3 and 5 marks, so inmates could earn 1 day toward early release for every 2 days of work.

In the 1890s, some jurisdictions in Canada began adopting indeterminate sentences and the mark system for juvenile offenders. For adults, reforms found expression in the concept of "ticket of leave." The Act to Provide for the Conditional Liberation of Penitentiary Convicts, known as the Ticket of Leave Act, was passed in 1899. This legislation allowed federal convicts to be at large from prison under specified conditions.

The Prison Gate Section of the Salvation Army undertook to help those on tickets of leave, there being no equivalents to the modern-day parole officers to supervise and assist reintegrating offenders. The first Dominion parole officer, a brigadier in the Salvation Army, was appointed in 1905.

An enormous change to the parole system occurred after a commission of inquiry in the mid-1950s.[1] The commission wanted an independent body affiliated with neither the penal system nor government to make release decisions. The National Parole Board, now known as the Parole Board of Canada, came into being with the passage of the Parole Act in 1959.

THE PURPOSE AND PRINCIPLES OF CONDITIONAL RELEASE

Section 100 of the Corrections and Conditional Release Act (CCRA) states:

> *The purpose of conditional release is to contribute to the maintenance of a just, peaceful and safe society by means of decisions on the timing and conditions of release that will best facilitate the rehabilitation of offenders and their reintegration into the community as law-abiding citizens.*

The act also sets out a number of principles to be followed by parole boards (as well as by the CSC when that agency makes release decisions) in pursuing the objectives of conditional release. These include that the protection of society is the primary consideration in every case and that the board must consider all relevant case information when making decisions. All parole decisions are predictive.

Release on parole is not a statutory right—it is a privilege. Although inmates have the right to apply for parole when eligible, there are no guarantees that an application will succeed.

With respect to the conditional releases decided by parole boards, Section 102 of the CCRA states:

> *The Board or a provincial parole board may grant parole to an offender if, in its opinion,*

> (a) *The offender will not, by reoffending, present an undue risk to society before the expiration according to law of the sentence the offender is serving; and*
>
> (b) *The release of the offender will contribute to the protection of society by facilitating the reintegration of the offender into society as a law-abiding citizen.*

The process of determining which inmates qualify for conditional release is forward looking, asking two basic questions: (1) If released, will the inmate commit an offence that he or she would not have committed if kept in confinement? (2) Will conditional release with supervision reduce the risk for reoffending compared to a **cold turkey release** with no supervision? Parole decision making can best be described as an inexact science: It is often difficult to be certain how offenders will respond if released into the community.

THE TYPES OF CONDITIONAL RELEASE

The specific conditional release options available to an inmate depend on the length of the sentence and on whether he or she is under the supervision and control of a provincial/territorial or federal system of corrections. Because the guidelines are broad, parole board members have considerable discretion in making decisions to grant or deny parole and may choose to disregard risk assessments.

The release of an offender from custody can occur at one of three points in the sentence: (1) the parole eligibility date, for either day parole or full parole; (2) the "statutory release" date, which is usually at the two-thirds point in a sentence; or (3) the **warrant expiry date**, which marks the end of the sentence imposed by the court.

The premise of conditional release programs is that the likelihood of recidivism is reduced if the offender is reintegrated back into the community under supervision. The absence of research studies, however, makes it difficult to determine the validity of that assumption.

Figure 11.1 illustrates the sentencing milestones for federal offenders. The release options for federal and provincial/territorial inmates are set out in Box 11.1.

Judicial Recognizances for Sex Offenders

Federal sex offenders not released on either parole or statutory release remain in custody until warrant expiry. These offenders are then released "cold turkey" and are not required to inform law enforcement or correctional agencies of their location. One response to this problem has been the use of community notification, discussed in Chapter 12. Another is the use of Section 810.1 of the Criminal Code to force the individual to enter into a **judicial recognizance**, often referred to in this context as a peace bond.

Cold turkey release
The discharge of an offender at the end of their sentence when no conditional release or supervision is possible, such as when an offender has served his or her entire sentence in custody or provincial/territorial offenders are released at the two-thirds point in their sentence.

Warrant expiry date
The end of an offender's sentence.

Judicial recognizance
An order of the court, often referred to as a peace bond, that requires the offender (most often sex offenders) to adhere to set conditions beyond the expiry of their sentence, including most often avoiding places where there are children.

Figure 11.1

Sentencing Milestones

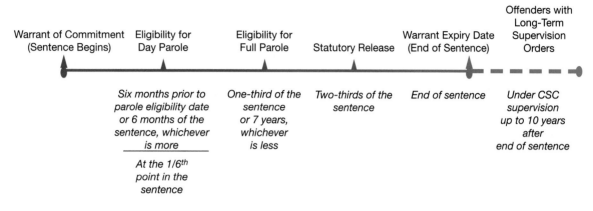

Sentencing Milestones for Federal Offenders (Fixed Sentences)

Warrant of Commitment (Sentence Begins)	Eligibility for Day Parole	Eligibility for Full Parole	Statutory Release	Warrant Expiry Date (End of Sentence)	Offenders with Long-Term Supervision Orders
	Six months prior to parole eligibility date or 6 months of the sentence, whichever is more	One-third of the sentence or 7 years, whichever is less	Two-thirds of the sentence	End of sentence	Under CSC supervision up to 10 years after end of sentence
	At the 1/6th point in the sentence				

Source: A Road Map to Strengthening Public Safety, http://www.publicsafety.gc.ca/csc-scc/cscrprprt-eng.pdf. (Correctional Service of Canada, 2007). Reproduced with the permission of the Minister of Public Works and Government Services Canada, 2013.

BOX 11.1

Release Options for Federal and Provincial/Territorial Inmates

Type of Release	Federal	Provincial/Territorial
Temporary Absences	Usually the first type of release granted; escorted (ETA) or unescorted (UTA); for medical, family, employment, education purposes	Most common type of release
Eligibility	ETA anytime; UTA varies with length and type of sentence; maximum security inmates not eligible for UTAs; sentences of 3 years or more: may apply for UTA after serving one-sixth of sentence; sentences of 2–3 years: may apply for UTA 6 months into sentence; life sentences: may apply for UTA 3 years before full parole eligibility date	Varies; in some jurisdictions inmate can apply immediately; others require waiting period May require EM

Temporary absence
A type of conditional release that allows an inmate to participate in community activities, including employment and education, while residing in a minimum security facility or halfway house.

(continued)

Day parole
The authority granted by a parole board that provides an opportunity for inmates to be at large in order to prepare for full release (e.g., for job search) while returning at night to an institution or, more typically, to a community residential facility.

Full parole
The authority granted by a parole board for an inmate to be at large under supervision in the community for the remainder of his or her sentence.

Statutory release
A provision that allows incarcerated federal offenders to be released at the two-thirds point in their sentence (unless the CSC makes the decision to recommend to the PBC that the offender be detained) and to serve the remaining one-third of their sentence under supervision in the community.

Type of Release	Federal	Provincial/Territorial
Day Parole	Prepares offender for release on full parole by allowing participation in community-based activities; offender must return nightly to an institution or halfway house unless otherwise authorized by the PBC or provincial parole boards.	
Eligibility	Sentences of 2 to 3 years: may apply after serving 6 months of sentence; sentences of 3 years or more: may apply for day parole 6 months prior to full parole eligibility; life sentences: eligible to apply 3 years before full parole eligibility date	Inmates may apply after serving one-sixth of their sentence
Full Parole	Provides an opportunity for offenders to serve remainder of the sentence under supervision in the community; parolee must report to a parole supervisor on a regular basis and abide by conditions	
Eligibility	After serving one-third of sentence (except for offenders serving life sentences for murder); after 25 years if serving a life sentence for first degree murder; between 10 and 25 years (set by judge at sentencing) for offenders serving life sentences for second degree murder	Inmates may apply after serving one-third of their sentence
Statutory Release	Provides for offenders who have not been granted parole or not applied for parole to be released to serve the remainder of their sentence under the supervision of a parole officer; a decision of CSC, not the PBC;[a] not available to offenders designated as Dangerous Offenders	Not available for provincial/territorial inmates who may serve their entire sentence in custody, minus **remission** that is earned at a rate of 1 day for every two days served and allows for discharge from the institution

Eligibility	By law, for most federal offenders after serving two-thirds of their sentence (if not released on parole); offenders serving life or indeterminate sentences not eligible; CSC may recommend that an offender be denied statutory release if it believes the offender is likely to (a) commit an offence causing death or serious harm to another person; (b) commit a sexual offence against a child; or (c) commit a serious drug offence before the end of the sentence[b]	Unless the offender has a probation order, there will be no supervision upon release

[a] PBC may attach residency requirements if the offender poses a risk to reoffend.

[b] PBC may detain the offender; this is **Detention During the Period of Statutory Release**; inmates detained in this manner will have their case reviewed on an annual basis.

Source: National Parole Board, Fact Sheet: Types of Release. http://pbc-clcc.gc.ca/infocntr/factsh/rls-eng.shtml. (Parole Board of Canada, 2010). Reproduced with the permission of the Minister of Public Works and Government Services Canada, 2013.

Remission/discharge
Available to provincial/territorial inmates who have served two-thirds of their sentence (often referred to as *cold turkey release* as there is no supervision by a parole officer).

Detention during the period of statutory release
A decision by the Parole Board of Canada (after an application by the CSC) that a federal inmate be denied statutory release and be detained in the institution until Warrant Expiry Date.

Judicial recognizance is most commonly used with pedophiles who have reached warrant expiry but who remain at a very high risk of offending against children under 16.[2] The applicant—who can be a police officer—need only have reasonable grounds to fear that the subject of the order may commit one of the designated offences in the near future. In other words—and this is somewhat unique in legal terms—it is applied proactively for offences that *may* be committed rather than in reaction to offences that *have* been committed.

The application is heard in a Provincial Court, where the judge can order the subject to enter into a recognizance to comply with set conditions, which can include a prohibition from engaging in any activity that involves contact with persons under 16. For example, the subject will not be permitted to visit a day care centre, schoolyard, playground, or any public park or swimming area where children are present or can reasonably be expected to be present. This order can be in effect for up to 12 months. A person who refuses to enter into the recognizance can be sent to prison for up to 12 months for the refusal, and an offender who violates a condition of the order commits an offence for which he or she is liable for up to two years in prison.

Section 810 raises the issue of how to balance the rights of ex-offenders with the need to protect the community.

Pre-Release Planning

Pre-release planning is an important part of the inmate's correctional plan and is directed toward managing the risk posed by offenders and, ideally, toward providing access to programs and services in the community. Despite its importance in the correctional process, pre-release planning is often minimal in provincial/territorial institutions. A small sample (N = 12) of provincial inmates in Nova Scotia, some of whom had also served federal time, found that they did not feel they were prepared for release. One respondent commented: "Because there is no support, you're back on the street and then soon back in the system."[3] The inmates indicated that there was no pre-release planning, and no information provided on support services in the community, and that they were not generally aware of the assistance that was available to them. There may also be a lack of pre-release planning for inmates with particular challenges, such as mental illness. This hinders successful reintegration into the community upon release.[4]

Federal inmates, who are incarcerated for longer periods of time than their provincial counterparts, have greater access to pre-release assistance. These inmates tend to be released in stages, beginning with escorted or unescorted temporary absences. Long-term studies have found that certain types of offenders who are gradually released from prison on conditional release are more likely to become law-abiding citizens than those who stay in prison until the end of their sentence.[5]

AT ISSUE

Issue 11.1: Statutory Release

Should statutory release be abolished?

While 60 percent of offenders on SR successfully complete their period of supervision, offenders on SR are responsible for nearly 80 percent of violent reoffending in the community.* Supporters contend that SR provides supervision for high-risk offenders that would not be available if they served their entire sentence in custody. Critics of SR point to the high rates of violent reoffending among offenders released on SR as evidence that it neither contributes to the rehabilitation of offenders nor protects the community and that offenders "play the clock" until the two-thirds mark of their sentence, cause disruptions in the prison, and are not motivated to participate in treatment programs. In your view, should SR be abolished?

* R. Sampson (Chair), *Report of the Correctional Service of Canada Review Panel* (Ottawa: Minister of Public Works and Government Services Canada, 2007), http://www.publicsafety.gc.ca/csc-scc/cscrprprt -eng.pdf.

The Changing Face of Conditional Release

Statistics indicate that conditional release is being used less often than in previous years. There have been steady decreases in the number of offenders granted temporary absence permits and in the grant rates for federal day parole (62 percent grant rate in 2010–2011, down 4 percent from the previous year) and full parole (39 percent, down 2 percent from the previous year).[6] See Figures 11.2 and 11.3.

Figure 11.2

Grant Rates for Federal and Provincial Day Parole, 2006–2007 to 2010–2011

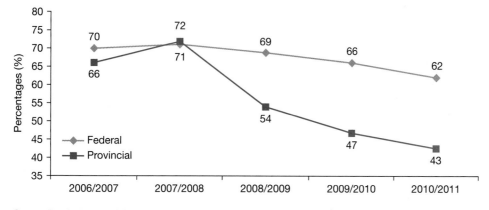

Source: Parole Board of Canada, *Performance Monitoring Report 2010/2011.* Found at: http://pbc-clcc.gc .ca/rprts/pmr/pmr_2010_2011/pmr_2010_2011-eng.pdf. (Parole Board of Canada, 2012). Reproduced with the permission of the Minister of Public Works and Government Services Canada, 2013.

Figure 11.3

Grant Rates for Federal and Provincial Full Parole, 2006–2007 to 2010–2011

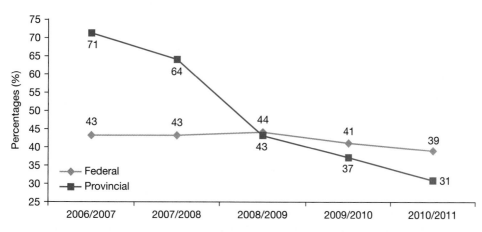

Source: Parole Board of Canada, *Performance Monitoring Report 2010/2011.* Found at: http://pbc-clcc.gc .ca/rprts/pmr/pmr_2010_2011/pmr_2010_2011-eng.pdf. (Parole Board of Canada, 2012). Reproduced with the permission of the Minister of Public Works and Government Services Canada, 2013.

In 2012 the PBC full parole grant rate was the lowest in 30 years.[7] That year, female offenders were more likely to succeed with their day parole applications, while black offenders were the least likely. Federal Aboriginal offenders were the least successful in obtaining full parole, while black offenders had the lowest grant rate for provincial full parole. The reasons for these disparities in grant rates have yet to be explored.[8]

Changes in legislation have also affected conditional release. For example, accelerated parole review has been abolished. Such reviews had been a mechanism for releasing nonviolent federal offenders from custody after one-sixth of sentence for first-time federal offenders unlikely to commit a violent crime.

Given how very recent these changes have been, it is difficult to determine what impact they will have on prison populations, corrections costs, and rates of reoffending. What *is* clear is that there is an increasing emphasis on punishment rather than rehabilitation and that there are ever fewer opportunities for conditional release.[9] Low grant rates for parole strongly suggest a "get tough" approach; they also indicate that parole boards have become more risk-averse in their decision making.[10] In a significant number of cases—nearly 15 percent regarding day parole, and 8 percent regarding full parole—the PBC has overridden the CSC's own recommendation that parole be granted.[11]

VICTIMS AND CONDITIONAL RELEASE

The role of crime victims in the conditional release process has been tenuous. Except in Québec, the victim of the offence committed by the inmate-applicant may observe the hearing and make a statement in person, in writing, or by pre-recorded video.

It is not common for victims to submit statements to parole boards or to attend hearings. The Ontario Parole Board heard 1,063 cases in 2011–2012; victim impact statements were submitted in only 53 of them, and victims attended only 16 parole hearings.[12] This is quite dissimilar to restorative justice approaches, where the victim is a key player in the discussions.

The institution where the parole hearing is held may be a considerable distance from the victim's home, or the victim may not have access to a victim support worker. Most victims have little knowledge of the parole process or of how hearings are conducted. Besides this, it can also be very intimidating for them to sit in a hearing room with the offender present and to speak candidly about the offender's potential release. The victim may fear reprisals if and when the offender is released. For these and a variety of other reasons, some victims choose to make a written submission to the parole board to be considered during the hearing; a smaller number submit videotaped statements for parole board members to view. Box 11.2 presents an excerpt from a victim's written submission to a parole board.

BOX 11.2

Excerpts from a Victim's Written Submission to a Parole Board

I have just received notification that [   ], if granted parole, will be released as soon as [   ]. I am writing this letter to express my opposition to his parole. I am the victim of the crimes for which [Mr.   ] was convicted. I was in an on-off relationship with [Mr.   ] that spanned for six months. During that time he was severely emotionally abusive and increasingly physically abusive. My last encounter with him resulted in a serious concussion, multiple bruises and lacerations and my fleeing the province. Several incidents prior to that last one also resulted in physical injury of varying severity. The emotional wounds were far more severe and it took a long time for me to recover from them.

If [Mr.   ] claims that he must be released from the correctional facility to receive treatment he is merely being manipulative. I am absolutely certain that [Mr.   ] will re-offend. I believe that he should, at least, fulfill his entire sentence. I believe that the more time he is kept from society, then the safer it will be. It is only a matter of time before he will appear before the courts again. If [Mr.   ] is released early, then it will re-affirm to him that he is able to act inappropriately without any significant fear of punishment.

Source: Anonymous. Provided to the authors.

To share information with crime victims regarding the movement and release of their perpetrators, the CSC operates a National Victim Services Program. This program provides registered crime victims with updated information on the offender's status, notifications of parole board hearings, and release dates and conditions. An evaluation of the program found that it was succeeding in its objectives.[13] Similar programs are operated by provincial/territorial systems of corrections, but the effectiveness of these initiatives is unknown.

THE PAROLE FILE

In its deliberations, the parole board considers a number of documents contained in the inmate-applicant's parole file. These generally include, but are not limited to, police reports, an official record of convictions, reports from institutional staff on the inmate's behaviour and performance, victim impact statements, pre-sentence reports, letters of support, and a community assessment (CA) prepared by a probation or parole officer.

"Bad news. The mailman is going to attend the parole-board hearing."

Community assessment

A document prepared by probation or parole officers for the parole board and containing information on the feasibility of the inmate-applicant's proposed community plan in terms of the level of supervision required, employment/residential/education plans, and the availability of community resources.

A key document in the parole file is the **community assessment (CA)**, which is prepared by parole officers (probation/parole officers in Québec and Ontario). The CA is best described as an investigation to evaluate the feasibility of the inmate-applicant's proposed community plan in terms of the level of supervision required and the availability of community resources. The CA (or Pre-Parole Report) typically includes input from the police as well as the inmate's response to previous corrections interventions (including community supervision), if any. And it includes information about family relationships and friendship networks; proposed treatment or counselling programs; and an assessment of the components of the proposed release plan, including the proposed residence and education/employment activities. The CA may recommend that special conditions be attached to the release certificate that will help manage the level of risk the offender poses to the community.

Many offenders find it a challenge to develop a viable release plan. Family support may be lacking, and there may be no arrangements for employment or accommodation. Also, access to specialized community-based treatment programs for addiction, sex offending, and mental health issues may be limited, particularly for provincial/territorial inmates and for offenders from rural and remote communities. Because many treatment programs will not accept offenders who have a history of violence, it is often difficult to ensure throughcare for high-risk offenders.

THE DYNAMICS OF PAROLE BOARD DECISION MAKING

A Journalist's Observations of the Parole Board of Canada, Ontario Region

Like Santa, a parole board is supposed to know who's been good or bad, and so by the time the hearing arrives parole panelists (called directors) already know more about the prisoner than they perhaps care to—and a lot of it is not very nice.

On this particular day, three board directors—former prison warden Kenneth Payne, career correctional-service employee Sheila Henriksen, and social worker John Brothers—have the final say.

Armed with documents describing the parole-seeker's criminal history, psychological assessments, education, family situation, other relationships, behaviour while in prison and the recommendation from Correctional Services Canada, the members try to evaluate what risk these individuals pose to society and determine if that risk is manageable in the community.

The first up to bat on this day is a 36-year-old Kingston man who was sentenced to life on a charge of second-degree murder for killing a friend in a dispute over a woman.

At 8:30 a.m., the slight, frail-looking man is waiting outside the hearing with his case management officer and a university law student as the morning announcements play over the intercom. The atmosphere is weirdly like high school.

When the door to the hearing room opens, the brief window of opportunity has arrived that the convict has been waiting for—make-or-break time. The parole panel will soon begin its grueling interview. No holds are barred, and no part of a convict's life is off limits.

Sitting a couple of metres from the convicts, looking them in the face, panel members have to sift through what they're hearing and judge what is sincere and what is contrived, remembering that people seldom get to this point in their lives by being totally honest.

The members take in the convict's appearance and mannerisms, dissect his answers, ask questions in different ways to get a better read and compare the answers to facts provided by the professions.

They often caution the convicts against lying, because their replies must be consistent with what's in their files.

This morning, the murderer from Kingston slouches, his hair slicked back tightly like people wore in the 1950s. He is wearing dark clothes, a tweed sports jacket and unmatching light-coloured socks.

The case management officer sits at a table to his left. Right as the hearing starts, the convict withdraws his application for full parole. He says day parole will suffice.

The man has spent time in a number of jails and prisons since the murder. He stares straight ahead as the case management officer outlines his criminal record, all of it minor and non-violent up to the killing. He also relates how the convict was granted full parole twice, in 1992 and again in 1995, and violated it both times.

A doctor's report rates the probability he will reoffend within a year of release at 40 per cent, saying he suffers from an anti-social personality disorder.

A panel member asks why he withdrew his application for full parole. In a low, frail voice, the convict states the obvious: "In a realistic view, I don't think you guys would send me to full parole."

A member jokes, "You have already done some of our work for us." Mr. Payne asks the convict about the bad choices he has made through his life, and there are many. The convict says his worst was getting involved in a relationship with the woman he killed for and, as he puts it, his "negative thinking."

The focus shifts to what he might have learned from his failures. "I needed to change the way I view things," the convict says. "I used to go through distorted thinking patterns. I have a problem over-complicating things. I used to take on other people's problems and make them my own."

In discussing an anger-management course he has just repeated, he is asked: "When was the last time you felt really angry?" "When I got the letter from the parole board that media would be at my hearing," he answers. He adds, "Nothing personal," as he turns toward the observers behind him.

Asked about the killing, the convict says he doesn't recognize the man who did it, that there are "some pretty blank spots surrounding that time."

Ms. Henriksen questions his integrity. "I have got a sense you have an ability to fool people," she says. He replies: "Sitting in the position I am in, it doesn't seem right for me to say, 'Trust me.'"

But the board chooses to trust him anyway. Following brief deliberations it grants the man once-a-month [unescorted temporary absences]. If he does well on those, the next step will be day parole and then full parole without any further hearing.

"The board is satisfied you have benefited from our programs," says Mr. Payne.

The convict thanks the directors and, as he leaves, passes the bank robber waiting outside. And the process repeats itself.

The day ends with the case of the Stratford father, a 29-year-old first time offender who smashed up his truck after a night of partying and nearly killed his passenger. His sentence was two years for criminal negligence causing bodily harm. He has served about a year.

If there is a common thread among these convicts it is the way they handle stress: Drugs and alcohol are their mainstays.

Oddly enough, the convict doesn't do a very good job of selling his case. Lucky for him it sells itself.

The case management officer gives an exemplary report on his prison behaviour, noting he attends night school and wants to pursue a trade in college.

The convict shakes as he appears before the panel members, who at times try to relax him.

One thing that works against him is a compelling victim impact statement. The victim is suing the convict. "I know he's mad but I have gone and tried to talk with him and all he does is yell at me or make rude gestures when he drives by," the convict explains. "I just wish it was me who got injured that night."

"All I know is I have two young kids I haven't seen in a month and I want to get back to them," says the man. "I can't wait."

Another quick verdict: immediate full parole. The directors deliver their judgment. And then they just hope.

Source: D. Campbell, "A Journalist Goes to Prison to See for Himself How Parole Boards Decide Which Convicts Are Good Risks and Which Ones Are Not," *Ottawa Citizen*, November 3, 1997, A3.

Video Link
A Day in the Life of a Parole Board Member
pbc–clss.gc.ca/org/ bmlife-eng.shtml

Parole board decision making is an inexact science. Parole hearings are usually presided over by two board members and are generally convened at the institution where the inmate is being held. In federal parole hearings, the inmate-applicant is accompanied by his or her case manager, who serves as an assistant.

Before the hearing, the board members review the parole file and make notes on key points. During the hearing, the board members ask the inmate about the release plan (and other questions) to ascertain suitability for release. The board may pay a great deal of attention to the inmate's version of the offence, looking for some insight into why it was committed and why it would not happen again. (The inmate's participation in treatment programs and skills/trades training, as well as any other positive steps taken while in custody, are key factors here.) Board members are interested in the insights the offender has gained about the offence, the decisions that led to the criminal behaviour, and the steps the offender has taken to address the issues that were associated with the criminal activity. Often, this involves addressing issues related to alcohol or drug abuse, anger management, or life skills. Indications of remorse and of empathy for the victim are considered important by board members. The file review and the interview are meant to determine whether the offender can be managed at an acceptable level of risk in the community.

To conduct an effective interview with the inmate-applicant, the board members must be aware of their own biases and avoid moralizing. As well, they must appreciate the pressure that is on the inmate-applicant. Most applicants appear without assistants or family members present and may have limited verbal skills. Parole boards are administrative tribunals, not courts of law. That said, the onus is on these boards to be fair, and they must follow specific procedures (see the grounds for appeal, discussed below). Lawyers may attend hearings on the inmate's behalf, but there is no provision for the adversarial approaches found in criminal courts. Lawyers may provide additional information to the board and/or speak in support of the inmate's application.

After the interview, the inmate is asked to wait outside the hearing room while the members deliberate and decide. The inmate returns to the room to be told the outcome—whether the release has been granted, or denied, or deferred pending the gathering of additional information. If it has been denied, specific reasons must be given so that the inmate can understand how to increase the likelihood of success if another application is made—for example, by participating in a treatment program, completing a program already in progress, or developing a different release plan. For instance, if the plan had been to live with friends who might not be a good influence, the board might recommend that the inmate secure alternative, more suitable accommodations. Provincial parole boards in Ontario and Québec follow a decision-making process similar to that of the PBC, except that victims who attend hearings of the Québec board cannot make oral statements to the board.

If the parole board determines that the level of risk the inmate-applicant presents is not manageable in the community, the application for release on day parole or full parole will be denied. A decision of the Ontario Parole Board to grant parole is presented in Appendix 11.1.

Many provincial/territorial inmates do not apply for parole; instead, they serve out their sentences in custody. These inmates are eligible to be released after serving two-thirds of their time in custody, at their remission/discharge date. In contrast to federal offenders, provincial/territorial inmates remission/discharge release are not supervised by parole officers. Provincial parole boards often must decide between releasing an offender on parole who may present a risk, or whose plan is not optimal, or having the inmate leave at their remission/discharge date and reenter the community with no plan or supervision.

Another concern is that in jurisdictions where the PBC is responsible for provincial/territorial parole hearings (i.e., everywhere but Ontario and Québec, which operate their own provincial parole boards), "paper decisions" are common and there is no hearing. This denies inmate-applicants the opportunity to meet face to face with the board and discuss their application. It also denies the victims of crime the chance to appear before the parole board and to discuss the impact of the crime and to offer their opinion on the application.

The decision of a parole board to release an inmate back into the community is, along with the verdict of the Criminal Court, perhaps the most important decision that is made in the correctional process. Yet little attention has been given to the composition of parole boards, the relationship between member characteristics and conditional release decisions, how board members use the information contained in offender case files, and the consequences of decisions for the offender, the victims, and the community.

Video Link
Virtual Hearing: A Parole Board of Canada (PBC) Hearing Room
pbc–clss.gc.ca/ hearing/index –eng.shtml

THE PAROLE CERTIFICATE

If parole is granted, a certificate of parole is prepared. The **parole certificate** contains both mandatory conditions and additional ones. Mandatory conditions include reporting regularly to a parole officer, obeying the law, and securing permission from the supervising parole officer prior to leaving a specified geographic area.

Parole certificate
A document that contains the mandatory and, often, additional conditions of a conditional release.

The parole board may add additional conditions to the parole certificate to address issues specific to the offender. These conditions may require the parolee to participate in a treatment program, to maintain employment, and not to have contact with certain persons. Sex offenders may have prohibitions against being alone with children or residing within a certain distance of a school or playground. The board can also direct that the offender live in a community residential facility or other approved residence. A parole certificate issued by the Ontario Parole Board and Earned Release Board is presented in Appendix 11.2.

THE INMATE AND PAROLE HEARINGS

For inmates applying for conditional release, the appearance before the parole board can be stressful, intimidating, and anxiety-provoking. Even inmates who have previously appeared before a parole board are uncertain what questions will be asked and how individual board members will weigh the information contained in the parole file and the responses provided by the inmate during the interview. There are often great socioeconomic disparities between board members and inmates; there may also be cultural differences (including language barriers) that make it difficult for board members and the inmate to communicate. Many inmates have little or no understanding of the parole board's role and may be intimidated by the more sophisticated language skills of board members. Parole board members, for their part, may not realize that the inmate-applicant is mentally disordered or is still in withdrawal following a relapse into drug use while on conditional release.

Inmates have only a short time to make their case to the board. Most likely, they have never seen the board members before and never will again. They are allowed to have legal representation or other persons in attendance for support, but in many provinces, legal aid will not pay for lawyers to attend board hearings. So most parole applicants appear on their own.

Board members can ask the inmate-applicant literally anything. The questions may relate to past criminal activities and convictions, the present offence, and participation in treatment programs. Also within bounds are more personal questions about family members and current friendships. For most inmates who plead guilty in Criminal Court, this is the first time they have been asked detailed questions about their crimes, their personal history, and their future intentions. The severe time constraints under which many parole boards operate place an added burden on both board members and the inmate-applicant, and this may lead to superficial coverage of some topics.

Some inmate-applicants play the parole "game"—that is, they manipulate the system to create the impression that they addressing their issues and moving toward a law-abiding life. There is more knowledge of the role of the parole board and of the dynamics of parole hearings among federal offenders who have served multiple terms in custody. A lifer on parole who had appeared before the parole board on many occasions offered the following opinion:

> *Parole hearings for me now are old hat. I know how to present myself, what to do, what they want to hear, why they want to hear it. I have a good understanding of what their role is, and what they think their role is and how to approach that ... I think they have a really difficult job in trying to gauge the threat to society of the people who are there. They're responsible for the decisions they make. Just looking at a file doesn't give you a very good indicator of who people are. But if you put a person in a stressful situation and crank them up a bit and see how they react and see how they handle a situation, then you get a pretty good view of who that person is. I think the board does that quite often ... If you're able to handle yourself in those situations and still be able to supply the things that are necessary, and make them feel comfortable with the idea of actually letting the person out, then you've done your job as a presenter to the board of your case.*[14]

AT ISSUE

Issue 11.2: Parole

Should parole be abolished?

Many American states have abolished parole, replacing it with fixed sentences. The majority of offenders are released at the two-thirds point of their sentence. High-risk offenders are generally required to be under supervision, including GPS monitoring for sex offenders. Proponents of parole argue that it provides a way to reintegrate offenders back into the community under the supervision of a parole officer who can help the offender access programs and services. Also, that the discretionary decisions of parole boards can be improved with the appointment of persons with specialized professional competence. Critics of parole contend that abolishing the parole board eliminates uncertainty and discretionary decision making, which may be politically influenced, and that there is no evidence that jurisdictions without parole have higher rates of reoffending than those with parole. What additional arguments could be made in support of, or in opposition to, parole? Which arguments do you find most persuasive?

INMATE APPEALS

Section 147 of the CCRA sets out a number of grounds for appeal by the inmate-applicant. Parole boards are not courts of law, but they are bound by policies relating to administrative tribunals. In cases where the proper procedures are not followed, the inmate may have grounds for an appeal. The appeal division may reverse or vary the decision.

A review of successful appeals of PBC decisions culled these reasons for their being modified: the board failed to provide reasons for the decision; it relied on false or incomplete information; it failed in its duty to act fairly (e.g., it was rude and disrespectful to the inmate-applicant); it used information that had not been shared with the offender; and it acted with bias toward the applicant.[15]

ISSUES IN PAROLE BOARD DECISION MAKING

A number of issues surround parole board decision making, including the following:

Boards May Be Subject to Public and Political Influence

Parole board members are appointed by governments, and positions on parole boards have long been patronage appointments—that is, rewards for supporters of the government. Members are not required by legislation to have any special training or expertise in law, criminology, psychology, or corrections. As concerns about risk management increase along with negative publicity over high-visibility crimes committed by offenders on conditional release, this is likely to affect the PBC's decision making.[16]

A notable trend on the PBC is the appointment of retired police officers as parole board members. Some observers contend that this is meant to inject more conservatism into the board's decision making. Critics argue that it is yet another expression of the federal government's "get tough" approach to crime. Proponents of parole have argued that there is a need to staff parole boards with persons with specialized competence.[17] See At Issue 11.3.

There is little doubt that the move toward punitive penology in Canada has had a significant impact on the provisions for releasing offenders from correctional institutions. That same shift also seems to be affecting the decision making of provincial parole boards and the PBC. Overall, rates of conditional release have been declining. The Ontario board grants parole in around 30 percent of the cases it hears; the grant rate of Québec's provincial parole board is just under 50 percent.[18]

The Absence of Clearly Defined Release Criteria

One criticism often levelled against parole boards is that too much discretion has been vested in nonjudicial, unscrutinized decision makers. Board members have access to a great deal of information on each inmate-applicant—including police reports, pre-sentence reports, the presiding judge's reasons for the sentence, materials produced by case managers (including risk/needs assessments), and parole officers' CAs—yet it is often difficult for them to prioritize this information.

AT ISSUE

Issue 11.3: Politics and Justice

Should justice ever be political?

Addressing the appointment of ex-police officers to the PBC, an opinion piece in the *Ottawa Citizen* stated: "What is troubling about the appointment is the apparent attempt to create a perception that the current federal government is going to be tough on prospective parolees by putting their fate in the hands of enforcement-minded individuals ... The integrity and impartiality of our quasi-judicial tribunals must transcend the government of the day and remain unassailable from partisan political influence."* How would you respond to this editorial? Also, should persons appointed to parole boards have certain qualifications? If yes, what types of qualifications?

* J. Morton and M. M. Persaud, "Justice Shouldn't be Political," *Ottawa Citizen*, February 23, 2011, A13.

This lack of guidance, combined with the discretion exercised by board members, can result in individual styles of decision making that may, in turn, lead to disparity in decisions on applications for conditional release between boards as well as among board members, even within the same jurisdiction. Whether a particular inmate-applicant is successful may depend upon which board members happen to be sitting at the hearing.

The Absence of Case Information Feedback to Parole Board Members

Few if any mechanisms are in place for parole board members to receive feedback on the outcomes of their decisions—that is, on what happens to offenders while they are under supervision in the community and after warrant expiry and the end of supervision. This prevents individual board members from developing their knowledge of the factors that may facilitate, or hinder, successful reintegration with the community. Generally, parole board members learn of an inmate's behaviour on conditional release only when that person commits a high-profile crime or by happenstance reappears during a parole suspension hearing before one of the board members involved in the original decision.

Research on the effectiveness of conditional release is presented in Research File 11.1.

RESEARCH FILE 11.1

The Effectiveness of Conditional Release

Do TA's work? Yes. The rates of successful completion of UTAs have consistently been in the 95 percent+ range.[a]

Is day parole an effective conditional release option? Yes. Day parole is an important part of the graduated release of offenders from confinement. It provides inmates with access to community services, employment, and educational opportunities. The successful completion rates for day parole are around 90 percent.[b]

Is parole an effective conditional release option? Yes. Even though grant rates are declining, supervision in the community provides offenders with the best chance to address their needs, while at the same time managing the risk posed to the community. Statistics indicate that federal and provincial/territorial offenders who are released on some form of conditional release do quite well. Rates of successful completion for full parole are in the 80 percent range.[c]

It could be argued that these high rates of completion are due in part to the more restrictive release policies of federal and provincial parole boards, although this perspective has yet to be validated by research. Even so, the use of conditional release

(continued)

has been declining, due in some measure to the rise of punitive penology in Canada. And the media's focus on sensational incidents involving offenders on parole have tended to obscure the successes of most offenders on conditional release.

Is statutory release a useful strategy? Yes. Although the PBC is generally not involved in this decision, SR does provide for supervision of the highest risk offenders. Without SR, these offenders would serve their entire sentence in custody and be released without any supervision (unless they are subject to a long-term supervision order). The successful completion rate of offenders on SR is around 60 percent. The success rate of SR releases who had a period of day parole or full parole supervision prior to SR is 13 percent higher, around 72 percent. This indicates the value of providing offenders, even those who are high risk, the opportunity for community supervision.[d]

Are parole boards effective in their decision making? Hard to tell. The effectiveness of parole boards should be measured by more than rates of reoffending. The lack of standardized criteria for board membership, the potential impact of public and political influences, the absence of feedback, and broad decision-making guidelines all potentially undermine the effectiveness of parole boards. As well, offenders with FASD or mental illness, or who are a visible minority or who are Aboriginal, may be at a disadvantage in parole hearings.

[a] Parole Board of Canada, *Performance Monitoring Report 2010-2011* (Ottawa: 2012), xi, http://pbc-clcc.gc.ca/rprts/pmr/pmr_2010_2011/pmr_2010_2011-eng.pdf; Public Safety Canada, Portfolio Corrections Statistics Committee, *Corrections and Conditional Release Statistical Overview* (Ottawa: Ottawa: Public Works and Government Services Canada, 2010), http://www.publicsafety.gc.ca/res/cor/rep/_fl/2010-ccrso-eng.pdf.

[b] Parole Board of Canada, *Performance Monitoring Report 2010-2011*, 30.

[c] Ontario Parole Board, *2011–2012 Annual Report* (Toronto: Ministry of Community Safety and Correctional Services, 2012), 11, http://www.opb.gov.on.ca/english/publications/publications.html; Public Safety Canada, *Corrections and Conditional Release Statistical Overview*, 89.

[d] Parole Board of Canada, *Performance Monitoring Report 2010-2011*, 37.

SUMMARY

This chapter has focused on one of the most important stages of the corrections process: the release of offenders from confinement. The purpose and principles of conditional release, which are set out in the CCRA, provide only a broad framework for release decisions. In recent years, conditional release has been granted to inmates less often, reflecting the emergence of a punitive penology. A variety of types of release have been designed to reintegrate offenders back into the community. For inmate-applicants, the parole hearing can be intimidating, and there are often socio-economic and cultural disparities between board members and inmate-applicants. A number of issues surround parole board decision making, which makes it, at best, an inexact science.

KEY POINTS REVIEW

1. The purpose and principles of conditional release are set out in the CCRA.

2. The specific conditional release options available to inmates depend on the length of the offender's sentence and whether he or she is under the supervision and control of provincial/territorial or federal systems of corrections.

3. There is often little pre-release planning for provincial/territorial offenders.

4. Federal inmates, who are incarcerated for longer periods of time than their provincial counterparts, tend to be released in gradual stages, and long-term studies show that offenders who are gradually released from prison are more likely to become law-abiding citizens than offenders who remain in prison until the end of their sentence.

5. The role of crime victims in conditional release is sporadic and is most often limited to providing written impact statements to the board.

6. The parole file contains many types of information, including the CA, that board members use in reaching a decision.

7. Parole certificates contain both mandatory and additional conditions to which the inmate must adhere.

8. Issues surrounding parole board decision making include these: boards may be subject to public and political influence; there is an absence of clearly defined release criteria; and a lack of feedback on case decisions to parole board members.

9. Predicting which offenders will reoffend upon release is a difficult task.

10. The consequences of parole board decisions can be significant if the offender reoffends.

KEY TERM QUESTIONS

1. What is the *warrant expiry date*?

2. Define the following types of conditional release: *temporary absence, day parole, full parole, remission/discharge*, and *statutory release*.

3. What is *cold turkey release* and what issues does it raise?

4. Describe the procedures and objectives of *detention during the period of statutory release*.

5. Describe the purpose and conditions of a *judicial recognizance*.

6. Discuss the role of the *community assessment* in the conditional release process.

7. Describe the *parole certificate*.

APPENDIX 11.1

Ontario Parole Board

Commission ontarienne des libérations conditionelles

Parole Decision of Board
Décision de la Commission
En matière de libération
Conditionnelle

Last Name, First, Middle/ Nom de famille, Prénom, deuxième	Client ID/ N° matricule	DOB/ Date de naissance	FPS No./ Numéro de SED

Institution/Établissement *Monteith Correctional Centre*	Date of Decision/Date de décision

Parole Eligibility Date d'admissibilité à la libération conditionnelle 09/15/2007	Discharge Possible Date Date possible de libération 11/17/2007	Final Warrant Expiry Date Date d'échéance finale du mandat 01/16/2008

After careful review of all available information about your case, the Ontario Parole Board has decided:
/Après avoir étudié attentivement tous les renseignements disponibles sur votre cause, la commission ontarienne des libération conditionnelles et des mises en libertés méritées a conclu la décision suivante:

☒ Parole Granted/ Libération conditionnelle accordée	☐ Parole Terminated/ Libération conditionnelle Terminée	☐ Hearing Denied/ Audience refusée
☐ Parole Denied/ Libération conditionnelle refusée	☐ Parole Continued/ Libération Conditionnelle prolongée	☐ Parole Granted Decision Rescinded/ Décision de libération conditionnelle annulée
☐ Parole Decision Deferred/ Décision ajournée	☐ Hearing Granted/ Audience accordée	☐ Conditions Varied/ Conditions modifiées
☐ Parole Revoked/ Libération conditionnelle révoquée	☐ Hearing Rescheduled/ Audience remise à une autre date	☐ Conditions Not Varied/ Conditions maintenues
Details/Détails		☐ Remission Recredited/ Remise de peine reportée au dossier
Parole Granted effective September 26, 2007		☐ Remission Not Recredited/ Remise de peine non reportée au dossier

REASON FOR DECISION/RAISONS QUI MOTIVENT LA DÉCISION:

a) Risk to society by re-offending/Danger de récidive pour la société :

Your custody sentence relates to a very serious assault offence that occurred while you were under the influence of alcohol after a lengthy period of consumption. You have no prior convictions and you have maintained a successful and lawful interim release period prior to coming into custody. It is apparent that the offence and related charge caused you to realize that you required assistance in dealing with personal issues which include alcohol consumption and anger management. In response to your issues, you have completed an anger management program and additional, more intensive, counselling sessions at the North of Superior Community Mental Health Programs. It is also noted by the Board that you have maintained institutional program invlovement and institution work while in custody.

b) Protection of society through reintegration/Protection de la société grâce à la réinsertion sociale :

Your release plan includes sponsor support and your plans to return to your employment. You also intend to continue counselling sessions with the North of Superior Community organization. The Board believes that your plan contains sufficient support to ensure a successful parole release. Your request is granted to become effective September 26, 2007.

Standard Parole Conditions
/Conditions générales de libération conditionnelle

You have agreed to the following standard conditions/Vous avez accepté les conditions générales suivantes:

Pursuant to Section 48 ss(a) to (e) of the Ministry of Correctional Services Act and Regulations (1990)/Conformément aux alinéas a) à c) de la *Loi de 1990 sur le ministère des Services correctionnels* et ses règlements.

48.   It is a condition of every grant of parole, unless the Board orders otherwise that the parolee shall/ À moins d'avis contraire par la Commission, tout libéré conditionnel doit respecter les conditions suivantes:

1)   remain within Jurisdiction of the Board/vous devez rester dans la jurisdiction territoriale de la Commission

Ontario Parole Board

Commission ontarienne des libérations conditionelles

**Parole Decision of Board
Décision de la Commission
En matière de libération
Conditionnelle**

2) keep the peace and be of good behaviour/vous ne devez pas troubler l'ordre public et vous devez vous conduire convenablement

3) obtain the consent of the Board or the parole supervisor for any change of residence or employment/vous devez obtenir l'autorisation de la commission ou de votre surveillant de libération conditionnelle pour tout changement de domicille ou d'emploi

4) report immediately upon release to your parole supervisor and the local police force. Report thereafter as required by your parole supervisor./ vous devez vous présenter au bureau de votre surveillant de libération conditionnelle et au poste de police immédiatement après liberation. Et par après vous presenter tel que convenu avec votre surveillant de liberation conditionnelle.

5) refrain from associating with any person who is engaged in criminal activity or unless approved by the parole supervisor, with any person who has a criminal record/Il vous est interdit de fréquenter des personnes ayant des activités criminelles ou, sauf avec autorisation du surveillant de libération conditionnelle, des personnes ayant un casier judiciaire

6) carry your parole certificate at all times and present it to any police officer or probation and parole officer upon request./Porter sur vous,en tout temps, votre document de liberation conditionnelle et le presenter à tout agent de probation et liberation conditionnelle ou à tout agent de police qui vous le demande

**Special Parole Conditions
/Conditions spéciales de libération conditionnelle**

You have also agreed to the following special conditions/Vous avez aussi accepté les conditions spéciales suivantes:

1. Upon release abide by your approved travel plan.
2. Abstain from the purchase, possession or consumption of alcohol or other intoxicating substances.
3. Not to enter or be found in any establishment whose primary source of business is the sale of alcohol.
4. Not to associate or hold any communication directly or indirectly with (named individual) except within circumstances approved of by the Parole Officer in writing.
5. Abstain from owning, possessing or carrying any weapon as defined by the criminal code.
6. Continue to attend for and actively comply with any counselling program for anger management issues and substance use issues with the North of Superior Community Health Program and provide written verification of same to your Parole Officer, or any such programming as may be recommended by your Parole Officer and provide proof of same to your Parole Officer.

Release Plans/Plans de Libération

Residence/Domicile	
Employment/Education/Other/Emploi, éducation et autre(s)	
Parole Supervisor/Name & Address	
Police Reporting	
Vice Chair or Designate/Vice-président ou mandataire	**Member Signature/Signature du membre**

PROVISO: The Board's decision to grant parole is conditional upon your good behaviour and the continuation of your Board approved release plan.
/La Commission accorde la libération temporaire à la condition que votre comportement demeure convenable et que vous vous conformiez à votre plan de libération approuvé par la Commission.

DISTRIBUTION: Inmate/Parolee
Board Case File
I.L.O./Parole Supervisor
Superintendent

Source: © Queen's Printer for Ontario, 2011. Reproduced with permission.

APPENDIX 11.2

Ontario Parole Board

Commission ontarienne des libérations conditionnelles

**Certificate of Parole/
Certificat de mise en liberté
conditionnelle**

Date(s) Issued/ Date d'émission	Warrant Expiry/ Expiration du mandat	Release Date/ Date de mise en liberté
	01/16/2008	09/26/2007
Supervision Service Sector/ Secteur de Service superviseur	Released from/Mise en liberté de	

Under the **Ministry of Correctional Services Act 1990**, and the regulations, the Ontario Parole Board releases:
/En vertu de la **Loi de 1990 sur le ministère des services correctionnels** et des règlements y afférents, la commission des libération conditionnelles et des mises en liberté méritées libère:

Last Name/ Nom de famille	First, Middle/ Prénom, deuxième	Client ID/ N° matricule	DOB/ Date de naissance	FPS No./ Numéro de SED

Under the following standard conditions/sous réserve du respect des conditions normales suivantes:

1) Remain within jurisdiction of the Board.
   /Vous devez rester dans la jurisdiction de la Commission des libérations conditionnelles.
2) Keep the peace and be of good behaviour.
   /Vous ne devez pas troubler l'ordre public et vous devez vous conduire convenablement.
3) Obtain the consent of the Board or the Parole Supervisor for any change of residence or employment.
   /Vous devez obtenir l'autorisation de la commission ou de votre surveillant de libération conditionnelle si vous désirez changer d'emploi ou de résidence.
4) Report immediately upon release to your Parole Supervisor and local Police force. Report thereafter as required by your parole supervisor.
   /Vous devez vous présenter au bureau de votre surveillant de libération conditionnelle et au poste de police immédiatement après votre libération. Et par après vous presenter tel que convenu avec votre surveillant de libération conditionnelle.
5) Refrain from associating with any person who is engaged in criminal activity or unless approved by the Parole Supervisor with any person who has a criminal record.
   /Il vous est interdit de fréquenter des personnes impliquées dans des activités criminelles. D'autant plus, vous ne devez fréquenter des personnes ayant un casier judiciare, sans l'autorisation du surveillant de libération conditionnelle.
6) You must carry your parole certificate at all times and present it to any police officer or Parole Supervisor upon request.
   /Vous devez porter votre certificat de libération conditionnelle en tout temps et le présenter, sur demande, à tous officier de police ou agent de probation.

Special Conditions/ Conditions spéciales

1. Upon release abide by your approved travel plan.
2. Abstain from the purchase, possession or consumption of alcohol or other intoxicating substances.
3. Not to enter or be found in any establishment whose primary source of business is the sale of alcohol.
4. Not to associate or hold any communication directly or indirectly with (named individual) except within circumstances approved of by the Parole Officer in writing.
5. Abstain from owning, possessing or carrying any weapon as defined by the criminal code.
6. Continue to attend for and actively comply with any counselling program for anger management issues and substance use issues with the North of Superior Community Health Program and provide written verification of same to your Parole Officer, or any such programming as may be recommended by your Parole Officer and provide proof of same to your Parole Officer.

**Upon Release you shall
/Lors de votre libérations vous devrez**

Report immediately to a Parole Supervisor/ Lors de votre libération vous devrez vous présenter immédiatement à surveillant de libération
Reside at address/ Adresse d'habitation
Report to Police at/ Vous présenter au poste de police de

Parole Declaration/Déclaration de mise en liberté conditionnelle

I have carefully read or had read to me the conditions of this certificate. I understand the conditions and contents of this certificate of Parole. I accept my release and pledge myself honestly to comply with the conditions. I also understand that if I violate the conditions of my Parole, I may be returned to a correctional institution to serve the portion of my term of imprisonment, including any remission that remained unexpired at the time Parole was granted less the period of time spent on Parole.
/Je déclare avoir lu attentivement ce certificat ou en avoir reçu lecture. Je déclare voir lu attentivement ce certificat ou en avoir reçu lecture. Je comprends les conditions et la teneur de ce certificat de mise en liberté conditionnellle. J'accepte ma libération en ces termes et je promets en toute honnêteté d'observer ces conditions. Je sais également que, si je commets une infraction aux conditions stipulées pour ma libération conditionnelle, on peut me renvoyer dans un établissement corrrectionnel pour y purger le reste de ma peine d'emprisonnement, y compris toute réduction de peine, non encore purgée au moment où la libération conditionnelle m'a été accordée, moins la période de liberté conditionnelle.

Valid only when signed by Parolee/Ce certificat n'est valide que s'il est signé par la personne en liberté conditionnelle Parolee's Signature/Signature de la personne en liberté conditionnelle	
	Date

Given in triplicate by the authority of the Ontario Parole Board.
/Établi en triple examplaire avec l'autorisation de la commission ontarienne des libérations conditionnelles et des mises en liberté méritées.
Vice Chair or Designate/Vice-Président ou mandataire

Signature	Date

DISTRIBUTION: Parolee (after signing)
  Probation and Parole Office
  Board Case File

Source: © Queen's Printer for Ontario, 2011. Reproduced with permission.

NOTES

1. G. Fauteux, *Report of a Committee Appointed to Inquire into the Principles and Procedures Followed in the Remission Service of the Department of Justice of Canada* (Ottawa: Queen's Printer, 1956).

2. P. Lussier, N. DesLauriers-Varin, and T. Ratel, "A Descriptive Profile of High-Risk Sex Offenders Under Intensive Supervision in the Province of British Columbia, Canada," *International Journal of Offender Therapy and Comparative Criminology* 54, no. 1 (2010): 71–91.

3. C. Marshall, *HIV/AIDS and Hepatitis in Correctional Facilities: Reducing the Risks* (Halifax: Nova Scotia Advisory Commission on AIDS, 2008), 26, http://www.gov.ns.ca/AIDS/documents/HIV-AIDS-Hepatitis-C-Correctional%20Facilities.pdf.

4. Schizophrenic Society of Ontario, *Provincial Correctional Response to Individuals with Mental Illnesses in Ontario: A Review of Literature* (Toronto, 2012), 4, http://cefso.ca/wwdnews/uploads/Provincial_Corrections_Literature_Review_Final_March_2012.pdf.

5. M.D. Schlager and K. Robbins, "Does Parole Work - Revisited: Reframing the Discussion of Postprison Supervision on Offender Outcome," *The Prison Journal* 88, no. 2 (2008): 234–51.

6. Parole Board of Canada, *Performance Monitoring Report 2010-2011* (Ottawa: 2012), xi, http://pbc-clcc.gc.ca/rprts/pmr/pmr_2010_2011/pmr_2010_2011-eng.pdf; Public Safety Canada, *Portfolio Corrections Statistics Committee, Corrections and Conditional Release Statistical Overview* (Ottawa: Public Works and Government Services Canada, 2010), http://www.publicsafety.gc.ca/res/cor/rep/_fl/2010-ccrso-eng.pdf.

7. M. Dauvergne, "Adult Correctional Statistics in Canada, 2010/2011," 15, http://www.statcan.gc.ca/pub/85-002-x/2012001/article/11715-eng.pdf.

8. Parole Board of Canada, *Performance Monitoring Report 2010–2011*, 19.

9. I. Zinger, "Conditional Release and Human Rights in Canada: A Commentary," *Canadian Journal of Criminology and Criminal Justice* 54, no. 1 (2012): 117–35 at 120.

10. Ibid.

11. Ibid., 122.

12. Ontario Parole Board, *2011–2012 Annual Report* (Toronto: Ministry of Community Safety and Correctional Services, 2012), 13, http://www.opb.gov.on.ca/english/publications/publications.html.

13. M. K. Olotu and M. G. Beaupre, *Evaluation Report: National Victim Services Program* (Ottawa: Correctional Service of Canada, 2010), http://csc-scc.gc.ca/text/pa/nvsp/index-eng.shtml.

14. P. J. Murphy, L. Johnsen, and J. Murphy, *Paroled for Life: Interviews with Parolees Serving Life Sentences* (Vancouver: New Star, 2002), 93.

15. Parole Board of Canada, *Performance Monitoring Report 2010–2011*, 22–23.

16. Zinger, "Conditional Release and Human Rights in Canada," 121.

17. M. A. Paparozzi and R. Guy, "The Giant That Never Woke: Parole Authorities as the Lynchpin to Evidence-Based Practices and Prisoner Reentry," *Journal of Contemporary Justice* 25, no. 4 (2009): 397–411.

18. Ontario Parole Board, 2011–2012 Annual Report, 12.

CHAPTER 12

REENTRY AND LIFE AFTER PRISON

CHAPTER OBJECTIVES

After reading this chapter, you should be able to:
- *Describe reintegration as a process rather than as an event.*
- *Discuss what is meant by the pains of reentry.*
- *Describe the activities of parole officers and, in particular, their dual function in supervision.*
- *Discuss the unique challenges of supervising high-risk offenders, mentally ill offenders, and sex offenders on parole.*
- *Discuss the key issues that surround the practice of community notification (CN).*
- *Describe the structure and dynamics of circles of support and accountability (COSAs).*
- *Describe the procedures that apply when a parolee commits a new offence or violates the conditions of the parole certificate.*
- *Address the issue of the effectiveness of supervision and control strategies used for offenders reentering the community.*

THE REINTEGRATION PROCESS

Reintegration is a process, not an event. It has been defined as "all activity and programming conducted to prepare an offender to return safely to the community as a law-abiding citizen."[1]

It begins with the treatment programs described in Chapter 10 and includes the development of a release plan that sets out where the inmate will live, work, go to school, and, if required, participate in post-release treatment programs. The goal of reintegration is to avoid recidivism in the short term (i.e., until the warrant expiry date) as well as afterward. When required, yet another goal is to address the interests of crime victims.

For reintegration to succeed, there should be continuity between institutional programs and the services an offender receives on conditional release in the community.[2] This is the concept of **throughcare**. A seamless transition in treatment from the institution to the community is especially important for offenders with special needs, such as substance abuse issues.[3]

Reintegration
The process whereby an inmate is prepared for and released into the community after serving time in prison.

Throughcare
The notion that there should be continuity between institutional treatment programs and community-based services for offenders.

Most inmates who reoffend do so within the first 3 years following release from a correctional institution. This highlights the importance of providing support in the community. The ICPM in federal corrections (see Chapter 10) is one initiative that has been designed to provide continuity of care from the institution to the community. The short time that provincial/territorial offenders spend in custody works against this type of planning. There is often a lack of resources, especially for groups with special needs. A study ($N = 671$) of offenders with mental illness in detention in Québec found, for example, that these individuals were poorly prepared to reenter the community and had difficulty accessing services; also, there was little program continuity between the institution and the community.[4]

The term "reintegration" is problematic, for it suggests that offenders had been successfully integrated into the community before their incarceration. In fact, many inmates come from marginalized backgrounds and have never acquired the attitudes and behaviours necessary to live as productive members of society.[5] The reintegration process for federal offenders is illustrated in Figure 12.1.

Figure 12.2 breaks down the federal correctional release population in 2011. Note the high number of offenders who are on statutory release. If PBC

Figure 12.1

The Reintegration Process for Federal Offenders

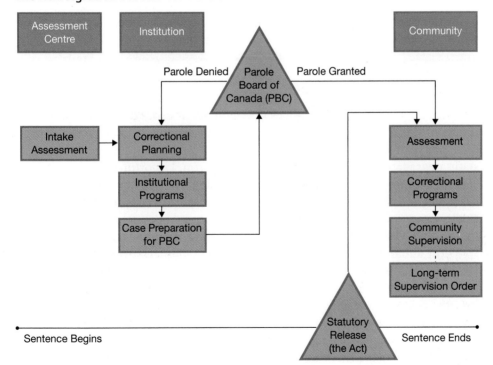

Source: Adapted from 1996 November Report of the Auditor General of Canada, http://www.oag-bvg .gc.ca/internet/English/parl_oag_199611_e_1152.html. (Office of the Auditor General of Canada, 1996). Reproduced with the permission of the Minister of Public Works and Government Services Canada, 2013.

Figure 12.2

Federal Conditional Release Population, April 10, 2011

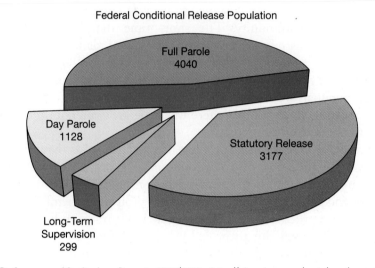

Federal Conditional Release Population

Full Parole
4040

Day Parole
1128

Statutory Release
3177

Long-Term
Supervision
299

Source: Performance Monitoring Report, 2010/2011, http://pbc-clcc.gc.ca/rprts/pmr/pmr_2010_2011/index-eng.shtml. (Parole Board of Canada, 2012). Reproduced with the permission of the Minister of Public Works and Government Services Canada, 2013.

grant rates continue to decline, the numbers of offenders on statutory release will continue to increase, placing an additional burden on parole officers.

COMING BACK: THE PAINS OF REENTRY

Pains of reentry
The difficulties that inmates released from correctional institutions encounter in attempting to adjust to life in the outside, free community.

Chapter 9 noted that many inmates in confinement experience pains of imprisonment. Similarly, on being released from confinement, offenders may experience **pains of reentry**. Persons who are sent to custody undergo a variety of status degradation ceremonies as they enter prison. Unfortunately, there are no status *restoration* ceremonies and "rituals of reintegration" that would build on the offender's accomplishments while incarcerated; instead, the focus is solely on risk to the community.[6] As a consequence, newly released offenders are left largely to their own devices as they attempt to adapt and survive in the community.

Put another way, a prison sentence triggers a process whereby individuals are extracted from society and forced to adjust to a closed, structured, and artificial environment, one in which an antisocial value system predominates and inmates have little responsibility. Then, upon release, these same inmates are expected to resume/assume law-abiding lives in the community and to hold prosocial values, exercise independence of thought and decision making, and display life skills that enable them to cope with the complexities of daily life in a fast-paced society. A transition this dramatic would challenge even the most gifted individual, and it is especially difficult for marginalized and socially isolated offenders who have been incarcerated for long periods. One long-term offender

Video Link
"The Probation Process," "On the Rebound," "Confession and Change"
www.homecomer .weebly.com/vi –confession–and –change.html

told C. T. Griffiths: "The values, attitudes and behaviours that I learned inside were just the opposite of what I needed to make it in the free world." Complicating this, offenders tend to have few, if any, noncriminal friends and little access to legitimate opportunities.

PERSPECTIVE

An Ex-offender Reflects on Reentry

The moment offenders step off the bus they face several critical decisions. Where will they live, where will they be able to find a meal, where should they look for a job, how will they get to a job interview, and where can they earn enough money to pay for necessities? These returning inmates are also confronted with many details of personal business, such as obtaining identification cards and documents, making medical appointments, and working through the many everyday bureaucratic problems that occur during any transition. These choices prompt feelings of intense stress and worry over the logistics of their return to the outside world. To those who have had no control over any aspect of life for many years, each of these problems can be difficult. In accumulation, they can be overwhelming.

My own experience is a good example. Shortly after my release from prison to the halfway house, some friends took me to lunch at a local deli. The waiter came over to take our orders. Everyone else told him what they wanted, but I kept poring over the menu. My eyes raced over the columns of choices. I knew that I was supposed to order, but the number of options overwhelmed me. My friends sat in embarrassed silence. I was paralyzed. The waiter looked at me impatiently. I began to panic. How ridiculous that I wasn't able to do such a simple thing as order lunch. Finally, in desperation, I ordered the next item my eyes landed on, a turkey sandwich. I didn't even want it, but at least it put an end to this embarrassing incident.

For 2 years I hadn't been able to make any choices about what I ate. Now I was having a hard time making a simple choice that most people make every day. If I had this much difficulty after only a couple of years in prison, think how hard it is for those inmates who haven't made any choices for 5, 10, or 15 years. And what about those who didn't have the wonderful home, the loving family, the strong faith, and the good education that I had? They face a baffling array of options and little preparation. Is it any surprise that so many newly released prisoners make some bad choices and end up back in prison? If we do not prepare these inmates for their return to the community, the odds are great that their first incarceration will not be their last.

Source: P. Nolan, "Prepared Statement Presented to the Committee on the Judiciary, U.S. House of Representatives," November 3, 2005, http://www.gpo.gov/fdsys/pkg/CHRG-109hhrg24372/pdf/CHRG-109hhrg24372.pdf.

THE CHALLENGES OF THE NEWLY RELEASED

Most federal offenders on conditional release have difficulties associated with one or more of the seven dynamic need domains: attitudes, community functioning, employment, marital/family, personal and emotional, associates, and substance abuse.[7] Newly released offenders may face social, economic, and personal challenges that make it difficult for them to avoid returning to criminal activity. Offenders often find themselves in a Catch-22 situation. One released explained: "You need to meet with a worker first to get money, you need to get out of jail to meet with a worker … You need an address to get a cheque, and a cheque to get an address."[8] There is often a lack of continuity between the institution's programs and those in the community. Offenders who were in a Methadone maintenance program in the institution, for example, may not have access to this program in the community. All of this is especially true for offenders from rural and remote communities.[9] Additional challenges may exist owing to mental illness and the presence of FASD.[10]

Homelessness poses a severe challenge to newly released offenders. There is evidence that homelessness is related to reoffending: four out of ten homeless persons admitted to one Toronto-area jail during one year were returnees.[11] It is estimated that 30 percent of released offenders are homeless and have no stable residence to go to after they are released.[12] Compounding this problem are provincial laws that allow landlords to deny accommodation to persons with a criminal record.[13]

A study of inmates in Toronto-area jails ($N = 363$) found that 22 percent were homeless before *and* after being incarcerated and that, overall, 32 percent anticipated being homeless upon release.[14] Ninety-seven percent of these offenders were men; 22 percent were over 50 years old; and 43 percent faced serious medical issues. High percentages of this sample group needed help with transportation, housing, and employment and skills training, not to mention assistance replacing their IDs. All of this was in addition to their need for counselling, addiction services, and legal assistance. None of the offenders in this group said that the institution had provided them with pre-release planning.[15] Now add to all of this the "collateral effects" of confinement, which include the loss of personal relationships and social networks, the acquisition of self-defeating habits and attitudes, and the loss of personal belongings.[16] It is likely that these had been problems even before they were incarcerated.

Ironically, studies also show that providing social housing for these people would have been cheaper than providing them with medical and social services.[17]

Perspectives of Clients and Service Providers on Community Corrections Services in Hamilton, Ontario: A Case Study

Interviews with clients ($N = 35$; [16 men, 19 women]) of a number of community corrections organizations in Hamilton, including the Elizabeth Fry Society, the St. Leonard's Society, the John Howard Society, and the Native

Women's Centre, identified a number of challenges for offenders returning to the community. Housing was one of these: many offenders had nowhere to go upon release and relied on family and friends for shelter. Other needs they identified were for drug-free shelter, employment opportunities, mental health and counselling supports, and addiction services.

One client stated: "I didn't overcome these challenges. I went back to sex trade work. Most girls, that's what they do."[18] Another commented on what happens when the ex-offender's needs are not met: "They wander the streets. They don't know how to address their needs."[19] One particular challenge was staying away from old friendship networks. Comments on this from the clients included the following:

> *People have big plans coming out of jail but they don't happen because of the time lag between being released from jail and arriving at the first service provider.*

> *A girl gets out of jail, she want to get into rehab right away. She can't go so she gets frustrated and decides, "Well, if I can't get clean now I might as well still do drugs."*[20]

Personnel in community corrections organizations noted the need for housing, for gender-specific programs and services, and for more collaboration and sharing of resources among agencies. Many of their clients had multiple issues, one of these often being addiction. It was proposed that a "wrap-around model" of services be developed so that one facility could provide addiction counselling, mental health services, and housing and employment assistance.

Strangers in a Strange Land: The Isolation of Offenders Returning to the Community

A newly released offender can feel like the proverbial "stranger in a strange land"—embarrassed and inadequate, and convinced that every person on the street can tell at a mere glance that he or she has been in prison. One female parolee with a life sentence commented: "I didn't feel like I was back. I didn't feel like I belonged … I didn't feel part of this world anymore, I was still inside. In some respects, part of me will always be inside."[21] Ironically, offenders may experience paranoia and fear for their safety upon reentering the community. Another offender commented, "I was always more nervous getting out than going in."[22]

There is concern that offenders who have been incarcerated for lengthy periods of time may suffer from **post incarceration syndrome (PICS)**. The symptoms of this include post-traumatic stress, which arises from trauma experienced prior to incarceration and during confinement; and an institutionalized personality, which develops as a result of life inside the prison.[23]

Post incarceration syndrome (PICS) A condition of offenders in custody and in the community that is caused by prolonged exposure to the dynamics of life inside correctional institutions.

The "State-Raised" Offender and Reentry

The stress of reentry may be especially acute for state-raised offenders (see Chapter 9). These individuals have very little experience living in the outside community, have few or no family ties, and—a key point—have no "stake" in the community. Their friends, identity, status, and power are all inside the correctional institution. Out in the community, they have no guarantees of status, of security, or of a routine that will provide for their basic needs. For these people, the pull of the institution may be stronger than that of the outside world.

Close friendships forged in the prison are in danger of being lost; indeed, the inmate may feel that he or she is abandoning close friends, confidants, and/or lovers. One ex-offender who had spent many years in federal prisons confided to C. T. Griffiths: "I have never had the intensity of friendships, the trust, the companionship, in the outside community that I had when I was incarcerated." These feelings may be especially acute when the soon-to-be-released inmate realizes that he or she has no friends on the outside who can be relied on for help, protection, and security. One parolee, who had been incarcerated almost continuously from a young age for more than three decades, related an incident that illustrates the anxiety and panic that ex-offenders may experience when attempting tasks that people on the outside take for granted. It happened during his first trip to the grocery store after being released on day parole to live in a halfway house:

> *I wanted to buy some groceries, so I went to Safeway. I must have been in the store for hours. There were so many choices, I had no idea of what to put in my cart. Finally, my cart was full and I pushed it up to the checkout counter. The store was really crowded, and I was so focused on deciding what to buy that I hadn't given any thought to the price of the things I was putting in the cart. I think I had about $50 in my pocket. When the cashier rang up the total, it came to over $150. When she told me the total, I just froze. Everyone was looking at me. I stood there for what seemed like an eternity and then, without saying a word, ran out of the store. At the bus stop, my heart was racing and I was sweating. I never went back to that store. And, it was a long time before I went grocery shopping for more than one or two items.*
>
> Personal communication with C. T. Griffiths

Even offenders who, prior to confinement, had relatively conventional lifestyles (except for their lawbreaking) can find it hard to unlearn the automatic responses they have acquired in an environment where physical aggression is necessary for survival.

To cope with the pains of reentry, the parolee may revert to high-risk behaviour, including heavy drinking, drug use, resuming friendships with former criminal associates, and spending time with old friends from prison. Although most will complete their period of conditional release without committing a new offence, many will be reconvicted of a criminal offence within three years of release.

PAROLE OFFICERS AND THE SUPERVISION OF OFFENDERS

Offenders on parole are generally required to report regularly to a correctional agent such as a parole officer. All federal parolees are supervised by parole officers employed by or under contract to the CSC. By agreement, the CSC also supervises provincial parolees released by the PBC. In two jurisdictions—Ontario and Québec—provincial probation and parole officers provide supervision for offenders on parole as well as for many inmates on temporary absence. Parole officers are also involved in supervising offenders who are placed on long-term supervision orders by the court.

In provincial/territorial corrections, few distinctions are made between parole and probation, except with regard to provisions for enforcement. For example, the breach of a probation condition is a new offence, whereas the violation of a parole condition can (but does not always) lead to suspension of the release and to a return of the parolee to custody.

Not all offenders who are released into the community require the same level of supervision. An assessment is made to determine the offender's need and risk levels—low, medium, or high—and the results are used to determine the level and intensity of supervision. Supervision by parole officers may range from periodic telephone calls to the offender's residence to the requirement that the parolee reside in a community-based residential facility with 24-hour monitoring and attend frequent face-to-face meetings with a parole officer.

The various activities of parole officers are set out in Box 12.1.

BOX 12.1

The Activities of Parole Officers

Assessment

- Risk assessment and case management planning, for example, interviewing offenders and collateral contacts to make evidence-based assessments regarding offender risk and needs areas.
- Determining appropriate interventions to address risk and needs areas, supported by maintaining close collaboration with other members of the Case Management Team as well as with community service providers (e.g., mental health and addiction services).

Offender Pre- and Post-Release Decision Making

- Preparation of comprehensive reports involving the evaluation of offender progress against the Correctional Plan; risk assessment drawing upon available actuarial measures, contained in psychological reports, and so on; the creation of a tailored risk management strategy based on case specifics and

(continued)

dynamics; and delivery of a recommendation in relation to the decision at hand.

- Case preparation in relation to specific offender populations, for example, Section 84 planning for those Aboriginal offenders who have applied for such a release type.
- Presentation of offenders' cases before review boards for screening for residency at community residential facilities and treatment centres, and completion of the associated Community Strategy, documenting screening results.
- Gathering relevant case-related information from post sentence to warrant expiry.
- Active participation in PBC hearings, in the context of which the parole officer's formulated recommendation is delivered, newly gathered information is outlined, and the provision of justification/rationale for case management decisions is offered.

Surveillance/Enforcement

- Supervision of offenders based on assessed level of intervention.
- Monitoring compliance with parole conditions and adherence to Correctional Plan.
- Arranging urinalysis testing schedule and completing ongoing follow-up with staff at the relevant Community Residential Facility or other testing site.
- Methadone coordination and completion of ongoing follow-up with staff at the relevant pharmacy and clinic.
- Ongoing collateral contact with police and security staff.
- Integral role in decision making with regard to case management strategy following offender breach activity coming to light; that is, case conferencing with Parole Officer Supervisor results in the determination to issue a warrant of suspension and apprehension to effect offender arrest and reincarceration or maintain offender release to the community with the implementation of an enhanced release plan involving the implementation of interventions to manage risk.
- Documenting violations/breach activity and providing analysis in relation to offender crime cycle.
- Preparing progress and violation reports for submission to the CSC and the PBC.

Counselling

- Motivational interviewing, challenging difficult client attitudes and behaviour.
- Rapport building.
- Completion of the initial interview (institution and community).
- Completion of the post-suspension interview.
- Individual supervision as well as supervision involving the presence of collaterals (e.g., employers, intimate partners, family members, other associates).

Officer of the Court

- Testifying in relation to a supervised offender's new charges.
- Preparation of documents submitted to the court in relation to offender progress and case status for offenders facing new or outstanding charges.

Source: Federal parole officer, personal communication with C. T. Griffiths.

The Dual Function of Parole Supervision

Like probation officers, parole officers have a dual role in their relations with clients. The first involves being a resource person and confidant to counter the pains of reentry. The supportive activities of parole officers can include offering job search advice, referring clients for counselling, and advocating with welfare authorities on their behalf. The second role involves monitoring and enforcing parole conditions.

Each parole officer has his or her own style of supervision. Some are more lenient and give the parolees assigned to them a longer "leash"; others are much stricter. The style of supervision also depends on the level of risk the parolee poses to the community. Ideally, a balance between the two roles is achieved, with more control/surveillance during the early phases of release and more assistance as the supervision period draws to an end. Not surprisingly, research studies have found that parole officers with more authoritarian attitudes are more inclined to enforce the conditions of parole and to send an offender to a parole board revocation hearing.[24]

To be effective, a parole officer must adapt his or her supervision style to the offender's risk and needs. A number of factors may damage the relationship between the two, including the perceptions that each brings to the relationship. Parole officers may believe, for example, that offenders make a rational choice to follow (or not) the conditions of their release. A parole officer who treats the offender with disrespect can actually hinder the latter's good-faith efforts to succeed in the community.[25] Offenders, on the contrary, may perceive that parole officers don't understand "where they're coming from" and that they aren't able to appreciate the pressures and challenges they face.[26] High-risk offenders, such as sex offenders, may be unlikely to disclose their urges to reoffend to their parole supervisor for fear of being returned to custody.

The increasing emphasis on risk management in corrections and the rise of punitive penology may soon transform the role of parole officers into one of monitoring and enforcing compliance with release conditions and periodically reassessing changes in risk and need.[27] The paperwork burden of conducting these assessments and recording them in computerized, centralized databases has had a strong impact on the amount of time that parole supervisors can spend in face-to-face contact with clients.

Parole Officer Safety: A Death in Yellowknife

The death of a federal parole officer in Yellowknife highlighted issues surrounding the safety of parole officers as well as the decision making of the PBC. On October 6, 2004, CSC parole officer Louise Pargeter went to the home of Eli Ulayuk, one of the parolees she supervised. She failed to return to her office as scheduled, and her coworkers were unable to locate her. The following day, the RCMP made a gruesome discovery: they found her body at Ulayuk's apartment. During the trial, the court learned that Ulayuk had wanted to kill Pargeter since 2001 when she revoked his day parole. The court heard that Ulayuk had struck Pargeter with a hammer five times, strangled her with twine, and had sex with her body. In February 2006, Ulayuk was found guilty of second-degree murder and sentenced to life in prison, with the recommendation that he be ineligible for parole for 25 years.

A CSC inquiry into the incident identified a number of factors that may have led to Pargeter's death.[28] Earlier, Ulayuk had been convicted of the murder of a woman in his home community of Igloolik, Nunavut, and had been diagnosed as a necrophiliac, a form of sexual deviance. The sentencing judge in that case commented that Ulayuk was one of the most dangerous offenders ever to have come before the court. The Board of Investigation (BOI) found that while Ulayuk was in confinement, the CSC had not completed sufficient clinical assessments of him, nor had sufficient attention been given to his sexual deviancy in the treatment plan. The BOI also stated that there had not been sufficient analysis of Ulayuk's case file prior to his release; it then made numerous recommendations with respect to the CSC's information-gathering process, case preparation for PBC hearings, and the supervision of offenders in the community. The BOI also recommended that the PBC change the format of its decisions to make it more structured, with a focus on specific risk factors.

In 2012, the federal government announced that it was exploring the possibility of providing parole officers and other staff who work with offenders in the community with GPS-linked panic buttons.[29]

INNOVATIONS IN COMMUNITY ASSISTANCE AND SUPERVISION

Across the country, a number of programs have been developed to increase community involvement in helping released offenders. These programs are generally staffed by trained volunteers, whose activities include assisting parole officers and offenders and participating in COSAs (discussed below). The Community Parole Project in London, Ontario, and the Community Adult Mentoring and Support (CAMS) Program in Victoria, British Columbia, are two examples.

REENTRY COURTS: A PROBLEM-SOLVING APPROACH

The emergence of problem-solving courts as an alternative to the traditional criminal justice process was discussed in Chapter 4. The research evidence suggests that this approach can be effective in addressing the needs of offenders while providing protection to the community and reducing reoffending.

A similar approach could be taken with respect to offenders reentering the community following incarceration. Reentry courts have been established in a number of American jurisdictions to provide judicial oversight of offenders released from prison (e.g., Superior Court of Delaware; http:courts.delaware. gov/Superior/reentry.stm). These courts review the progress and problems of offenders, assist in the continuity of treatment from the institution to the community, monitor compliance with release conditions, and apply sanctions when offenders do not comply with treatment requirements.

In reentry courts, judges actively involve themselves in the offender's transition from prison to the community, either by retaining jurisdiction over the offender from sentencing to warrant expiry or by assuming jurisdiction once the offender is released. The activities of reentry courts include designing reintegration plans based on offenders' assessed needs, providing active oversight, and coordinating services and community supports. The courts can be especially helpful for women offenders who are attempting to reunite with their children following a period of incarceration.[30] Not enough research has been done to determine the effectiveness of reentry courts at reducing rates of recidivism.[31]

SPECIAL OFFENDER POPULATIONS ON PAROLE

As noted earlier in the chapter, offenders vary in the specific types of problems they encounter on reentry. This disparity requires that correctional systems adapt their policies and programs to meet the needs of special offender populations and to manage the risks they present.

High-Risk Offenders

One Canadian program for high-risk offenders is a collaborative effort between the CSC and several police departments across the country (including the Regina Police Service and the Hamilton Police Service). It involves police officers being hired as community corrections liaison officers (CCLOs). These officers monitor the activities of high-risk/high-needs offenders in the community and liaise between police officers and parole officers.[32]

Mentally Ill Offenders

Mentally disordered parolees returning to the community face special challenges: they tend to be socially isolated and to be more prone to substance abuse, and they have even more difficulty finding suitable employment and housing. As is often the case, provincial/territorial programs for these populations are less developed than federal ones. Mentally ill offenders released to northern and remote communities are likely to face particular challenges, though corrections scholars have done little research on this.

Video Link
The Released
**www.pbs.org/
wgbh/pages/
frontline/released/
etc/synopsis.html**

Sex Offenders

Video Link

All Sex Offenders on GPS Under California Parole Division Supervision **www.youtube .com/ watch?v=BWyY -ZIBMXU**

No group of offenders has attracted more interest from the public, politicians, and correctional authorities than sex offenders. Their release from prison is often front-page news in the local press or even announced over the Internet. Correctional systems use a variety of techniques to manage the risks of this offender group. These techniques include treatment, drugs such as antiandrogens to reduce sex drive, CN, registration, and supervision and monitoring strategies, including polygraph testing.[33] The monitoring of sex offenders by means of GPS systems is commonplace in the United States and may be adopted in Canada.

The challenges that sex offenders face in avoiding situations that may lead to relapse are captured by the comments of an offender convicted of raping and killing a young girl. He is on parole for life:

> *Sometimes when I'm driving down the road and I see some well-developed 15-year-old and I think, "Oh yeah, she's cute," I kind of mentally give myself a slap and say, "Yeah, she's cute. Let her stay cute, you stupid bastard." I have to give myself the height of shit … I'm motivated by her memory not to do that sort of garbage.*[34]

The CSC operates a high-risk offender program as well as a maintenance program for managing sex offenders on release in the community. The *high-risk offender program* is cognitive-behaviour oriented and includes individual and group counselling. Group therapy is used to address the four "F's" related to sexual offending: feelings, fantasy, future, and follow-through. This multidisciplinary program involves monthly case conference meetings attended by the supervising parole staff, treatment staff, and the program director. These case conferences provide an opportunity to discuss supervision of the offender and any concerns relating to the offender's no-contact orders, family relationships, employment, and attitude and behaviour. Sex offenders who have admitted their guilt and who require lower intensity relapse prevention participate in the *maintenance program*. These offenders receive individual or group therapy designed to maintain their institutional treatment gains. Research findings suggest that there are lower rates of recidivism for sex offenders who are supervised via a case management approach and who are offered individualized treatment services in combination with an appropriate level of parole supervision.[35]

In provincial/territorial programs the potential effectiveness of sex offender treatment programs may be severely compromised by the short period of time these offenders are confined. Inmates may not be able to access programs in a timely manner and may not complete all of the prescribed sessions of a treatment intervention prior to being eligible for parole or reaching their remission/discharge date (at the two-thirds point in their sentence). There may also be a lack of throughcare due to the absence of community-based resources. Provincial/territorial offenders who are discharged at their remission date do not have access to corrections programs and services in the community.

The federal government and several provinces (including British Columbia and Ontario) have established sex offender registries to track high-risk sex offenders. Sex offenders must register fifteen days prior to release into the community (or upon conviction if they receive a noncustodial sentence) and must then reregister annually as well as 15 days prior to any change of address. The register database includes information on the offender, such as their name, date of birth, current address, and identifying marks, as well as photographs. Offenders remain on the registry indefinitely unless they are acquitted on appeal or receive a pardon.

COMMUNITY NOTIFICATION: CREATING A FALSE SENSE OF SECURITY?

It was noted in Chapter 11 that the victims of incarcerated offenders have the right to request that they be informed of the timing of the release. In some cases this information can help the victims take the necessary steps to ensure their safety. The large majority of crime victims are not harassed or threatened by offenders on conditional release; however, some victims are at great risk. It is in these cases that victim notification is most crucial, for both officially sanctioned releases and unauthorized absences from community supervision.

The use of **community notification (CN)** when high-risk offenders are released into the community is a key component of various attempts to manage risk and protect the community. This strategy may also be viewed as a hardening of attitudes against certain categories of offenders and as reflective of a punitive penology.

Community residents protest against a sex offender released from prison taking up residence in their neighbourhood.

CP PHOTO/Red Deer Advocate/Randy Fiedler

Video Link
Tracked: A Week Under GPS Supervision
www.youtube.com/watch?v=QBAT07UEWug

Community notification
The practice, usually carried out by police agencies, of making a public announcement that a high-risk offender has taken up residence in an area.

The premise of CN policies is that when potential victims and the community at large are warned, the community is better able to protect itself; also, offenders who know they are being watched will be deterred from reoffending.[36] The negative aspects of CN are that it may prevent the offender from re-establishing a stable residence and relationships in the community, thereby increasing the possibility of reoffending.

Decisions about CN are most often made by a committee composed of a police representative, a private citizen, a specialist in medical/therapeutic interventions, and representatives from provincial and federal corrections. See At Issue 12.1.

AT ISSUE

Issue 12.1: Community Notification

Should the practice of community notification be continued in Canada?

Proponents of CN make these arguments: that CN will alert the neighbourhood to a potential risk, thereby reducing the likelihood of another offence; that public safety overrides any expectation the offender has for privacy; and that it protects victims. Opponents of CN counter that it is not an innovative correctional practice, but rather reflective of penal populism; that there is no evidence that it is effective at reducing reoffending; that it increases public fear and paranoia; and that it makes it difficult for offenders to reintegrate into the community and, in so doing, raises the risk of reoffending. Which arguments do you find most persuasive?

Sources: A. Bain, "Please Recycle: Continuities in Punishment," *International Journal of Law, Crime, and Justice* 39, no. 2 (2011): 121–35; Y. N. Brannon, J. S. Levenson, T. Fortney, and J. N. Baker, "Attitudes About Community Notification: A Comparison of Sexual Offenders and the Non-Offending Public," *Sexual Abuse: A Journal of Research and Treatment* 19, no. 4 (2007): 369–79; G. Duwe and W. Donnay, "Impact of Megan's Law on Sex Offender Recidivism: The Minnesota Experience." *Criminology* 46, no. 2 (2008): 411–46.

MAKING IT OR GOING BACK: FACTORS IN THE SUCCESS OR FAILURE OF OFFENDERS ON RELEASE

It took me 34 years to get lucky, a lot of people don't get that opportunity, and they get really frustrated and they get really angry and down on themselves. They resort to alcohol and drugs, and that is sometimes why they are there in the first place, and then they just get out of control, they don't care about their life. They don't care if they get into trouble. When I look back in my life, going out on those mandatory supervision releases, I would be doing things like getting really drugged and getting high, and then hurting somebody. I

think people, a lot of people, are doing that just because they don't have any
positive things happening in their life, and they can't see a positive future.

A state-raised ex-offender, personal communication with C.T. Griffiths

Even the most institutionalized state-raised inmate does not leave a correctional institution with the intent of returning. Furthermore, correctional systems have as a primary objective the reduction of recidivism among offenders released into the community.

There are several ways in which the supervision of an offender on conditional release comes to an end: (1) successful completion of sentence to the end of the supervision period; (2) revocation for a breach of a condition of release; and (3) revocation due to a conviction for a new offence.[37] The successful completion rates for federal offenders in 2010–2011 were as follows: day parole: 89 percent; full parole: 77 percent; and statutory release: 62 percent.[38]

For provincial offenders, the successful completion rates in 2010–2011 were 83 percent for day parole and 82 percent for full parole.[39] Provincial parolees are more likely to breach a condition of their release rather than to be convicted of a new offence. Offenders on statutory release have higher rates of revocation with offences and with violent offences than offenders on full parole.[40] The outcome rates for provincial offenders indicate that there are very few revocations of parole resulting from the commission of a violent offence.

Among the factors that increase the likelihood of success on parole are a supportive network of family and friends, stable housing and employment, participation in treatment programs, and a conscious decision to move out of a criminal lifestyle.[41] Incarceration is hard on families, and couples can encounter challenges in reunification after the offender's release from custody. This is reflected in the comments of a male offender and an offender's spouse:

Male offender: A lot of women don't understand that what we go through
as men and being incarcerated. They say, "You ain't there no more, you
know. Just forget about it." It's not that easy.

Female partner: Even though we have trust and loyalty there, it's still a big
gap … It's almost like a whole relationship all over again … The biggest
thing right now is just getting back to reality, have everything set back in,
trying to get back to who we were from before.[42]

Unfortunately it is the handful of offenders who commit heinous crimes again who receive the attention of the media. It is they who often have a strong impact on corrections policies and practices—who encourage tougher sentencing laws and tighten the decision making of parole boards. The "silent majority" of offenders who successfully complete conditional release is invisible to the community. When asked about the connotations attached to the word "parolee," community residents tend to respond in one of two ways: "got out too soon," or "dangerous to the public." These responses reflect the fact, noted in Chapter 1, that most citizens get their information on crime, criminal justice, and corrections from the media.

Contrary to what media reports would have us believe, the rate of reconviction for violent offences for offenders under community supervision has declined over the past decade. The highest failure rate is among those offenders who were not granted parole but instead were released on statutory release by the CSC after serving two-thirds of their sentence. As a group, these offenders are at high risk to reoffend, which perhaps is one reason why they were not granted release on parole. Statistics also indicate that offenders released on day parole had significantly higher completion rates than offenders released on full parole or statutory release.[43]

Suspension and Revocation of Conditional Release

Failing to abide by any of the set conditions, including committing a new criminal offence or failing to adhere to the conditions of the parole certificate, may result in a **suspension of conditional release**.

When a parolee is suspended, two outcomes are possible: (1) the parole supervisor cancels the suspension and releases the person from custody, or (2) the case is referred back to the provincial parole board or the PBC for a hearing to determine whether there should be a **revocation of conditional release** (which usually means a transfer back to a correctional facility).

Parole officers have considerable discretion in the use of suspensions. The law states that officers *may* suspend a parolee for violating a parole condition or when new offences are alleged. The number of cases in which technical violations occur or new offences are alleged but a suspension is not imposed is unknown.

An understudied area of corrections is the decision making of staff in community corrections centres and other facilities where offenders may reside while on release. These staff may facilitate or hinder an offender's efforts to abide by conditions of release. A staff member at a federal halfway house stated: "Sometimes a staff member won't like the offender and will find any little reason to have them violated and returned to prison. There is definitely favouritism at work" (personal communication with C. T. Griffiths).

Offenders who have had their conditional release suspended are returned to the correctional facility to await a post-suspension hearing before the parole board. The board will review the report on the incident that triggered the suspension and the post-suspension report prepared by the supervising parole officer. The parole board has a number of options, including cancelling the suspension and reinstating the parole (with additional conditions if required), or ending the parole, which means that the offender remains in confinement.

CIRCLES OF SUPPORT AND ACCOUNTABILITY: A RESTORATIVE, REINTEGRATIVE PRACTICE FOR HIGH-RISK OFFENDERS

COSAs were first developed by the Canadian Mennonite Community in the early 1990s. They were based on the traditional indigenous practice of healing circles. COSAs provide support for sex offenders who are released from federal

---

Suspension of conditional release
A process initiated by the supervising parole officer (or in some instances by the parole board) in cases where the parolee has allegedly failed to abide by the conditions of release.

Revocation of conditional release
A decision by a releasing authority, such as a parole board, made in connection with an offender whose release has been suspended.

Circles of support and accountability (COSAs)
Community-based committees composed of criminal justice personnel and community members that provide mentoring for high-risk sex offenders whose sentences have expired.

institutions at warrant expiry or whose period of supervision on conditional release has ended due to warrant expiry. COSAs are a counterweight to the professionalization of corrections and penal populism.[44]

These offenders are the most likely targets of judicial recognizances and CN. Any offender who participates in the program does so on a voluntary basis; there is no legal mechanism that can compel him or her to be subject to monitoring.

COSAs are centred on the principles of restorative justice, including the importance of positive relationships that can facilitate positive change in the offender while at the same time addressing the injury caused to the victim and the community.[45] COSAs are designed to extend contact with the offender beyond the Warrant Expiry Date (end of sentence and parole supervision) and to engage the community in efforts to reintegrate high-risk offenders.[46] Figure 12.3 sets out the four key principles on which COSAs are based: reintegration/restoration, support, monitoring, and maintenance. Figure 12.4 illustrates the relationships of COSAs.

Figure 12.3

The Key Principles of COSAs

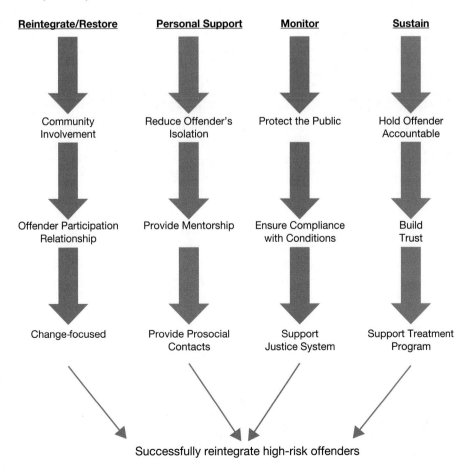

Reintegrate/Restore	Personal Support	Monitor	Sustain
Community Involvement	Reduce Offender's Isolation	Protect the Public	Hold Offender Accountable
Offender Participation Relationship	Provide Mentorship	Ensure Compliance with Conditions	Build Trust
Change-focused	Provide Prosocial Contacts	Support Justice System	Support Treatment Program

Successfully reintegrate high-risk offenders

Figure 12.4

Conceptual Model of a Circle of Support: Relationships of the Circle within the Community

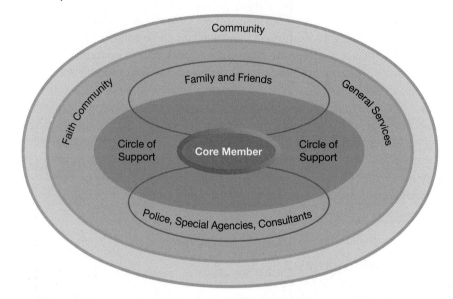

Source: E. Heise, L. Horne, H. Kirkegaard, H. Nigh, I. P. Derry, and M. Yantzi. *Community Reintegration Project.* (Toronto: Mennonite Central Committee, 1996). Pg. 14. Reprinted by permission of Mennonite Central Committee Ontario.

A circle of support is a team of five or six volunteers assigned to an offender to assist him as he or she takes up residence in their community. Volunteers can include teachers, social workers, police officers, businesspeople, and other community residents. They help with all facets of reintegration, including housing, employment, budgeting and financial management, spiritual development, and moral support. The offender may call only in times of stress or may have daily contact with the circle members. Circle members can also mediate between the offender and the community, as suggested in the conceptual model in Figure 12.4. In Ontario, the Mennonite Central Committee operates the Community Reintegration Project (CRP), which provides the Circles of Support and Accountability program, which in turn offers support for sex offenders who are released from federal institutions at warrant expiry. Mediation took place in the case of Joe, whose arrival in the community was the subject of a CN (see Box 12.2).

BOX 12.2

Joe and His Circle of Support

It began with a telephone call. "Can you help me?" the caller asked. "I'm just out of prison, and the police have already been warning everyone that I am in town. Where am I going to find a quiet place to live?" Joe, 54, had been released at warrant expiry from prison after serving a 6-year sentence for sexual assault against a child. It was his 8th conviction.

Joe wanted to come to our city for several reasons. He knew us, he had met public resistance in another town when he attempted to settle there before his parole was revoked, and he suspected that he could get help in relapse prevention. We agreed to help him find accommodation, help him to find a job, and try to build a Circle of friendship and support in his new city. We thought of people that we knew who could help him in each of these areas and who would be willing to work with us. We also agreed to make contact with the police.

The detectives, when we met with them, candidly said, "We don't want him here." Based on institutional reports, the police felt that Joe was likely to reoffend. There had been a lot of negative publicity recently about released prisoners reoffending, and they didn't want any of that kind of publicity for their department.

When Joe came to stay with us for the weekend while beginning the apartment search, the police quickly made his picture available to the media and warned the community of his presence among us.

The media descended upon us because we had been identified as providing support for Joe. Pickets of irate and concerned parents arrived in front of our home. After a number of angry and threatening phone calls, we finally bought a telephone answering machine.

The police mounted a plan of surveillance. They felt sure he would reoffend within a short period. They were concerned about the safety of the children in the neighbour-hood, but they also wanted to ensure Joe's safety.

One of the neighbours had called the police and had a lengthy discussion with the detective. She later called to talk with me. Ann had small children and was very concerned for their safety and that of the many other children living in the area. After a discussion with her, and later with Joe, we agreed that he would meet with her to discuss her concerns. Lengthy negotiations ensued, finally resulting in a meeting proposed in a neutral site, and several other neighbours were invited to participate. The police detectives would also be present. They would be there not only as a resource, but as people who could add to the participants' feelings of security.

Joe, accompanied by two of his friends, was the first to arrive at the meeting and take a seat on the far side of the room. Soon the neighbours began to arrive. Then the detectives entered. The ground rules of the meeting were outlined. We would go around the circle to allow everyone an opportunity to share their first name and a particular concern they brought with them. We would have a statement from the neighbourhood group, followed by an opportunity for Joe to share, and from there we would move to addressing the issues presented. Only one person at a time would

(continued)

speak, and they would follow our direction and instructions for the orderly addressing of the issues. Before the end of the meeting, we would decide together what of this meeting would be appropriate to share with other people, outside of this meeting.

As we began to go around the circle, the first person began by saying how much she appreciated the willingness of Joe and his friends to attend such a meeting. Ann outlined the questions she had heard the others discussing with her. There was a long list of questions: they wanted to know what had happened, what the sentence was, what treatment he had obtained, and what treatment he planned to receive now that he was released. "From your experience, what is the best way to avoid the behaviour you were charged with?" "How do you plan to deal with the negative reactions and anger of some individuals in the community?"

Joe responded, outlining in general terms his offences. Appreciation was expressed for the constructive method the residents had chosen to address their concerns, which he acknowledged were understandable. He indicated that he had received some treatment while in the institution and was planning to arrange suitable community-based therapy and had indeed made arrangements for that already. He had also set up an accountability system through his Circle of Support, by which he had daily contact with us, and we were able to make inquiry as to his faithfulness to his commitments in specific relevant areas.

We talked, and the earlier tension in the room eased as we got on with the task of problem solving around the various issues at hand. Though all the questions were not answered, by the end of the 2½- hour meeting, there was a feeling of accomplishment and a readiness to move on.

Out of that meeting and others we had, some bridges were built. Neighbourhood residents, some of whom were vocally angry, began to see Joe as a person and recognized the difficulties with which he coped.

Throughout this time, Joe's Circle of Support met regularly with him. At least one of the Circle Members contacted him every day. After a year, we still talk to him daily. We took him to do his laundry, to shop for groceries and furnishings for his apartment.

The police have been partners with us in Joe's Circle of Support. Without the patient, humorous, understanding commitment of the detectives with whom we dealt most frequently, our efforts might not have reached this point. They came to our Circle meetings. They checked in with us frequently and we trusted their openness with us. Similarly, the police served as a buffer with the community, correcting rumours and diffusing problems.

Joe's life has settled into a comfortable pattern. He maintains a clean, comfortable apartment and has developed some close relationships. He is finding ways to spend his time and is slowly developing a small network of friends, although trust takes a long time.

Source: E. Heise, L. Horne, H. Kirkegaard, H. Nigh, I. P. Derry, and M. Yantzi, *Community Reintegration Project,* (Toronto: Mennonite Central Committee, 1996). Pg. 14. Reprinted by permission of Mennonite Central Committee Ontario.

The effectiveness of selected supervision/control strategies for offenders in the community are summarized in Research File 12.1.

RESEARCH FILE 12.1

The Effectiveness of Selected Supervision/Control Strategies

Does parole work? Hard to say. Most parolees successfully complete their sentence. However, there is little information on whether the needs of offenders have been addressed and whether their quality-of-life issues (e.g., addiction issues, housing, family stability, employment) have been addressed. Ex-offenders may remain marginal and vulnerable. The primary measure is recidivism rates, which consider none of these items. There is a need for studies on post-supervision recidivism and other measures of success.

Which offenders benefit most from parole? Lower risk offenders. Success rates are generally higher for low-risk offenders without lengthy criminal histories and those who have not committed a sexual offence or another crime of violence. There is evidence from American studies that low-risk offenders benefit most from parole supervision and community programs, while those offenders with lengthy criminal histories and who had committed crimes of violence were the least impacted by parole.[a]

Do EM and GPS tracking reduce reoffending? Unknown. There is no conclusive evidence that GPS technology either increases public safety, lowers rates of reoffending, or, in particular, helps sex offenders successfully reintegrate back into the community.[b] Studies have found that GPS programs are very time consuming for parole officers. A preliminary study of the use of EM with federal offenders in Canada found no impact of reoffending.[c] However, since this study, the federal government has created legislative provisions for the use of EM for federal offenders.

Do COSAs work? Yes. Research studies of the experiences of COSA participants (including offenders) have found lower rates of reoffending and a positive view of the program by all participants.[d] In a study of sex offenders released from confinement at the expiry of their sentence, half the sample ($N = 44$) participated in COSAs and the other half ($N = 44$) did not. The offenders were followed for nearly 3 years, and success/failure was measured by incurring a new charge or being convicted of a new offence. Among the findings of the study: compared to the offenders who did not participate in COSAs, the sex offenders who participated in the program had lower rates of sexual reoffending (85 percent reduction), other types of violent crimes (73 percent reduction), and overall reoffending (71 percent reduction).[e]

(continued)

Does CN work? Not likely. Although CN appears to have strong support from the public, there have been few studies (none of them Canadian) about the impact of CN on reoffending among high-risk offenders. Nor have there been any about whether CN improved feelings of personal safety in the community. An American study found no differences in the recidivism rates (commission of new offences and/or violations of release conditions) of male sex offenders.[f] A study that compared the perceptions of sex offenders with those of the general public as to the fairness of the CN law in that state found (not surprisingly) that sex offenders viewed the law as more unfair than did the general public; also, the sex offenders stated that they experienced more vigilantism than was publicly known and that notification had had a negative impact on their efforts to reintegrate into the community.[g] Similarly, sex offenders who were required to register with the police in the community felt stigmatized and experienced difficulties in social relationships and in finding housing and employment.[h]

[a] B. M. Huebner and M. T. Berg, "Examining the Sources of Variation in Risks for Recidivism," *Justice Quarterly* 28, no. 1 (2011): 146–73; A. L. Solomon, V. Kachnowski, and A. Bhati, *Does Parole Work? Analyzing the Impact of Postprison Supervision on Rearrest Outcomes* (Washington, DC: Urban Institute, 2005), http://www.urban.org/publications/311156.html.

[b] California Sex Offender Management Board, *Recommendations Report* (Sacramento, 2010), 48, http://www.casomb.org/docs/CASOMB%20Report%20Jan%202010_Final%20Report.pdf.

[c] M. Olotu, M. Beaupre, and P. Verbrugge, *Evaluation Report: Electronic Monitoring Program Pilot* (Ottawa: Correctional Service of Canada, 2009), http://www.csc-scc.gc.ca/text/pa/empp/index-eng.shtml.

[d] R. J. Wilson, J. E. Picheca, and M. Prinzo, *Circles of Support and Accountability: An Evaluation of the Pilot Project in South-Central Ontario* (Ottawa: Correctional Service of Canada, 2005), http://www.csc-scc.gc.ca/text/rsrch/reports/r168/r168_e.pdf.

[e] R. J. Wilson, F. Cortoni, and A. J. McWhinnie, "Circles of Support and Accountability: A Canadian National Replication of Outcome Findings," *Sexual Abuse: A Journal of Research and Treatment* 21, no. 4 (2009): 412–30.

[f] R. G. Zevitz, "Sex Offender Community Notification: Its Role in Recidivism and Offender Reintegration," *Criminal Justice Studies* 19, no. 2 (2006): 193–208.

[g] Y. N. Brannon, J. S. Levenson, T. Fortney, and J. N. Baker, "Attitudes About Community Notification: A Comparison of Sexual Offenders and the Non-Offending Public," *Sexual Abuse: A Journal of Research and Treatment* 19, no. 4 (2007): 369–79.

[h] R. Tewksbury, "Collateral Consequences of Offender Registration," *Journal of Contemporary Criminal Justice* 21, no. 1 (2005): 67–81.

SUMMARY

The reentry of offenders into the community after serving time in custody is one of the most important, and challenging, stages of the corrections process. While society has perfected the process for removing offenders from the community, far less attention has been given to how to reintegrate them back into the community. This may be particularly challenging as many offenders were marginal prior to their conviction and incarceration. Offenders may find adjusting to life in the outside community stressful. Unique challenges are encountered by special groups of offenders, including the mentally ill and sex offenders. The majority of offenders are on some form of conditional release, and parole officers have a dual role: to provide assistance *and* oversight. Restorative justice practices such as COSAs hold considerable promise and provide an alternative to strategies that may hinder an offender's reintegration, such as CN.

KEY POINTS REVIEW

1. To succeed, reintegration should involve continuity between the inmate's institutional programs and the services that person receives on conditional release in the community (the notion of throughcare).

2. Incarceration has a number of collateral effects, including the loss of personal relationships and social networks, the acquisition of self-defeating habits and attitudes, the loss of personal belongings, and the loss of the ability to maintain housing.

3. Persons on conditional release are subject to differing levels of supervision by corrections officials, ranging from periodic reporting to electronic monitoring, to frequent face-to-face contacts with a parole officer.

4. Parole officers have a dual role in their relations with clients: they serve as resources and confidants while also monitoring them and enforcing conditional release conditions.

5. The general approach of correctional systems is to manage the risk of sex offenders on conditional release through drug therapy, CN, registration, and various supervision and monitoring strategies.

6. Statistics indicate that most federal offenders successfully complete their conditional sentences and do not reoffend prior to warrant expiry.

7. The reconviction rate for violent offences for offenders under community supervision has declined in recent years.

8. A number of factors complicate attempts to assess the effectiveness of parole.

9. CN may not be an effective strategy for ensuring the safety and security of the community and may hinder offender reintegration.

10. COSAs are an effective strategy for reducing re-offending among high-risk sex offenders.

KEY TERM QUESTIONS

1. Define **reintegration** and its objectives.

2. What is meant by **throughcare** and why is this notion important in the study of prisoner reentry?

3. How do the ***pains of reentry*** and ***post incarceration syndrome (PICS)*** affect offenders returning to the community?

4. Describe ***community notification*** and discuss the issues surrounding its use.

5. Define ***suspension of conditional release*** and ***revocation of conditional release*** and explain how these affect the status of an offender on conditional release.

6. Describe ***circles of support and accountability (COSAs),*** how these circles operate, and what the research suggests regarding their effectiveness.

NOTES

1. A. Thurber, "Understanding Offender Reintegration," *Forum on Corrections Research* 10, no. 1 (1998): 14–18 at 14.

2. K. Bumby, M. Carter, S. Gibel, L. Gilligan, and R. Stroker, *Increasing Public Safety Through Successful Offender Reentry: Evidence-Based and Emerging Practices in Corrections* (Washington, DC: Center for Effective Public Policy and Bureau of Justice Assistance, 2007), http://www.cepp.com/documents/CEPPSVORI_final.pdf; P. B. Burke, *TPC Reentry Handbook: Implementing the NIC Transition for Prison to the Community Model* (Washington, DC: National Institute of Corrections, U.S. Department of Justice, 2008), http://static/nicic.gov/Library/022669.pdf.

3. L. Gideon, "What Shall I Do Now? Released Offenders' Expectations for Supervision Upon Release," *International Journal of Offender Therapy and Comparative Criminology* 53, no. 1 (2009): 43–56.

4. Le Protecteur du Citoyen, *Report by the Québec Ombudsman: Toward Services That Are Better Adjusted to Detainees with Mental Disorders* (Québec City: 2011), 6, http://www.protecteurducitoyen.qc.ca/fileadmin/medias/pdf/rapports_speciaux/10-05-11_Rapport_sante_mentale_FINAL_EN.pdf.

5. C. T. Griffiths, Y. Dandurand, and D. Murdoch, *The Social Reintegration of Offenders and Crime Prevention* (Ottawa: National Crime Prevention Centre, Public Safety Canada, 2007), http://www.publicsafety.gc.ca/res/cp/res/soc-reint-eng.aspx.

6. S. Maruna, "Reentry as a Rite of Passage," *Punishment and Society* 13, no. 1 (2011): 3–28.

7. M. Olotu, D. Luong, C. MacDonald, M. McKay, S. Heath, N. Allegri, and E. Loree, "Correctional Interventions," Chapter 1 in *Report of the Evaluation of CSC's Community Corrections* (Ottawa: Correctional Service of Canada, 2011), 47, http://www.csc-scc.gc.ca/text/pa/ev-cci-fin/ev-cci-fin-eng.pdf.

8. S. Poirier (Chair), *Decades of Darkness, Moving Towards the Light: A Review of the Prison System in Newfoundland and Labrador* (St. John's: Government of Newfoundland and Labrador, 2008), 27, http://www.cbc.ca/news/pdf/nl-corrections-report-20081208.pdf.

9. Ibid., 30.

10. Griffiths, Dandurand, and Murdoch, *The Social Reintegration of Offenders and Crime Prevention*.

11. S. Novac, J. Herner, E. Paradis, and A. Kellen, *Justice and Injustice: Homelessness, Crime, Victimization, and the Criminal Justice System*, Research Paper no. 207 (Toronto: Centre for Urban and Community Studies, University of Toronto, 2006), http://www.citiescentre.utoronto.ca/Assets/Cities+Centre+Digital+Assets/pdfs/publications/Research+Papers/207+Novac+et+al.pdf.

12. R. Zorzi, S. Scott, D. Doherty, A. Engman, C. Lauzon, M. McGuire, and J. Ward, *Housing Options upon Discharge from Correctional Facilities* (Ottawa: Canada Mortgage and Housing Corporation, 2006), http://www.cmhc-schl.gc.ca/odpub/pdf/65340.pdf?fr=1343101698796.

13. H. Echenberg and J. Jensen, *Risk Factors for Homelessness* (Ottawa: Social Affairs Division, Parliamentary Information and Research Service, 2009), 2, http://www.parl.gc.ca/Content/LOP/ResearchPublications/prb0851-e.pdf.

14. John Howard Society of Toronto, *Homeless and Jailed; Jailed and Homeless* (Toronto: 2010), 20, http://www.johnhoward.ca/document/JHS-Toronto%20Report%20Homeless%20and%20Jailed.pdf.

15. Ibid., 27.

16. M. Borzycki, *Interventions for Prisoners Returning to the Community* (Canberra: Australian Institute of Criminology, 2005), http://www.crimeprevention.gov.au/NationalCrimePreventionProgramme/Pages/Interventions_for_Prisoners_Returning_to_the_Community.aspx.

17. City of Toronto, *Street Needs Assessment Results* (Toronto: Toronto Shelter, Support, and Housing Administration, 2009), http://www.toronto.ca/legdocs/mmis/2010/cd/bgrd/backgroundfile-29123.pdf.

18. Social Planning and Research Council of Hamilton, *Hamilton Community Correctional Services Needs Assessment* (Hamilton: 2010), 15, http://www.sprc.hamilton.on.ca/wp-content/uploads/2010/02/Hamilton-Community-Correctional-Services-Needs-Assessment-February-2010.pdf.

19. Ibid., 16.

20. Ibid., 16.

21. P. J. Murphy, L. Johnsen, and J. Murphy, *Paroled for Life: Interviews with Parolees Serving Life Sentences* (Vancouver: New Star, 2002), 166–67.

22. Poirier, *Decades of Darkness*, 26.

23. T. T. Gorski, *Post Incarceration Syndrome and Relapse* (2002), http://www.tgorski.com/criminal_justice/cjs_pics_&_relapse.htm.

24. B. Steiner, L. F. Travis, M. D. Makarios, and T. Brickley, "The Influence of Parole Officers' Attitudes on Supervision Practices," *Justice Quarterly* 28, no. 6 (2011): 903–27.

25. E. Gunnison and J. B. Helfgott, "Factors That Hinder Offender Reentry Success: A View from Community Corrections Officers," *International Journal of Offender Therapy and Comparative Criminology* 55, no. 2 (2011): 287–304 at 296.

26. J. Helfgott, "Ex-Offender Needs Versus Criminal Opportunity in Seattle, Washington," *Federal Probation* 61, no. 2 (1997): 12–24.

27. M. Lynch, "Waste Managers? The New Penology, Crime Fighting, and Parole Agent Identity," *Law and Society Review* 32 (1998): 839–69.

28. Correctional Service of Canada and National Parole Board, *National Joint Board of Investigation into the Release and Supervision of an Offender on Full Parole Charged with First-Degree Murder of a Parole Officer on October 7, 2004, in Yellowknife, Northwest Territories* (Ottawa, 2006), http://www.csc-scc.gc.ca/text/pblct/ci-report05-06/report-eng.pdf.

29. B. Cheadle, "Feds Explore GPS-Linked Panic Buttons for Parole Officers, Other Staff," *iPolitics*, October 1, 2012, http://www.ipolitics.ca/2012/10/01/feds-explore-gps-panic-buttons-for-parole-officers.

30. E. McGrath, "Reentry Courts: Providing a Second Chance for Incarcerated Mothers and Their Children," *Family Court Review* 50, no. 1 (2012): 113–27.

31. D. J. Farole, *The Harlem Parole Reentry Court Evaluation: Implementation and Preliminary Impacts* (New York: Center for Court Innovation, 2003), http://www.courtinnovation.org/pdf/harlem_reentry_eval.pdf; S. Maruna and T. LeBel, "Welcome Home? Examining the 'Reentry Court' from a Strengths-Based Perspective," *Western Criminology Review* 4, no. 2 (2003): 91–107, http://wcr.sonoma.edu/v4n2/manuscripts/marunalebel.pdf.

32. M. Axford and R. Ruddell, "Police–Parole Partnerships in Canada: A Review of a Promising Programme," *International Journal of Police Science and Management* 12, no. 2 (2010): 274–86.

33. R.J. Wilson, L. Stewart, T. Stirpe, M. Barrett, and J.E. Cripps, "Community-Based Sex Offender Management: Combining Parole Supervision and Treatment to Reduce Recidivism," *Canadian Journal of Criminology* 42, no. 2 (2000): 177–88.

34. Murphy, Johnsen, and Murphy, *Paroled for Life* 117.

35. Wilson et al., "Community-Based Sex Offender Management," 177–88.

36. R.G. Zevitz, "Sex Offender Community Notification: Its Role in Recidivism and Offender Reintegration," *Criminal Justice Studies* 19, no. 2 (2006): 193–208.

37. Parole Board of Canada, *Performance Monitoring Report 2010–2011*, 29.

38. Ibid., 30.

39. Ibid., 32.

40. Ibid.

41. S.J. Bahr, L. Harris, J.K. Fisher, and A.H. Armstrong, "Successful Reentry: What Differentiates Successful and Unsuccessful Parolees?", *International Journal of Offender Therapy and Comparative Criminology* 54, no. 5 (2010): 667–92; M. Makarios, B. Steiner, and L.T. Travis, "Examining the Predictors of Recidivism Among Men and Women Released from Prison in Ohio," *Criminal Justice and Behavior* 37, no. 12 (2010): 1377–91; C.A. Visher, S.A. Debus-Sherrill, and J. Yahner, "Employment After Prison: A Longitudinal Study of Former Prisoners," *Justice Quarterly* 28, no. 5 (2011): 698–718.

42. J.J. Harman, V.E. Smith, and L.C. Egan, "The Impact of Incarceration on Intimate Relationships," *Criminal Justice and Behavior* 34, no. 6 (2007): 794–815 at 801.

43. Public Safety Canada, Corrections Statistics Committee, *Corrections and Conditional Release Statistical Overview* (Ottawa: Public Works and Government Services Canada, 2011), http://www.publicsafety.gc.ca/res/cor/rep/_fl/2010-ccrso-eng.pdf.

44. A. Bates, R. Saunders, and C. Wilson, "Doing Something About It: A Follow-Up Study of Sex Offenders Participating in Thames Valley Circles of Support and Accountability," *British Journal of Community Justice* 5, no. 1 (2007): 19–42; A. Bates, R. Macrae, C. Webb, and D. Williams, "Ever-Increasing Circles: A Descriptive Study of Hampshire and Thames Valley Circles of Support and Accountability 2002–2009," *Journal of Sexual Aggression* 18, no. 3 (2012): 355–73.

45. C. Wilson, "The Realities of Practice," in *A Community-Based Approach to the Reduction of Sexual Reoffending*, ed. S. Hanvey, T. Philpot, and C. Wilson (London: Jessica Kingsley, 2011), 58–71.

46. Hanvey, Philpot, and Wilson, *A Community-Based Approach to the Reduction of Sexual Reoffending*.

PART V

SPECIAL POPULATIONS
IN CORRECTIONS

Systems of corrections have a responsibility to supervise and assist a diverse population of offenders. The next three chapters focus on three special populations: women (Chapter 13), Aboriginals (Chapter 14), and youth (Chapter 15).

Correctional policy for women offenders has been driven by critical events as well as by a recognition that women's needs—and their pathways to crime—are different than for men. Aboriginal persons are overrepresented in the criminal justice and corrections systems. In part, this reflects the legacy of colonization and the destruction of Aboriginal cultures, communities, and families. A number of specialized facilities, programs, and services have been developed in an effort to meet the unique needs of Aboriginal offenders; many of these utilize Aboriginal traditions and spirituality. For young offenders, there is a separate system of justice and corrections that strongly emphasizes alternatives to incarceration, including various community-based initiatives. Many of these initiatives are based on restorative justice principles.

The move toward a punitive penology, as evidenced by Bill C-10, threatens to have a strong negative impact on women and Aboriginal offenders; for example, it may increase the number of offenders in custody and result in lengthier periods of incarceration. For young offenders, the legislation represents a shift away from the principles of the Youth Criminal Justice Act toward a "get tough" approach.

CHAPTER 13

WOMEN OFFENDERS

CHAPTER OBJECTIVES

After reading this chapter, you should be able to:

- *Describe the profile of women offenders in corrections.*
- *Discuss the evolution of correctional policies for women offenders.*
- *Note the importance of the Arbour Report and the Creating Choices report for women's corrections.*
- *Discuss the dynamics of doing time in women's correctional institutions.*
- *Describe the pains of imprisonment for women offenders.*
- *Discuss the death of Ashley Smith and its implications for women's corrections.*
- *Describe correctional programming for women offenders.*
- *Describe the challenges women that offenders encounter upon release from custody.*

Women offenders present unique challenges for systems of corrections. The pathways to crime for women offenders are in many ways distinct from those for male offenders, and as a result, gender-specific programs and interventions have had to be developed. A review of the correctional response to women points to instances when their human rights, including Canada's obligations under international law, have been violated.[1] Box 13.1 sets out some of the general attributes of women offenders.

BOX 13.1

A Profile of Women Offenders in Corrections

- Women offenders represent about 1 in 10 offenders admitted to custody and, in many respects, present a different profile than male offenders.
- The number of women admitted to federal custody has increased 40 percent in the past decade, and the number of Aboriginal women admitted to federal correctional facilities has increased 90 percent during that time.
- More and more women are being admitted to custody for violent crimes.
- One in 10 women are gang-affiliated, compared to 1 in 6 for male offenders.

- One in four federal women inmates have been incarcerated on drug-related charges, and HIV and HCV infection is generally higher among women inmates.
- Federal women offenders are twice as likely to have been previously hospitalized for psychiatric reasons and to have mental health issues.
- Women offenders generally have greater health and mental health needs and are more likely to have experienced sexual or physical victimization prior to incarceration.
- The number of federal women offenders over the age of 50 has increased over the past decade. Compared to younger women, these offenders have lower overall risk/needs and are less likely to have substance abuse issues, but are more likely to have personal/emotional issues.

Sources: Canadian HIV/AIDS Legal Network, *Women in Prison, HIV, and Hepatitis C* (Toronto: 2012), http://www.aidslaw.ca/publications/interfaces/downloadFile.php?ref=2008; D. Calverley, "Adult Correctional Services in Canada, 2008–2009," *Juristat* 30, no. 3 (Ottawa: Statistics Canada, 2010), http://www.statcan.gc.ca/pub/85-002-x/2010003/article/11353-eng.htm; D.D. DeHart, "Pathways to Prison: Impact of Victimization in the Lives of Incarcerated Women," *Violence Against Women* 14, no. 12 (2008): 1362–81; L. Greiner and K. Allenby, *A Descriptive Profile of Older Women Offenders* (Ottawa: Correctional Service of Canada, 2010), http://www.csc-scc.gc.ca/text/rsrch/reports/r229/r229-eng.shtml; L. Stone, "Gangs Starting to 'Infect' Women's Prisons," *Calgary Herald*, May 25, 2012.

THE EVOLUTION OF CORRECTIONS POLICY FOR WOMEN OFFENDERS

Little attention has been paid to the specific issues facing women offenders on probation or to their participation in restorative justice programs and in problem-solving courts (see Chapter 5). Instead, discussions of women's corrections have tended to focus on institutions where they are incarcerated. The defining events in women's corrections have all occurred in federal correctional facilities. Note also that most of the materials on women's corrections are on federally-sentenced women (FSW). Little is known about women in provincial/territorial corrections.

Two reports have had an especially significant impact on corrections policy for FSW. The first was **Creating Choices**, produced in 1990 by the Task Force on Federally Sentenced Women. This inquiry examined correctional policies and programs for federal women offenders. Among its recommendations were that a separate system of corrections be created for women, that the Kingston Prison for Women be closed (which it was, in 2000), that small regional facilities be built for women, including a healing lodge for Aboriginal women, and that the CSC appoint a Deputy Commissioner for Women.[2]

The second influential report was produced by Madame Justice Louise Arbour.[3] It was precipitated by an incident in 1994 at the now-closed Kingston Prison for Women, discussed below.

Creating Choices
The report of the Task Force on Federally Sentenced Women that had a significant impact on the structure and operation of women's corrections.

Video Link
Women Behind Bars
www.youtube.com/
watch?v=
-8QrjbtYktc

The Incident at the Kingston Prison for Women (P4W): A Watershed Event in Women's Corrections

On April 22, 1994, a brief but violent physical confrontation took place between six inmates and several COs at the Kingston Prison for Women (which has since been closed). As a result of the incident, the women were placed in segregation and criminally charged (five of the six inmates later pleaded guilty). Immediately after the incident, a high level of tension developed in the institution, compounded by the presence of a large number of overworked, overstressed, and relatively inexperienced correctional staff and COs. A lack of leadership from the prison's warden contributed to the events that unfolded over the next several days.

Two days later, on April 24, three other inmates who were housed in the segregation unit caused further disruption by slashing, taking a hostage, and attempting suicide. On April 26, COs from the institution demonstrated outside its walls, demanding that the inmates involved in the clash on April 22 be transferred to a higher security institution.

On the evening of that same day, the warden sent an all-male IERT to extract eight inmates in the segregation unit from their cells and strip-search them. Six of the eight had been involved in the initial confrontation on April 22. The IERT did not complete the cell extractions until early the following morning, at which time the eight women were left in empty cells in the segregation unit. The women had been stripped (in the presence of male members of the IERT), dressed in paper gowns, and placed in restraints and leg irons. All of the cell extractions and strip searches were recorded on videotape as per routine procedure. The following evening, seven of the eight inmates were subjected to body cavity searches. Six of the women involved in the original April 22 incident then were placed in segregation for many months.

The CSC investigated the incidents, but the report it issued left out many details. In February 1995, the report of the Correctional Investigator was tabled in the House of Commons. This report criticized the CSC's actions, the correctional staff, and the IERT. Pressure on the federal government to take action increased when portions of the videotape, showing the cell extractions and strip searches by the IERT, were shown on national television. An independent judicial inquiry was demanded, and one was appointed in April 1995. It was headed by the Honourable Louise Arbour, a highly respected member of the Québec judiciary.

The **Arbour Report** was extremely critical of the actions taken by correctional staff, the IERT personnel, and the warden.[4] The same report sharply criticized the response of senior CSC officials. In the end, the Commissioner of Corrections resigned.

The inquiry's report documented numerous violations of policy, the rule of law, and institutional regulations. For example, it criticized the use of segregation, the use of force by the IERT, and the manner in which the women had been strip-searched and subjected to body-cavity searches. The same report raised serious concerns regarding whether, without intervention and monitoring, the CSC was capable of implementing the necessary reforms to ensure adherence to

Arbour Report
The report of an inquiry into events at the Kingston Prison for Women in April 1994, which documented violations of policy, the rule of law, and institutional regulations and had a significant impact on the development of women's corrections.

justice and the rule of law. The Arbour Report made 14 key recommendations relating to the following: cross-gender staffing in correctional institutions for women; the use of force and of IERTs; the operations of segregation units; the needs of Aboriginal women in correctional institutions; ways of ensuring accountability and adherence to the rule of law by correctional personnel; and procedures for handling inmate complaints and grievances.

The Arbour Report had a significant impact on the CSC's operations and on the development of women's corrections.[5] A Deputy Commissioner for Women was appointed; a use-of-force policy was developed that stipulated that all-male IERT teams were never to be used as a first response in women's correctional institutions; and it is now forbidden for male staff to be present when female inmates are being strip-searched. The report also accelerated the closing of the Prison for Women in the year 2000 and the opening of smaller, regional facilities for federal female offenders.[6]

THE CURRENT STATE OF CORRECTIONS POLICY AND PRACTICE FOR WOMEN OFFENDERS

Despite these reforms, a number of scholars have argued that the CSC has failed to develop a correctional practice for women that is empowering and rehabilitative.[7] Although senior corrections officials did transform many of the recommendations from the *Creating Choices* (1990) and Arbour (1996) reports into policy, it has been argued that the experience of women offenders in institutions has remained largely unchanged and that the focus of the system is on punishment and control.[8, 9]

The closing of the Kingston Prison for Women and the opening of smaller regional facilities across the country was heralded as a new era in women's corrections. However, in the view of feminist scholars and others, systems of corrections continue to pursue a punitive penology based on "an oppressive hierarchical structure of gender equality" in which women who resist traditional roles are viewed as a threat to male patriarchy as embodied by corrections.[10] Specifically, attention is called to how traditional views of femininity affect correctional policy and practice. Within this perspective, women offenders who commit crime ("misbehave") are severely punished. There have also been feminist criticisms of community-based programs and services, as well as calls for practices that are gender responsive.[11]

Others dispute this interpretation, nothing that the number of women committing violent offences has increased, as have women who are gang affiliated. These observers also point to the development of women-specific assessment instruments and of treatment programs that have been designed to empower women offenders.

ALTERNATIVES TO CONFINEMENT

Women offenders participate in a variety of specialized courts that are intended to divert them from the traditional criminal justice process (See

Chapter 5). Women offenders generally do better on probation than their male counterparts and have lower rates of reoffending. There is some evidence that probation officers view women offenders as more challenging to supervise than male offenders.[12] These challenges often include addressing the needs of the children of women probationers, many of whom are single parents. This requires gender-specific programs and services.

DOING TIME: INSIDE WOMEN'S CORRECTIONAL FACILITIES

Historically, scholars have given little attention to the dynamics of life inside women's correctional institutions. The research literature on inmate social systems has focused primarily on men's institutions. There are unique features of life inside women's institutions that have significant implications for the women, correctional staff, and treatment programs. These include the patterns of interaction among the women.

It appears that the pains of imprisonment may be much more severe for female offenders than for their male counterparts. This is for a number of reasons, including these: many FSW are housed in facilities that are far from home; many are mothers who have been separated from their children; and confinement can have a strong impact on women who have experienced physical and emotional abuse as children and/or adults. For insightful, first-person accounts of female offenders in prison, see Lamb.[13]

Female offenders adapt to life inside correctional institutions differently than their male counterparts. Generally speaking, women inmates are far less likely than male inmates to verbally and/or physically assault correctional staff, regardless of their criminal history, mental health, and addiction issues.[14] This may change with the influx of increasing numbers of women offenders convicted of violent crimes and women who are gang-affiliated.

Research has also identified a number of different types of adjustment to confinement: some women adjust poorly to the prison regimen and remain entrenched in criminal thinking patterns; others are state-raised offenders who adhere to and enforce the traditional convict code; and still others access programs and resources in an effort to make significant changes in their attitudes and behaviour.[15] The argot roles inside a correctional facility for men include "right guys," "snitches," and "square Johns" (see Chapter 9). Inside the women's prison, the argot roles include "cherries," "butches," and "tricks."[16]

These roles are not readily apparent in Canadian women's prisons, though the absence of research precludes any definitive conclusions about the structure of the social system among women inmates. Women inmates may refer to having a "street mother" or "street sister"—that is, women with whom they have had relationships in the community, often associated with gang or criminal activity (warden, federal women's prison, personal communication with C.T. Griffiths). Other differences in the dynamics inside men's and women's institutions are set out in Box 13.2.

BOX 13.2

A Comparison of the Dynamics Inside Men's and Women's Correctional Institutions

	Men's Institutions	Women's Institutions
Security	More static, particularly in maximum security	More dynamic, interaction in maximum security between staff and inmates
Drugs	Generally imported from the outside	Often in-institution prescription drugs
Family visiting	Frequent; extensive use of family visitation unit; women "stand by their man"	Infrequent; men don't "stand by their women"; family visit units rarely used
Inmate interaction	Conflicts often short-lived; men internalize emotions	Conflicts endure; "assault with tongue"; emotional management a key issue
Personal relationships	Hidden; covert	Often overt

Source: Warden, Federal Women's Prison, personal communication with C.T. Griffiths.

Violence Inside Women's Institutions

The closing of the Kingston Prison for Women and the opening of smaller regional facilities across the country was heralded as a new era in women's corrections. In recent years, however, there appears to have been an increase in violence among women inmate populations. Overcrowding is often a factor in violence. During 2009–10, there was a 50 percent increase in disciplinary incidents, fights between inmates, assaults on COs, and other incidents in federal women's prisons.[17]

As in men's facilities, the social system in women's prisons appears to be changing, due in part to an increasing number of women being admitted to custody for crimes of violence. More women are self-identifying as gang-affiliated. Ten percent of women admitted to federal correctional facilities have gang ties, and this may lead to violence between inmates, placing correctional staff at more risk and compromising treatment efforts.

When first constructed, the regional facilities for federal women did not include maximum security units. That changed after a series of critical incidents, including the death of Denise Fayant (see Box 13.3). This incident occurred in 1996 at the then recently opened Edmonton Institution for Women (one of the small regional facilities built for federal female offenders). At the time, minimum, medium, and maximum security inmates were mixed into one population. For one inmate, this had fatal consequences.

BOX 13.3

The Murder of Denise Fayant

Thirty hours after arriving at the Edmonton Institution for Women, 21-year-old Denise Fayant was strangled by her former lover with a bathrobe sash. She died two days later in hospital. An investigation into the death, which was originally ruled a suicide, found that she had been slain by two inmates, one of whom had been her former lover and against whom she was scheduled to testify. A subsequent inquiry conducted by an Alberta Provincial Court judge found that Fayant had repeatedly told corrections officials that she would fear for her safety if they transferred her to the newly opened institution. Thirty hours after arrival, she was dead. Two inmates were later convicted and sentenced to additional federal time for the death. The investigating judge concluded that Fayant's death was a result of "callous and cavalier" actions on the part of the CSC and that she was a "victim of a process intent upon implementing an untested concept to manage federally sentenced women inmates. She was the test. The process failed tragically and inhumanely. Her death was avoidable."[a] Prison officials insisted that they had been assured by inmates in the prison that no harm would come to Fayant.

Fayant's death was only one of a number of critical incidents that occurred in the Edmonton Prison for Women within four months of its opening. Others included inmate-on-inmate assaults, assaults on a nurse and a physician, a completed suicide, and two attempted suicides.

[a] P. Cowan and D. Sheremata, "Death in Experimental Prison Unit—'She Was Helpless,'" *Edmonton Sun*, February 9, 2000.

A Pain of Imprisonment: Women Inmates and Their Children

I have pictures of my kids under my pillow, but I don't take them out, they make me cry.[18]

Women inmates are likely to be the sole custodial parent of their children.[19] When they are incarcerated, their children are usually cared for by relatives, most commonly grandparents. When no surrogate caretaker is available, the children may be taken in by provincial/territorial child welfare authorities and placed in foster care. If the period of incarceration is long and the children are young, they may be candidates for adoption. Because of these factors, the incarceration of a mother typically results in greater disruption in the lives of children than is the case if a father is incarcerated.

Inmate mothers have varying levels of contact with their children. That contact can include day visits, overnight family visits, on-site part-time residency, and live-in programs that allow the inmate-mother to have her child stay in the institution. Private family visits are generally available only in federal facilities. These visits, which allow the spouse and family members to spend up to 72 hours in a trailer unit or small house on the prison grounds, provide the opportunity for more normal parent–child interaction than is possible on a four-hour day visit.

Mother–child programs generally allow infants to reside with their mothers in open living units. Despite support for mother–child programs by the CSC and various provincial/territorial correctional systems, implementation has been slow and uneven across the country. A number of issues have been raised by these programs. See At Issue 13.1.

AT ISSUE

Issue 13.1: Mothers in Prison

Should there be mother–child programs in correctional institutions?

Proponents of such programs argue that they create or strengthen the bonds between mothers and their children, provide inmate mothers with the opportunity to learn parenting skills, and facilitate the development of prosocial attitudes and behaviours. Critics of mother–child programs counter that they are not in the best interests of children, that the prison environment, with its attendant illicit activities such as drug use, is no place for young children, and that the prison is an artificial environment that bears little resemblance to the outside community in which the inmate-mother and her child will ultimately have to adjust. To date, there have been no published studies on mother–child programs in Canadian correctional institutions. What do you think?

Psychological Health and Self-Injurious Behaviour (SIB)

Recall from Chapter 9 that many inmates are at risk of engaging in SIB, or self-harm, as a means of coping with confinement. These behaviours may include cutting, burning, ligature use, and head banging.[20] Note that self-harm is distinct from suicide and is most appropriately viewed as a coping mechanism.[21] This is particularly true for female offenders, who appear, as a group, to be at high risk.

Between 80 and 90 Percent
Have Been Physically
or Sexually Abused

Leah Hennel, Calgary Herald. Reprinted with permission of The Calgary Herald.

The arm of an incarcerated federally-sentenced woman.

Interviews with a sample (N = 54) of federal female offenders revealed that the most common reasons for this behaviour were to deal with negative emotions and as a cry for help to draw attention to their issues.[22] In the words of an inmate in the Edmonton Institution for Women, "I sliced my arms up because my brother passed away and I didn't know what to do."[23] Increasing attention is being given to identifying women offenders who are at risk of SIB. The risk of suicide may be higher for women who are placed in segregation and for those who have spent lengthy periods in relative isolation from the general population.[24] The Depression Hopelessness and Suicide Screening Form, for example, is used to screen for the presence of depression and suicide risk.[25]

The CSC has been severely criticized for its response to FSWs with mental health issues. An in-depth study of the topic found the following: (1) the CSC's mental health strategy is focused on assessment rather than treatment; (2) FSWs with mental health problems are treated as a risks; (3) the CSC does not consider the women's history of abuse; and (4) women with mental health problems are often overclassified, which results in their confinement in secure environments that limit their access to programs and services.[26] In addition, many FSWs with mental health issues are moved frequently between facilities, which undermines the continuity of what little treatment is available. This occurred in the case of Ashley Smith (see Box 13.4).

BOX 13.4

The Death of Ashley Smith

On October 19, 2007, 19-year-old Ashley Smith was found unconscious in her segregation cell at the Grand Valley Institution for Women. She died later that day. The official cause of death was self-initiated asphyxiation (suicide). However, a CSC report, made known in 2010, concluded that her death was accidental and the result of a desperate attempt for attention and interaction after she had been confined to isolation for many months.[a] At the time of her death, Ms. Smith was serving a sentence of six years and one month for a variety of weapons and assault offences.

As a young offender, Ms. Smith was initially sent to the New Brunswick Youth Centre. Her initial offences were minor and included throwing crabapples at a letter carrier. During her stay in that facility, before being transferred to the Saint John Regional Correctional Centre, she accumulated more than 800 incident reports, more than 500 institutional charges, and 168 self-harm incidents.

Ms. Smith was transferred to the penitentiary at age 19 and was subsequently moved 17 times between 9 different federal correctional facilities. She was in segregation during her entire confinement in the federal system.

The final report of the Office of the Correctional Investigator (2008) found that the CSC's actions violated the law and its own policy. Specifically, it found that Ms. Smith's mental health issues had not been addressed either in the youth facility or in the federal institutions in which she had been confined. There had been no psychological assessment. The Correctional Investigator concluded that her death might have been prevented had she been provided with proper care.

Among the recommendations in the Correctional Investigator's final report were that the CSC comply with the law and policy in its operations; that it improve its response to medical emergencies; that it review its segregation policy and practices; and that it ensure the delivery of adequate healthcare, including mental health services.[b]

A report on Ms. Smith's confinement in youth facilities was completed by the New Brunswick Ombudsman and Child and Youth Advocate,[c] and the Union of Canadian

(continued)

Correctional Officers has prepared a report on the incident as well, criticizing what it views as a "rush to judgment" to implicate the COs involved in the incident.[d]

An investigation of the incident by the Waterloo Regional Police resulted in three COs and a supervisor being charged with criminal negligence causing death. Police documents filed in court alleged that the guards and supervisor were responsible for the death of Ashley Smith in that they were negligent in failing to come to her aid when she was in distress in her cell. These four correctional personnel were fired and four other COs were suspended without pay for 60 days. The acting warden and deputy warden were also fired. In 2008, an Ontario judge, on recommendation from Crown counsel, dismissed all charges of criminal negligence causing death against the three COs.

The initial coroner's inquest into Ashley Smith's death collapsed in 2011 due to legal wrangling and the resignation of the coroner. A second inquest commenced in late 2012; it too was beset by legal challenges and delays, and continued into 2013. In 2011, the family of Ashley Smith settled an $11 million lawsuit against the CSC. For a timeline of Ashley Smith's involvement in the corrections system, related documents, and interviews, refer to the video links provided below.

[a] K. Makin, "Ashley Smith's Death Was an Accident, Not Suicide, Report Says," *Globe and Mail*, October 29, 2010, A4.

[b] Office of the Correctional Investigator, *A Preventable Death* (Ottawa: 2008), http://www.oci-bec.gc.ca/rpt/oth-aut/oth-aut20080620-eng.aspx.

[c] New Brunswick Office of the Ombudsman and Child and Youth Advocate, *Ashley Smith: A Report of the New Brunswick Ombudsman and Child and Youth Advocate on the Services Provided to a Youth Involved in the Youth Justice System* (Fredericton: 2008), http://www.gnb.ca/0073/PDF/AshleySmith-e.pdf.

[d] Union of Canadian Correctional Officers, *Rush to Judgment: A Report on the Death in Custody of Ashley Smith, an Inmate at Grand Valley Institution for Women* (Ottawa: 2008), http://www.ucco-sacc.csn.qc.ca/scriptorweb/scripto.asp?resultant=261990.

Video Links

Out of Control
www.cbc.ca/fifth/2009–2010/out_of_control

Behind the Wall: The Ashley Smith Story
www.cbc.ca/fifth/2010–2011/behindthewall

These practices are viewed as violations of international law—for example, as violations of the right to health, the right not to be discriminated against, the right not to be deprived of liberty and security, and the right not to suffer cruel, inhuman, and degrading treatment.[27] Of particular concern is the absence of judicial oversight of management policies and decisions with respect to FSWs with mental health problems.

CROSS-GENDER STAFFING IN WOMEN'S INSTITUTIONS

The incident at the Kingston Prison for Women in 1994 involved an all-male IERT extracting female inmates from their cells and stripping them of their clothing. This rekindled the debate over male staff in women's correctional facilities. Men work at all levels in Canadian women's institutions, from senior management positions down to the line level.

In 1998, the CSC appointed a Cross-Gender Monitor to conduct an independent review of **cross-gender staffing** in federal women's correctional facilities. The review's final report included the recommendation that male COs working in women's facilities not be permitted to carry out security functions in living and segregation units or to serve as members of cell-extraction teams.[28] An evaluation of a pilot project that involved introducing male correctional workers into front-line positions in a provincial institution for women in Saskatchewan reported positive views among inmates and staff and support for continuing the program.[29] See At Issue 13.2.

Cross-gender staffing
The practice of staffing correctional institutions with male and female officers. Most often discussed in terms of whether male COs should work inside correctional facilities for women.

AT ISSUE

Issue 13.2: Male COs in Women's Prisons

Should male COs work in women's prisons?

Proponents of cross-gender staffing argue that the presence of male COs helps normalize daily institutional life and provides positive relationships for women who in the past may not have been treated with respect. Opponents contend that the presence of male COs and treatment staff has a negative impact on female inmates who have histories of abuse by men and that the presence of men as front-line correctional workers increases the risk of privacy violations and sexual misconduct. Can you think of other arguments in support of or opposition to cross-gender staffing? What is your view on this issue? If you were a female offender in custody, would you have any difficulties with the presence of male COs?

Sources: The Honourable L. Arbour (Commissioner), *Commission of Inquiry into Certain Events at the Prison for Women in Kingston* (Ottawa: Public Works and Government Services Canada, 1996), http://www.elizabethfry.ca/arbour/ArbourReport.pdf; C. Glube (Chair), *Moving Forward with Women's Corrections* (Ottawa: Correctional Service of Canada, 2006), http://www.csc-scc.gc.ca/text/prgrm/fsw/wos29/wos29-eng.shtml; T. Lajeunesse, C. Jefferson, U.J. Nuffield, and D. Majury, *The Cross Gender Monitoring Project: Third and Final Report* (Ottawa: Correctional Service of Canada 2000), http://www.csc-scc.gc.ca/text/prgrm/fsw/gender3/toc-eng.shtml.

TREATMENT INTERVENTIONS

Female offenders as a group have greater needs in the areas of emotional stability, marital and family relations, academic/vocational skills, and employment. The relatively small population of federal female offenders and their geographic dispersal on release together make it difficult to provide gender-specific health and residential services and programs. The annual cost of

PERSPECTIVE

Treatment Therapist

We have encouraged them [women] to be victims, we've encouraged them to believe that they have no control over their lives; that they have no control over the decisions that they have made, and we have to get them past that stage. And they have been victims—don't get me wrong. But we have to help all offenders to get past the victim stage and take responsibility for what they did. Women offenders do generally come from very dysfunctional backgrounds. There has been a lot of abuse. Many are addicted. And there is difficulty in accepting the fact that they have committed a criminal offence. (personal communication with C.T. Griffiths)

incarcerating each federal women offender is more than $200,000, which is nearly double that for federal male offenders in custody.[30] Despite these costs, there are serious questions as to whether systems of corrections are successfully addressing the issues confronting women offenders.

A number of task forces have identified the need for a gender-specific approach to treatment, one that centres on empowerment and that recognizes the broader, systemic barriers facing women in general: poverty, unemployment, lack of education, and sexism.[31]

The Classification of Women Offenders

Considerable controversy has surrounded the use of assessment instruments such as the LSI-R (see Chapter 10) to assess the risk and needs of women offenders. These instruments were originally developed for use with male offenders and, it is argued, do not consider the different pathways to crime of women offenders—pathways that often include sexual abuse and victimization. This may result in women offenders being overclassified with respect to their level of risk and not having their needs identified.

Research studies have found that assessment instruments such as the LSI-R (discussed in Chapter 10) produce valid predictions of the risk that women offenders will reoffend. Indeed, it is just as valid as it is for men.[32] Even so, the prevailing view is that the assessments provided by the LSI-R, and by other instruments, could be enhanced through the use of gender-specific instruments.

It is argued that the addition of variables specifically related to women offenders would increase the predictive power of the LSI-R and other risk assessments.[33] These variables include the impact of sexual, physical, and mental/emotional victimization and the role that women's social relationships play in their involvement in criminal behaviour. One of the strongest predictors of risk, for example, is whether the woman's partner/spouse is involved in criminal activity.[34] Co-offending is an important facet of women's involvement in criminal activity and often leads to women becoming involved in more serious offences.[35] The increasing involvement of Aboriginal women in gangs is one example of this.

Treatment Programs for Women Offenders

The principles of RNR have been found to be equally important for male and female offenders.[36] American researchers have found that women offenders who are exposed to intensive treatment interventions have lower rates of reoffending than women who are not.[37] Several evaluations of gender-specific interventions targeting high-risk/needs women offenders in Canada have found that RNR programs may reduce reoffending.[38]

Less conclusive results were found in an evaluation of the CSC's Intensive Intervention Strategy (IIS) for women offenders. This program was developed to address the needs of higher risk offenders and women with identified mental health disabilities. Two of the core components of the IIS are structured living environments (SLEs) designed to support and empower minimum and medium security women with mental health issues or low cognitive functioning; and secure units (SUs) to address the needs of high-risk women offenders.[39]

A statistical analysis of the IIS failed to indicate any changes in correctional outcomes for women participants; however, qualitative data gathered in interviews indicated that the SLEs provided women with increased coping and communication skills that helped them manage their behaviour and emotions.[40] Even so, participation in the SU program did not appear to have any significant impact on the attitudes or behaviour of women participants.[41]

At the federal level, gender-responsive substance abuse programs have produced lower rates of reoffending among women. The Women Offender Substance Abuse Program (WOSAP) is a gender-specific program designed to empower women to make healthy lifestyle choices in order to reduce reoffending upon release. WOSAP offers three modules in the institution: education and engagement; intensive therapeutic treatment (ITT); and relapse prevention and maintenance. A fourth module—community relapse prevention and maintenance (CRPM)—is offered to women once they have been released into the community.

An evaluation of WOSAP ($N = 560$) found that one year after release into the community, the women who completed the ITT module and the community-based CRPM module had much lower rates of reoffending than the other women in the sample who had participated in the other modules.[42] Two other gender-specific corrections programs are highlighted in Box 13.5. These and most other gender-specific programs for women offenders have not been evaluated. This makes it uncertain whether programming efforts have reduced rates of reoffending.

BOX 13.5

Two Gender-Specific Programs for Women Offenders

Emotions Management for Women (EMWO)

Rationale	Participants develop basic techniques for managing emotions and achieving positive outcomes
Objectives	Improve self-awareness Promote self-confidence Understand how to make healthy decisions to keep themselves and others safe
Trained facilitators	Correctional staff in correctional centres
Targeted population	Female inmates
Duration	Ten 150-minute sessions

Relationship Skills for Women (RSWO)

Rationale	Participants gain confidence in their ability to develop positive relationships and make decisions that keep themselves and other people safe
Objectives	Promote understanding of healthy relationships Promote being held accountable for behavioural choices Support efforts to work on change
Trained facilitators	Correctional staff in correctional centres
Targeted population	Female inmates
Duration	Thirteen 150-minute sessions

REENTRY AND LIFE AFTER PRISON

Video Link
How Women
Behind Bars Came
to Be
www.youtube.com/
watch?v=kGGvr
-t5xyM&feature
=relmfn

The system doesn't support reintegration ... You see them being released into the community with nothing. And how surprised should we be that they reoffend?[43]

Executive Director, Elizabeth Fry Society

Like their male counterparts, women offenders reentering the community must attempt to find stability in their lives. This requires supportive family and friendship networks as well as access to programs and services. Finding employment may be even more challenging for women than for men, because women are less likely to have completed their education, often have little job experience, and may have to find and pay for day care.[44] Women released from confinement may also have to address difficult issues with respect to their partners/spouses, who also may have been involved in criminal activity. This may place additional strains on women and increase the "pains of reentry." Women offenders may be more likely to experience gender discrimination and more stigma as ex-offenders than their male counterparts, in part because of societal attitudes toward "misbehaving women."[45]

Among the factors that appear to be associated with women's reoffending are a high-risk rating, unemployment, substance abuse, and failure to complete community-based programs.[46] Successful reintegration is facilitated by a conscious decision on the part of the woman offender to live a crime-free and drug-free life, as well as by support from families, partners/spouses, and children and by a positive relationship with their parole officer.[47]

For inmate-mothers, the challenges may include re-establishing contact with their children, finding suitable accommodation with sufficient space, and attempting to regain custody if the children have been placed in care during the mother's confinement. Especially when the inmate-mother is the sole caregiver, child protection authorities may require that she obtain stable employment and suitable accommodation before being allowed to reapply for custody. The frustrations that mothers may encounter upon release are reflected in the following comments of an ex-offender on parole in Ontario:

I took parole to get my kids back. Parole agreed to my present location, but now the Children's Aid Society is saying it's not suitable for the kids. I can't rent before I know whether I am going to get my kids, and I can't get them back until I rent. I can't get mother's allowance until I have my kids, and without it I can't rent. I never know what I have to do for who. There are just so many hoops to jump through.[48]

It can be assumed that the challenges are even greater for women released from provincial/territorial institutions. These women, who may have extensive histories of abuse, addiction, and mental health disabilities, frequently do not have access to programs and services either while incarcerated or when released from confinement. This is a vastly underresearched area in Canadian corrections.

Surprisingly, the CSC and provincial/territorial corrections systems have given little attention to officially tracking the annual rates of reoffending among women released from custody. It is estimated that around 40 percent of federal female offenders will return to custody, either for a violation of release conditions or for having committed a new offence.[49]

SUMMARY

Women offenders have a different profile than their male counterparts. Also, Canada's women's correctional system has been strongly influenced by critical incidents and investigations. Despite the development of smaller regional facilities and gender-specific treatment programs, feminist scholars and others decry the system as punitive and oppressive. Life inside women's prisons has a number of unique features, and there have been a number of high-profile incidents involving the death of women inmates. Women experience the pains of imprisonment differently from men; this is reflected in their high rates of self-injurious behaviour. A key challenge facing women upon reentry into the community is reuniting with their children.

KEY POINTS REVIEW

1. Women offenders present unique challenges for correctional systems.
2. The profile of women offenders is changing; these changes include an increase in the number of women convicted of violent crimes and of women who are gang-affiliated.
3. The defining events in women's corrections have all occurred in federal correctional institutions.
4. The incident at the Kingston Prison for Women in 1994 was a watershed event in women's corrections.
5. The dynamics of life inside women's correctional institutions are different in many respects from those of men's institutions.
6. Women may experience the pains of imprisonment differently from men.
7. The death of Ashley Smith raised a number of questions about the treatment of women offenders—specifically, of women offenders with mental health issues.
8. The relatively small number of women offenders makes it a challenge to develop and deliver gender-specific programs.
9. The principles of RNR are just as important for women's treatment interventions as they are for men's.

10. Among the factors associated with reoffending among women offenders are a high-risk rating, being unemployed, having substance abuse issues, and failing to complete community-based programs.

11. Re-establishing contact with their children is a major source of stress for women offenders returning to the community.

KEY TERM QUESTIONS

1. Describe the impact of *Creating Choices* and the *Arbour Report*.
2. What issues have surrounded *cross-gender staffing* in women's correctional institutions?

NOTES

1. E. Bingham and R. Sutton, *Cruel, Inhuman, and Degrading? Canada's Treatment of Federally Sentenced Women with Mental Health Issues* (Toronto: International Human Rights Program, University of Toronto, 2012), http://media.thestar.topscms.com/acrobat/ba/55/3c47d5da4a599c0f879c56ebe3e6.pdf.

2. S. Hayman, *Imprisoning Our Sisters: The New Federal Women's Prisons in Canada* (Montréal and Kingston: McGill–Queen's University Press, 2006).

3. The Honourable L. Arbour (Commissioner), *Commission of Inquiry into Certain Events at the Prison for Women in Kingston* (Ottawa: Public Works and Government Services Canada, 1996), http://www.elizabethfry.ca/arbour/ArbourReport.pdf.

4. Ibid.

5. C. Glube (Chair), *Moving Forward with Women's Corrections* (Ottawa: Correctional Service of Canada, 2006), http://www.csc-scc.gc.ca/text/prgrm/fsw/wos29/wos29-eng.shtml.

6. Hayman, S. 2006. *Imprisoning Our Sisters: The New Federal Women's Prisons in Canada*. Montréal and Kingston: McGill-Queen's University Press.

7. J. Ferrari, *Federal Female Incarceration in Canada: What Happened to Empowerment?*, M.A. thesis, 2011, Department of Sociology, Queen's University, Kingston, http://qspace.library.queensu.ca/bitstream/1974/6352/3/Ferrari_Jacqueline_201104_MA.pdf.

8. Task Force on Federally Sentenced Women, *Creating Choices: The Report of the Task Force on Federally Sentenced Women* (Ottawa: Correctional Service of Canada, 1990), http://www.csc-scc.gc.ca/text/prgrm/fsw/choices/toce-eng.shtml.

9. Ferrari, J. 2011. *Federal Female Incarceration in Canada: What Happened to Empowerment?* Unpublished M.A. thesis. Kingston, ON: Department of Sociology, Queen's University. http://qspace.library.queensu.ca/bitstream/1974/6352/3/Ferrari_Jacqueline_201104_MA.pdf.

10. C. A. Dell, C. J. Filmore, and J. M. Kilty, "Looking Back 10 Years After the Arbour Inquiry: Ideology, Policy, Practice, and the Federal Female Offender," *Prison Journal* 89, no. 3 (2009): 286–308 at 286 and 291; S. T. Marcus-Mendoza, "Feminist Therapy Behind Bars," *Women's Studies Quarterly* 32, nos. 3–4 (2004): 49–60.

11. M. Morash, *Women on Probation and Parole: A Feminist Critique of Community Programs and Services* (Boston: Northeastern University Press, 2010).

12. M. Seng and A. Lurigio, "Probation Officers' Views on Supervising Women Probationers," *Women and Criminal Justice* 16, nos. 1–2 (2005): 65–85.

13. W. Lamb, *Couldn't Keep It to Myself: Wally Lamb and the Women of York Correctional Institution* (New York: HarperCollins, 2004); W. Lamb, *I'll Fly Away: Further Testimonies from the Women of York Prison* (New York: HarperCollins, 2007).

14. M. Solinas-Saunders and M. J. Stacer, "Prison Resources and Physical/Verbal Assault in Prison: A Comparison of Male and Female Inmates," *Victims and Offenders* 7, no. 3 (2012): 279–311 at 302.

15. D. R. van Tongeren and K. J. Klebe, "Reconceptualizing Prison Adjustment: A Multidimensional Approach to Exploring Female Offenders' Adjustment to Prison Life," *Prison Journal* 90, no. 1 (2010): 48–68.

16. A. Pardue, B. A. Arrigo, and D. S. Murphy, "Sex and Sexuality in Women's Prisons: A Preliminary Typological Investigation," *Prison Journal* 91, no. 3 (2011): 279–304 at 283.

17. L. Stone, "Violence Spikes in Cramped Women's Prisons," *Calgary Herald*, May 25, 2010.

18. Woman Offender in Newfoundland/Labrador Correctional Centre for Women, in B. Fleming, *Alone Among the Few: A Report on Facilities and Supports for Female Offenders from Labrador* (St. John's: Office of the Citizens' Representative, Government of Newfoundland and Labrador, 2007), 16, http://www.citizensrep.nl.ca/pdfs/FacilitiesSupportsFemale OffendersLabrador_Report.pdf.

19. A. Brown, B. Miller, and E. Maguin, "Prevalence and Severity of Lifetime Physical and Sexual Victimization Among Incarcerated Women," *International Journal of Law and Psychiatry* 22 (1999): 301–22.

20. J. Power and A. Usher, *A Qualitative Study of Self-Injurious Behaviour in Women Offenders*, Research Brief (Ottawa: Correctional Service of Canada, 2010), http://www.csc-scc.gc.ca/text/rsrch/reports/r225/r225-eng.shtml.

21. C. A. Dell, *Fact Sheet: "Self-Harm Among Criminalized Women"* (Ottawa: Canadian Centre for Substance Abuse, 2006), http://www.ccsa.ca/2006%20CCSA%20Documents/CCSA -011338-2006-e.pdf.

22. Ibid., 20 at 28.

23. L. Stone, "On the Winding Road to Redemption in Canada's Women's Prison System," *Calgary Herald*, October 11, 2011, 6.

24. J. Martel, *Solitude and Cold Storage: Women's Journeys of Endurance in Segregation* (Edmonton: Elizabeth Fry Society of Edmonton, 1999).

25. J. F. Mills and D. F. Kroner, *Concurrent Validity and Normative Data of the Depression Hopelessness and Suicide Screening Form with Women Offenders*, Research Brief (Ottawa: Correctional Service of Canada, 2010), http://www.csc-scc.gc.ca/text/rsrch/briefs/b47/b47-eng.shtml.

26. Bingham and Sutton, *Cruel, Inhuman, and Degrading?*, 2.

27. Ibid., 2.

28. T. Lajeunesse, C. Jefferson, U. J. Nuffield, and D. Majury, *The Cross Gender Monitoring Project: Third and Final Report* (Ottawa: Correctional Service of Canada, 2000), http://www .csc-scc.gc.ca/text/prgrm/fsw/gender3/toc-eng.shtml.

29. G. Gilroy, *Evaluation of Cross-Gender Staffing Pilot Project* (Regina: Ministry of Corrections, Public Safety and Policing, Government of Saskatchewan, 2009).

30. Ibid., 23 at 6.

31. Glube, *Moving Forward with Women's Corrections*; Task Force on Federally Sentenced Women, *Creating Choices*.

32. P. Smith, F. T. Cullen, and E. J. Latessa, "Can 14,737 Women be Wrong? A Meta-Analysis of the LSI-R and Recidivism for Female Offenders," *Criminology and Public Policy* 8, no. 1 (2009): 183–208.

33. P. van Voorhis, E. M. Wright, E. Salisbury, and A. Bauman, "Women's Risk Factors and Their Contributions to Existing Risk/Needs Assessment," *Criminal Justice and Behavior* 37, no. 3 (2010): 261–88.

34. K. Heilbrun, D. DeMatteo, R. Fretz, J. Erickson, K. Yasuhara, and N. Anumba, "How 'Specific' Are Gender-Specific Rehabilitation Needs? An Empirical Analysis," *Criminal Justice and Behavior* 35, no. 11 (2008): 1382–97 at 1387.

35. S. Becker and J. A. McCorkel, "The Gender of Criminal Opportunity: The Impact of Male Co-Offenders on Women's Crime," *Feminist Criminology* 6, no. 2 (2011): 79–110.

36. Heilbrun, K., D. DeMatteo, R. Fretz, J. Erickson, K. Yasuhara, and N. Anumba. 2008. "How 'Specific' Are Gender-Specific Rehabilitation Needs? An Empirical Analysis," *Criminal Justice and Behavior* 35(11), 1382–97.

37. L. B. Lovins, C. T. Lowenkamp, E. J. Latessa, and P. Smith, "Application of the Risk Principle to Female Offenders," *Journal of Contemporary Criminal Justice* 23, no. 4 (2007): 383–98.

38. N. Messina, C. E. Grella, J. Cartier, and S. Torres, "A Randomized Experimental Study of Gender-Responsive Substance Abuse Treatment for Women in Prison," *Journal of Substance Abuse Treatment* 38, no. 2 (2010): 97–107; S. J. Tripodi, S. E. Bledsoe, J. S. Kim, and K. Bender, "Effects of Correctional-Based Programs for Female Inmates: A Systematic Review," *Research on Social Work Practice* 21, no. 1 (2011): 15–31.

39. A. Nolan, N. Allegri, and M. Olotu, *Evaluation Report: Intensive Intervention Strategy for Women Offenders* (Ottawa: Correctional Service of Canada, 2011), v, http://www.csc-scc.gc.ca/text/pa/ev-iiswo-394-2-88/ev-iiswo-394-2-88-eng.pdf.

40. Ibid., viii.

41. Ibid., viii.

42. F. I. Matheson, S. Doherty, and B. A. Grant, *Women Offender Substance Abuse Programming and Community Reintegration* (Ottawa: Correctional Service of Canada, 2009), http://www.csc-scc.gc.ca/text/rsrch/reports/r202/r202-eng.shtml.

43. L. Stone. "After an Inmate's Release, the Struggle Begins" (*Calgary Herald*), May 25.

44. Glube, *Moving Forward with Women's Corrections*; R. Sampson (Chair), *Report of the Correctional Service of Canada Review Panel* (Ottawa: Minister of Public Works and Government Services Canada, 2007), http://www.publicsafety.gc.ca/csc-scc/cscrprprt-eng.pdf.

45. T. P. LeBel, "'If One Doesn't Get You Another One Will': Formerly Incarcerated Persons' Perceptions of Discrimination," *Prison Journal* 92, no. 1 (2011): 63–87.

46. Matheson, Doherty, and Grant, *Women Offender Substance Abuse Programming*.

47. R. Gobiel, *Staying Out: Women's Perceptions of Challenges and Protective Factors in Community Reintegration* (Ottawa: Correctional Service of Canada, 2008), http://www.csc-scc.gc.ca/text/rsrch/reports/r201/r201-eng.shtml.

48. S. Wine, *A Motherhood Issue: The Impact of Criminal Justice System Involvement on Women and Their Children* (Ottawa: Solicitor General, 1992), 111.

49. Stone, "After an Inmate's Release."

CHAPTER 14

ABORIGINAL OFFENDERS

CHAPTER OBJECTIVES

After reading this chapter, you should be able to:
- *Discuss the impact of colonization on Aboriginal involvement in the criminal justice and corrections systems.*
- *Provide a profile of Aboriginal women in corrections.*
- *Discuss the initiatives that have been taken in an attempt to reduce Aboriginal overrepresentation in corrections.*
- *Discuss the role of Aboriginal healing lodges and centres in corrections.*
- *Describe Aboriginal-specific treatment interventions.*
- *Discuss the CSC Continuum of Care for Aboriginal offenders.*
- *Discuss the challenges that Aboriginal offenders experience in applying for conditional release and upon reentry into the community.*
- *Discuss the effectiveness of various Aboriginal-specific programs.*

ABORIGINAL PEOPLES IN CANADIAN SOCIETY: THE LEGACY OF COLONIZATION

Many Aboriginal people live on the margins of Canadian society. (Note: for purposes of this discussion, the term "Aboriginal" will be used to include First Nations, Métis, and Inuit). This is reflected in pervasive poverty, high rates of unemployment, low levels of formal education, and high death rates from accidents and violence. More than half of Aboriginal students fail to graduate from high school, and the unemployment rate among Aboriginals is twice that of non-Aboriginals. Aboriginal youth may be prime targets for gang recruitment, which may result in involvement in the criminal justice and corrections systems.[1]

The subordinate political and economic condition of Aboriginal peoples is a consequence of their colonization by Europeans and of Canadian government policies that have exerted control over virtually every aspect of Aboriginal life. Under the residential school system, Aboriginal children were forcibly removed from their families, often for many years. This resulted in widespread sexual victimization; it also fractured Aboriginal families, helped destroy traditional cultures and values, and shredded the fabric of many First Nations.[2]

Racism and discrimination toward Aboriginal people have intensified their marginality and vulnerability. Poverty, poor healthcare, and inadequate housing are all pervasive in First Nations across Canada, where Third World conditions prevail. More and more Aboriginals residing in urban areas are facing significant challenges, which include finding adequate housing and accessing programs and services.[3]

ABORIGINAL OVERREPRESENTATION IN THE CRIMINAL JUSTICE SYSTEM

At all stages of the criminal justice system, from arrest to incarceration, Aboriginal people are overrepresented in proportion to their numbers in Canada. The CSC has seen significant increases in the numbers of incarcerated Aboriginal men and women.[4] Aboriginal people are 3 percent of the Canadian adult population but around 20 percent of federal offenders and 27 percent of provincial/territorial inmates (see Figure 14.1). The figure for Aboriginal women in custody is even higher, at 41 percent.[5] Federal Aboriginal offenders are more likely to be incarcerated than on conditional release.[6]

Video Links
Matthew Coon Come on Canada's Handling of Aboriginal Peoples **www.youtube .com/watch?v= 5MJ6mqUoelw**

8th Fire Dispatch: Sacred Heart Residential School—Part 1 **www.cbc.ca/ doczone/8thfire/ 2011/12/ painful-legacy .html**

Figure 14.1

Aboriginal Adult Admissions to Custody, by Province and Territory, 2010–11

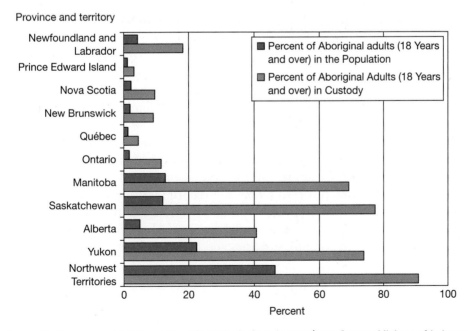

Source: M. Dauvergne, *Adult Correctional Statistics in Canada, 2010/2011*. Ottawa: Minister of Industry, 2012). Pg. 12. Found at: http://www.statcan.gc.ca/pub/85-002-x/2012001/article/11715-eng.pdf.

Aboriginal youth are approximately 6 percent of the Canadian population but account for nearly one-quarter (23 percent) of admissions to remand custody and almost one-third (31 percent) of admissions to sentenced custody.[7]

Federal Aboriginal offenders are more likely than non-Aboriginals to be classified as a medium or maximum level security risk; fewer are designated as a minimum security risk. A greater proportion of Aboriginal men and women offenders are currently serving a sentence for a violent offence; the difference is especially evident for Aboriginal versus non-Aboriginal women (75 vs. 47 percent). Aboriginal offenders are also disproportionately designated as Dangerous Offenders (DOs), accounting for 26 percent of the 458 active DOs in Canada in 2011.[8]

The statistics are even more compelling in provincial/territorial correctional facilities, although there is variation among jurisdictions. Aboriginal representation in sentenced custody in Saskatchewan is seven times greater than for the general population, whereas in Québec it is two times greater.[9] There has been an increase in the number of Aboriginals entering custody with gang affiliations.[10]

Aboriginal organizations have expressed concern about recent legislation that has increased the number of mandatory minimum sentences. The Assembly of First Nations (AFN) has argued that such sentences deviate from Sections 718.2(d) and 718.2(e) of the Criminal Code, which requires Criminal Court judges to consider the unique circumstances of Aboriginal offenders and to make every effort to find alternatives to confinement (recall here the *Gladue* decision, discussed in Chapter 5). Mandatory minimum sentences do not allow judges to follow the principles set out in *Gladue*. The AFN's concern is that this will lead to a further increase in Aboriginal offenders in custody.[11]

It appears that the *Gladue* decision has done little to stem the rising tide of Aboriginal overrepresentation in corrections systems. This is for a variety of reasons, including the absence of viable community-based alternatives. Also, the high rates of violent crime among Aboriginal offenders limit the options available to Criminal Court judges at sentencing.

There is concern that the overrepresentation of Aboriginals in corrections systems will continue in both the federal and provincial/territorial systems, because the Aboriginal rate of population growth is higher than for non-Aboriginals, with the result that the Aboriginal population is, overall, younger than the non-Aboriginal.[12] It is also possible that the increasing focus on risk in corrections will work to the detriment of Aboriginal offenders, given that many have violent offence histories and higher risk assessment ratings.

Aboriginal Women Offenders

Aboriginal women are a high and growing proportion of women in remand and sentenced custody and are over-represented. Women Aboriginal offenders are more overrepresented in the federal correctional population than their male counterparts. Around one in three incarcerated women is Aboriginal.[13]

Nearly one-third of women Aboriginal offenders admitted to federal custody have an identified mental health disability; that is double the number from a decade ago. Also, over 75 percent reported abusing both alcohol and drugs. Box 14.1 provides a composite description of an Aboriginal woman serving time in a federal correctional institution.

Research indicates that Aboriginal women in federal corrections tend to be "overclassified"—that is, given a higher than appropriate security rating.[14] This may result in less access to treatment programs and a reduced likelihood of release on parole.[15] There are also concerns that the punitive penology

BOX 14.1

Profile of an Aboriginal Woman Serving Time in a Federal Correctional Institution

The Aboriginal women offender is generally 27 years old with a grade nine education. She is also single, with two or three children. She has limited education and employment skills and is usually unemployed at the time of her crime. Contributing factors that may negatively affect the life of an Aboriginal woman include moving to an urban centre (isolation and loneliness); alcoholism and violence in the family home; lack of family support and supervision; lack of financial resources; and lack of opportunities to become involved in positive interactions with others.

Generally the Aboriginal offender experimented with drugs and alcohol at a young age. Often she came into conflict with the law as a youth; more recently, because of lack of intervention, she has continued into the adult system. She is likely to have left school at a young age to associate with friends who are streetwise. On the street, her abuse of drugs and alcohol continued to the point where she became a prostitute to continue her addiction. Under the influence of her associates and a negative lifestyle, she became more streetwise and committed more serious crimes such as robberies, assaults, or murder.

She may have left home because she experienced violence (whether she was abused or she witnessed abuse) and her home life became unbearable. Or she may have lived under very rigid conditions that she fled because she wanted to become independent. Or she may have been lured away by friends who were living a life of drugs, alcohol, and partying. She may have worked the streets because she needed money to live on and did not have the education, skills, and training to get a job. She may have been subjected to racism, stereotyping, and discrimination because she was Aboriginal. Her experience on the streets became violent as she continued to experience sexual, emotional, and physical abuse. She probably became involved in

(continued)

an abusive relationship. There usually have been children born from this relationship, and the social, emotional, and economic struggle has continued. The cycle of an unhealthy family continues.

A high percentage of Aboriginal women who come into conflict with the law are convicted of crimes committed while under the influence of drugs and alcohol. These contributing factors are often related to their history of physical, psychological, and emotional abuse, and they have not dealt with the effects of this abuse. This harmful way of dealing with the past history of dysfunctional behaviour may continue unless these past abuses and effects are dealt with.

Source: Facts and Figures: Aboriginal Initiatives, "Profile of an Aboriginal Woman Serving Time in a Federal Correctional Institution," http://www.csc-scc.gc.ca/text/prgrm/abinit/know/5-eng.shtml. (Correctional Service Canada, 2000). Reproduced with the permission of the Minister of Public Works and Government Services Canada, 2013.

evident in the early 21st century—including an increase in the number of mandatory minimum sentences—will result in even greater overrepresentation of Aboriginal women in correctional institutions.

ADDRESSING ABORIGINAL OVERREPRESENTATION IN THE JUSTICE SYSTEM

Over the past three decades, governments, not-for-profit organizations, and First Nations have made a variety of attempts to address the disproportionate involvement of Aboriginal persons at all stages of the criminal justice system. These include Aboriginal policing programs and autonomous Aboriginal police services, diversion programs, Native Court Worker and Liaison programs, Aboriginal-focused community-based corrections programs, and institutional programs designed to address the unique needs of Aboriginal offenders.

An example is the Community Council Program in Toronto, which is a diversion program for urban Aboriginal offenders designed to reduce recidivism, increase offender responsibility, and return a greater degree of responsibility to the Aboriginal community. The options offered by this program include fines, restitution to the victim, community service hours, and referral to treatment resources.

INITIATIVES IN ABORIGINAL CORRECTIONS

To address the needs of Aboriginal offenders, a variety of programs have been developed by systems of corrections and also by Aboriginal organizations and communities.

First Nations and Native Organizations

It has been argued that European methods of justice, which are predominantly adversarial, are ill suited to address Aboriginal crime and that efforts should focus on programs developed by Aboriginal people to address their communities' unique needs.[16]

First Nations and various Native organizations are designing and delivering correctional services in both communities and institutions. The justice system often partners with them in delivering these services, many of which incorporate Aboriginal spirituality and principles of restorative justice. These programs include sentencing circles, community mediation, and sentencing advisory committees. Many of them employ Native personnel—for example, Native Liaison Workers.

These initiatives vary widely with regard to the types of offences and offenders; the procedures for hearing cases, reaching dispositions, and imposing sanctions; and the extent to which these programs involve justice system personnel.

Other initiatives are more independent of the justice system and are controlled by communities. In Manitoba, for example, First Nations and Métis community correctional agencies are involved in probation supervision, fine option programs, the preparation of PSR for the courts, and a variety of community-based treatment programs.

The Community Holistic Circle Healing Program on Hollow Water First Nation in Manitoba, profiled in Box 14.2, is one example of a community-controlled program.

BOX 14.2

Community Holistic Circle Healing Program, Hollow Water, Manitoba

The Community Holistic Circle Healing Program has been designed as a community-based response to the high rates of sexual and family abuse that afflict the community. It includes a 13-phase process, illustrated in Figure 14.2.

The Special Gathering in the Hollow Water program is a public event that shares many similarities with the traditional justice ceremony described below. Traditional healing practices are used in an attempt to restore the community, the family, and individual peace and harmony. The offender signs a healing contract and apologizes publicly to the victims and to the community for the harm done. The circle healing process is designed to consider the needs of all of the parties to the abuse—the victim, the offender, and the community—and is directed beyond merely punishing the offender for a specific behaviour.

(continued)

Figure 14.2

The Thirteen Phases of the Hollow Water Community Holistic Circle Healing Process

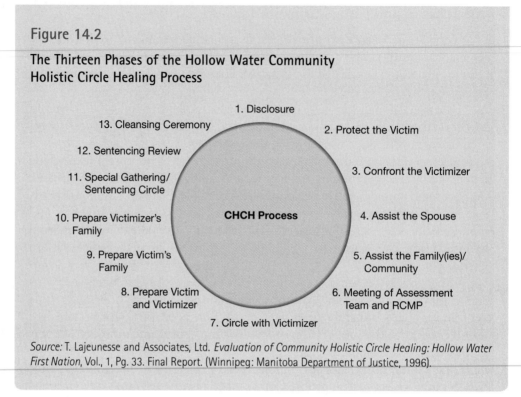

Source: T. Lajeunesse and Associates, Ltd. *Evaluation of Community Holistic Circle Healing: Hollow Water First Nation*, Vol., 1, Pg. 33. Final Report. (Winnipeg: Manitoba Department of Justice, 1996).

Aboriginal Healing Centres and Lodges

Corrections systems have made some efforts to address the specific treatment needs of Aboriginal offenders. Among the more common Aboriginal-specific programs found in correctional institutions across the country are sweat lodges, healing circles, and modules that focus on cultural awareness, substance abuse, and family violence.

Under Section 81 of the CCRA, the federal government has entered into agreements with First Nations groups across the country to develop and operate healing lodges. These include Pê Sâkâstêw (Cree for "new beginnings" and pronounced "Bay Sah-ga-stay-o"), a minimum security facility for male offenders near Hobbema, Alberta, on the Samson Cree Nation; the Prince Albert (Saskatchewan) Grand Council Spiritual Healing Lodge for male Aboriginal offenders on the Wahpeton Dakota First Nation; the Okimaw Ohci Healing Lodge (Saskatchewan) for federal Aboriginal women offenders, which incorporates Aboriginal culture and spirituality; and the Waseskun Healing Centre, near Montréal, which offers residential therapy for men and women referred from First Nations and from provincial and federal correctional institutions. Healing lodges operate under the CSC but are also accountable to a governing council composed of elders and other First Nations representatives.

At healing lodges, the needs of Aboriginal offenders are addressed in a holistic manner. They receive individualized programming, engage with the community, partake in Aboriginal teachings and ceremonies, and engage with elders.[17]

Elders play a key role in most programs. At the Waseskun Healing Centre near Montréal, for example, elders use the Medicine Wheel to promote balance, addressing the physical, mental, spiritual, and emotional health of each individual.[18] One resident commented on the value of one-on-one sessions with the elders: "[They] really helped me gain ground. With the Native Elders, they have this passion, they have a different technique. They thrive off the sincerity of the individual."[19] The Pê Sâkâstêw Centre is profiled in Box 14.3.

BOX 14.3

The Pê Sâkâstêw Centre

Pê Sâkâstêw (Cree for "new beginning" and pronounced "Bay Sah-ga-stay-o") is a minimum security facility near Hobbema, Alberta, on the Samson Cree Nation. Aboriginal elders are directly involved in developing the treatment programs, which focus on healing and culturally appropriate practices and include a sweat lodge. Inmates in the minimum security facility are called *owiciiyisiwak*, which in the Cree language means "here to learn." Offenders are screened carefully before being sent to the institution and must be classified as minimum security. Also, they must demonstrate an interest in rehabilitation programs, have a genuine interest in learning more about Aboriginal culture and traditions, and have a history of positive interactions with correctional staff.

The primary objectives of the centre are to prepare the offenders for their eventual release as safe and law-abiding citizens and to encourage Aboriginal community participation and organizational support of offenders' reintegration.

Source: S. Trevethan, N. Crutcher, J.P. Moore, and J. Mileto, *Pê Sâkâstêw Centre: An In-Depth Examination of a Healing Lodge for Federally Incarcerated Offenders* (Ottawa: Correctional Service of Canada, 2007), http://www.csc-scc.gc.ca/text/rsrch/reports/r170/r170-eng.pdf.

CSC ABORIGINAL STAFF POSITIONS

The CSC provides opportunities for Aboriginals to serve as role models in correctional facilities. Some Aboriginal people become COs; other CSC positions are specific to Aboriginal people (see Table 14.1).

Inmates at the Aboriginal Healing Range at the Stony Mountain Institution, Manitoba, participate in a drum ceremony.

Table 14.1 Aboriginal-Specific Positions in the CSC

Title	Description
Aboriginal Liaison Officers	Ensure that Aboriginal offenders and their communities' histories are understood and that their needs are met; liaise between non-Aboriginal staff and Aboriginal offenders to guarantee that offenders' cultural and spiritual needs are met
Aboriginal Correctional Program Officers	Facilitate culturally appropriate institutional programs for Aboriginal offenders to address their risk factors; work with contractors and other CSC employees to facilitate Aboriginal programs that are based on Aboriginal beliefs
Aboriginal Community Development Officers	Help Aboriginal offenders who want to return to their communities; help communities develop plans for Aboriginal offenders reentering their communities under a Section 84 release
Aboriginal Community Liaison Officers	Provide support to Aboriginal offenders reintegrating into urban communities

Source: CSC, 2nd. *Strategic Plan for Aboriginal Corrections: Innovation, Learning & Adjustment 2006–2007 to 2010–2011.* Found at: http://www.csc-scc.gc.ca/text/prgrm/abinit/plan06-eng.shtml.

ABORIGINAL INMATES AND TREATMENT INTERVENTIONS

> *So, prison is no place to recover. From anything, either the grief of memory, or loss, or abuse, or the diseases of addiction. But if you're Native and you can get the help to seek and find and claim your spiritual name, a lot can be changed. You can discover your destiny. Your life can bridge back to the origins of your family and people, you can seek out your colours, your clan, your spirit keepers. You may find the self you never knew you were.*[20]

Aboriginal offenders generally have greater criminogenic needs than non-Aboriginal offenders.[21] The risk factors for chronic Aboriginal offenders—whose deviant behaviour typically begins in childhood, escalates in the adolescent years, and continues throughout adulthood—include substance abuse, a dysfunctional family environment, and negative peer group associations.[22] All of these issues require specialized programs.[23] Aboriginal offenders present challenges for the correctional staff who facilitate treatment groups. One Aboriginal Correctional Program Officer stated: "A lot of inmates coming in are really young—like 19, 20, 21, 22, and they don't have their basic knowledge of having respect when an Elder comes into the room. They don't give a shit. They don't" (personal communication with D. Murdoch).

Aboriginal offenders have access to the same treatment programs as other inmates, including interventions focusing on substance abuse, domestic violence, sexual offending, violence prevention, emotions management, and cognitive skills training.[24] There are also specific interventions directed toward Aboriginal inmates. Among the more common Aboriginal-specific programs in facilities across the country are sweat lodges, healing circles, and modules that focus on

Aboriginal sweat lodge and ceremonial grounds.

© Mikael Karlsson / Alamy

cultural awareness, substance abuse, and family violence. Provincial and territorial systems of corrections have far fewer programs and services for Aboriginal inmates, even though these offenders may account for as much as 90 percent of the inmate population. Given the short time that offenders are in confinement, the greatest promise is for programs in the community, either post-release or as part of an alternative to confinement. Unless otherwise indicated, the programs discussed below are operated by the CSC. Box 14.4 profiles the Ma Mawi Wi Chi Itata Family Violence Program in Stony Mountain Institution.

BOX 14.4

The Ma Mawi Wi Chi Itata Family Violence Program, Stony Mountain Institution (Manitoba)

This program for male Aboriginal inmates is designed to address the issues related to violent behaviour and attempts to alter inmates' patterns of violent behaviour toward spouses and family members, as well as disruptive behaviour in the institutional setting. The program focuses on education, counselling, healing, and prevention and incorporates contemporary and traditional treatment approaches.

The program has four sections, each representing a geographical direction on the Medicine Wheel:

- *The East.* Represented by the eagle. The primary objective is "to see." The focus is on the cycle of violence, the role of socialization in committing violence, and the relationship between violence and substance abuse.
- *The South.* Represented by the mouse. The primary objective is "to do." The focus is on the offender's expressing negative emotions, including those related to childhood experiences and family origin; and on exploring feelings of shame and guilt for past behaviour, which includes discussion of the inmate's most violent incident.
- *The West.* Represented by the bear. The primary objective is "to think." The focus is on the impact of violence on children and families. Also addressed are the various dimensions of relationships, as well as skills in substituting assertiveness for aggression.
- *The North.* Represented by the buffalo. The primary objective is "to know." The focus is on taking the middle way. Inmates meet in sharing circles to establish goals, share stories, and relate feelings.

On completion of the program, there are a number of ceremonies, including a sweat lodge ceremony and a feast. These ceremonies and the program itself are designed to provide the Aboriginal inmate with a new identity.

Source: J. Proulx and S. Perrault. *An Evaluation of the Ma Mawi Wi Chi Itata Centre's Family Violence Program, Stony Mountain Project.* (Winnipeg, MB: Ma Mawi Wi Chi Itata, 1996).

The CSC ICPM Initiative

Recall from Chapter 10 that the objectives of the new ICPM are to provide more timely access to programs upon admission, facilitate greater program enrollment, increase program completion rates, and increase the rates of discretionary conditional release.[25] The ICPM has a separate module for Aboriginal offenders called the Aboriginal Multi-Target Stream. This module is designed to address the criminogenic factors related to offending and to develop a variety of skill sets in offenders, including coping skills, goal setting, and self-management. A small group of inmates meet with facilitators. The High-Intensity Program is designed for Aboriginal inmates in high-security institutions and involves more than 100 sessions up to 2.5 hours in length, while the Moderate-Intensity Program is for inmates in medium security correctional facilities and has 62 sessions up to 2.5 hours in length.

Following is the perspective of a CSC Aboriginal Correctional Program Officer (ACPO).

PERSPECTIVE

An Aboriginal Correctional Program Officer

As an ACPO, I work with the Elders and other Case Management Team members, such as the Institution Parole Officers, and ALOs to help rehabilitate Aboriginal offenders. During programs, I teach culturally appropriate healing and treatment programs to Aboriginal and Métis offenders. The Elder and I work hard to motivate and guide the Aboriginal inmates to move forward on their Healing Journey, which is also referred to as their path to rehabilitation. In programs, I teach the Aboriginal inmates skills and competencies, such as problem solving, and challenging distorted thinking, which are necessary for a safe reintegration back into the community. (personal communication with D. Murdoch)

The CSC Aboriginal Corrections Continuum of Care

The CSC introduced its **Aboriginal Corrections Continuum of Care** in 2003 after extensive consultation with Aboriginal stakeholders. This program begins at intake with the identification of Aboriginal offenders, who are encouraged to reconnect with their communities, traditions, and cultures. It then provides programming that will enable them to cascade down to lower security levels until they receive a conditional release. First Nations are engaged throughout this process, providing support to facilitate their successful reintegration as law-abiding citizens beyond their warrant expiry date (see Figure 14.3).[26]

Aboriginal Corrections Continuum of Care
An initiative of the CSC designed to connect Aboriginal offenders with their communities, traditions, and cultures, beginning in the institution and continuing on conditional release in the community.

Figure 14.3

The CSC Corrections Continuum of Care for Aboriginal Offenders

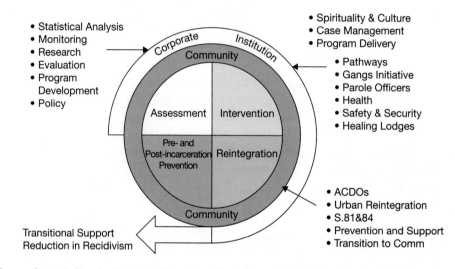

Corrections Continuum of Care

- Statistical Analysis
- Monitoring
- Research
- Evaluation
- Program Development
- Policy

- Spirituality & Culture
- Case Management
- Program Delivery

- Pathways
- Gangs Initiative
- Parole Officers
- Health
- Safety & Security
- Healing Lodges

- ACDOs
- Urban Reintegration
- S.81&84
- Prevention and Support
- Transition to Comm

Transitional Support
Reduction in Recidivism

Source: Strategic Plan for Aboriginal Corrections, Pg. 9, Correctional Services Canada, 2007. Reproduced with the permission of the Minister of Public Works and Government Services Canada, 2013.

PROGRAMS FOR ABORIGINAL WOMEN OFFENDERS

The Aboriginal Women Offender Circle of Care

Aboriginal Women Offender Circle of Care
A CSC program designed to provide women with coping strategies in preparation for release into the community.

The **Aboriginal Women Offender Circle of Care** helps federal women offenders return to their communities to live crime-free lives. It does so by helping them develop strategies to cope with daily life. Each program in the Circle of Care is assisted full time by an elder. The theme that connects all programs in the circle is healing through cultural identity. A woman's movement throughout the Circle of Care Program is dictated by availability, risk level, and sentence duration. Not all women will complete the cycle.

The circle is composed of the Program Intake Interview, the Aboriginal Women's Engagement Program, the Aboriginal Women Offender–Moderate Intensity Program, the Aboriginal Women's High Intensity Program, the Aboriginal Women Offender–Self Management Program, and Pre-Release Transition Sessions. Connections are made with Aboriginal women early in their sentence to encourage them to change. Each stage of the process has different objectives, which include helping them develop Healing Plans; helping them understand how their thoughts affect their emotions and behaviours; encouraging them to explore their spirituality to achieve balance in their lives; and helping them access community resources (Aboriginal Correctional Program Officer, personal communication with D. Murdoch).

CHALLENGES IN TREATMENT FOR ABORIGINAL OFFENDERS

Aboriginal offenders generally have higher risk/needs ratings than their non-Aboriginal counterparts.[27] Despite this, their participation rates in treatment programs are low overall. Many Aboriginal offenders are classified as high risk and are placed in maximum security institutions where programming opportunities may be more limited. Offenders who are classified as high risk and who have a history of violence may not qualify for residence in an Aboriginal healing lodge.[28] Also, Aboriginal inmates spend more time in administrative segregation, which further limits program opportunities. This is especially the case in the CSC's Prairie region, where Aboriginal gangs are a prominent feature of correctional institutions.[29]

In the past, the CSC has been criticized for failing to ensure that Aboriginal offenders have equal access to its programs. The ICPM is designed to address this. There has also been a lack of appropriate staff to deliver Aboriginal programs. Because of challenges in recruiting and retaining those staff, many institutions are forced to operate their Aboriginal programs without elders or Aboriginal correctional personnel.[30]

ABORIGINALS AND CONDITIONAL RELEASE

Aboriginal inmates are less likely than others to succeed in their applications for conditional release; they also have lower parole grant rates.[31] The day parole and full parole grant rates for federal Aboriginal offenders (53 percent and 24 percent, respectively) have been declining; they are also lower than for non-Aboriginal offenders (64 percent and 42 percent, respectively).[32] In addition, they serve a higher proportion of their sentence before being released on parole, partly because of the seriousness of the crimes they have committed but also because of the lack of community supports available to them, especially in rural and remote communities.[33]

Many parole-eligible Aboriginal inmates do not apply for conditional release. This is for a number of reasons: they feel alienated, they don't understand the parole process, they lack confidence in their ability to complete conditional release, or they lack help in applying for parole. Lack of access to Aboriginal programming is another factor: if Aboriginal offenders have not been able to work on their correctional plan because their institution does not provide programs for them to do so, the PBC is unlikely to perceive them as a good risk.[34] For all of these reasons, Aboriginal offenders are more likely than non-Aboriginal inmates to be on statutory release or to be held in custody until warrant expiry.

Compared to their non-Aboriginal counterparts, Aboriginal inmates are younger, more likely to be gang-affiliated, more likely to be suffering from FASD, and more likely to have served a previous youth and/or adult sentence. Also, more Aboriginal offenders are serving a sentence for a violent offence.[35]

Finally, individual parole board members may be biased toward Aboriginals, although this has not been documented by research.

Aboriginal Inmates and the Parole Board

There may be particular difficulties between Aboriginal inmate-applicants and parole boards. Only 5 percent of PBC staff are Aboriginal. The PBC does not disclose how many board members are Aboriginal, but it can be assumed that few of them are. To qualify for appointment to the PBC, board members are not required to have any special knowledge of Aboriginal cultures and communities. This raises the possibility of a lack of cultural sensitivity among non-Aboriginal board members, as well as inequities in the hearing process, leading to poor decisions. These problems are reflected in the observations of a non-Aboriginal former member of the PBC in the Prairie region:

> *When I found myself sitting opposite Samuel Grey Hawk, or Amos Morning Cloud, or Joseph Brave Bear, or when I caught the shy, uncertain eyes of a Cree-speaking teenager from the far North attempting to follow, through an interpreter, our ritualistic procedures and answer our thoroughly white middle-class questions, I felt a little like a fraud. It seemed incalculably unfair that these men had the misfortune to have to depend upon the decisions of people who might as well have come from another planet, as far as the similarities in culture and lifestyle were concerned.*[36]

Efforts have been made to address concerns about a lack of cultural sensitivity among board members. For example, they must undergo cultural sensitivity and awareness training, learn about the traditions and cultures of the Inuit, Métis, and First Nations populations, and complete training with elders.[37] How this training is applied in parole hearings and the impact it has had on parole board decisions has not been examined.

The PBC has a number of initiatives designed to improve parole hearings for Aboriginal offenders. Federal Aboriginal offenders have the opportunity to participate in parole hearings with an Aboriginal Cultural Adviser, and there are also elder-assisted parole hearings. The elder may say a prayer or perform a ritual (such as smudging) to open and/or close the parole hearing. He or she may also provide board members with general information regarding Aboriginal experiences, traditions, and cultures as well as, hopefully, information specific to the culture of the Aboriginal parole applicant. In 2010–11, 37 percent of all Aboriginal parole hearings ($N = 490$) involved a cultural adviser. Interestingly, 11 percent of those hearings ($N = 56$) involved non-Aboriginal offenders, which raises a number of unexplored questions.[38] The Aboriginal Cultural Adviser is involved throughout the parole hearing but does not have authority in the release decision.

There is also provision for parole hearings to be held in the community rather than the penitentiary, as a means to restore the relationship between the offender and the community, thereby contributing to the "traditional sense of responsibility felt by every community member for each other and for the creatures and forces that sustain all human life."[39] The Ontario Parole Board also conducts Aboriginal Circle Hearings, which are designed to be culturally sensitive and to involve elders. There are no evaluations, however, as to whether these hearings contribute to better decisions by parole boards or to reduced rates of reoffending among Aboriginal offenders (http://pbc-clcc.gc.ca/infocntr/ethnobklt-eng.pdf).

Aboriginal Community Corrections

In recent years, a variety of community-based services and programs for offenders on conditional release have been developed by First Nations across the country. Many of these programs are grounded in traditional Aboriginal culture and spirituality and incorporate elements of restorative justice.

An example of specialized residential services for Aboriginals on conditional release is the O-Chi-Chak-Ko-Sipi Healing Lodge. The CSC refers men (most of them Aboriginal) over the age of 18 to this lodge in Brandon, Manitoba. The program helps Aboriginal offenders through Aboriginal teachings. The offender's physical, mental, emotional, and spiritual well-being is addressed by elders, who provide guidance to program participants. The program follows traditional Aboriginal practices, including sweat lodges and sharing circles.[40]

In Montréal, the 20-week residential program at the Wasekun Healing Centre for Aboriginal men provides individual and group counselling as well as programs in life skills, conflict resolution, family awareness, and women's issues. Sweat lodges and talking circles are also offered (http://www.waseskun.net).

A major issue is the lack of community-based programs and services for Aboriginal offenders from remote northern communities. This may affect the decision making of the parole board and present challenges for those offenders who are released. A former member of the PBC recalled:

> *Sometimes the inmate was ready to go out, and if he was from a city, we would release him. Another inmate, just as ready, would be denied release simply because he was from a community in the Far North with no supports available to him—not only no work, but also no self-help group of former alcoholics, no local hospital with a mental health program, no drug counselors, no sex offender programs.[41]*

Aboriginal offenders on release may encounter unique challenges in addition to those experienced by other offenders (see Chapter 12). Many of them are from rural and remote communities, which makes it difficult for them to access programs and services. Parole supervision may be sporadic, and there may be a lack of continuity regarding their parole officers, further under-mining case management. Little is known about the challenges faced by Aboriginal offenders with mental health disability, FASD, and addictions upon reentry into the community. Many will be returning to communities that are highly troubled and where there are few if any supports. The challenges encountered by corrections personnel in providing supervision and support for these offenders have not been studied, and they badly need to be.

Aboriginal offenders are more likely than others to have their parole revoked. They are also more likely than non-Aboriginals to have their conditional release revoked due to a breach of conditions or a new offence. And they are the most likely to be convicted of an offence involving violence while on conditional release.[42] The same pattern holds with Aboriginal women as for Aboriginal men.[43]

Several provisions in the CCRA are designed to increase the involvement of First Nations communities in the release and reintegration of federal Aboriginal offenders. **Section 81** authorizes the federal government to enter into agreements with First Nations communities whereby the community will take over the "care and custody" of some Aboriginal inmates. **Section 84** provides an opportunity for First Nations to participate in a Community-Assisted Hearing in front of the PBC, to propose a plan for the conditional release and reintegration of the Aboriginal offender into their community. This provision also allows for offenders under a Long-Term Supervision Order to be supervised in an Aboriginal community.[44]

THE EFFECTIVENESS OF SELECTED ABORIGINAL-FOCUSED CORRECTIONAL PROGRAMS AND INTERVENTIONS

Most Aboriginal-focused programs and interventions, be they community-based or in correctional facilities, have not been evaluated. What research studies have been conducted have generally focused on *program dynamics*, rather than on assessing the impact of the intervention on quality of life, subsequent reoffending, and the extent to which the offender's specific risks and needs have been addressed. This is evident in the materials presented in Research File 14.1. Note that a positive program dynamic may not translate into lower rates of re-offending once offenders are released from custody.

An evaluation of the healing lodges operated by the CSC-reported mixed results. In interviews, offenders and staff reported that the healing lodges had "positive transformative effects" on offenders, modified their attitudes and behaviour, and increased their knowledge of Aboriginal spirituality and culture. However, an analysis revealed that these perceived changes did not result in improved outcomes once the offenders were released into the community.[45] The challenges of maintaining throughcare and accessing support in the community were cited as contributing to the lack of positive correctional outcomes.

Section 81 (CCRA)
Authorizes the federal government to enter into agreements with First Nations communities whereby the community assumes the "care and custody" of some Aboriginal offenders upon their release from custody.

Section 84 (CCRA)
Provides for First Nations communities to participate in parole hearings and propose a plan for offender reintegration and includes a provision for First Nations communities to supervise long-term offenders.

RESEARCH FILE 14.1

The Effectiveness of Selected Aboriginal-Focused Programs/Interventions

Program/Intervention	Approach	Outcomes
Hollow Water Community Holistic Healing Program (Hollow Water First Nation, Manitoba)	A community-based response to sexual and family abuse that uses traditional healing practices in an attempt to restore the community, the family, and individual peace and harmony.	An evaluation found that the program has increased community awareness of sexual abuse and family violence and the rates of disclosure by offenders. It has also significantly reduced the rates of alcoholism in the community, improved educational standards, and increased services for at-risk children and youth. Impact on reoffending unknown.[a]
Pé Sâkâstêw Centre (Samson Cree Nation, Alberta)	A minimum security institution where federal Aboriginal elders are directly involved in developing the treatment programs, which focus on healing, culturally appropriate practices, and the use of a sweat lodge.	Research indicates that staff and residents believe the centre is effective in supporting offender reintegration into the community. The centre's residents made significant gains in many need areas following their time there and were assessed as having a higher potential for community reintegration. However, a comparable number of the centre's residents and offenders in the comparison offender group were readmitted to federal custody for new offences. Program may be becoming more effective, with recent statistics indicating that a smaller number of the centre's residents were readmitted to federal custody than in the comparison group.[b]

(continued)

Program/ Intervention	Approach	Outcomes
Ma Mawi Wi Chi Itata Family Violence Program (Stony Mountain Prison, Manitoba; CSC)	A program for Aboriginal inmates designed to address issues related to violent behaviour toward spouses/ partners and family members.	An evaluation found high levels of inmate and staff satisfaction with the program and a widely shared view among the inmates that the program had significantly affected their behaviour, attitudes, and emotions. Impact on reoffending, post-release quality of life, and the extent to which specific issues (e.g., addiction) were addressed is unknown.[c]
CSC ICPM Aboriginal Multi-Target Stream	Targets criminogenic factors using cognitive-behavioural strategies.	Preliminary results indicate that Aboriginal inmates had significantly higher rates of program completion and accessed their first program earlier— within six months of admission— in their sentence this year than in the previous year. Impact on reoffending and post-release quality of life, and the extent to which the offender addressed specific issues (e.g., addiction) are unknown.[d]
Aboriginal Women Circle of Care (CSC)	Institutional and community-based program to improve coping skills, attitudes, and behaviour.	No evaluation. Effectiveness unknown.
Corrections Continuum of Care for Aboriginal Offenders	Focus on reconnecting with traditions and culture and on involvement of First Nations communities in assisting with reintegration.	No evaluation. Several studies of specific programs. See Pé Sâkâstêw Centre.

Program/ Intervention	Approach	Outcomes
Spirit of a Warrior Program (CSC)	Violence prevention program for federal Aboriginal women offenders. Offers a cognitive-behavioural approach and culturally centred intervention strategies that target attitudes, beliefs, and behaviour related to violence and anger.	An evaluation found that program facilitators and participants identified cultural awareness, as well as self-awareness, as the most effective elements of the program. Assessments conducted by the facilitators indicated that the women achieved improvement in the following areas of healing: mental, spiritual, and physical, with the greatest change in the emotional domain. Impact on reoffending, quality of life, and other post-release indicators is unknown.[e]
In Search of Your Warrior (CSC)	Intervention focused on Aboriginal offenders with a history of violence; combines Western treatment approaches with traditional Aboriginal spirituality in an attempt to break the cycle of violence.	An evaluation found that a significantly smaller number of offenders who had participated in the program were returned to prison for committing a violent offence within a year of being released; rates of readmission were not significantly different from those of Aboriginal offenders who did not participate in the program.[f]
Aboriginal Offender Substance Abuse Program (AOSAP) (CSC)	A 16-week high-intensity program to address addiction using a holistic approach that considers the physical, mental, emotional, and spiritual dimensions of addiction. Sessions involve elders and are designed to increase awareness, motivation, skill enhancement, and spirituality.	CSC conducted an evaluation with respect to post-release success up until warrant expiry and found evidence that AOSAP is an effective correctional intervention. Aboriginals who participated in AOSAP performed better than their counterparts who participated in the mainstream substance abuse program; they also returned to the correctional system at a lower rate.[g]

(continued)

Program/ Intervention	Approach	Outcomes
Tupiq program (CSC)	High intensity, culturally based program for moderate to high-risk Inuit sex offenders; provides teachings based on Inuit knowledge and culture, using Inuit elders and facilitators.	Evaluation found that program participants had lower rates of general and violent recidivism than a comparison group approximately four years after they had been released from confinement.[h]
Aboriginal Gang Initiative (AGI) (CSC)	AGI teams, including Aboriginal facilitators guided by Aboriginal elders. An effort is made to help gang members find new identities in their Aboriginal culture and to provide them with a positive foundation with which to reenter the community.	Evaluation found no differences between Aboriginal offenders who participated in the program and a matched group (e.g., static and dynamic risk level ratings, etc.). A follow-up study found that AGI participants ($N = 13$) were more likely to return to prison with a new offence (100 percent) compared to the matched group (25 percent).[i]
Pathways Units (selected CSC institutions)	Living units in federal institutions led by small teams composed of Aboriginal elders and correctional staff. The approach is grounded in Aboriginal culture and spirituality and issues, including residential schools and reserve life. Broken families are addressed through individual counselling, sweat lodge ceremonies, and other culturally based activities.	An evaluation found that Pathway participants were more likely to be transferred to lower security and had enhanced opportunities for early release than a matched group. A high level of inmate and staff support for the program. A one-year post-release review of Pathway participants ($N = 44$) with a matched group found no significant differences in outcome measures (technical revocations and new offences), although Pathway unit offenders reoffended at a lower rate than offenders in the matched group (17 percent *v.* 35 percent respectively).[j]

Program/ Intervention	Approach	Outcomes
Okimaw Ohci Healing Lodge (O-Chi-Chak-Ko-Kipi First Nation, Brandon, Manitoba; federal women offenders)	Program for Aboriginal offenders centred on Aboriginal culture and teachings. Involvement of elders in traditional practices, including sharing circles and sweat lodges.	An evaluation found that the lodge was an appropriate alternative to incarceration, was cost-effective compared to correctional institutions, and had established effective relationships with the local community. A number of operational difficulties, however, limited its effectiveness, including a lack of programs and the need for staff development. No data on post-release reoffending, on the impact of the program on quality of life, or on specific issues (e.g., addiction, violence).[k]
Aboriginal Community Development Officers (CSCs)	Facilitate CCRA Section 84 consultations with First Nations communities and help develop plans to help Aboriginal offenders reintegrate with the community.	An evaluation found that the work of ACDOs had increased the number of Section 84 plans submitted to the PBC. There were no significant differences in reoffending between Aboriginal offenders released with a Section 84 plan and a matched group with no Section 84 plan.[l]
Waseskun Healing Centre (Montréal, CSC)	Program centred on the teachings of the Medicine Wheel to help offenders reintegrate with the community. Elders involved in group and one-on-one sessions.	Evaluation of the program found Waseskun is "a successful therapeutic healing community" that helps offenders address their issues. No information on the impact of the program on reoffending, quality of life, or other issues (e.g., addiction, violence).[m]

[a] J. Couture, T. Parker, R. Couture, and P. Laboucane, *A Cost–Benefit Analysis of Hollow Water's Community Holistic Circle Healing Process* (Ottawa: Solicitor General of Canada, 2001), http://www.publicsafety.gc.ca/res/cor/apc/_fl/apc-20-eng.pdf.

[b] S. Trevethan, N. Crutcher, J.P. Moore, and J. Mileto, *Pé Sâkâstêw Centre: An In-Depth Examination of a Healing Lodge for Federally Incarcerated Offenders* (Ottawa: Correctional Service Canada, 2007), http://www.csc-scc.gc.ca/text/rsrch/reports/r170/r170-eng.pdf.

(continued)

[c] J. Proulx and S. Perrault, *An Evaluation of the Ma Mawi Wi Chi Itata Centre's Family Violence Program Stony Mountain Project* (Ottawa and Winnipeg: Ma Mawi Wi Chi Itata Family Violence Program, 1996).

[d] CSC, *Departmental Performance Report 2010–2011* (Ottawa: Treasury Board Secretariat, n.d.), 29–31, http://www.tbs-sct.gc.ca/dpr-rmr/2010-2011/inst/pen/pen-eng.pdf.

[e] A. Bell and J. Flight, *An Evaluation of the Spirit of a Warrior Program for Woman Offenders* (Ottawa: Correctional Service of Canada, 2006), http://www.csc-scc.gc.ca/text/rsrch/reports/r180/r180-eng.shtml.

[f] S. Trevethan, J.-P. Moore, and N. Allegri, *The "In Search of Your Warrior" Program for Aboriginal Offenders: A Preliminary Evaluation* (Ottawa: Correctional Service of Canada, 2005), http://www.csc-scc.gc.ca/text/rsrch/reports/r172/r172-eng.shtml.

[g] D. Kunic and D. Varis, *The Aboriginal Offender Substance Abuse Program (AOSAP): Examining the Effects of Successful Completion on Post-Release Outcomes* (Ottawa: Correctional Service of Canada, 2009), http://www.csc-scc.gc.ca/text/rsrch/reports/r217/r217-eng.shtml.

[h] L. Stewart, E. Hamilton, G. Wilton, C. Cousineau, and S. Varrette, *An Examination of the Effectiveness of Tupiq: A Culturally Specific Program for Inuit Sex Offenders* (Ottawa: Correctional Service Canada, 2009), http://www.csc-scc.gc.ca/text/rsrch/reports/r213/r213-eng.pdf.

[i] M.J. Burrowes and P. McIntyre, *Final Report—Effective Corrections Initiative—Aboriginal Reintegration* (Ottawa: Correctional Service Canada, 2004), http://www.csc-scc.gc.ca/text/pa/ev-eci-ar-394-2-32/ECI_Aboriginal_Reintegration_e.pdf.

[j] M.J. Burrowes and P. McIntyre, *Final Report—Effective Corrections Initiative—Aboriginal Reintegration* (Ottawa: Correctional Service Canada, 2004), http://www.csc-scc.gc.ca/text/pa/ev-eci-ar-394-2-32/ECI_Aboriginal_Reintegration_e.pdf.

[k] J. Wheatley and I. Roberts, *Evaluation Report: The Section 81 Agreement between the O-Chi-Chak-Ko-Sipi First Nation and the Correctional Service of Canada—The O-Chi-Chak-Ko-Sipi Healing Lodge* (Ottawa: Correctional Service of Canada, 2007), http://www.csc-scc.gc.ca/text/pa/ev-ohl/ev-ohl-eng.pdf.

[l] M.J. Burrowes and P. McIntyre, *Final Report—Effective Corrections Initiative—Aboriginal Reintegration* (Ottawa: Correctional Service Canada, 2004), http://www.csc-scc.gc.ca/text/pa/ev-eci-ar-394-2-32/ECI_Aboriginal_Reintegration_e.pdf.

[m] S. Bell, *The History, Lessons and Observations of Waseskun Healing Centre, a Successful Therapeutic Healing Community* (Ottawa: Public Safety Canada, 2008), http://www.publicsafety.gc.ca/res/cor/apc/_fl/apc-28-eng.pdf.

The results from this study suggest that there is a disconnect between the perceptions of program staff and those of Aboriginal offenders as to the benefits of such programs, including as they relate to outcomes on conditional release. It appears that whatever changes occur in the healing lodges, they do not, for whatever reason, empower Aboriginal offenders to reintegrate successfully back into the community. This may be because, as noted in previous chapters, these offenders were not "integrated" into the community prior to being incarcerated.

The Need for Evaluation and the Development of Evidence-Based Treatment

Culturally appropriate programming for Aboriginal offenders, centred on Aboriginal traditions, culture, and spirituality, has an important role to play in addressing the needs of Aboriginal offenders and in reducing the levels of Aboriginal crime and involvement in corrections. However, the belief that Aboriginal-specific interventions work "is often anecdotal and often put forward by the people who write policy or deliver programs."[46]

Research should examine not only program dynamics but also outcomes, and it should include quality-of-life indicators, the extent to which offenders have reconnected with their community and culture, and their skill levels. At present, the absence of published evaluations of these programs has hindered the development of evidence-based practices for responding to the needs of Aboriginal offenders. One problem is that systems of corrections have not put in place processes to facilitate the analysis of program outcomes on an ongoing basis. "One-off" evaluation studies may provide some insights into program dynamics and outcomes, but they do not provide the basis for the development of evidence-based practice.

Despite the efforts of correctional systems and First Nations and other organizations, the number of Aboriginal persons in conflict with the law and in systems of corrections continues to increase. In the decade between 2000 and 2010, for example, the number of Aboriginal women in federal institutions rose by nearly 86 percent.[47] Aboriginal people continue to become involved in the criminal justice system and corrections systems at higher rates than their non-Aboriginal counterparts.[48]

This suggests that there are larger *structural issues* facing Aboriginal peoples in Canadian society, including racism, discrimination, social inequality, poverty, unemployment, and the Third World conditions of many communities. All of these must be addressed before there will be any appreciable impact on the rates of Aboriginal crime and conflict with the law. It could be argued that, in the absence of these initiatives, the rates of Aboriginal involvement in the criminal justice and corrections systems would be even greater, although the validity of this perspective is difficult to verify.

AT ISSUE

Issue 14.1 Aboriginals in Corrections

Why are so many Aboriginal persons involved in the corrections system?

Despite a variety of initiatives over the past three decades, the numbers of Aboriginal persons involved in corrections and in correctional institutions have continued to increase. Make some suggestions regarding policies and programs to address this situation.

SUMMARY

This chapter has examined the issues surrounding the involvement of Aboriginal peoples in corrections and the initiatives that have been undertaken to address the specific needs of this group. Aboriginal people are overrepresented at all stages of the criminal justice process far beyond their percentage of the national population. This is the result of a variety of historical and contemporary factors. The CSC has developed a number of Aboriginal-specific programs and services; also, many First Nations communities and organizations themselves are involved in responding to the needs of Aboriginal persons in conflict with the law. Many of these programs centre on Aboriginal traditions and spirituality. An absence of evaluations often makes it difficult to assess the effectiveness of these initiatives in addressing the needs of Aboriginal offenders and reducing reoffending.

KEY POINTS REVIEW

1. The subordinate political and economic position of Aboriginal peoples is a consequence of their colonization by Europeans and Canadian government policies.

2. Aboriginal peoples are overrepresented at all stages of the criminal justice system and are disproportionately represented in correctional institutions.

3. Aboriginal women represent a substantial and increasing portion of women in remand and sentenced custody.

4. First Nations communities have been active in developing alternative approaches to responding to Aboriginal persons in conflict with the law, including programs based on the principles of restorative justice.

5. The CSC has developed a number of Aboriginal-specific programs, many of which involve Native elders and are premised on Aboriginal culture and spirituality.

6. There are unique challenges in supervising Aboriginal offenders in the community, and there has been an effort to involve First Nations communities in this effort.

7. Aboriginal offenders generally have higher treatment needs than non-Aboriginal offenders.

8. Aboriginal inmates are less likely than others to succeed in their applications for conditional release and serve a higher proportion of their sentence before being released on parole.

9. Aboriginal inmates often experience difficulties when they appear before parole boards.

10. Most community-based and institutional programs for Aboriginal offenders have not been evaluated, which makes it difficult to

determine their effectiveness in addressing the needs of offenders and their impact on reoffending.

11. To reduce the involvement of Aboriginal persons in the justice and corrections systems and to effectively address the needs of Aboriginal offenders, broader structural issues, such as racism, social inequality, and poverty, will need to be addressed.

KEY TERM QUESTIONS

1. Describe the *Aboriginal Corrections Continuum of Care* and the *Aboriginal Women Offenders Circle of Care* and discuss their role in Aboriginal corrections.
2. What is the importance of *Section 81* and *Section 84* of the CCRA?

NOTES

1. Native Women's Association of Canada, *Aboriginal Women and Gangs: An Issue Paper* (Newfoundland: 2007), http://www.laa.gov.nl.ca/laa/naws/pdf/nwac-gangs.pdf.

2. M.B. Castellano, L. Archibald, and M. Degagne, *From Truth to Reconciliation: Transforming the Legacy of Residential Schools* (Ottawa: Aboriginal Healing Foundation, 2008), http://www.ahf.ca/downloads/from-truth-to-reconciliation-transforming-the-legacy-of-residential-schools.pdf.

3. A. Webster, *Sheltering Urban Aboriginal Homeless People: Assessment of Situation and Needs* (Ottawa: Human Resources and Social Development Canada, 2007), http://pathprogram.samhsa.gov/ResourceFiles/NAFC-Homeless-Final-12-02-08%5B1%5D.pdf.

4. Public Safety Canada, Corrections Statistics Committee, *Corrections and Conditional Release Statistical Overview, 2010–2011* (Ottawa: Public Safety Canada, 2011), 61, http://www.publicsafety.gc.ca/res/cor/rep/_fl/2011-ccrso-eng.pdf.

5. M. Dauvergne, *Adult Correctional Statistics in Canada, 2010–2011* (Ottawa: Minister of Industry, 2012), 12, http://www.statcan.gc.ca/pub/85-002-x/2012001/article/11715-eng.pdf.

6. Parole Board of Canada, *Performance Monitoring Report 2010–2011* (Ottawa: Parole Board of Canada, 2011), http://pbc-clcc.gc.ca/rprts/pmr/pmr_2010_2011/index-eng.shtml.

7. S. Milligan, "Youth Custody and Community Services in Canada, 2005–2006," *Juristat* 28, no. 8 (2008): 1–22, http://www.statcan.gc.ca/pub/85-002-x/2008008/article/10655-eng.htm.

8. Public Safety Canada Portfolio Corrections Statistics Committee, *Corrections and Conditional Release Statistical Overview, 2010–2011* (Ottawa: Public Safety Canada Portfolio Corrections Statistics Committee, 2011), http://www.publicsafety.gc.ca/res/cor/rep/_fl/2011-ccrso-eng.pdf.

9. S. Perreault, "The Incarceration of Aboriginal People in Adult Correctional Services," *Juristat* 29, no. 3 (2009), (Ottawa: Minister of Industry, 2009), http://www.statcan.gc.ca/pub/85-002-x/2009003/article/10903-eng.htm.

10. Correctional Service of Canada, *Strategic Plan for Aboriginal Corrections: Innovation, Learning, and Adjustment 2006–07 to 2010–2011* (Ottawa: Correctional Service of Canada, 2007), http://www.csc-scc.gc.ca/text/prgrm/abinit/plan06-eng.shtml.

11. Assembly of First Nations, *Submission: Bill C-10 Safe Streets and Communities Act* (Ottawa: Assembly of First Nations, 2011), http://www.afn.ca/uploads/files/parliamentary/billc-10.pdf.

12. M.M. Mann, *Good Intentions, Disappointing Results: A Progress Report on Federal Aboriginal Corrections* (Ottawa: 2009), http://www.oci-bec.gc.ca/rpt/oth-aut/oth-aut20091113-eng.aspx.

13. D. Calverley, "Adult Correctional Services in Canada, 2008–2009," *Juristat* 30 no. 3 (2010), http://www.sstatcan.gc.ca/pub/85-002-x/2010003.article/1353-eng.htm; M. Wesley, *Marginalized: The Aboriginal Women's Experience in Federal Corrections* (Ottawa: Public Safety Canada, 2012), http://www.publicsafety.gc.ca/res/cor/apc/_fl/apc-33-eng.pdf.

14. M. Wesley, *Marginalized: The Aboriginal Women's Experience in Federal Corrections* (Ottawa: Public Safety Canada, 2012), http://www.publicsafety.gc.ca/res/cor/apc/_fl/apc-33-eng.pdf.

15. Ibid.

16. D. Milward, "Making the Circle Stronger: An Effort to Buttress Aboriginal Use of Restorative Justice in Canada Against Recent Criticisms," *International Journal of Punishment and Sentencing* 4, no. 3 (2008): 124–58; L. Monchalin, "Canadian Aboriginal Peoples Victimization, Offending and Its Prevention: Gathering the Evidence," *Crime Prevention and Community Safety* 12 (2010): 119–32.

17. M.M. Mann, *Good Intentions, Disappointing Results: A Progress Report on Federal Aboriginal Corrections* (Ottawa: 2009), http://www.oci-bec.gc.ca/rpt/oth-aut/oth-aut20091113-eng.aspx.

18. S. Bell, *The History, Lessons and Observations of Waseskun Healing Centre, a Successful Therapeutic Healing Community* (Ottawa: Public Safety Canada, 2008), http://www.publicsafety.gc.ca/res/cor/apc/_fl/apc-28-eng.pdf.

19. Ibid., 87.

20. R. Weibe and Y. Johnson, *Stolen Life: The Journey of a Cree Woman* (Toronto: Vintage Canada, 1998), 387.

21. S. Perreault, *The Incarceration of Aboriginal People in Adult Correctional Services* (Ottawa: 2009), http://www.statcan.gc.ca/pub/85-002-x/2009003/article/10903-eng.htm.

22. A.K. Yessine and J. Bonta, "The Offending Trajectories of Youthful Aboriginal Offenders," *Canadian Journal of Criminology and Criminal Justice* 51, no. 4 (2009): 435–72.

23. J.P. Moore, *First Nations, Métis, Inuit, and Non-Aboriginal Federal Offenders: A Comparative Profile*, Research Branch R-134 (Ottawa: Correctional Service of Canada, 2003), http://www.csc-scc.gc.ca/text/rsrch/reports/r134/r134_e.pdf.

24. Public Safety Canada Portfolio Corrections Statistics Committee, *Corrections and Conditional Release Statistical Overview, 2010–2011* (Ottawa: Public Safety Canada Portfolio Corrections Statistics Committee, 2011), http://www.publicsafety.gc.ca/res/cor/rep/_fl/2011-ccrso-eng.pdf.

25. CSC, *Revitalizing Correctional Programs to Enhance the Correctional Service of Canada's Contributions to Public Safety: Moving Towards an Integrated Correctional Program Model* (Ottawa: Correctional Service of Canada, 2011).

26. CSC, *Strategic Plan for Aboriginal Corrections*, http://www.csc-scc.gc.ca/text/prgrm/abinit/plan06-eng.shtml.

27. S. Perreault, *The Incarceration of Aboriginal People in Adult Correctional Services* (Ottawa: 2009), http://www.statcan.gc.ca/pub/85-002-x/2009003/article/10903-eng.htm.

28. T. Rugge, *Risk Assessment of Male Aboriginal Offenders: A 2006 Perspective* (Ottawa: Public Safety and Emergency Preparedness Canada, 2006), http://www.publicsafety.gc.ca/res/cor/rep/_fl/abo-offen-eng.pdf.

29. M.M. Mann, *Good Intentions, Disappointing Results: A Progress Report on Federal Aboriginal Corrections* (Ottawa: 2009), http://www.oci-bec.gc.ca/rpt/oth-aut/oth-aut20091113-eng.aspx.

30. Ibid.

31. Parole Board of Canada, *Performance Monitoring Report 2010–2011* (Ottawa: 2011), 78, http://pbc-clcc.gc.ca/rprts/pmr/pmr_2010_2011/index-eng.shtml.

32. Parole Board of Canada, *Performance Monitoring Report 2010–2011* (Ottawa: 2011), 78, http://pbc-clcc.gc.ca/rprts/pmr/pmr_2010_2011/index-eng.shtml.

33. Public Safety Canada Portfolio Corrections Statistics Committee, *Corrections and Conditional Release Statistical Overview, 2010–2011* (Ottawa: Public Safety Canada Portfolio Corrections Statistics Committee, 2011), http://www.publicsafety.gc.ca/res/cor/rep/_fl/2011-ccrso -eng.pdf, 61.

34. M.M. Mann, *Good Intentions, Disappointing Results: A Progress Report on Federal Aboriginal Corrections* (Ottawa: 2009), http://www.oci-bec.gc.ca/rpt/oth-aut/oth-aut20091113-eng.aspx.

35. Assembly of First Nations, *Submission: Bill C-10 Safe Streets and Communities Act* (Ottawa: 2011), http://www.afn.ca/uploads/files/parliamentary/billc-10.pdf.

36. L.H. Birnie, *A Rock and a Hard Place: Inside Canada's Parole Board* (Toronto: Macmillan), 195.

37. Parole Board of Canada, *From Confinement to Community: The National Parole Board and Aboriginal Offenders.* (Ottawa, n.d.) http://pbc-clcc.gc.ca/infocntr/bklt-eng.pdf.

38. Public Safety Canada Portfolio Corrections Statistics Committee, *Corrections and Conditional Release Statistical Overview, 2010–2011* (Ottawa: Public Safety Canada Portfolio Corrections Statistics Committee, 2011), http://www.publicsafety.gc.ca/res/cor/rep/_fl/2011-ccrso-eng.pdf, 61.

39. Parole Board of Canada. *From Confinement to Community: The National Parole Board and Aboriginal Offenders.* (Ottawa, n.d.) http://pbc-clcc.gc.ca/infocntr/bklt-eng.pdf.

40. J. Wheatley and I. Roberts, *Evaluation Report: The Section 81 Agreement between the O-Chi-Chak-Ko-Sipi First Nation and the Correctional Service of Canada—The O-Chi-Chak-Ko-Sipi Healing Lodge* (Ottawa: Correctional Service of Canada, 2007), http://www.csc-scc.gc.ca/text/pa/ev-ohl/ev-ohl-eng.pdf.

41. L.H. Birnie, *A Rock and a Hard Place: Inside Canada's Parole Board* (Toronto: Macmillan), 195.

42. Parole Board of Canada, *Performance Monitoring Report 2010–2011* (Ottawa: 2011), 78, http://pbc-clcc.gc.ca/rprts/pmr/pmr_2010_2011/index-eng.shtml.

43. R. Gobeil, *Rates of Recidivism for Women Offenders* (Ottawa: Correctional Service of Canada, 2007), http://www.csc-scc.gc.ca/text/rsrch/reports/r192/r192-eng.shtml.

44. Parole Board of Canada, *Elder-Assisted Hearings and Community-Assisted Hearings* (Ottawa: n.d.), http://pbc-clcc.gc.ca/rprts/eah-cah/eah-eng.pdf.

45. E. Didenko and B. Marquis, "Aboriginal Healing Lodges," Chapter 1 in *Evaluation Report: Strategies Plan for Aboriginal Corrections* (Ottawa: Correctional Service of Canada, 2011), vii, http://www.csc-scc.gc.ca/text/pa/ev-ahl-394-2-49/healing-lodge-final-eng.pdf.

46. C. Laprairie, *Examining Aboriginal Corrections in Canada* (Ottawa: Supply and Services Canada, 1996), http://www.publicsafety.gc.ca/res/cor/apc/_fl/apc-14-eng.pdf.

47. Public Safety Canada Portfolio Corrections Statistics Committee, *Corrections and Conditional Release Statistical Overview, 2010–2011* (Ottawa: Public Safety Canada Portfolio Corrections Statistics Committee, 2011), http://www.publicsafety.gc.ca/res/cor/rep/_fl/2011-ccrso-eng.pdf, 61.

48. L. Monchalin, "Canadian Aboriginal Peoples Victimization, Offending and Its Prevention: Gathering the Evidence," *Crime Prevention and Community Safety* 12 (2010): 119–132.

CHAPTER 15

YOUNG OFFENDERS

CHAPTER OBJECTIVES

After reading this chapter, you should be able to:
- *Discuss the evolution of youth corrections in Canada.*
- *Discuss how Bill C-10 may impact youth justice in Canada.*
- *Describe the profile of young offenders in Canada.*
- *Identify and describe noncustodial and custodial sentence options for young offenders.*
- *Identify and briefly describe the different types of correctional treatment programs offered to youth in custody.*
- *Describe the dynamics of life inside youth correctional facilities.*
- *Discuss restorative justice initiatives used in the youth criminal justice system.*
- *Discuss the importance of aftercare programs and informal social support networks.*
- *Discuss the effectiveness of youth justice interventions.*

THE EVOLUTION OF YOUTH CORRECTIONS

Recall from the discussion in Chapter 2 that in the 1800s, young offenders were confined along with adults in institutions. Reform efforts in the late 1800s were designed to segregate youth from adults. Successive legislation, beginning in the early 20th century, reflected changing philosophies as to how best to respond to young offenders.

Juvenile Delinquents Act (JDA; 1908)

Legislation centred on a social welfare approach to youth crime.

The first comprehensive legislation for young offenders was the **Juvenile Delinquents Act (JDA)**, enacted in 1908. This legislation set out a social welfare approach to youth crime. Youth who came into conflict with the law were viewed as misdirected and in need of assistance and intervention to address the factors that had contributed to their offending behaviour.[1] This meant that youth could be subject to supervision until the authorities decided they had been rehabilitated and that sentences could be changed midway to reflect the youth's progress.[2]

The JDA, however, raised concerns about lenient sentences, the abuse of child and parental rights, and the presence of "status offences"—that is, behaviour engaged in by a youth (e.g., sexual behaviour) that would not be against the law for an adult.[3]

PERSPECTIVE

The spouse of an offender convicted of a violent crime reflects on her experience with the criminal justice and corrections system:

One of the overarching conclusions I drew was that if a society wants to make a pickpocketing boy into a killer and his sister into a prostitute, the best way is to put them in jail at an early age, allow them to be physically and sexually assaulted by bigger children or adults, deny them contact with anyone who might care about them, and take away opportunities for education. Then, once the child is grown, release him or her back into the community with no money, no ability to trust, no skills for getting a job, and no adults he or she can rely on.

Source: S. Maroney, *Through the Glass* (Toronto: Doubleday Canada, 2011). P. 245.

The **Young Offenders Act (YOA)**, enacted in 1984, attempted to balance the protection of young offenders with ensuring they would be held accountable. The YOA was criticized for, among other things, placing too high a value on the rights and rehabilitation of youth; it was argued that this put the public at risk.[4]

The current legislation under which the youth justice system operates is the **Youth Criminal Justice Act (YCJA)** (2003; http://laws-lois.justice.gc.ca/PDF/Y-1.5.pdf). The objectives of the youth justice system are set out in Section 3(1)(a)(i–iii) of that act and include crime prevention, rehabilitation, and protection of the public through meaningful responses to young offenders.[5] The YCJA is intended to establish clear principles to guide decision making in youth courts; to ensure fairness in sentencing; to reduce the rate of youth incarceration through the increased use of extrajudicial measures; to reintegrate youth into their communities; and to distinguish clearly between serious (e.g., violent) offences and less serious ones.[6]

The YCJA's emphasis on extrajudicial measures is intended to provide more effective programming for young offenders, to address young offenders' multitude of needs, and to reduce reliance on courts and custody in order to save costs.[7] This legislation is in sharp contrast to the more punitive approaches taken by American youth justice systems. American policies have resulted in large numbers of youth serving lengthy sentences. Many are tried as adults and sentenced to custody.

The YCJA seems to have succeeded: fewer young people are serving custodial sentences, and the use of alternative measures has increased.[8] The youth justice system is illustrated in Figure 15.1.

Bill C-10 and the Youth Criminal Justice System

A prominent theme throughout this text has been the trend toward a punitive penology under the present Conservative federal government. A clear indicator of this is Bill C-10 (see Chapter 2), which is likely to result in more youth

Young Offenders Act (YOA; 1984)
Youth legislation that attempted to balance the protection of young offenders with ensuring accountability.

Youth Criminal Justice Act (YCJA; 2003)
The legislative framework for the youth justice system; it has as a key principle to use extrajudicial measures to reduce the rates of incarceration of young offenders.

Video Link
Young Kids, Hard Time Director's Cut
www.youtube.com/watch?v=g316PMjj40&feature=endscreen&NR=1

Figure 15.1

Structure of the Youth Justice System under the YCJA

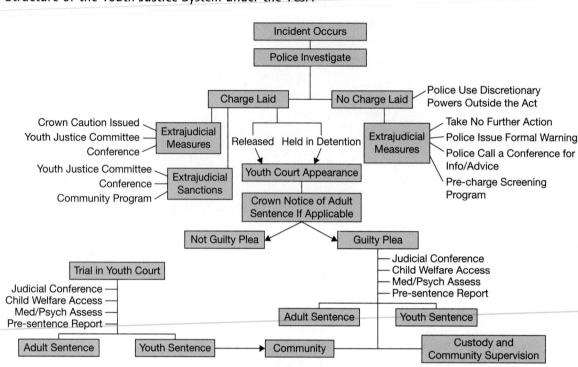

being sentenced to custody as a result of the shift in focus toward public security and risk management.

Specific concerns have been raised about Bill C-10's impact on Aboriginal youth, who are overrepresented in youth corrections. Also, the bill emphasizes public safety and protection, which makes it easier for judges to sentence young offenders to a period of imprisonment and to "promote" young offenders to adult court for trial. Other provisions compel police agencies to keep records of extrajudicial sanctions imposed on youth to document their criminal tendencies and allow the names of young offenders to be published if they have been convicted of a violent offence.[9] See At Issue 15.1.

AT ISSUE

Issue 15.1: Publicizing the Names of Young Offenders

Should the names of young offenders be published?

Opponents of this practice argue that publicizing the names of youth convicted of violent offences will increase the amount of public shaming that occurs and increase the youth's visibility in the community, making it more difficult for them to receive assistance and successfully integrate with the community. The provision may also violate Section 16 of the UN's *Convention on the Rights of the Child* (www2.ohchr.org/english/law/crc.htm), which addresses a child's right to privacy and to not be subjected to "interference or attacks" (s. 16(2)) "on his or her honour and reputation" (s. 16(1)), which arguably is an inevitable consequence of publicizing a young offender's name. Proponents counter that publishing the names of youth will serve as a specific and general deterrent and protect the community. What are your views?

A PROFILE OF YOUNG OFFENDERS

Several key attributes of young offenders are set out in Box 15.1.

Factors that place youth at risk for involvement in delinquent behaviour include drug consumption, substance abuse, poverty, a negative or disruptive family environment, a history of abuse, delinquent peers, educational difficulties, and gang membership.[10] Young female offenders typically experience higher rates of sexual, emotional, and physical abuse than young male

BOX 15.1

A Profile of Youth Crime and Offenders

- The rates of violent crime and property crime committed by youth ages 12 to 17 are declining.
- The rate of youth charged and cases being heard by Canadian youth courts have been declining over the past decade, due in large measure to the YCJA, which emphasizes diversion.
- The majority (60 percent) of youth court cases involve older youth (ages 16 and 17).
- Youth most often find themselves before the court for nonviolent offences (73 percent). The most common offences are theft under $5,000, mischief, common assault (level 1), and administration of justice offences (e.g., failure to appear, failure to comply with conditions of a court order).
- Youth are most frequently incarcerated for property offences (61 percent); the remainder are imprisoned for violent offences.

(continued)

- The rate of offending among female youth is around half the youth male rate of offending (4,011 per 100,000 versus 9,700 per 100,000 in 2010–2011).
- Cases that are heard in youth courts are less likely to involve females (23 percent) than males (77 percent).
- Young female offenders are sentenced to custody less often than young male offenders and receive, on average, shorter custodial sentences.
- Young male and female offenders receive noncustodial sentences (e.g., probation) at approximately the same rate.

Sources: J. Brennan, "Youth Court Statistics in Canada, 2010–2011," *Juristat* (Ottawa: Statistics Canada, 2012), http://www.statcan.gc.ca/pub/85-002-x/2012001/article/11645-eng.htm; C. Munch, "Youth Correctional Statistics in Canada, 2010–2011," *Juristat* (Ottawa: Canadian Centre for Justice Statistics, Statistics Canada, 2012), http://www.statcan.gc.ca/pub/85-002-x/2012001/article/11716-eng.htm; National Crime Prevention Centre, "A Statistical Snapshot of Youth at Risk and Youth Offending in Canada" (Ottawa: Public Safety Canada, 2012), http://www.publicsafety.gc.ca/res/cp/res/ssyr-eng.aspx; R. Kong and K. Aucoin, "Female Offenders in Canada," *Juristat* (Ottawa: Canadian Centre for Justice Statistics, 2008), http://www.statcan.gc.ca/pub/85-002-x/85-002-x2008001-eng.pdf.

offenders.[11] High levels of gang and drug involvement have been correlated with higher rates of gun use among at-risk youth in Montreal and Toronto.[12]

Refer to Chapter 1, Table 1.1, to review the conservative, liberal, and radical perspectives on crime: how it is defined, how people come to be involved in the criminal justice system, and what the objectives of corrections should be. These apply to young offenders as well.

Aboriginal Young Offenders

Aboriginal youth are around 6 percent of the Canadian population but account for 23 percent of admissions to remand, 22 percent of probationers, and 31 percent of admissions to sentenced custody.[13] The same pattern holds for Aboriginal youth, both male and female.[14] Young female Aboriginal offenders represent a higher proportion of the incarcerated female young offender population than male Aboriginal youth in comparison with the young male offender population.[15] One contributing factor may be the lack of community programs, resources, and extrajudicial measures in remote, rural communities.[16] Of particular concern is the plight of youth on First Nations reserves. Aboriginal youth living on reserves are charged with a criminal offence at a rate more than three times the average rate across the remainder of Canada, and they commit a greater proportion of violent and property crimes. These youth are eleven times more likely to be accused of committing homicide than non-Aboriginal youth living off-reserve.[17]

The higher rates of criminal offending among the youth Aboriginal population have been related to high rates of substance abuse, high rates of victimization and family violence, pervasive poverty, low educational attainment, gang membership, and high numbers of Aboriginal children witnessing abuse against their mothers.[18] Many of these factors relate to issues discussed in Chapter 14 with respect to colonization, racism, residential schools, and the destruction of Aboriginal communities and culture.

Aboriginal youth may be prime targets for gang recruitment, resulting in their involvement in the criminal justice and corrections systems.[19] Incarcerating gang members may not be an effective way to reduce recidivism among this population, because gang members may strengthen their bonds in the prison setting, further entrenching their antisocial tendencies and criminal offending upon release.[20] By contrast, early prevention strategies work for at-risk Aboriginals when they are tailored to address the multitude of factors that lead them to join gangs. Effective prevention strategies target the economic and social conditions of Aboriginal youth as well as the trauma, loss, and cognitive impairments (such as FASD) that many of them experience. Culturally appropriate youth crime prevention programs offered in conjunction with programs targeting anger management, substance abuse, and family violence may be effective at decreasing Aboriginal involvement with the criminal justice system.[21]

DIVERSION

Diversion is a key feature of the YCJA. Police officers and Crown counsel can divert youth from the formal court system. Section 6(1) of the YCJA has formalized the practice of police issuing warnings and cautions and referring youth to diversion programs. Young offenders may be diverted at the pre-charge stage to community organizations whose task is to ensure that they complete specified sanctions in a given time period. Once the young offender has satisfied the requirements as laid out, the police or Crown counsel are notified and charges are not laid for the original offence.

When extrajudicial sanctions are brought at the post-charge stage, youth are diverted to formal community diversion programs. When they have met the requirements of the program, the charges are withdrawn.[22] These sanctions include offering an apology to those impacted by their offence; providing restitution or personal services to the victim(s) of the offence; completing a period of community service; participating in community programs (e.g., counselling); and/or being subject to a period of community supervision.[23]

One of the more highly publicized prevention/intervention programs is Scared Straight. Through this "juvenile awareness" program, at-risk youth enter correctional institutions where they are subjected to intense "sit-downs" with inmates. The program's purpose, literally, is to "scare youth straight" by having inmates share, often in a confrontational manner, the realities of a life of crime and incarceration. The program, which is popular in the United States, has not succeeded in reducing the risk of offending/reoffending among youth and may even be harmful to youth.[24]

Video Link
Scared Straight 4
www.youtube
.com/watch?
v=jEiwmcicOu0

As with adults, there is concern that diversion programs may result in net widening, meaning that low-risk, nonviolent youth who would otherwise have received an informal warning from the police are finding themselves caught up in the justice system.[25]

So, do diversion programs work? Research studies suggest that they can. First-time young offenders who participate in diversion programs have been found to have lower rates of reoffending than first-time young offenders processed by the courts for similar offences.[26] However, the lower recidivism rates among diversion program participants may reflect their lower risk/needs profiles more than the effectiveness of those programs.

SENTENCING YOUNG OFFENDERS

The sentencing of young offenders under the YCJA has two objectives: rehabilitation and reintegration of the young offender, and the public's protection.[27] Sentencing tends to be progressive, so that first-time offenders are more likely to receive a community-based sanction and frequent offenders are more likely to receive an institutional sanction.[28] Sentence disparity may exist between and even within jurisdictions, with justice personnel tailoring sanctions to the circumstances, taking into account the young offender's social environment and unique risks and needs.[29] The noncustodial sentencing options for youth court judges are set out in Table 15.1.

Table 15.1 Noncustodial Sentence Options for Young Offenders

Sanction	Description
Judicial reprimand	A judge may issue a verbal "reprimand" to a young offender rather than an actual sentence. This is most often given to first-time offenders convicted of minor offences. These offenders do not receive a criminal record.
Absolute discharge	The youth is found guilty but is released and does not have a criminal record.
Conditional discharge	The youth is found guilty but discharged on the condition that he or she will follow conditions directed by the court. If the youth adheres to the conditions of the order—which may include reporting conditions—no criminal record will result.

Fine	The court can impose a fine not to exceed $1000, which is to be paid at a time and under the conditions the court determines to be appropriate. The judge is required to consider the ability of the youth offender to pay the fine. A youth who is unable to pay it can choose to work off the fine through community service as part of a fine option program.
Restitution	The court may order the youth to make restitution to any other person through money, in kind, or by way of personal services to compensate for a variety of consequences resulting from a criminal offence, including "for loss of or damage to property or for loss of income or support" (YCJA, 42(2)(e)).
Community Service Order	The court may impose an order for the youth to perform a maximum of 240 hours of community service work. It must be completed within 12 months of the date of the order. This period of free work cannot interfere with youth's school or normal work hours. Community Service Orders are commonly included as a condition of probation for young offenders.
Probation	This is the most frequently imposed sanction in the youth courts. Around 91 percent of young offenders serving a community supervision sentence are on probation. The maximum term of probation is two years. There are mandatory conditions and often additional ones. Breach of probation is a Criminal Code offence.
Intensive Support and Supervision Order	The provinces decide whether to use this sanction. It involves more intensive programming and assistance for young offenders as well as greater surveillance and control than youth experience on probation.
Nonresidential Attendance Order	A nonresidential order for a period not to exceed 240 hours over a 6-month period.

Sources: S. J. Bell, *Young Offenders and Youth Justice: A Century After the Fact*, 4th ed. (Toronto: Nelson, 2012); J. Brennan, "Youth Court Statistics in Canada, 2010–2011," *Juristat* (Ottawa: Statistics Canada, 2012), http://www.statcan.gc.ca/pub/85-002-x/2012001/article/11645-eng.htm; C. Munch, "Youth Correctional Statistics in Canada, 2010–2011," *Juristat* (Ottawa: Canadian Centre for Justice Statistics, Statistics Canada, 2012), http://www.statcan.gc.ca/pub/85-002-x/2012001/article/11716 -eng.htm.

Young offenders doing community service.

Richard Gardner/Rex Features

Youth Probation

As with adult corrections, the majority of youth under supervision in the community are on probation. Like their counterparts in the adult corrections systems, youth probation officers have a variety of tasks to perform: providing supervision to youth probationers; writing pre-sentence reports and attending court; making referrals to community services; and monitoring youth on bail, deferred custody, mandatory supervision, and community service. Youth probation officers typically have smaller caseloads than adult probation officers; in British Columbia, for example, they carry average caseloads of twenty probationers. Modes of contact with probationers include office, school, and home visits. These personnel often work with other community agencies.

Two important dimensions of youth probation are risk/needs assessment and case management. The former involves determining which youth are high-risk and therefore require greater supervision, as well as which criminogenic needs should be targeted through intervention. Case management refers to how supervision and services will be provided to youth.[30] Youth who are under an intensive support and supervision order receive more intensive programming and assistance.

Youth probation officers hold **integrated case management (ICM) conferences** with young offenders, their parents/guardians, and other

Integrated case management (ICM) conferences The primary strategy used for case management of young offenders on probation.

support people, such as mental health workers, social workers, and specialists in FASD. The objective of ICM conferences is to establish manageable goals and benchmarks that the youth can achieve while in custody and on probation as well as after completion of their sentence. When a youth's support network has helped develop and revise the case management plan, everyone is aware of its goals and can identify their role in helping the youth achieve them.

Custodial Sentences for Young Offenders

The various custodial sentences for young offenders are summarized in Table 15.2. Only a brief description is provided for each type of sentence.

Youth in custody are likely to have experienced problems or trauma in the family home resulting in their removal and placement in youth care. Many lack positive peer, school, and adult attachments in their lives.[31] These youth are more prone than their nonincarcerated peers to substance abuse, mental health disorders, learning disabilities, and HIV.[32]

Table 15.2 Custodial Sentences for Young Offenders

Sanction	Description
Custody and supervision order	The community supervision period following custody is half as long as the term of custody, and the youth is subject to supervision and conditions. The total term cannot exceed two years for offences, except for those involving imprisonment for life—for which the term cannot exceed three years.
Custody and conditional supervision	Applies to presumptive offences (e.g., manslaughter, attempted murder). The total term of custody and conditional supervision in the community cannot exceed three years from the date of committal.
Deferral of custody and supervision	The order cannot exceed 6 months. It excludes cases involving presumptive offences.
Intensive rehabilitative custody and supervision order	The first portion of the sentence is served in intensive rehabilitative custody, the second under conditional supervision in the community.

DOING TIME

Young offenders find imprisonment harder to take than adult offenders do, which makes a prison term a much more severe sentence for them. Making it even worse is that many young offenders lack survival strategies that might help them cope with the pains of imprisonment.[33] For youth, those pains typically include violence, the loss of freedom, and high anxiety due to severed family and social ties.[34] Violence in youth institutions may include bullying, verbal threats, theft, intimidation, physical abuse, predatory aggression, and coercion.[35]

Displays of bravado, masculinity, and strength may be especially prevalent in youth facilities. Interviews with 350 adolescent males in Canadian custody and detention facilities revealed the ways in which hegemonic masculinity is exhibited in youth facilities: the interview subjects endorsed behaving manly, not displaying emotion, and standing up for oneself.[36] Because the "prisoner" label comes with "connotations of weakness, conformity, and the relinquishing of power," it is not surprising that "manliness becomes the primary means of adaptation and resistance" in institutional settings.[37] It seems that many of the dynamics in adult correctional institutions are also found in youth facilities. For example, a youth may hesitate to ask COs for help, out of fear that his peers will label him a "rat."[38] Also, youth may resort to aggression to achieve status within the facility.[39]

Young offenders who do not cope well within the prison environment are at a higher risk of committing suicide, as are youth with pre-existing vulnerabilities such as family instability.[40]

TREATMENT PROGRAMS

Much like in the adult system, correctional intervention with young offenders begins with an assessment to identify risks and needs and to develop an appropriate correctional plan. Correctional programs can be general, offence-specific, or offender-specific.[41] Education, counselling, and recreation programs are offered to all young offenders; *offence*-specific programs target certain offenders (e.g., sex offenders); *offender*-specific programs (e.g., for substance abuse issues) target individual risks and needs.[42] Community-based interventions vary by province, but probation officers everywhere refer young offenders to community services, which range from detox centres to safe houses to psychiatric assessment facilities to educational and employment resources.

Treatment programs in youth custodial institutions are often designed to foster a sense of agency among youth—for example, to encourage self-control and self-discipline and to teach mastery skills.[43] But the closed nature of institutions means that youth have few meaningful opportunities to apply these new tools to increase their social mobility; as a result, they may use those skills to dominate one another, which can lead to more disciplinary infractions for some youth and increased bullying and victimization for others.[44]

Another concern is that youth in secure facilities are expected to defer entirely to authority figures and the institutional structure. This does not encourage them to take responsibility for their choices and to demonstrate their agency, which may make it harder for them to move forward upon their release in the community.[45]

Finally, youth may "do program" to show self-control, commitment to the objectives of the institution, and self-change; however, they may simply be faking it to achieve rewards by demonstrating "progress" to the administration.[46]

As mentioned, youth in institutions must confront the inmate code, the adolescent code, the pains of imprisonment, and the difficulties of adjusting to the institution. Their fear of victimization and of transgressing the inmate code may undermine treatment efforts. Research studies suggest that personal security is necessary if there is to be any hope of changing young offenders' attitudes and behaviour.[47] Other factors that may hinder the implementation and effectiveness of correctional programs for youth include these: security concerns that obstruct treatment efforts, poorly trained correctional staff, an absence of political and public support for rehabilitating young offenders, and counterproductive inmate–staff relationships.[48]

Some research suggests that youth who are sentenced to adult facilities receive more services—schooling, job training, caseworker assistance, counselling, and drug treatment—than youth who are sentenced to youth facilities.[49] Notwithstanding that, youth in juvenile facilities benefit more from the treatment that *is* available to them, largely because of more positive staff–inmate interactions, which can include mentoring.[50]

A meta-analysis of 195 studies investigating young offender treatment programs found that youth who participated in *any* form of treatment intervention were less likely to recidivate than youth who did not.[51] Participation in treatment interventions resulted in a 9 percent decrease in recidivism, which "theoretically prevented more than 1,300 offenders from reoffending."[52]

Incarcerated young female offenders typically have higher rates of disruptive disorders, major depression, PTSD, and separation anxiety than incarcerated young male offenders.[53] The unique risk/needs profiles and characteristics of young females (as identified above) point to a need for gender-specific programming. Evidence suggests, however, that the most effective programs in reducing young offender recidivism—gender-specific or not—are comprehensive, follow the RNR model, and target multiple risk factors.[54] Nevertheless, girl-specific programming may help achieve particular goals, such as empowerment and improved quality of life.[55] Further longitudinal research investigating girls' delinquency is required to develop effective programming for this offender population that reflects their unique socialization and development.[56]

Youth–Staff Relationships

Just as in adult facilities, COs play a prominent role in the incarceration experience for youth. Youth may require emotional support and practical assistance from staff as they adjust to life in the institution. Positive relationships with staff may alleviate depression, hopelessness, and anxiety among incarcerated young offenders.[57] Staff can help create a stable and secure environment where youth do not fear for their personal security. When the rules and boundaries are consistently enforced, positive social exchanges can develop between staff and offenders.[58]

COs can demonstrate prosocial modelling for troubled youth, which may encourage the youth's resocialization.[59] Research exploring relationships between prosocial adults and juveniles in custodial institutions found that most incarcerated youth turned first to a same-sex staff member, rather than to a case manager, for assistance and advice.[60]

Positive relationships with staff can affect youth perceptions of whether they will succeed on release.[61] Youth in the "balanced" relationship category—that is, who viewed their relationships with staff positively, as being built on trust, engagement, and effective problem solving—often anticipate succeeding on release.[62]

Instead of providing positive, prosocial modelling for youth, some COs may engage in negative behaviour that breaches the trust of the youth in their care. One study of young offenders in Ontario (*N* = 100) found that when COs put their safety at risk, it took the form of "letting bad things happen" (46 percent), jeopardizing an inmate's safety (47 percent), or bribing inmates to discipline one another (31 percent).[63] There have also been documented incidents of correctional staff abusing young offenders physically, sexually, and psychologically.[64]

Interviews with young male offenders (*N* = 350) in Canadian custody and detention centres found that youth felt that staff were inconsistent and unfair in their decision making. One youth reported that "some staff try to make their own rules and they change them depending on what staff are here—other rules that are supposed to be enforced, they don't enforce them—so you don't know what you will get in trouble for."[65]

RISK ASSESSMENT IN YOUTH CORRECTIONS

The principles of RNR are applied when assessing the risk and needs of young offenders and developing intervention plans for them. As noted, treatment programming that centres on the RNR model is generally effective at reducing reoffending among both young and adult offenders.[66] Risk assessment tools help practitioners classify young offenders and predict whether they will place the community at risk upon release.[67]

The **Youth Level of Service/Case Management Inventory (YLS/CMI)** is the most extensively used risk/needs measurement tool in youth justice systems.[68] It is based on RNR principles and is a variant of the Level of Service Inventory (LSI-R) used for adult offenders.[69] Youth probation officers,

Youth Level of Service/Case Management Inventory (YLS/CMI)

The primary risk/need assessment instrument in youth corrections.

psychologists, social workers, youth workers, and court workers use this risk/needs assessment tool to assess a youth's risk for general recidivism, to identify the factors that require intervention, and to develop a community supervision plan.[70] The YLS/CMI comprises 42 risk/needs factors that fall into the following eight domains: Prior and Current Offenses/Dispositions, Family Circumstances/Parenting, Education/Employment, Peer Relations, Substance Abuse, Leisure/Recreation, Personality/Behaviour, and Attitudes/Orientation.[71]

The YLS/CMI has been found to predict general recidivism among young offenders regardless of their gender, Aboriginal versus non-Aboriginal status, or offence type.[72] It has also been found to identify the needs of young male and female offenders and so it can be used to inform recommendations for probation interventions. However, the YLS/CMI, when used to identify RNR factors and to match them with interventions, was a more useful tool for male than for female young offenders. This suggests that it may be worthwhile to include gender-specific/sensitive factors in risk assessment tools to ensure that interventions with female young offenders are better matched to their needs.[73]

RESTORATIVE JUSTICE APPROACHES AND YOUNG OFFENDERS

As previously discussed, restorative justice initiatives bring together offenders, victims, families, and communities to mutually resolve conflicts and repair the harms that have been caused by crime. Restorative justice initiatives provide

© Michael Newman/PhotoEdit

Youth Justice Committee.

young offenders with the opportunity to make amends with those they have harmed and take responsibility for their behaviour; victims are given a voice in the process, which promotes their healing; and the community comes together to support the victims and offenders in addressing the harms that have been caused and in achieving peace in the community. Many restorative programs for young offenders are limited to first-time, nonviolent offenders, although some programs target more serious offenders.[74]

There are a variety of restorative justice initiatives across Canada designed to facilitate reparation, reconciliation, and relationship building. These may be particularly beneficial for Aboriginal young offenders, who can culturally identify with these principles. Several of these initiatives are presented in Table 15.3. Note that for all of the initiatives, the impact on re-offending is unknown.

Table 15.3 Selected Restorative Justice Programs for Young Offenders

Initiative	Participants	Approach/Outcomes
Aboriginal Youth Restorative Justice Committee (CAYRJC) (Calgary, Alberta)	Aboriginal youth in conflict with the law, their families, the victims and their families, legal system personnel, and the community.	Establish a suitable and meaningful consequence for the criminal behaviour. Participants receive culturally relevant teachings from respected elders. Offer youth hope and empower them by providing meaningful opportunities to engage with experienced and knowledgeable community members.[a] Impact on reoffending unknown.
Victoria Restorative Justice Society (Victoria, B.C.)	Pre-charge diversion cases for minor offences referred from the Victoria Police Department; post-charge referrals from Crown counsel for medium and serious offences; referrals from victims, social service agencies, and other RJ programs; public education and outreach; local schools.	Trained volunteers facilitate community justice conferences, panels, victim–offender mediation, peacemaking circles. Programs include a support group for at-risk youth (Girls' Circle) and a program that addresses the needs of shoplifters (Shoplifting Program). Certificate program, the Youth Restorative Practices Certificate, offered to school youth. In-house evaluations show positive outcomes, with victims, offenders, and police officers reporting being "very satisfied" or "satisfied" with the restorative justice processes.[b] Impact on reoffending unknown.

Windsor–Essex County Youth Justice Committee (Windsor, Ontario)	Pre-charge diversion cases; youth aged 12–18 who have committed low-risk or nonviolent offences; youth who accept responsibility and accountability for their actions.	Alternative to formal, court-based system. Victims, offenders, their families, and communities come together to address victim needs and offender accountability and community wellness; potential sanctions include a mandatory apology, curfew, donation to charity, community service work, and/or a reprimand.[c] Impact on reoffending unknown.
Island Community Justice Society (Nova Scotia)	Referrals are accepted at multiple stages of the youth justice process: pre-charge (police), post-charge/conviction (Crown counsel), post-conviction/pre-sentence (judges), and post-sentence (correctional services/victims' services). For youth aged 12 to 17 in conflict with the law.	Facilitate family group conferences, victim offender meetings, accountability meetings, and sentencing circles. Deliver a community service order program. Promote offender accountability. Provide victims with a voice in the process, and enable community support and input. Provide victim and volunteer support services.[d] Impact on reoffending unknown.

[a] Native Counselling Services of Alberta, *Corrections and Restorative Justice* (Edmonton: 2012), http://www.ncsa.ca/online/?page_id=46; Montreal Urban Aboriginal Community Strategy Network, *The Aboriginal Justice Research Project* (Montreal: Montreal Urban Aboriginal Strategy Network, 2012), http://www.crime-prevention-intl.org/uploads/media/Aboriginal_Justice_Research_Project_-_Final _Report.pdf.

[b] S. Warmald, *Victoria Restorative Justice Society: Annual Review 2010* (Victoria: 2011), http://rjvictoria .wordpress.com/about/annual-reports.

[c] Youth Justice Committees of Ontario, *Windsor–Essex County Youth Justice Committee* (n.d.), http://www .yjcontario.ca/committees/windsor.php.

[d] Island Community Justice Society, *Restorative Justice: A Program for Nova Scotia* (n.d.), http://island communityjustice.com/services.html.

The outcomes of most of these programs have not been evaluated, so it is difficult to assess their effectiveness at addressing the risk/needs of young offenders and in reducing reoffending.

A prominent role in restorative justice is played by **Youth Justice Committees (YJCs)**, which operate across the country. YJCs provide guidance about which extrajudicial measures would be most appropriate for

Video Link
Restorative v. Retributive Justice in Vermont and New Zealand: A Case Study Comparison **www.youtube .com/watch?v=s 967kBKEJowand feature=related**

Youth Justice Committee (JYC)
Community-based committees that sponsor a variety of initiatives for youth in conflict with the law, including extrajudicial measures centred on restorative justice.

individual young offenders. They also support the victim and facilitate victim–offender reconciliation; ensure community support for the young offender through services, short-term mentoring, and community supervision; and coordinate interactions between agencies (e.g., the local child protection agency and the youth criminal justice system).

YJCs may be involved in a variety of initiatives, including family group conferences, community/neighbourhood accountability panels, victim/offender mediation/reconciliation sessions, multidisciplinary case management conferences, and Aboriginal sentencing and healing circles.

AFTERCARE PROGRAMS

Aftercare programs are designed to address young offenders' unique needs and risks as they reenter society. They combine community restraint elements with community service strategies to facilitate offender change and increase public safety.[75] Young female offenders may be more amenable to therapeutic interventions (e.g., formal counselling services) than young male offenders when reentering society.[76] These findings suggest the importance of providing young female offenders with access to therapeutic community interventions to help them transition back to the community after a period of incarceration. The research evidence demonstrates the importance of providing young offenders with aftercare programming in community settings and at a lower intensity than the youth received in institutional settings.[77]

The Role of Informal Social Support Networks

Research suggests that informal social supports (e.g., friends and family) play a major role in the community reentry process for young offenders. The relationships that young offenders form with their peers are important in the community reentry process, for peers may provide young offenders with assistance such as support, camaraderie, and financial resources. However, peers may also encourage illicit behaviour, resulting in the youth returning to custody. Young offenders may thus find themselves "walking a fine line" as they limit their contacts with their old social groups so as to avoid trouble, while working to develop a new sense of identity and belonging.[78]

Family support is also important in the community reentry process for young offenders. Families are able to provide financial resources, emotional support, encouragement, and potentially, employment. But the family may also pose challenges for young offenders, for the environment at home may encourage previous patterns of criminal behaviour. Also, the pressure of expectations may generate a self-fulfilling prophecy, so that some youth fall back into old patterns of illicit behaviour.[79]

Materials on the effectiveness of selected interventions are presented in Research File 15.1. Most of these interventions have not been proven effective at reducing reoffending, and it is not certain whether these interventions address the needs of young offenders.

RESEARCH FILE 15.1

The Effectiveness of Selected Youth Justice Interventions

Noncustodial Interventions	Strategy	Outcomes
Boot camps	Used as a condition of probation or diversion program. Short-term residential program. Military model involves demanding exercise routines. Emphasis on labour, discipline, exercise, and drills. Some incorporate cognitive behavioural treatment and aftercare.	Generally do not have an impact on reoffending unless young offenders are voluntary participants. May improve young offenders' attitudes and impact their adjustment while in the facility. Young offenders view boot camps more favourably than correctional facilities. Decreases in recidivism are more likely to occur following participation in boot camps that target risk factors through rehabilitation components.[a]
Scared Straight programs	Target at-risk youth or youth who have come into conflict with the law, who are taken into correctional institutions for a "sit down" with inmates, who share their stories. Objective is to deter youth from criminal behaviour by showing them the punitive nature of imprisonment.	Research has found that the programs are ineffective as a general or specific deterrent to future offending.[b]
Probation	The most frequently used intervention. Places youth under supervision in the community, subject to general and, often, specific conditions designed to address their risk and needs.	The effectiveness of probation is enhanced when the principles of RNR are followed (e.g., low-intensity supervision for low-risk young offenders and high-intensity supervision for higher-risk youth).[c]

(continued)

Noncustodial Interventions	Strategy	Outcomes
Open custody and open detention facilities	Provide optimal programming opportunities for youth, prosocial role modelling opportunities, and community reintegration. Middle of the continuum between containment and reintegration.	Evaluation in Ontario found that these facilities can function as transitional programming to facilitate youth reintegration and opportunities for prosocial modelling and relationships between staff and youth.[d] Impact on reoffending unknown.
Intensive rehabilitative custody and supervision (IRCS)	Objectives include appropriate use of courts and correctional institutions for young offenders, as well as proportionality in the youth justice system's response to the offence and offender's level of responsibility. Greater opportunities for social reintegration and rehabilitation.	IRCS has increased provincial/territorial abilities to provide programming for young serious violent offenders with mental health issues. Each jurisdiction has developed the capacity to administer IRCS sentences.[e] Impact on reoffending unknown.
Serious and Violent Offender Reentry Initiative (SVORI) (U.S.)	Designed to improve youth access to comprehensive, integrated community services and to improve reentry outcomes in the education, employment, health, housing, and criminal justice domains.	In one study ($N = 337$), SVORI participants were more likely to have reentry plans, but there was no difference between SVORI and non-SVORI participants in rates of reoffending.[f]
Intensive Aftercare Programs (IAP) Denver, Las Vegas, Virginia	Attention to reintegration during incarceration. Intensive supervision and services post-release. Slow and steady transition between the institution and aftercare in the community. Objective is to reduce recidivism among high-risk parolees.[g]	Initial implementation and testing of IAP over a 12-month follow-up period found few statistically significant differences between the IAP and control groups in incidence, severity, or prevalence of reoffending.[h]

[a] B. Meade and B. Steiner, "The Total Effects of Boot Camps That House Juveniles: A Systematic Review of the Evidence," *Journal of Criminal Justice* 38, no. 5 (2010): 841–53; B. Steiner and A.L. Giacomazzi, "Juvenile Waiver, Boot Camp, and Recidivism in a Northwestern State," *Prison Journal* 87, no. 2 (2007): 227–40.

[b] P. M. Klenowski, K. J. Bell, and K. D. Dodson, "An Empirical Evaluation of Juvenile Awareness Programs in the United States: Can Juveniles Be 'Scared Straight'?", *Journal of Offender Rehabilitation* 49, no. 4 (2010): 254–72.

[c] D. Luong and S. Wormith, "Applying Risk/Need Assessment to Probation Practice and Its Impact on the Recidivism of Young Offenders," *Criminal Justice and Behavior* 38, no. 12 (2011): 1177–99.

ᵈ D. Cooke and J. Finlay, *Open Detention and Open Custody in Ontario* (Toronto: 2007), http://provincial advocate.on.ca/documents/en/Open%20Custody-OpenDetention%20Review.pdf.

ᵉ Department of Justice Canada, *The Youth Justice Initiative Funding Components Evaluation: Final Report* (Ottawa: Evaluation Division, Office of Strategic Planning and Performance Management, 2010), http://www.justice.gc.ca/eng/pi/eval/rep-rap/11/yjifc-vfijj/yjifc-vfijj.pdf.

ᶠ P. K. Lattimore and C. A. Visher, *The Multi-Site Evaluation of the Serious and Violent Offender Re-entry Initiative* (Washington: U.S. Department of Justice, 2009), https://www.ncjrs.gov/pdffiles1/nij/grants/230421.pdf.

ᵍ R. G. Wiebush, D. Wagner, B. McNulty, Y. Wang, and T. N. Le, *Implementation and Outcome Evaluation of the Intensive Aftercare Program: Final Report* (Washington: National Council on Crime and Delinquency, 2005), https://www.ncjrs.gov/pdffiles1/ojjdp/206177.pdf.

ʰ Wiebush, et al., "Implementation and Outcome Evaluation."

There are additional questions that can be asked with respect to the effectiveness of youth corrections, including these:

Do harsh penalties deter youth from committing crimes? In most cases, no. Research studies have found that, for a variety of reasons, punitive sanctions (including the threat to transfer young offenders to adult court) do not deter young offenders from committing crimes.[80] In one study (*N* = 53), 42 percent of the youth participants sentenced to either probation or custody indicated that their sentence would not deter them from reoffending, and 66 percent indicated that their sentence would be unlikely to deter their friends from committing the same crime.[81]

For which groups of young offenders are treatment programs most effective? The most positive outcomes tend to occur when violent and high-risk offenders are targeted for intervention. For most young offenders, the most effective correctional programs offered in the community and institutional settings are those that incorporate cognitive behaviour strategies, education, and vocational skills.[82]

THE JOURNEY OF AN EX-DANGEROUS OFFENDER

"It started out when I was at a group home which consisted of 30 other children. I was sent there because I was labeled as being 'incorrigible' under the Juvenile Delinquents Act. This was in the late 1960s. My dad was physically abusive and so they took me away from my family. But the group home was full and I was called into the office and told that I was going to a bigger school, a school which I would learn quite a bit and would become a responsible boy. Initially I would start at a place called Bowmanville which was kind of a reception centre for boys coming into the training school system. I would be there for approximately ten days, and I would be classified as being too young to be there and so I was sent to a place called Coburn. Coburn Training School: what would go on in that training school for me, I felt, was probably the hardest part in my whole life, because there was a lot of discipline and discipline was really forced on you.

"I mean physically forced. We were made to sit in lockers in houses of 30 boys; each house consisted of 30 boys, and there were seven houses at the school. Everything was done military style, and we would have to sit in our lockers and if anybody, you know, acted up or something like that the house would be put onto routines. Routines sometimes consisted of running up and down fire escapes with big parkas on during the summer. This was referred to as being the sweat box, because it was summer and we would be up and down the fire escape. Some of the routines would last three or four hours. If one of the boys, or any of the boys didn't make it or fell down or gave up or whatever, the house was put on more routines. As a consequence, whoever caused the house to be put on longer routines would get beat. Sometimes the staff would suddenly get up and say he heard the telephone ring. That was the key to go and he was leaving and that some guy was going to get beat up. So at an early age we learned that fighting was part of the way of life, and that if you wanted to survive that you had to be physical, and also the fact that you weren't going to inform on anybody there, because if you did, you were a rat. So at an early age we were learning not to be a rat and also to fight. And, if somebody escaped, the whole house would be put on routines until the boy came back, providing that it was not a long period. So anyway, when this boy came back he would sometimes be put into a potato sack and tied into it. Then everybody would scramble him.

"Sometimes when visitors came they would give candy and chocolate bars and stuff like that. Well we were only allowed to have it on Friday night. So all of this candy was put away in a closet and on Friday night if the house had been good then we were able to get whatever candy we had. People like myself were unfortunate not to have visitors; so, they would have a box of candy and what they used to do is put like jelly beans or Smarties or something like that; they would give you a cup, then throw the candy in the middle of the floor. Everybody would scramble for it. So everybody was beating each other up to get a couple of candies.

"For me training school was probably, as I said earlier, the worst part of my experience with the criminal justice system. My mother and father never came to visit me, ever. Not when I was a juvenile or adult. I never saw my mother again. Due to the fact that I was very young and had just been taken away from my family and having no loved ones, I started to build this out of control kind of person, you know, in the sense that I would fight at the drop of a hat. The thing is I realized by doing that then I was protecting myself, so for my own protection I was developing these skills that as I got older would become very harmful to me, and to most other people I would come into contact with." (personal communication with C. T. Griffiths)

These are the reflections of an ex–dangerous offender who entered the youth justice system as an "incorrigible" at age 7 in the 1960s under the JDA. He would go on to serve twenty-three years inside youth and adult correctional institutions; for his last series of offences, he would be designated a

"It seems like only yesterday you were a juvenile offender."

dangerous offender. His story, while perhaps extreme, is similar to those of many others who find themselves involved in the correctional system. It also highlights the difficulty of escaping what, for many, becomes a perpetual "revolving door": from the community to the justice system and (sometimes) incarceration and back into the community. The challenge for community-based and institutional correctional systems is to intervene in a positive way so as to reduce the likelihood of reoffending. When this challenge is met, the offender is helped and the community is protected. See At Issue 15.2.

AT ISSUE

Issue 15.2: Dangerous Offenders

The ex-dangerous offender's journey: what could have been done differently?

The journey of the ex–dangerous offender is an all-too-familiar story, especially for offenders who are "state-raised." From the materials presented in the preceding chapters, set out what, in your view, could have been done differently that might have produced a different outcome.

SUMMARY

This chapter provided an overview of young offenders and youth corrections. Like their adult counterparts, the majority of youth who become involved in provincial/territorial systems of correction have multiple needs and are often from unstable families and/or communities. For many observers, Bill C-10 reflects a shift toward more punitive corrections for young offenders. The chapter examined a variety of noncustodial and custodial options as well as the effectiveness of those interventions. Concerns were expressed about the effectiveness of youth custody and of a variety of noncustodial approaches, including Scared Straight and boot camps.

KEY POINTS REVIEW

1. The Juvenile Delinquents Act (JDA) set out a social welfare approach to youth crime; youth were viewed as misdirected and in need of assistance and intervention to address the factors that contributed to their offending behaviour.

2. The Young Offenders Act (YOA) simultaneously emphasized the protection of young offenders and their accountability.

3. At the core of the Youth Criminal Justice Act (YCJA) are extrajudicial measures to reduce the incarceration rates for young offenders.

4. The rates of violent crime, property crime, youth charged, and cases being heard by Canadian youth courts have declined over the past decade.

5. Females are less likely to become involved in the youth criminal justice system.

6. Factors that place youth at risk for involvement in delinquent behaviour include drug consumption, a history of abuse, delinquent peers, substance abuse, poverty, a negative or disruptive family environment, and gang membership.

7. Diversion involves the police issuing warnings and cautions and referring youth to diversion programs.

8. Probation is the most frequently imposed sanction in the youth courts.

9. Youth experience a variety of pains of imprisonment, including violence, bullying, the loss of freedom, and high levels of anxiety due to severed family and social ties.

10. A variety of correctional treatment programs are offered to youth in custodial and noncustodial settings; these may be general, or offence- or offender-specific.

11. COs play a key role in the incarceration experience for youth; positive relationships with staff members may alleviate depression, hopelessness, and anxiety among incarcerated young offenders.

12. Treatment programming centred on the RNR model is generally effective in reducing the rates of reoffending among young offenders.

13. YJC may be involved in family group conferences, community/neighbourhood accountability panels, victim/offender mediation/reconciliation sessions, multidisciplinary case management conferences, and Aboriginal sentencing and healing circles.

14. Aboriginal youth are overrepresented in youth custody facilities.

15. The most effective correctional programs offered to young offenders in community and institutional settings are those that incorporate cognitive-behavioural strategies, education, and vocational skills.

KEY TERM QUESTIONS

1. Briefly describe the evolution of youth justice legislation in Canada (*Juvenile Delinquents Act*, *Young Offenders Act*, *Youth Criminal Justice Act*).

2. Identify and describe the primary goals of the *Youth Criminal Justice Act*.

3. Identify and discuss the purpose of *integrated case management conferences* in the youth probation system.

4. Describe the *youth level of service/case management inventory (YLS/CMI)*, including the domains it assesses.

5. What role do *Youth Justice Committees (YJCs)* play in the youth justice system in Canada?

NOTES

1. L. Casavant, R. MacKay, and D. Valiquet, *Youth Justice Legislation in Canada*, Legal and Legislative Affairs Division, Library of Parliament, PRB-08-23E (Ottawa: 2008), http://www.parl.gc.ca/Content/LOP/researchpublications/prb0823-e.pdf.

2. Ibid.

3. Ibid.; S. J. Bell, *Young Offenders and Youth Justice: A Century After the Fact*, 4th ed. (Toronto: Nelson, 2012).

4. Ibid.

5. Ibid.

6. J. Latimer and N. Desjardins, *The 2008 National Justice Survey: The Youth Justice System in Canada and the Youth Criminal Justice Act* (Ottawa: Department of Justice, 2009), 1, http://www.justice.gc.ca/eng/pi/rs/rep-rap/2008/rr08_yj1-rr08_jj1/p3.html.

7. Department of Justice Canada, *The Youth Justice Initiative Funding Components Evaluation: Final Report* (Ottawa: Evaluation Division, Office of Strategic Planning and Performance Management, 2010), http://www.justice.gc.ca/eng/pi/eval/rep-rap/11/yjifc-vfijj/yjifc-vfijj.pdf.

8. B. DeGusti, *The Impact of the Youth Criminal Justice Act on Case Flow in Alberta and System Response in Calgary*, Canadian Research Institute for Law and the Family, University of Calgary, 2008. http://people.ucalgary.ca/~crilf/publications/Final_Case_Flow_and_Focus _Group_Report-September2008v3.pdf.

9. L. Barnett, T. Dupuis, C. Kirkby, R. MacKay, J. Nicol, and J. Béchard, *Bill C-10: An Act to enact the Justice for Victims of Terrorism Act and to amend the State Immunity Act, the Criminal Code, the Controlled Drugs and Substances Act, the Corrections and Conditional Release Act, the Youth Criminal Justice Act, the Immigration and Refugee Protection Act and other Acts*, Legislative Summary of Bill C-10, Publication no. 41-1-C10-E (Ottawa: Library of Parliament, 2012), http://www.parl.gc.ca/Content/LOP/LegislativeSummaries/41/1/c10-e.pdf.

10. J. Savoie, "Youth Self-Reported Delinquency, Toronto—2006," *Juristat* 27, no. 6 (Ottawa: Statistics Canada, 2007), http://www.statcan.gc.ca/pub/85-002-x/85-002-x2007006-eng.pdf; C. R. Trulson, M. DeLisi, and J. W. Marquart, "Institutional Misconduct, Delinquent Background, and Rearrest Frequency Among Serious and Violent Delinquent Offenders," *Crime and Delinquency* 57, no. 5 (2011): 709–31; D. J. Simourd and D. L. Andrews, "Correlates of Delinquency: A Look at Gender Differences," *Forum on Corrections Research* 6, no. 1 (Ottawa: Correctional Service of Canada, 1994), http://www.csc-scc.gc.ca/text/pblct/forum/e061/e061g-eng.shtml.

11. K. M. McCabe, A. E. Lansing, A. Garland, and R. Hough, "Differences in Psychopathology, Functional Impairment, and Familial Risk Factors among Adjudicated Delinquents," *Journal of American Academy of Child and Adolescent Psychiatry* 41, no. 7 (2002): 860–67.

12. J. E. Butters, J. Sheptycki, S. Brochu, and P. G. Erickson, "Guns and Sublethal Violence: A Comparative Study of At-Risk Youth in Two Canadian Cities," *International Criminal Justice Review* 21, no. 4 (2011): 402–26; National Crime Prevention Centre, *A Statistical Snapshot of Youth at Risk and Youth Offending in Canada* (Ottawa: Public Safety Canada, 2012), http:// www.publicsafety.gc.ca/res/cp/res/ssyr-eng.aspx.

13. S. Milligan, "Youth Custody and Community Services in Canada, 2005–2006," *Juristat* 28, no. 8 (2008): 1–22, http://www.statcan.gc.ca/pub/85-002-x/2008008/article/10655-eng.htm.

14. C. Munch, "Youth Correctional Statistics in Canada, 2010–2011," *Juristat* (Ottawa: Canadian Centre for Justice Statistics, Statistics Canada, 2012), http://www.statcan.gc.ca/pub/85-002-x/2012001/article/11716-eng.htm.

15. C. Munch, "Youth Correctional Statistics in Canada, 2010/2011," *Juristat* (Ottawa: Minister of Industry, 2012), http://www.statcan.gc.ca/pub/85-002-x/2012001/article/11716-eng.htm.

16. Bell, *Young Offenders and Youth Justice*.

17. National Crime Prevention Centre, *A Statistical Snapshot of Youth at Risk and Youth Offending in Canada* (Ottawa: Public Safety Canada, 2012), http://www.publicsafety.gc.ca/res/cp/res/ ssyr-eng.aspx.

18. J. Latimer and L. C. Foss, *A One Day Snapshot of Aboriginal Youth in Custody Across Canada: Phase II*, Department of Justice Canada, Research and Statistics Division, Youth Justice Policy (Ottawa: 2004), http://www.justice.gc.ca/eng/pi/rs/rep-rap/2004/yj2-jj2/yj2.pdf; M. Totten, *Preventing Aboriginal Youth Gang Involvement in Canada: A Gendered Approach*, paper prepared for the Aboriginal Policy Research Conference, 2009, http://www.nwac.ca/sites/default/files/ reports/TottenAPRCGangGenderpaperFeb2609.pdf.

19. Native Women's Association of Canada, *Aboriginal Women and Gangs: An Issue Paper* (St. John's: 2007), http://www.laa.gov.nl.ca/laa/naws/pdf/nwac-gangs.pdf.

20. M. Totten, *Preventing Aboriginal Youth Gang Involvement*, http://www.nwac.ca/sites/default/ files/reports/TottenAPRCGangGenderpaperFeb2609.pdf.

21. Montreal Urban Aboriginal Community Strategy Network, *The Aboriginal Justice Research Project* (Montreal: 2012), http://www.crime-prevention-intl.org/uploads/media/Aboriginal _Justice_Research_Project_-_Final_Report.pdf.

22. C. T. Greene, *Creating Consensus: An Exploration of Two Pre-Charge Diversion Programs in Canada*, PhD dissertation, University of Toronto, 2011, https://tspace.library.utoronto.ca/ bitstream/1807/29733/11/Greene_Carolyn_T_201106_PhD_Thesis.pdf.

23. Bell, *Young Offenders and Youth Justice*, 241.

24. A. Petrosino, C. Turpin-Petrosino, and J. Beuhler, "Scared Straight and Other Juvenile Awareness Programs for Preventing Juvenile Delinquency: A Systematic Review of the Randomized Experimental Evidence," *Annals of the American Academy of Political and Social Science* 589, no. 1 (2003): 41–62.

25. Greene, *Creating Consensus*.

26. D. K. Forgays, "Three Years of Youth Court Offender Outcomes," *Adolesence* 43, no. 171 (2008): 473–84; A. P. Logalbo and C. M. Callahan, "An Evaluation of Teen Court as a Juvenile Crime Diversion Program," *Juvenile and Family Court Journal* 52, no. 2 (2011): 1–11.

27. Youth Justice Committees of Ontario, *Windsor-Essex County Youth Justice Committee* (n.d.), http://www.yjcontario.ca/committees/windsor.php.

28. D. P. Mears, J. C. Cochran, S. J. Greenman, A. S. Bhati, and M. A. Greenwald, "Evidence on the Effectiveness of Juvenile Court Sanctions," *Journal of Criminal Justice* 39, no. 6 (2011): 509–20.

29. Ibid.

30. D. Luong and S. Wormith, "Applying Risk/Need Assessment to Probation Practice and Its Impact on the Recidivism of Young Offenders," *Criminal Justice and Behavior* 38, no. 12 (2011): 1177–99.

31. B.C. Representative for Children and Youth and B.C. Office of the Provincial Health Officer, *Kids, Crime, and Care: Health and Well-Being of Children in Care: Youth Justice Experiences and Outcomes* (Victoria, 2009), http://www.rcybc.ca/Images/PDFs/Reports/ Youth%20Justice%20Joint%20Rpt%20FINAL%20.pdf.

32. N. Freudenberg, "Jails, Prisons, and the Health of Urban Populations: A Review of the Impact of the Correctional System on Community Health," *Journal of Community Health* 78, no. 2 (2009): 214–35; A. J. Sedlak and K. S. McPherson, *Youth's Needs and Services: Findings from the Survey of Youth in Residential Placement* (Washington, DC: Office of Juvenile Justice and Delinquency Prevention, 2010), https://www.ncjrs.gov/pdffiles1/ ojjdp/227728.pdf.

33. J. V. Roberts, "Harmonizing the Sentencing of Youth and Adult Offenders: A Comparison of the Youth Criminal Act and Part XXII of the Criminal Code," *Canadian Journal of Criminology and Criminal Justice* 46, no. 3 (2004): 301–26; R. Maynard, "Incarcerating Youth as Justice: An In-Depth Examination of Youth, Incarceration, and Restorative Justice," *Canadian Dimension* 45, no. 5 (2011): 25–27.

34. Roberts, "Harmonizing the Sentencing of Youth and Adult Offenders"; G. Beck, "Bullying Among Young offenders in Custody," *Issues in Criminological and Legal Psychology* 22 (1995): 54–70.

35. Office of the Child and Family Service Advocacy, *Review of Toronto Youth Assessment Center (TYAC)* (Toronto: 2003); cf. C. Cesaroni and M. Peterson-Badali, "Understanding the Adjustment of Incarcerated Young Offenders: A Canadian Example," *Youth Justice* 10, no. 2 (2010): 107–25; and C. Cesaroni and S. Alvi, "Masculinity and Resistance in

Adolescent Carceral Settings," *Canadian Journal of Criminology and Criminal Justice*, 52 no. 3 (2010): 303–20.

36. Cesaroni and Alvi, "Masculinity and Resistance in Adolescent Carceral Settings."

37. Y. Jewkes, "Men Behind Bars: 'Doing' Masculinity as an Adaptation to Imprisonment," *Men and Masculinities* 8, no. 1 (2005): 61.

38. M. Peterson-Badali and C. Koegl, "Juvenile Experiences of Incarceration: The Role of Correctional Staff in Peer Violence," *Journal of Criminal Justice* 29, no. 1 (2001): 1–9.

39. Jewkes, "Men Behind Bars."

40. A. Liebling, "Suicides in Prison: Ten Years On," *Prison Service Journal* 138 (2001): 35–41.

41. Bell, *Young Offenders and Youth Justice*.

42. Ibid., 321.

43. A. Cox, "Doing the Programme or Doing Me? The Pains of Youth Imprisonment," *Punishment and Society* 13, no. 5 (2011): 592–610.

44. Ibid.

45. Ibid.

46. Ibid., 592.

47. R. McCorkle, "Living on the Edge: Fear in a Maximum Security Prison," *Journal of Offender Rehabilitation* 20, nos. 1–2 (1993): 73–91.

48. A. Kupchik, "The Correctional Experiences of Youth in Adult and Juvenile Prisons," *Justice Quarterly* 24, no. 2 (2007): 247–70.

49. Ibid.

50. Ibid.

51. J. Latimer, C. Dowden, and K. E. Morton-Bourgon, *Treating Youth in Conflict with the Law: A New Meta-Analysis* (Ottawa: Department of Justice, 2003), http://www.justice.gc.ca/eng/pi/rs/rep-rap/2003/rr03_yj3-rr03_jj3/rr03_yj3.pdf.

52. Ibid., 11.

53. McCabe et al., "Differences in Psychopathology."

54. M. A. Zahn, J. C. Day, S. F. Mihalic, and L. Tichavsky, "Determining What Works for Girls in the Juvenile Justice System: A Summary of Evaluation Evidence," *Crime and Delinquency* 55, no. 2 (2009): 266–93; T. D. Akoensi, D. Humphreys, and F. Lösel, *What Works in Reducing Reoffending: Strengthening Transitional Approaches to Reducing Reoffending (STARR)*, European Youth Centre, Budapest, June 20–23, 2010, http://www.cepprobation.org/uploaded_files/Thomas%20Akoensi.pdf.

55. S. Peters, *Guiding Principles for Promising Female Programming: An Inventory of Best Practices* (Washington, DC: U.S. Department of Justice, Office of Juvenile Justice and Delinquency Programs, 1998); cf. D. Hubbard and B. Matthews, "Reconciling the Differences Between the 'Gender-Responsive' and the 'What Works' Literatures to Improve Services for Girls," *Crime and Delinquency* 54, no. 2 (2008): 225–58.

56. Hubbard and Matthews, "Reconciling the Differences."

57. F. H. Biggam and K. G. Power, "Social Support and Psychological Distress in a Group of Incarcerated Offenders," *International Journal of Offender Therapy and Comparative Criminology* 41 (1997): 213–30.

58. C. Cesaroni and M. Peterson-Badali, "Young Offenders in Custody: Risk and Adjustment," *Criminal Justice and Behaviour* 32, no. 3 (2005): 251–77; A. Liebling, D. Price, and G. Schefer, *The Prison Officer* (New York, NY: Willan, 2011).

59. M. Inderbitzin, "A Look from the Inside: Balancing Custody and Treatment in a Juvenile Maximum-Security Facility," *International Journal of Offender Therapy and Comparative Criminology* 51, no. 3 (2007): 348–62.

60. S. C. Marsh and W. P. Evans, "Youth Perspectives on Their Relationships with Staff in Juvenile Correction Settings and Perceived Likelihood of Success on Release," *Youth Violence and Juvenile Justice* 7, no. 1 (2009): 46–67.

61. Ibid., 59.

62. Ibid.

63. A. Doob, *The Experiences of Phase II Male Young Offenders in Secure Facilities in the Province of Ontario* (Toronto: Canadian Foundation for Children, Youth and the Law, 1999); Cesaroni and Peterson-Badali, "Understanding the Adjustment of Incarcerated Young Offenders."

64. Law Commission of Canada, *Restoring Dignity: Responding to Child Abuse in Canadian Institutions* (Ottawa: 2000); Cesaroni and Alvi, "Masculinity and Resistance."

65. Cesaroni and Alvi, "Masculinity and Resistance," 312.

66. F. T. Cullen, "It's Time to Reaffirm Rehabilitation," *Criminology and Public Policy* 5, no. 4 (2006): 665–72; Akoensi, Humphreys, and Lösel, "What Works in Reducing Reoffending."

67. D. Ballucci, "Subverting and Negotiating Risk Assessment: A Case Study of the LSI in a Canadian Youth Custody Facility," *Canadian Journal of Criminology and Criminal Justice* 54, no. 2 (2012): 203–28.

68. R. D. Hoge and D. A. Andrews, *Youth Level of Service/Case Management Inventory (YLS/CMI)* (Toronto: Multi-Health Systems, 2002).

69. N. A. Vitopoulos, M. Peterson-Badali, and T. A. Skilling, "The Relationship Between Matching Service to Criminogenic Need and Recidivism in Male and Female Youth: Examining the RNR Principles in Practice," *Criminal Justice and Behavior* 39, no. 8 (2012): 1025–41; M. E. Olver, K. C. Stockdale, and J. S. Wormith, "Risk Assessment with Young Offenders: A Meta-Analysis of Three Assessment Measures," *Criminal Justice and Behavior* 36, no. 4 (2009): 329–53.

70. Ibid.

71. Ibid., 331.

72. Ibid.; Vitopoulos, Peterson-Badali, and Skilling, "The Relationship"; C. S. Schwalbe, "A Meta-Analysis of Juvenile Justice Risk Assessment Instruments," *Criminal Justice and Behavior* 35, no. 11 (2008): 1367–81.

73. Vitopoulos, Peterson-Badali, and Skilling, "The Relationship."

74. Canadian Resource Centre for Victims of Crime, *Restorative Justice in Canada: What Victims Should Know* (2011), http://www.rjlillooet.ca/documents/restjust.pdf.

75. J. A. Bouffard and K. J. Bergseth, "The Impact on Reentry Services on Juvenile Offenders' Recidivism," *Youth Violence and Juvenile Justice* 6, no. 3 (2008): 295–318.

76. D. Fields and L. S. Abrams, "Gender Differences in the Perceived Needs and Barriers of Youth Offenders Preparing for Community Reentry," *Child Youth Care Forum* 39 (2010): 253–69.

77. P. R. Jones and B. R. Wyant, "Target Juvenile Needs to Reduce Delinquency," *Criminology and Public Policy* 6, no. 4 (2007): 763–72.

78. D. J. Martinez and L. S. Abrams, "Informal Social Support Among Returning Young Offenders: A Metasynthesis of the Literature," *International Journal of Offender Therapy and Comparative Criminology* 57, no. 2 (2013): 169–90.

79. Ibid.

80. R. G. Wiebush, D. Wagner, B. McNulty, Y. Wang, and T. N. Le, *Implementation and Outcome Evaluation of the Intensive Aftercare Program: Final Report* (Washington: National Council on Crime and Delinquency, 2005), https://www.ncjrs.gov/pdffiles1/ojjdp/206177.pdf.

81. Ibid.

82. Akoensi, Humphreys, and Lösel, "What Works in Reducing Reoffending."

PART VI

GOING FORWARD: REFORMING CORRECTIONS

In the Preface, we promised that this text would avoid the doom and gloom that often accompanies discussions of corrections. Tracing the evolution of the response to criminal offenders over the past 200 years and identifying the obstacles to correctional change and the ongoing challenges of corrections could lead one to conclude that not much has changed. Of particular concern in Canada is legislation that appears to have moved toward a more punitive penology based not on evidence but rather on the view that a "get tough" approach is the best strategy for protecting the community. This may prove to be a costly and ineffective approach, particularly if the well-documented needs of criminal offenders are not addressed at the same time that their risk is being managed. There are, however, areas where corrections have produced positive outcomes, and these should be highlighted and strengthened.

CHAPTER 16

CREATING EFFECTIVE SYSTEMS OF CORRECTIONS

CHAPTER OBJECTIVES

After reading this chapter, you should be able to:
- *Discuss the challenges of implementing evidence-based practices in corrections and the strategies for overcoming these challenges.*
- *Identify and discuss areas where correctional reform is required.*
- *Identify and discuss the opportunities for corrections.*

I n this, the final chapter, we take a step back from the specific components of the corrections process to reflect on areas where reform is required to create more effective systems of corrections. Addressing these areas will strengthen the foundations of correctional practice, increase the effectiveness of responses to criminal offenders, and protect communities better.

REFORMING CORRECTIONS: A WAY FORWARD

For systems of corrections to address the risk and needs of offenders more effectively, and to ensure the safety of communities, a number of areas must be examined, including the following:

Evidence-Based Policies and Programs: Overcoming the "Panacea" Phenomenon

Historically, systems of corrections have lacked a well-developed body of empirical knowledge that could be used to formulate policies and guide programs. There is often a disconnect between correctional policy and practice and scholarly research. Too often, correctional laws and policies are affected by political considerations and public opinion. For example, Bill C-10—perhaps the most significant piece of legislation in years—will have a powerful impact on systems of corrections, yet it was not informed by research or by the experiences of other jurisdictions (such as the United States) that have found punitive penology to be both expensive and largely ineffective.

One consequence of this has been the susceptibility of corrections to **panaceas**—that is, the search for a "magic bullet" that will reduce recidivism, lower costs, and deter offenders from future criminal behaviour. Systems of corrections, buffeted by a political environment that is focused strongly on penal populism, remain susceptible to simple, "quick fix" solutions that neither protect the community nor assist offenders.[1]

A review of initiatives over the past century reveals that systems of corrections have stumbled from one strategy to another and that most of these strategies have not achieved any of their intended objectives. Systems of corrections have been slow to adopt evidence-based strategies and to discard ineffective policies and programs. The challenge, for Canadians, their governments, and their systems of corrections, is to undertake the fundamental structural changes that are required so that the next 50 years of corrections do not produce the same outcomes as the present ones and so that correctional policies and practices do not continue to reel from crisis to crisis.

This text has identified community and institution-based programs and strategies that do not help offenders and protect communities. There is plenty of research evidence that supports discontinuing a number of correctional practices, including community notification for sex offenders released into the community and (for most offenders) lengthy sentences of incarceration.

Panaceas
In corrections, the search for the "magic bullet" that will reduce recidivism, lower costs, and deter offenders from future criminal behaviour.

Confronting the Challenges to Developing Evidence-Based Practice

Even with an increasing body of knowledge as to "what works," the adoption of evidence-based practices faces multiple challenges. These are set out in Table 16.1.

Table 16.1 Challenges to Developing Evidence-Based Practices

Challenge	Why the Challenge Exists	How to Overcome the Barrier
Policy makers resistant to new strategies	Policy makers are responsive to public opinion and may be unwilling to try new things.	Engage in an awareness campaign informing policy makers of the utility of evidence-based strategies.
Concerns about cost	Because many evidence-based practices are new, start-up costs may generate resistance among the public and policy makers.	Cost–benefit analyses can demonstrate whether the start-up costs are less than the continued costs for ineffective practices.

(continued)

Challenge	Why the Challenge Exists	How to Overcome the Barrier
Public desire for retribution	The public demands that offenders be punished; many evidence-based policies appear to be "slaps on the wrist."	Even less severe sanctions are experienced as punitive by offenders. Those developing evidence-based practices should demonstrate the punitive nature of those practices to the public.
Complacency among line staff	Some workers implementing policies may be accustomed to old practices and resistant to change.	Leaders must demonstrate how and why new practices will make the line officers' job more practical, without adding unnecessary work.
Defining success	It is sometimes difficult to develop measures of success for evidence-based practices when individuals are focused on punishment as the definition of success.	Indicators of success should be broadly defined so that all advantages of evidence-based practices are recognized and evaluated thoroughly.
Lack of awareness about evidence-based practices	Criminal justice officials may not be aware of practices that are deemed most effective.	Through collaborative efforts, practitioners can share information about effective and promising strategies.
Cooperating with researchers	In some places a gap exists between researchers and practitioners.	Partnerships and relationships can be developed with research agencies and college/university researchers.
Fear of the unknown	Because evidence-based practices are new, leaders and practitioners may see untested practices as risky.	Pilot-test the program and demonstrate to leaders and practitioners that the principles of the new practice are based on evidence that suggest the new practice should be effective.

Source: Adapted from M. DeMichele and B. Payne. *Offender Supervision with Electronic Technology. Community Corrections Resource.* (Washington, DC: U.S. Department of Justice, 2009). Pg. 62. http://www .appa-net.org/eweb/docs/APPA/pubs/OSET_2.pdf.

There are additional challenges to promoting evidence-based practices in systems of corrections. Determining the effectiveness of specific interventions is a challenge because of the need to follow large groups of offenders over a long period of time to assess whether and how those interventions work.

Reducing the "Pains" Experienced by Offenders and Their Families

The discussion in this book has documented a variety of "pains" that many offenders experience after becoming involved in the criminal justice and corrections systems. These difficulties may be most pronounced for offenders confined in correctional institutions, although probationers, parolees, and ex-offenders and their families may struggle as well.

The offender's family may break down under the stress of incarceration and supervision in the community. The damage to the children of offenders may manifest itself in subsequent conflict with the law. There is little doubt that society (i.e., the state) has a right to sanction offenders found guilty of committing criminal offences. But it can be argued that systems of corrections have an obligation to mitigate the ancillary pains that offenders experience and the collateral damage to the families of offenders.

Addressing the Needs of Offenders

Recall that a large number of persons who come into conflict with the law are marginal with respect to their employment skills, education, and other capacities. Many are mentally ill, and many have few community supports.

Do correctional systems do anything to reduce this marginality? The answer is "generally, no." Specific interventions may reduce reoffending, there is no conclusive evidence that the marginality of offenders—that is, their substance abuse issues, homelessness, and mental illness, all of which are closely related to their conflict with the law—are being addressed successfully in the long term. Neither governments nor correctional systems compile longitudinal data to track changes in these factors among ex-offenders. For some offenders, involvement in corrections may *increase* their marginality and the likelihood of reoffending.

Addressing the Needs of Victims

Systems of corrections have made some progress in recognizing and addressing the needs of crime victims. The evidence suggests, however, that victims are still marginalized in the criminal justice and corrections processes. Many victims do not understand how the justice and corrections systems work and have little opportunity to play a meaningful role in the response to criminal offenders. Contrast this with restorative justice programs, which provide an opportunity for crime victims to be part of the dialogue with and about offenders.

Acknowledging the Limits of Technology

Systems of corrections are making increasing use of technology, not only with respect to gathering and managing information, but also for control and surveillance. The rise of **techno-corrections** has been accompanied by the expansion of EM and GPS to monitor offenders and by the use of the media (including social media) to notify communities about high-risk offenders.

Techno-corrections
The application of technology to the supervision and control of offenders.

The challenge is to ensure that corrections does not come to rely too heavily on technology. Techno-corrections, in themselves, do not ensure public safety. The danger is that the increasing use of technology will come at the expense of developing human and helping relationships, which have been shown to reduce reoffending and to help offenders reintegrate with the community.

Adhering to the Rule of Law and Respecting the Rights of Offenders

A continuing challenge for systems of corrections is to ensure that responses to offenders adhere to the rule of law and that the rights of offenders are protected. This is crucial to ensuring the legitimacy of corrections and is a fundamental requirement for a democratic society. A common thread in the various commissions of inquiry into corrections over the past 200 years has been that corrections personnel did not abide by the **rule of law** and the **duty to act fairly**.

Rule of law
The requirement that governments, as well as individuals, be subject to and abide by the law.

The federal Office of the Correctional Investigator and its provincial counterparts provide a degree of oversight into the activities of correctional systems, though their recommendations are not binding. Canadian courts are hearing more and more cases centred on inmate rights, and the resulting decisions are having a significant impact on correctional practice.

Duty to act fairly
In corrections, the right of inmates to be heard and to have an impartial hearing.

Improving the Effectiveness of Community Corrections

The majority of offenders are under some form of supervision in the community, yet only a very small portion (about 10 percent) of the $4 billion consumed by correctional systems annually is spent on community corrections. The expansion of effective community programs could be cost effective, by keeping offenders out of prison; it could also reduce risk to communities and help offenders address their needs.[2]

More research is required on community corrections. Within the current framework of probation practice, for example, there is little information about how probation officers spend their time and how effective their interventions are. From the perspective of one corrections scholar, "probation and parole agents spend a considerable amount of time writing reports, receiving training, going to court, attending probation and parole revocation hearings, talking with program providers, all of which take time away from actually supervising their caseload."[3] The STICS model of probation practice, profiled in Chapter 6, has shown potential. It remains to be seen whether this success can be sustained, and replicated in other jurisdictions.

For offenders released from custody, systems of correction struggle to provide throughcare. The challenges are especially difficult for offenders with special needs, including addicted persons and those with a mental illness or FASD. When significant community resources are absent, the likelihood of reoffending is high. Research could lead to the development of best practices of community supervision.

Reforming Correctional Institutions

Prison reform is difficult to achieve for many reasons. First, many people view prisons as places of punishment, so they may be opposed to prison reforms that entail providing treatment and rehabilitation for offenders.[4] Another major challenge can be opposition from those working within correctional systems; these individuals may feel threatened by the proposed reforms if, for example, they think the reforms will reduce their importance or change the way they have been "doing business."[5] Consultation between reformers and correctional officials might ensure that reforms are designed and implemented in a realistic manner that accounts for the realities facing practitioners on the ground. Also, consultation with management personnel may help identify operational realities that reformers overlook; for example, those personnel may be better equipped to identify potential issues pertaining to competing demands for monetary and human resources.[6] Consultation could also secure "buy-in" from corrections staff and management, which might increase the effectiveness of reform efforts.

Financial constraints may impede reform efforts, both their implementation and their sustainability. When money and resources are scarce in correctional systems, treatment programs and services for offenders are unlikely to receive adequate funding.[7] Although reform initiatives often include resources to bring about the changes initially, ongoing maintenance of reform efforts may be impossible due to financial shortfalls in subsequent years. Also, an absence of administrative accountability may impede the thorough implementation and success of reform initiatives, for agencies may not be monitored to assess whether changes have actually be made and whether outcomes are being achieved.

Even if all of these challenges are addressed, some people argue that correctional reform will be impossible without fundamental changes in society's beliefs and values.[8] This is because, as was discussed in Chapter 2, politicians win votes for "tough on crime" approaches to reducing the "crime problem," and political decision making strongly influences criminal justice agencies and their operations.[9]

Addressing the Unique Challenges of Provincial/Territorial Systems of Corrections

This book has made it clear that provincial/territorial systems of corrections face unique challenges. These are largely a consequence of the very short periods of time that offenders spend in custody, the high risk/needs of many offenders, and the difficulties of providing services in rural and remote communities.

Despite this, there is relatively little published research on community and institutional corrections at the provincial/territorial level. It cannot be assumed that research findings from federal corrections are applicable to provincial/territorial corrections. Little is known, for example, about the dynamics of life inside provincial/territorial institutions or about the effectiveness of various treatment programs. Given that most offenders in Canada fall under the jurisdiction of the provinces/territories, much more needs to be known about how these systems of corrections are operating.

THE OPPORTUNITIES FOR CORRECTIONS

Discussions of corrections are often surrounded by negativism, even though there is an evolving literature pointing to strategies and interventions that can effectively address the risk and needs of criminal offenders.

Expanding Effective Interventions

There are promising correctional strategies that should be enhanced. One is the use of the RNR principles as the basis for correctional interventions. Another is the STICS model for probation practice. Yet another is restorative justice, which can take a number of forms, including circles of support and accountability (COSAs). Recall from the programs reviewed in the various Research Files throughout the text that while many created positive program dynamics, this was not translated into reduced rates of reoffending. This suggests that much more attention must be given to throughcare—ensuring that positive gains achieved in confinement are used as a foundation for success upon release into the community. This will require programs and services to assist offenders with the challenges that are encountered in reentry.

The jury is still out on the effectiveness of some initiatives, including the various problem-solving courts discussed in Chapter 4. These courts hold considerable promise; however, an absence of evaluations precludes a determination of their effectiveness. It has been noted several times in this book that lack of evaluation often makes it impossible to assess the effectiveness of specific interventions.

Corrections as a Restorative Process: Time for a Rethink?

Recall from Chapter 1 that restorative justice is an alternative framework for holding offenders accountable while at the same time addressing the needs of victims and the community—and the offenders themselves.

As this book has shown, Canadian corrections is far from a restorative process. Both in the community and in correctional institutions, offenders are managed in ways that often do more harm than good, that do not hold offenders accountable for their behaviour, and that often increase their likelihood of reoffending.

Mobilizing the Community: Maintaining Human and Helping Relationships

A strong force in today's correctional systems is penal populism, whereby politicians point to public pressure as their justification for enacting tougher laws and correctional policies. Meanwhile, criminal justice and corrections authorities have done little to educate the public about the system and the offenders it houses. Too often, this has placed the public in a reactive role.

The success of COSAs, which target high-risk offenders, illustrates the potential for criminal justice professionals, working with community residents, to reduce reoffending among high-risk offenders. There is a vast, untapped reservoir in the community that, if mobilized and supported, could play a significant role in the corrections process.

The success of COSAs is evidence that human and helping relationships with ex-offenders (even high-risk ones) can be at least as effective as interventions based on risk assessment instruments, or supervision based on surveillance and control.

Developing Models of Correctional Practice for a Diverse Society

Diversity is a defining characteristic of Canada. Cultural diversity poses challenges to the criminal justice system and to systems of corrections as well. Canada is a multicultural society, yet we know very little about the experiences of Indo-Canadian offenders, black offenders, or offenders from "new comer" groups.

Similarly, little attention has been paid to the challenges faced by probation officers, COs, treatment personnel, parole boards, and parole officers when it comes to supervising and making decisions about these groups of offenders. Language and cultural barriers, community resistance and suspicion, and a lack of knowledge about the cultures and communities of minority offenders can all undermine intervention efforts. There has been no research, for example, on the role that mosques or Sikh temples might play in helping offenders return to the community on conditional release, or on the potential for community-based alternatives, programs, and services.

Police services across Canada have made the recruitment of visible and cultural minorities a priority. Corrections should do the same and, like their police counterparts, publish information on the ethnicity of their personnel to track these changes.

FINAL THOUGHTS

The discussion in Chapter 2 documented the rise in the early 21st century of a new punitive penology in Canada. It is uncertain how this shift in government policy will affect the design and delivery of programs, the work of the correctional personnel who are charged with managing and assisting offenders in the community and in correctional institutions, and the offenders and inmates themselves. Subsequent editions of this text will track the impact of this legislation as well as other developments in Canadian corrections.

The materials presented in this text have been designed to stimulate informed discussion both in the classroom and in the community and, as well, to inform correctional policy and practice. Any examination of Canadian corrections should consider the lessons learned as well as chart a path forward. Ideally, the lessons of experience, along with research findings, will increasingly inform correctional policy and practice. See At Issue 16.1.

AT ISSUE

Issue 16.1: Change

Have punishments really changed over the years?

In a discussion of crime and justice, the British criminologist Alan Bain has stated: "[In] relation to crime and punishment I would argue that a change in development has not taken place, that society (and by definition punishment) remains in a state of confusion; changes reflecting little more than a renaming and recycling, of institutional roles and practices which make it more appealing to the public in terms of a 'tough on crime' rhetoric, and which seek to reduce an unhealthy fear of crime ... The punishments we observe are little more than a reflection of the past." Discuss.

Source: A. Bain. 2011. "Please Recycle: Continuities in Punishment." *International Journal of Law, Crime, and Justice,* 39 (2), 131.

SUMMARY

This chapter has identified and discussed the challenges and opportunities that systems of corrections face in becoming more effective at responding to criminal offenders and protecting the community. A key requirement is that corrections move toward the use of evidence-based practices, although a number of obstacles will be encountered. Similarly, there is a need to reduce the pains experienced by offenders and their families, to improve the effectiveness of strategies designed to address the needs of offenders, to focus greater attention on the needs of crime victims, and to acknowledge the limits of technology.

Throughout history, systems of corrections have struggled to adhere to the rule of law and to abide by the duty to act fairly in their responses to offenders. While the federal Office of the Correctional Investigator and provincial ombudspersons provide a certain level of oversight, their recommendations are not binding. It is the courts that provide a measure of accountability.

Strategies such as probation and parole have been in place for more than a century. The majority of offenders are under some form of supervision in the community, yet community corrections receives only a very small portion of overall corrections budgets. There is an urgent need for evidence-based practices such as the STICS initiative in probation.

Canada is a multicultural society, yet little is known about the experiences of offenders from visible and cultural minorities, their families, and the potential role their communities could play in reintegration.

Systems of corrections must discard ineffective strategies, expand effective interventions, explore the potential for integrating restorative justice approaches with the corrections process, and develop strategies for mobilizing community residents as change agents.

KEY POINTS REVIEW

1. Historically, systems of corrections have lacked a well-developed body of empirical knowledge that could inform policy and practice.

2. Systems of corrections are subject to panaceas—the "magic bullet" that will reduce recidivism, lower costs, and deter offenders from future criminal behaviour.

3. There are challenges in implementing evidence-based practices in corrections, but there are also strategies for overcoming these challenges.

4. Offenders and their families experience a number of "pains" that should be reduced for corrections to become more effective.

5. It is unlikely that systems of corrections are effective at reducing the marginality of most offenders.

6. Despite various initiatives, crime victims are largely marginalized in the criminal justice and corrections processes.

7. There is a danger that overreliance on the use of technology for supervision and control in corrections will undermine human and helping relationships.

8. Systems of corrections have faced challenges in adhering to the rule of law and in fulfilling their obligation to act fairly in the treatment of offenders.

9. The expansion of community-based corrections could reduce costs, help offenders address their needs, and reduce the risks to the community.

10. There is a need to develop models of correctional practice that consider the diversity of Canadian society.

11. Reforming correctional institutions is a difficult task that will require extensive consultations with all stakeholders.

12. Provincial/territorial systems of corrections face unique challenges as a consequence of short custodial times, the presence of high needs/high risk offenders, and a lack of resources.

13. To increase effectiveness, systems of corrections should discard ineffective strategies and expand effective interventions.

14. There is considerable potential to expand the use of restorative justice approaches in corrections.

15. To increase effectiveness, systems of corrections should facilitate the proactive involvement of the community.

KEY TERM QUESTIONS

1. What is meant when it is said that systems of corrections are subject to *panaceas*?

2. What are the challenges of an overreliance on *techno-corrections*?

3. What are the requirements of the *rule of law* and of the *duty to act fairly*?

NOTES

1. A. J. Harris and A. J. Lurigio, "Introduction to Special Issue on Sex Offenses and Offenders: Toward Evidence-based Public Policy," *Criminal Justice and Behavior* 37, no. 5 (2010): 477–81 at 480.

2. A. L. Solomon, J. W. L. Osborne, L. Winterfield, B. Elderbroom, P. Burke, R. P. Sroker, E. E. Rhine, and W. D. Burrell, *Putting Public Safety First: 13 Parole Strategies to Enhance Reentry Outcomes* (Washington, DC: Urban Institute, 2008), http://www.urban.org/uploadedpdf/411791_public_safety_first.pdf.

3. J. I. Ross, "Debunking the Myths of American Corrections: An Exploratory Analysis," *Critical Criminology* 20, no. 4 (2012): 409–27.

4. K. Hannah-Moffat, "Creating Choices: Reflecting on Choices," in *Women and Punishment: The Struggle for Justice*, ed. P. Carlen (London: Willan, 2002).

5. N. Shover, *Sociology of American Corrections* (Homewood: Dorsey Press, 1979).

6. H. Toch, *Corrections: A Humanistic Approach* (Albany: Harrow and Heston, 1997).

7. J. B. Jacobs, "Prison Reform amid the Ruins of Prisoners' Rights," in *The Future of Imprisonment*, ed. M. Tonry (New York, NY: Oxford University Press, 2004).

8. Shover, *The Sociology of American Corrections*.

9. P. Chevigny, "The Populism of Fear: Politics of Crime in the Americas," *Punishment and Society* 5, no. 1 (2003): 77–96.

Aboriginal Corrections Continuum of Care: An initiative of the CSC designed to connect Aboriginal offenders with their communities, traditions, and cultures, beginning in the institution and continuing on conditional release in the community. **(p. 313)**

Aboriginal Women Offender Circle of Care: A CSC program designed to provide women with coping strategies in preparation for release into the community. **(p. 314)**

Arbour Report: The report of an inquiry into events at the Kingston Prison for Women in April 1994, which documented violations of policy, the rule of law, and institutional regulations and had a significant impact on the development of women's corrections. **(p. 284)**

Auburn model (for prisons): A system that allowed prisoners to work and eat together during the day and housed them in individual cells at night. **(p. 25)**

Brown Commission: An investigation into the operations of Kingston Penitentiary that condemned the use of corporal punishment and emphasized the need for rehabilitation. **(p. 26)**

Canadian Charter of Rights and Freedoms: The primary law of the land, which guarantees basic rights and freedoms for citizens, including convicted offenders. **(p. 52)**

carceral: That portion of systems of corrections relating to confinement in correctional institutions. **(p. 46)**

case management: The process by which the needs and abilities of offenders are matched with correctional programs and services. **(p. 204)**

circle sentencing: An approach to sentencing based on the principles of restorative justice. **(p. 77)**

circles of support and accountability (COSAs): Community-based committees composed of criminal justice personnel and community members that provide mentoring for high-risk sex offenders whose sentences have expired. **(p. 270)**

classical (conservative) school: A perspective on criminal offenders and punishment based on the view that offenders exercise free will and engage in criminal behaviour as a result of rational choice and that punishment must be swift, certain, and severe. **(p. 5)**

classification: Using various assessment instruments to categorize inmates in order to determine the appropriate security level and programs. **(p. 199)**

cold turkey release: The discharge of an offender at the end of sentence when no conditional release or supervision is possible, such as when an offender has served his or her entire sentence in custody or provincial/territorial offenders are released at the two-thirds point in their sentence. **(p. 230)**

community assessment: A document prepared by probation or parole officers for the parole board and containing information on the feasibility of the inmate-applicant's proposed community plan in terms of the level of supervision required, employment/residential/education plans, and the availability of community resources. **(p. 238)**

community notification: The practice, usually carried out by police agencies, of making a public announcement that a high-risk offender has taken up residence in an area. **(p. 267)**

concurrent sentences: Sentences that are amalgamated and served simultaneously. **(p. 68)**

conditional sentence: A sentence imposed on an offender who would otherwise be incarcerated for a period of less than two years but whose risk is determined to be manageable in the community. **(p. 101)**

consecutive sentences: Sentences that run separately and are completed one after the other. **(p. 68)**

Constitution Act (1867): Legislation that includes provisions that define the responsibilities of the federal and provincial governments with respect to criminal justice. **(p. 52)**

continuity of supervision: The requirement that, to be effective, offenders be supervised by the same probation officer during their term of probation. **(p. 117)**

continuum of correctional institutions: The differences in institutional environments among correctional institutions located at either end of the security spectrum—minimum to maximum. **(p. 133)**

correctional agenda: The activities of correctional officers as change agents using their authority to help inmates cope with the problems of living in confinement. **(p. 160)**

correctional plan: A key component of the case management process that determines the offender's initial institution placement, specific treatment or training opportunities, and preparation for release. **(p. 206)**

corrections: The structures, policies, and programs to punish, treat, and supervise persons convicted of criminal offences. **(p. 50)**

Corrections and Conditional Release Act (CCRA): The primary legislation under which the federal system of corrections operates. **(p. 53)**

Creating Choices: The report of the Task Force on Federally Sentenced Women that had a significant impact on the structure and operation of women's corrections. **(p. 283)**

Criminal Code: Federal legislation that sets out the criminal laws of Canada and the procedures for administering justice. **(p. 53)**

criminogenic risk factors: Risk/needs factors that contribute to a person's propensity to commit criminal offences, including substance abuse problems and the acceptance of antisocial values. See also *dynamic risk factors*. **(p. 202)**

critical incident stress debriefing (CISD): A procedure for assisting COs following a critical incident. **(p. 168)**

critical (radical) school: A perspective on crime, offenders, and punishment that highlights the role of economics, politics, power, and oppression in the formulation of laws and the administration of justice. **(p. 10)**

cross-gender staffing: The practice of staffing correctional institutions with male and female officers. Most often discussed in terms of whether male COs should work inside correctional facilities for women. **(p. 293)**

custodial agenda: The activities of correctional officers that centre on control and enforcement of regulations. **(p. 160)**

dangerous offender: A designation made by the judge after conviction that results in an indeterminate term of imprisonment in a federal correctional institution. **(p. 72)**

day parole: The authority granted by a parole board that provides an opportunity for inmates to be at large in order to prepare for full release (e.g., for job search) while returning at night to an institution or, more typically, to a community residential facility. **(p. 232)**

deprivation theory: An explanation which holds that the inmate social system develops as a consequence of inmates' attempts to mitigate the pains of imprisonment. **(p. 180)**

detention during the period of statutory release: A decision by the Parole Board of Canada (after an application by the CSC) that a federal inmate be denied statutory release and be detained in the institution until Warrant Expiry Date. **(p. 233)**

differential amenability to treatment: The notion that, for a variety of reasons, not all inmates are receptive to treatment and/or that they require interventions tailored to meet their specific needs, abilities, and interests. **(p. 211)**

differential treatment availability: The recognition that, within systems of corrections, not all inmates have equal access to treatment programs. **(p. 215)**

differential treatment effectiveness: The requirement that, to be effective, treatment interventions be multifaceted and matched to the specific needs of individual offenders. **(p. 210)**

diversion: Programs designed to keep offenders from being processed further into the formal criminal justice system. **(p. 89)**

duty to act fairly: The obligation of corrections to ensure that offenders are treated fairly by corrections personnel. **(p. 52)** *Also*, the right of inmates to be heard and to have an impartial hearing. **(p. 364)**

dynamic risk factors: Attributes of the offender that can be altered through intervention, including level of education, employment skills, addiction issues, and cognitive thinking abilities. **(p. 202)**

dynamic security: A variety of ongoing, meaningful interactions between staff and inmates. **(p. 132)**

electronic monitoring: A correctional strategy that involves using electronic equipment to ensure that the conditions of supervision are fulfilled. **(p. 99)**

evidence-based practice: Policies, strategies, and programs that have been shown by evaluation research to be effective in achieving specified objectives. **(p. 59)**

fetal alcohol spectrum disorder (FASD): A condition of mental impairment due to the birth mother drinking alcohol while pregnant. **(p. 139)**

full parole: The authority granted by a parole board for an inmate to be at large under supervision in the community for the remainder of his or her sentence. **(p. 232)**

general deterrence: An objective of sentencing designed to deter others from engaging in criminal conduct. **(p. 66)**

importation theory: An explanation which holds that the inmate social system develops as a consequence of pre-prison attitudes and behaviours that are brought by inmates into the institution. **(p. 181)**

inmate code: A set of behavioural rules that govern interactions among inmates and with institutional staff. **(p. 181)**

institutionalized: Inmates who have become prisonized to such a degree that they are unable to function in the outside, free community. **(p. 181)**

integrated case management (ICM) conferences: The primary strategy used for case management of young offenders on probation. **(p. 338)**

Integrated Correctional Program Model (ICPM): An interdisciplinary approach to correctional programming operated by the CSC. **(p. 207)**

intensive supervision probation (ISP): An intermediate sanction (between the minimal supervision of traditional probation and incarceration) that generally includes reduced caseloads for probation officers, increased surveillance, treatment interventions, and efforts to ensure that probationers are employed. **(p. 119)**

interdiction strategies: Efforts to reduce the use of illegal drugs and other high-risk behaviours in order to prevent HIV/AIDS and other infectious diseases. **(p. 145)**

intermediate sanctions: A wide range of correctional programs that generally fall between probation and incarceration, although specific initiatives may include either of these penalties as well. **(p. 99)**

intermittent sentence: A sentence that is served on a "part-time" basis, generally on weekends. **(p. 68)**

judicial determination: An order by the sentencing judge that the offender serve one-half of his or her sentence before being eligible to apply for parole. **(p. 71)**

judicial recognizance: An order of the court, often referred to as a peace bond, that requires the offender (most often sex offenders) to adhere to set conditions beyond the expiry of their sentence, including most often avoiding places where there are children. **(p. 230)**

Juvenile Delinquents Act (JDA; 1908): Legislation centred on a social welfare approach to youth crime. **(p. 330)**

long-term offender: A designation under Section 752 or 753 of the Criminal Code that requires the offender to spend up to 10 years under supervision following the expiry of his or her sentence. **(p. 72)**

mature coping: A positive approach taken by inmates to adjust to life inside correctional institutions. **(p. 186)**

maximum security institutions: Federal correctional institutions with a highly controlled institutional environment. **(p. 131)**

medical model of corrections: The view that criminal offenders were ill—physically, mentally, and/or socially and that treatment and diagnosis would ensure rehabilitation. **(p. 29)**

medium security institutions: Federal correctional facilities that have a less highly controlled institutional environment than maximum security institutions and in which the inmates have more freedom of movement. **(p. 131)**

minimum security institutions: Federal correctional facilities that generally have no perimeter fencing and allow unrestricted inmate movement except at night. **(p. 131)**

moral architecture: The term used to describe the design of the first penitentiary in Canada, the intent of which was to reflect themes of order and morality. **(p. 25)**

motivational interviewing (MI): An interview technique used by probation officers designed to empower offenders to change their attitudes and behaviour. **(p. 117)**

multilevel institutions: Federal correctional institutions that contain one or more security levels (minimum, medium, and maximum) in the same facility or on the same grounds. **(p. 131)**

need principle: To be effective, correctional interventions must address the criminogenic needs of offenders. **(p. 61)**

net widening: A potential, unanticipated consequence of diversion programs in which persons who would otherwise have been released outright by the police or not charged by Crown counsel are involved in the justice system. **(p. 90)**

NIMBY (Not In My Back Yard): The resistance of community residents to efforts of corrections systems to locate programming and residences for offenders in the community. **(p. 15)**

noncarceral: That portion of systems of corrections relating to offenders in noninstitutional settings. **(p. 46)**

normative code of behaviour: The behavioural rules that guide interaction and contribute to solidarity among correctional officers. **(p. 156)**

pains of imprisonment: The deprivations experienced by inmates confined in correctional institutions, including the loss of autonomy, privacy, security, and freedom of movement and association. **(p. 180)**

pains of probation: The emotional and economic challenges that probationers may experience while under probation supervision in the community. **(p. 119)**

pains of reentry: The difficulties that inmates released from correctional institutions encounter in attempting to adjust to life in the outside, free community. **(p. 256)**

panaceas: In corrections, the search for the "magic bullet" that will reduce recidivism, lower costs, and deter offenders from future criminal behaviour. **(p. 361)**

parole certificate: A document that contains the mandatory and, often, additional conditions of a conditional release. **(p. 243)**

penal populism: Corrections policies formulated in pursuit of political objectives, often in the absence of an informed public or in spite of public opinion and that are centred on being "tough on crime." **(p. 13)**

Pennsylvania model (for prisons): A separate and silent system in which prisoners were completely isolated from one another; eating, working and sleeping in separate cells. **(p. 24)**

positivist (liberal) school: A perspective on criminal offenders and punishment based on the view that criminal behaviour is determined and that offenders require individualized treatment. **(p. 9)**

post incarceration syndrome (PICS): A condition of offenders in custody and in the community that is caused by prolonged exposure to the dynamics of life inside correctional institutions. **(p. 259)**

post-traumatic stress disorder (PTSD): An extreme form of critical incident stress that includes nightmares, hypervigilance, intrusive thoughts, and other forms of psychological distress. **(p. 168)**

pre-sentence report (PSR): A document prepared by the probation officer for the sentencing judge that contains information on the convicted offender, including sociobiographical information, offence history, victim impact, and risk assessments. **(p. 111)**

prevention strategies: Efforts to prevent and reduce high-risk behaviour among inmates and to reduce the levels of infection of HIV/AIDS and other infectious diseases. **(p. 143)**

prisonization: The process by which inmates become socialized into the norms, values, and culture of the prison. **(p. 181)**

probation: A sentence imposed on an offender by a Criminal Court judge that provides for the supervision of the offender in the community by a probation officer, either as an alternative to custody or in conjunction with a period of incarceration. **(p. 92)**

problem-solving courts: Specialized courts designed to divert offenders with special needs from the criminal justice system. **(p. 92)**

program drift: The extent to which a treatment program as delivered has moved away from the original design, with a potential impact on program effectiveness. **(p. 215)**

program fidelity: The extent to which a treatment program is delivered in accordance with the original program design. **(p. 215)**

protective custody: A section of the prison that holds inmates who are at risk in the general inmate population. **(p. 141)**

R. v. Gladue: A decision by the SCC that held that in cases where a term of incarceration would normally be imposed, judges must consider the unique circumstances of Aboriginal people. **(p. 69)**

recidivism rates: The number of offenders released from confinement who, once released from confinement, are returned to prison. **(p. 212)**

reintegration: The process whereby an inmate is prepared for and released into the community after serving time in prison. **(p. 254)**

remission/discharge: Available to provincial/territorial inmates who have served two-thirds of their sentence (often referred to as *cold turkey release* as there is no supervision by a parole officer). **(p. 233)**

responsivity principle: Correctional interventions should be matched to the learning styles of individual offenders. **(p. 61)**

restorative justice: An approach to responding to offenders based on the principle that criminal behaviour injures victims, communities, and offenders and that all of these parties should be involved in efforts to address the causes of the behavior and its consequences. **(p. 17)**

revocation of conditional release: A decision by a releasing authority, such as a parole board, made in connection with an offender whose release has been suspended. **(p. 270)**

risk principle: Correctional interventions are most effective when matched with the offender's level of risk, and higher risk offenders benefit from interventions more than medium- and low-risk offenders. **(p. 61)**

rule of law: The requirement that governments, as well as individuals, be subject to and abide by the law. **(p. 364)**

Section 81 (CCRA): Authorizes the federal government to enter into agreements with First Nations communities whereby the community assumes the "care and custody" of some Aboriginal offenders upon their release from custody. **(p. 318)**

Section 84 (CCRA): Provides for First Nations communities to participate in parole hearings and propose a plan for offender reintegration and includes a provision for First Nations communities to supervise long-term offenders. **(p. 318)**

self-injurious behaviour (SIB): Deliberate self-inflicted bodily harm or disfigurement. **(p. 191)**

social (or argot) roles: Roles that inmates assume based on their friendship networks, sentence length, and other factors related to their criminal history and activities in the institution. **(p. 182)**

Special Handling Unit (SHU): A federal correctional facility that houses inmates who pose such a high risk to inmates and staff that they cannot be confined in maximum security institutions. **(p. 131)**

specific deterrence: An objective of sentencing designed to deter the offender from future criminal conduct. **(p. 66)**

state-raised offenders: Inmates who have spent most of their youth and adult lives confined in correctional institutions. **(p. 181)**

static risk factors: Attributes of the offender that predict the likelihood of recidivism and that are not amenable to change, including criminal history, prior convictions, seriousness of prior offences, and performance on previous conditional releases. **(p. 202)**

static security: Fixed security apparatus in correctional institutions, including fixed security posts to which correctional officers are assigned, such as a control room. **(p. 132)**

status degradation ceremonies: The processing of offenders into correctional institutions whereby the offender is psychologically and materially stripped of possessions that identify him or her as a member of the "free society." **(p. 178)**

statutory release: A provision that allows incarcerated federal offenders to be released at the two-thirds point in their sentence (unless the CSC makes the decision to recommend to the PBC that the offender be detained) and to serve the remaining one-third of their sentence under supervision in the community. **(p. 232)**

suspension of conditional release: A process initiated by the supervising parole officer (or in some instances by the parole board) in cases where the parolee has allegedly failed to abide by the conditions of release. **(p. 270)**

techno-corrections: The application of technology to the supervision and control of offenders. **(p. 364)**

temporary absence: A type of conditional release that allows an inmate to participate in community activities, including employment and education, while residing in a minimum security facility or halfway house. **(p. 231)**

therapeutic integrity: The importance of the training, skill sets, and supervision of treatment staff for the effectiveness of correctional treatment programs. **(p. 216)**

therapeutic justice: The use of the law and the authority of the court as change agents in promoting the health and well-being of offenders. **(p. 93)**

throughcare: The notion that there should be continuity between institutional treatment programs and community-based services for offenders. **(p. 216 and 254)**

total institution: Correctional institutions, mental hospitals, and other facilities characterized by a highly structured environment in which all movements of the inmates/patients are controlled 24 hours a day by staff. **(p. 133)**

two-year rule: The basis for the division of responsibility for convicted offenders between the federal and provincial/territorial governments. **(p. 53)**

Unit Management Model: The supervisory arrangement in many provincial/territorial correctional institutions. **(p. 134)**

Use of Force Management Model: The framework that guides the use of force by correctional officers. **(p. 162)**

warrant expiry date: The end of an offender's sentence. **(p. 230)**

Young Offenders Act (YOA; 1984): Youth legislation that attempted to balance the protection of young offenders with ensuring accountability. **(p. 331)**

Youth Criminal Justice Act (YCJA; 2003): The legislative framework for the youth justice system; it has as a key principle to use extrajudicial measures to reduce the rates of incarceration of young offenders. **(p. 331)**

Youth Justice Committee (YJC): Community-based committees that sponsor a variety of initiatives for youth in conflict with the law, including extrajudicial measures centred on restorative justice. **(p. 345)**

Youth Level of Service/Case Management Inventory (YLS/CMI): The primary risk/need assessment instrument in youth corrections. **(p. 342)**

INDEX

Note: Page numbers followed by *f* and *t* denote figures and tables. Boldface page numbers denote key terms.